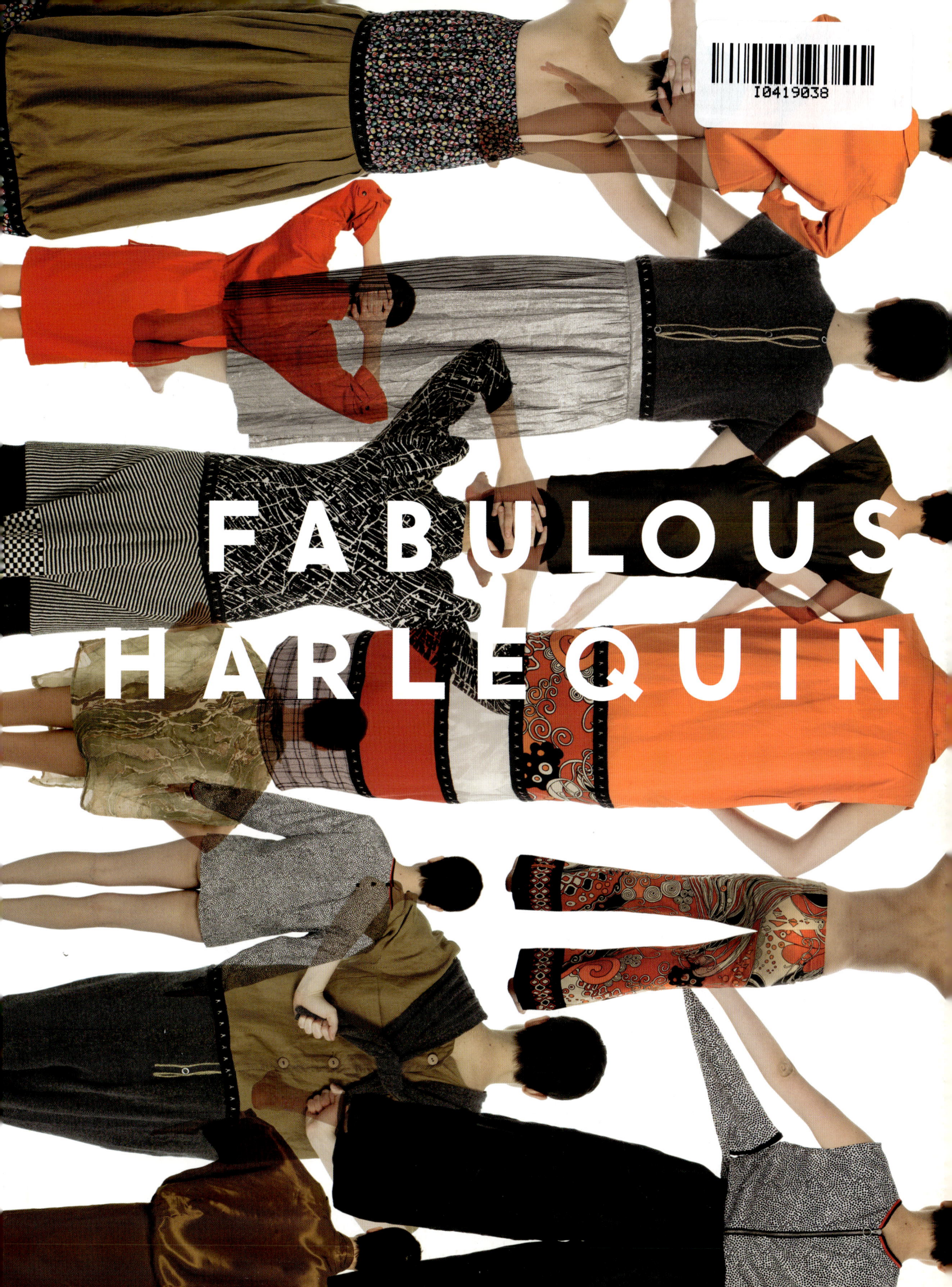

FABULOUS
HARLEQUIN

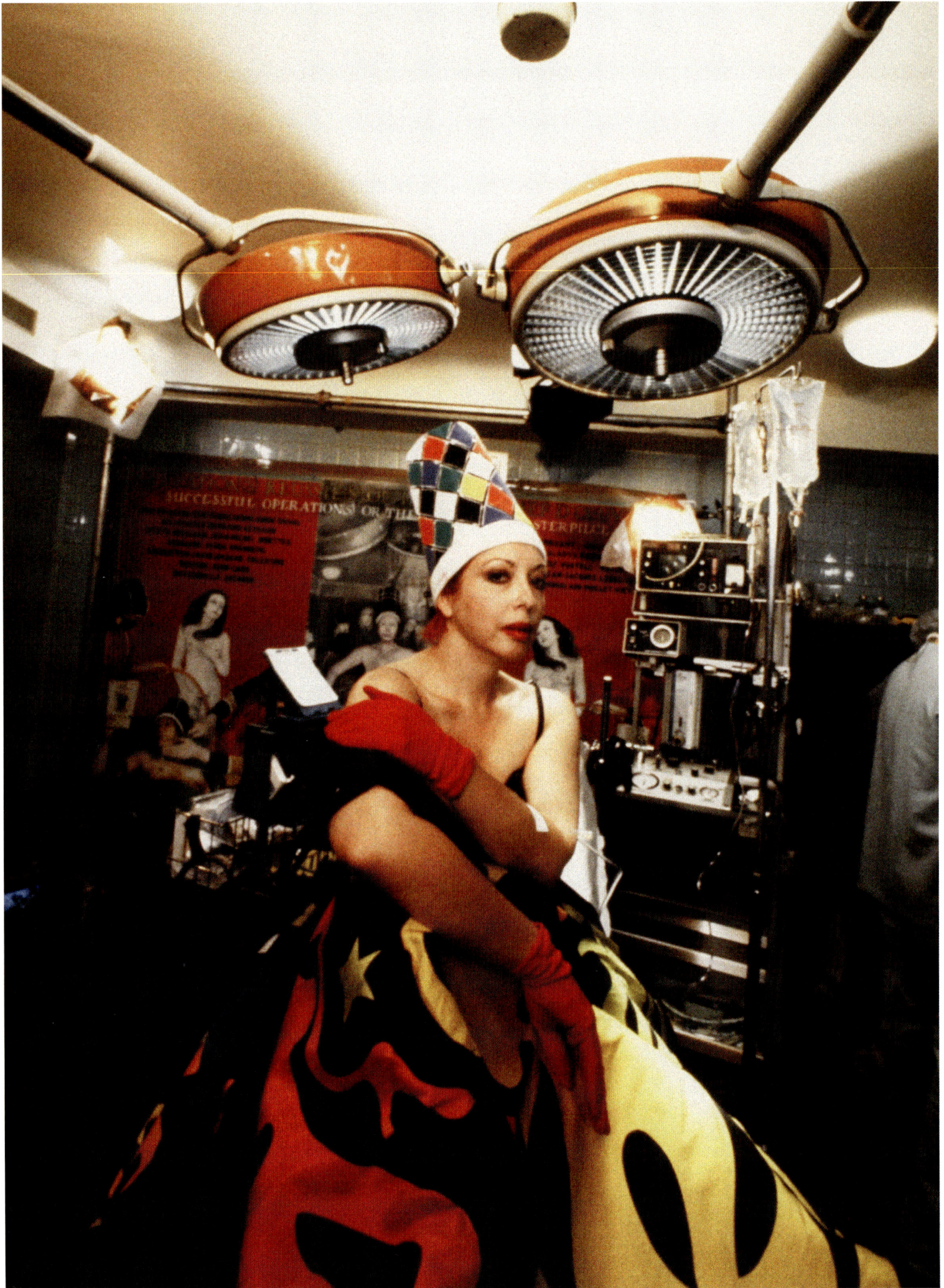

FABULOUS
ORLAN AND THE
HARLEQUIN
PATCHWORK SELF

EDITED BY JORGE DANIEL VENECIANO AND RHONDA K. GARELICK

UNIVERSITY OF NEBRASKA PRESS | LINCOLN AND LONDON

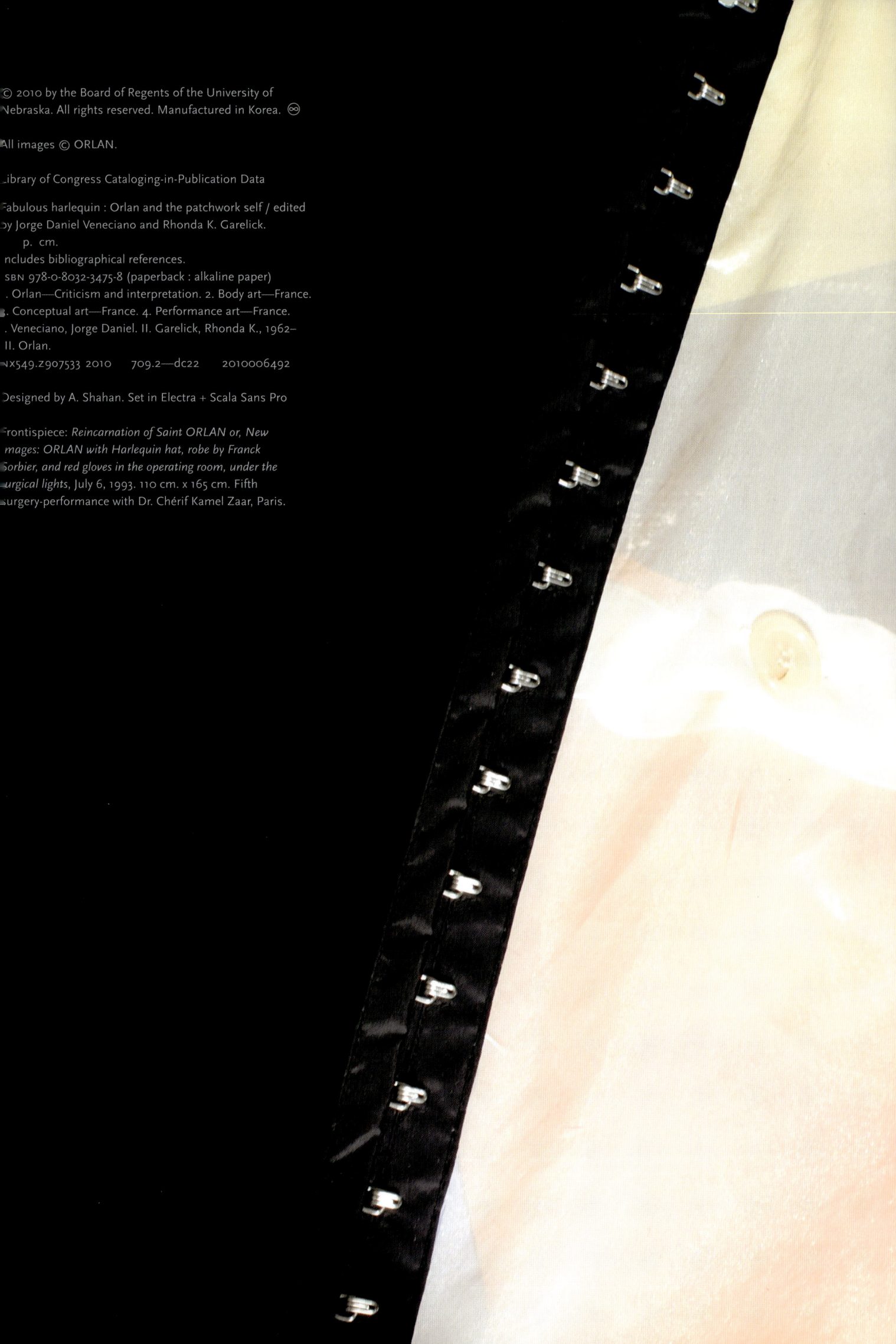

All images © ORLAN.

Library of Congress Cataloging-in-Publication Data

Fabulous harlequin : Orlan and the patchwork self / edited
by Jorge Daniel Veneciano and Rhonda K. Garelick.
        p. cm.
Includes bibliographical references.
ISBN 978-0-8032-3475-8 (paperback : alkaline paper)
1. Orlan—Criticism and interpretation. 2. Body art—France.
3. Conceptual art—France. 4. Performance art—France.
I. Veneciano, Jorge Daniel. II. Garelick, Rhonda K., 1962–
III. Orlan.
NX549.Z907533 2010   709.2—dc22   2010006492

Designed by A. Shahan. Set in Electra + Scala Sans Pro

Frontispiece: *Reincarnation of Saint ORLAN or, New
images: ORLAN with Harlequin hat, robe by Franck
Sorbier, and red gloves in the operating room, under the
surgical lights*, July 6, 1993. 110 cm. x 165 cm. Fifth
surgery-performance with Dr. Chérif Kamel Zaar, Paris.

CONTENTS

FOR FOUR DECADES FRENCH artist ORLAN has interrogated every defining aspect of being human—gender, ethnicity, religion, beauty, physiognomy, and even physiology itself—through an endlessly mutating oeuvre that itself defies categorization. Performance, sculpture, photography, poetry, design—ORLAN not only creates within these media, she disappears into them, willfully dissolving and reconfiguring her identity through her work. Most famous for her 1990s series of plastic-surgery performances, in which she remade her face and body into a living mise-en-scène of the potential for human (especially female) agency, ORLAN created a changing yet highly recognizable look that became her trademark, her signature. Even in her later experiments in self-hybridization, in which she merged her own features digitally with those belonging to African, Pre-Columbian, and American Indian portraiture, we always knew ORLAN when we saw her, however transformed she was.

In 2008, in a seemingly radical departure for her, ORLAN chose to disappear from her work entirely, effacing her famously protean features from her creations. In fact, she had chosen an even more dramatic way to dismantle her identity and perform it anew: with her Harlequin Coat project ORLAN adopts the commedia dell'arte trickster hero, the Harlequin, as her alter ego, using the Harlequin's patchwork motif as a metaphor for the fragmented, multicolored, multilayered performance of the human signature. The project is her most collaborative work to date, involving, at different stages, artists from the worlds of fashion, design, film, and technology. In reaching back to this Italian Renaissance character, ORLAN simultaneously reaches forward into the most pressing of contemporary concerns: How can we be sure of who and what we are?

RKG

ORLAN HAS A QUALITY OF omnipresence about her. She is everywhere, and everywhere she melds into and out of her milieu. Into and out of faces that situate her in North America, ORLAN has been something of a migrant artist, working in Los Angeles and Mexico City. She lived in Los Angeles for two years, conducting research at the Getty Center on the paintings of George Catlin and creating a new body of work: *Self-Hybridizations, American Indian*, 2005–2008. She returned repeatedly to Mexico City for extended periods of time in the late 1990s to study pre-Columbian art and artifacts for her first series of self-hybridization portraits.

The *Harlequin Coat* installation, created in Spain and tested in Australia, now comes to America as the Continent of Hybridity. The installation allows us to trace a concept that runs like a thread through much of ORLAN's work, from the early performances of the 1970s to her current work. This concept operates as kind of hunch or cumulative effect we call *the impossibility of sameness*: the impossibility, for instance, of containing the measure of "woman" or the essence of sexual or ethnic identity or the Western hegemony on standards of beauty. This idea of impossibility becomes the countermeasure with which to tease out the disciplinary unconscious of society. It is what *Self-Hybridizations* demonstrate and what *Harlequin Coat* turns to metaphor—the Harlequin as metaphor of multiculturalism. His magic and folly prefigure society's comic struggle with its own impossibility of sameness: its contradictory desires for both cultural distinction and cultural pluralism.

The essays and interviews in this volume explore and expand on ORLAN's contributions to the questioning of identity in and through multiculturalism, which was relevant across America, a colonized continent, long before it arose as an issue in Europe. This line of questioning is now intercontinental, transnational, and global. We thank the international contributors to this volume: Homi K. Bhabha, davidelfin, ORLAN, Michel Serres, Isabel Tejeda, Paul Virilio, and Lan Vu.

We are especially indebted to the artists ORLAN and davidelfin, who made their work and images of it available to us; to Raphael Cuir and Adeline Jeudy, who assisted with the organization of this publication; and to Vanessa Clairet and Pascaline Monier at Galerie Michel Rein in Paris, who assisted in getting the *Harlequin Coat* installation to the United States.

This project was born of a collaboration between the Sheldon Museum of Art and the Interdisciplinary Arts Symposium based in the Hixson-Lied College of Fine and Performing Arts at the University of Nebraska–Lincoln. The museum installation and IAS artist residency resulting from this collaboration coincide with the Textile Society of America's 12th Biennial Symposium, "Textiles and Settlement: From Plains Space to Cyber Space," held at UNL in October 2010.

The Sheldon Museum of Art is a program of the University of Nebraska–Lincoln. We thank Harvey Perlman, chancellor, Susan Poser, associate to the chancellor, and Giacomo Oliva, dean of the Hixson-Lied College of Fine and Performing Arts, for their support. The Sheldon's programs and exhibitions, including the *Harlequin Coat*, receive funding support from the Sheldon Art Association, the museum's dedicated membership and support group. General operating support is also provided in part by funds from the Nebraska Arts Council.

At the University of Nebraska Press we would like to thank director Donna Shear; editor in chief Heather Lundine; managing editor Ann Baker; acquisitions editor Bridget Barry; and designer Andrea Shahan, for the well-conceived design of the book. At the Sheldon Museum of Art several individuals were instrumental in seeing the installation to completion. They are collections manager Stacey Walsh, senior gallery technician Ed Rumbaugh, gallery tech Neil Christensen, and curatorial assistant Meghan Gilbride.

JDV

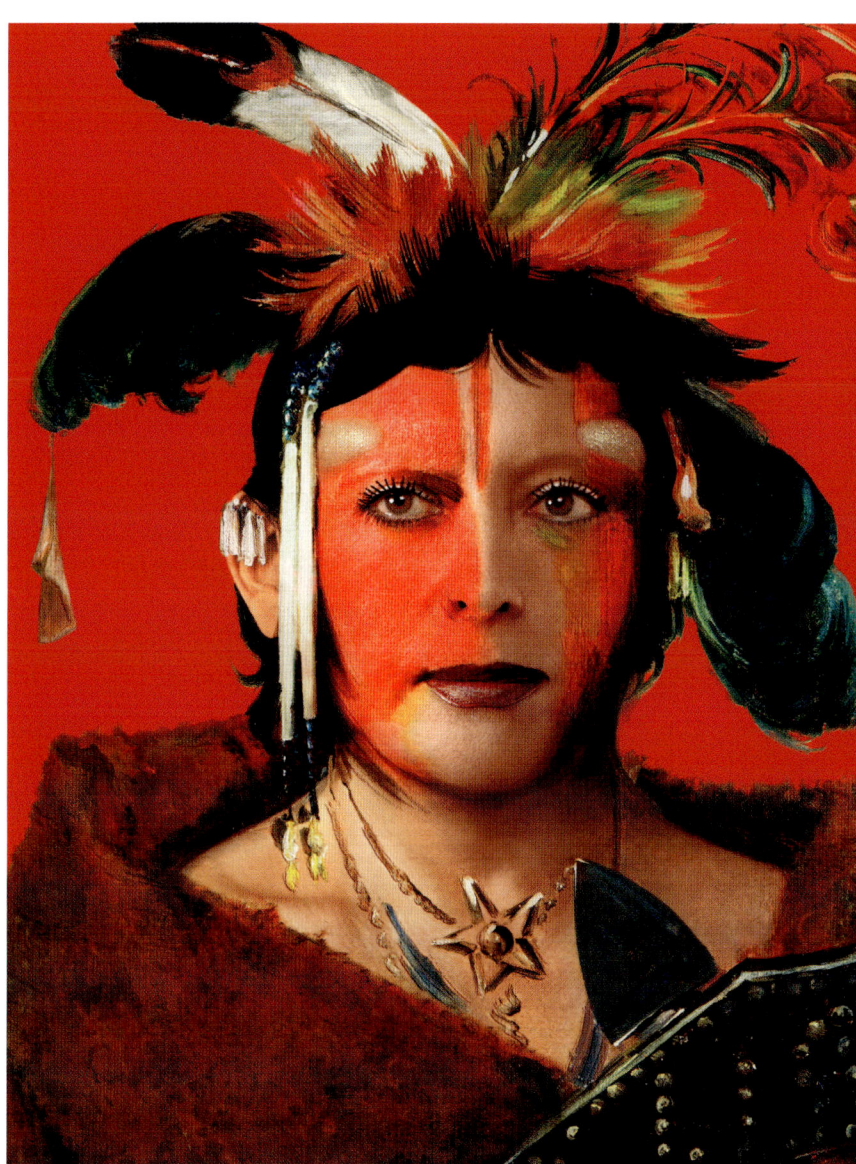

Refiguration Self-Hybridization, American Indian Series #12: "Painted portrait of Chee-me-nah-na-quet, Great Cloud, Son of Grizzly Bear, with photographic portrait of ORLAN," 2006. Digital photograph, 122.4 x 152.4 cm. Musée du Nouveau Monde, La Rochelle, France.

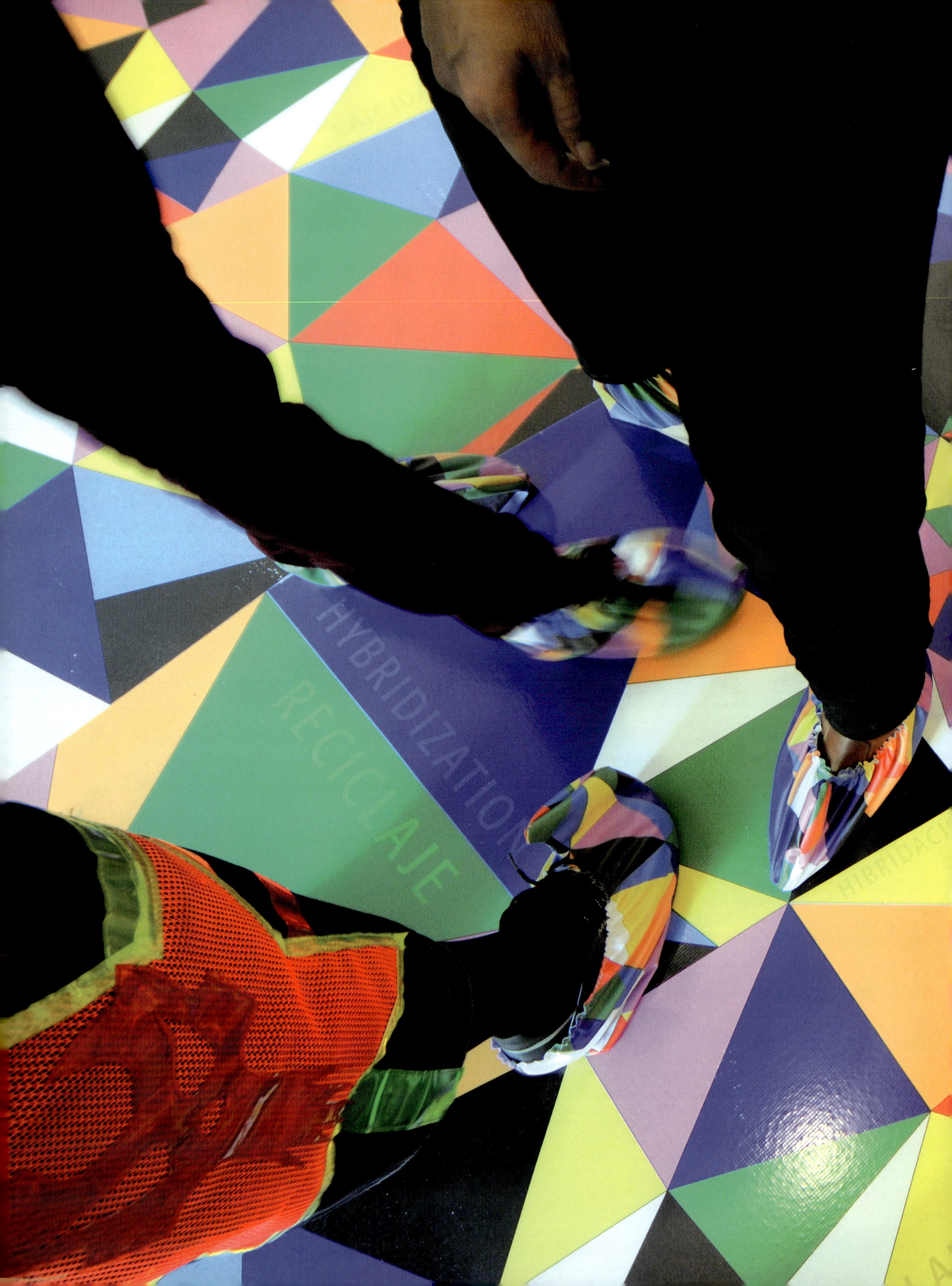

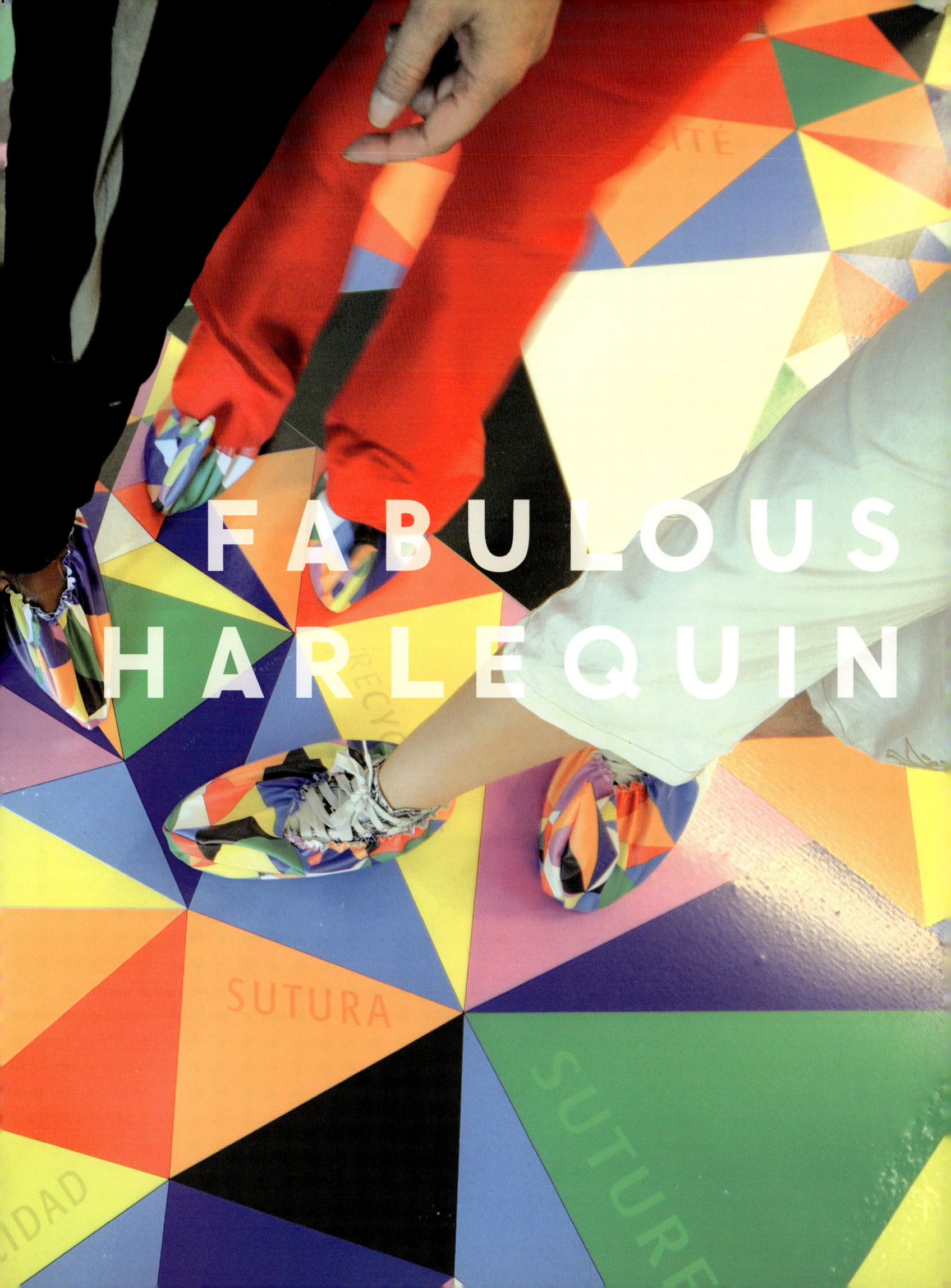

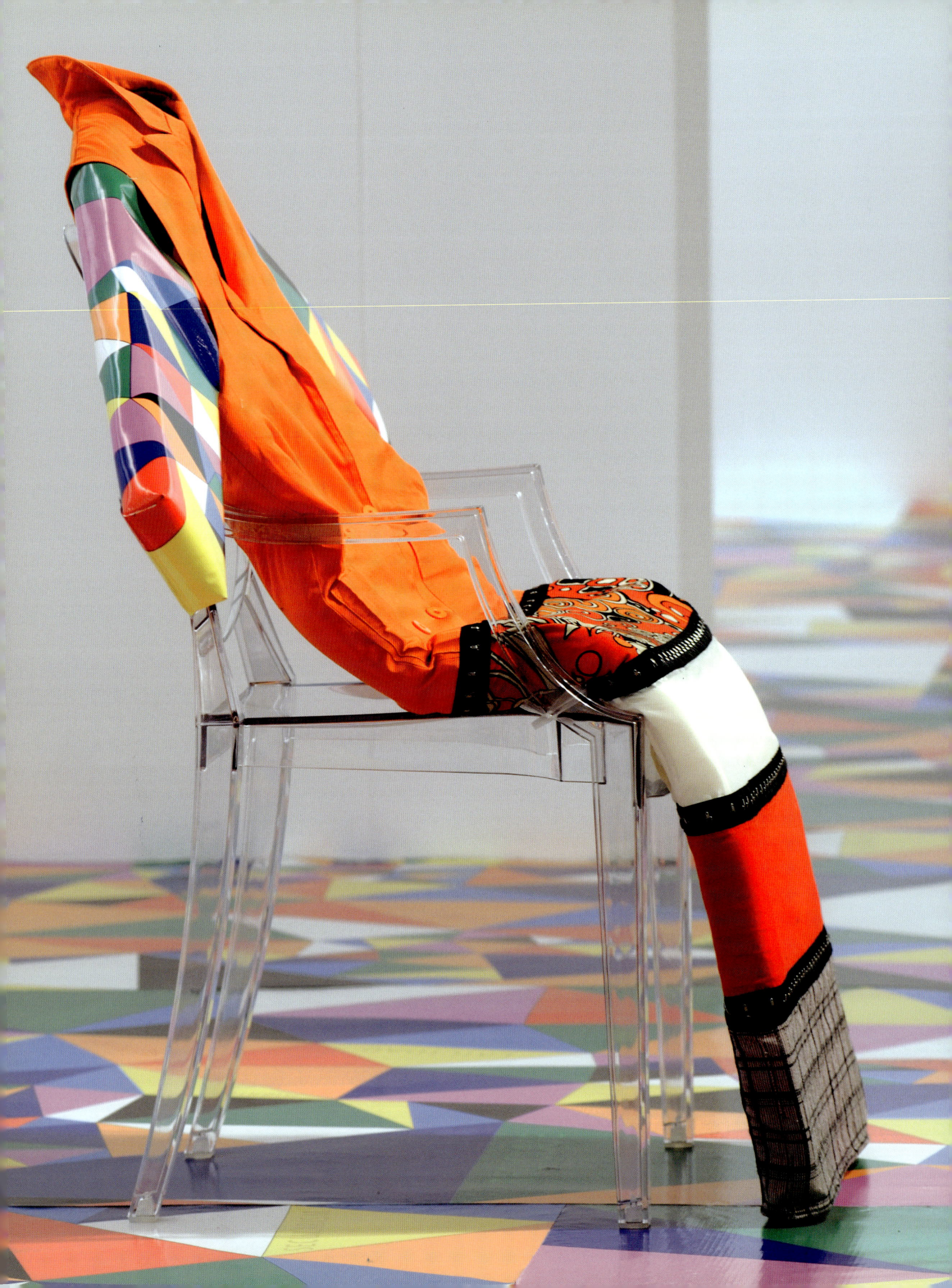

I don't believe in ghosts, I believe in warm exchange between bodies. I play at miscasting Starck's masterly designed Louis Ghost chairs, dressing them in hybridised and recycled clothing.

Offering these altered, inviting ready-mades to spectators so that they can sit on them. Making these non-bodies, these non-objects appear and at once disappear with the aid of garments that formerly covered a body that is no longer there. Those dresses that are ghosts of times, of stories, of forms, and of materials that have been masterised by others, worn by me and therefore chosen among others; by others and by myself. Relic-dresses from different times, now intertwined one with the other.

These hybridized-recycled dresses—here in Murcia with the collaboration of fashion designer davidelfin—have not been draped over the chairs like rags, they have been turned into comfortable objects: cushion and interfaces between a body-object, a chair, and a body-subject, a human being that is invited to sit, covering with her own body the dress which is at once covering the Louis Ghost chair. These bodies-subjects are sitting around the harlequin coat, in itself a hybridisation made out of three of my dresses (a piece made in 2007 in collaboration with the fashion designer Maroussia Rebecq from Andrea Crews).

Sitting requires a moment of pause, of rest . . . when there are other individuals in the space, it is possible to talk, to communicate with each other, to exchange impressions and views; gathering together opens up more possibilities, more openings to the world, and more hybridisations.

Sitting on a pleasant chair for a while is enjoyable. The foam cushions inside the dresses provide the softness the chairs lack. The cushions caress the bodies, provide pleasure, relaxation, and the libre parole . . .

TRANSLATED BY LAMBE AND NIETO

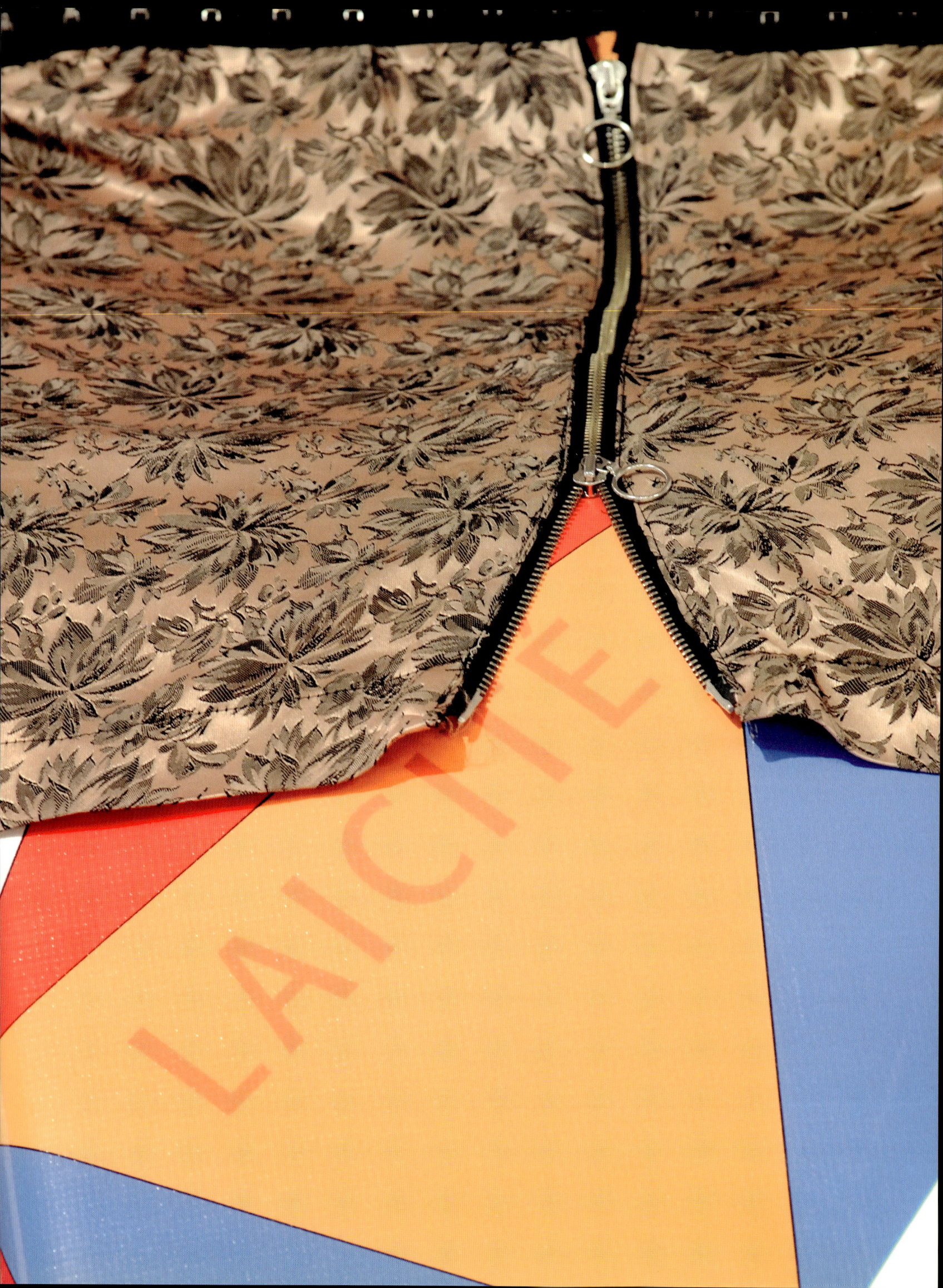

PREFACE TO *THE TROUBADOUR OF KNOWLEDGE*

BACK FROM THE INSPECTION of his lunar lands, Harlequin, emperor, appears on stage for a press conference. What marvels did he see in traversing such extraordinary places? The public is hoping for wondrous eccentricities.

"No, no," he responds to the questions that are fired at him, "everywhere everything is just as it is here, identical in every way to what one can see ordinarily on the terraqueous globe. Except that the degrees of grandeur and beauty change."

Disappointed, the audience cannot believe its ears: elsewhere must surely be different. Was he incapable of observing anything in the course of his voyage? At first silent, dumbfounded, they begin to stir once Harlequin pedantically repeats his lesson: nothing new under the sun or on the moon. The word of King Solomon precedes that of the satellite potentate. There is nothing more to be said, no need for commentary.

Whether royal or imperial, whoever wields power, in fact, never encounters in space anything other than obedience to his power, thus his law: power does not move. When it does, it strides on a red carpet. Thus reason never discovers, beneath its feet, anything but its own rule.

Haughtily, Harlequin looks the spectators up and down with ridiculous disdain and arrogance.

From the middle of the class, which is becoming unruly, a true and troublesome wit rises and extends his hand to designate the Harlequin's cape.

"Hey!" he cries. "You who say that everywhere everything is just as it is here, can you also make us believe that your cape is the same in every part; for example, in front as it is on the back?"

Shocked, the public no longer knows whether to be silent or to laugh; and, in fact, the king's clothing announces the opposite of what he claims. A motley composite made of pieces, of rags or scraps of every size, in a thousand forms and different colors, of varying ages, from different sources, badly basted, inharmoniously juxtaposed, with no attention paid to proximity, mended according to circumstance, according to need, accident, and contingency—does it show a kind of world map, a map of the comedian's travels, like a suitcase studded with stickers? Elsewhere, then, is never like here, no part resembles any other, no province could be compared to this or that one, and all cultures are different. The map-cum-greatcoat belies what the King of the Moon claims.

Gaze with all your eyes at this landscape—zebrine, tigroid, iridescent, shimmering, embroidered, distressed, lashed, lacunar, spotted like an ocelot, colorfully patterned, torn up, knotted together, with overlapping threads, worn fringe, everywhere unexpected, miserable, glorious, so magnificent it takes your breath away and sets your heart beating.

Powerful and flat, speech, monotonous, reigns and vitrifies space; superb in its misery, this improbable garment dazzles. The derisory emperor, who chatters like a parrot, is enveloped in a world map of badly bracketed multiplicities. Pure and simple language or a composite and badly matched garment, glistening, beautiful like a thing: which to choose?

"Are you dressed in the road map of your travels?" says the perfidious wit.

Everyone titters. The king is caught out and discomfited.

Harlequin quickly figured out the only escape from the ridicule his position invites: all he can do is to take off the coat that belies him. He gets up, hesitating, looks, gaping, at the panels of his outfit, then, devoutly, looks at his public, then looks again at his coat, as if seized with embarrassment. The audience laughs, a bit foolishly. He takes his time, everyone waits. The Emperor of the Moon finally makes up his mind.

Harlequin gets undressed; after much grimacing and graceless contortion, he finally lets the motley coat drop to his feet.

Another iridescent envelope then appears: he is wearing another rag beneath the first veil. Disconcerted, the audience laughs again. Thus, it is necessary to start again, because the second envelope, similar to the coat, is composed of new pieces and old bits. It's impossible to describe the second tunic without repeating, like a litany, tigroid, iridescent, zebrine, studded.

Harlequin keeps getting undressed. Another shimmering dress, a new embroidered tunic, then a kind of striated veil appear successively, and still another colorfully patterned body stocking spotted like an ocelot . . . The audience guffaws, increasingly stupefied; Harlequin never gets to his last outfit, while the one before last resembles the antepenultimate as closely as could be desired: motley, composite, torn up . . . Harlequin is wearing a thick layer of these harlequin coats.

Indefinitely, the naked retreats beneath the masks, and the living beneath the doll or the statue swollen with bits of cloth. Certainly, the first coat makes the juxtaposition of pieces visible, but the multiplicity, the overlap of successive, implied envelopes shows and also conceals it. Onion, artichoke, the Harlequin never ceases to shed his layers or to peel off his knotted capes; the public never stops laughing.

All of a sudden, silence; seriousness, even gravity, descends on the audience—the king is naked. Discarded, the last screen has just fallen.

Stupefaction! Tattooed, the Emperor of the Moon exhibits a colorfully patterned skin, more a medley of colors than skin. His whole body looks like a fingerprint. Like a painting on a curtain, the tattooing—striated, iridescent, embroidered, damasked, shimmering—is an obstacle to looking, as much as the clothing or the coats that fall to the ground.

Let the last veil fall and the secret be revealed; it is as complicated as all the barriers that protected it. Even the Harlequin's skin belies the unity presumed in what he says, because it, too, is a harlequin's coat.

The audience tries to laugh again, but it can't anymore: perhaps the man should strip himself—whistles, jeers. Can someone be asked to skin himself?

The audience has seen, it holds its breath. You could hear a pin drop. The Harlequin is only an emperor, even a derisory one; the Harlequin is only a Harlequin, multiple and diverse, undulating and plural, when he dresses and gets undressed: thus named and titled because he protects himself, defends himself, and hides, multiplies, indefinitely. Suddenly, the spectators, as a whole, have managed to see right through the whole mystery.

Here he is now unveiled—and delivered, defenseless—to intuition. Harlequin is a hermaphrodite, a mixed body, male and female. Scandalized, the audience is moved to the point of tears. The naked androgyne mixes genders to the extent that it is impossible to locate the vicinities, the places, or borders where the sexes stop and begin: a man lost in a female, a female mixed with a male. This is how he or she shows him/herself: as a monster.

Monster? A sphinx, beast and girl; centaur, male and horse; unicorn, chimera, composite and mixed body; where and how to locate the site of suture or of blending, the groove where the bone is knotted and tightens, the scar where the lips, the right and the left, the high and the low, but also the angel and the beast, the vain, modest, or vengeful victor and the humble or repugnant victim, the inert and the living,

Black box. Espacio AV, Murcia, Spain, 2008.

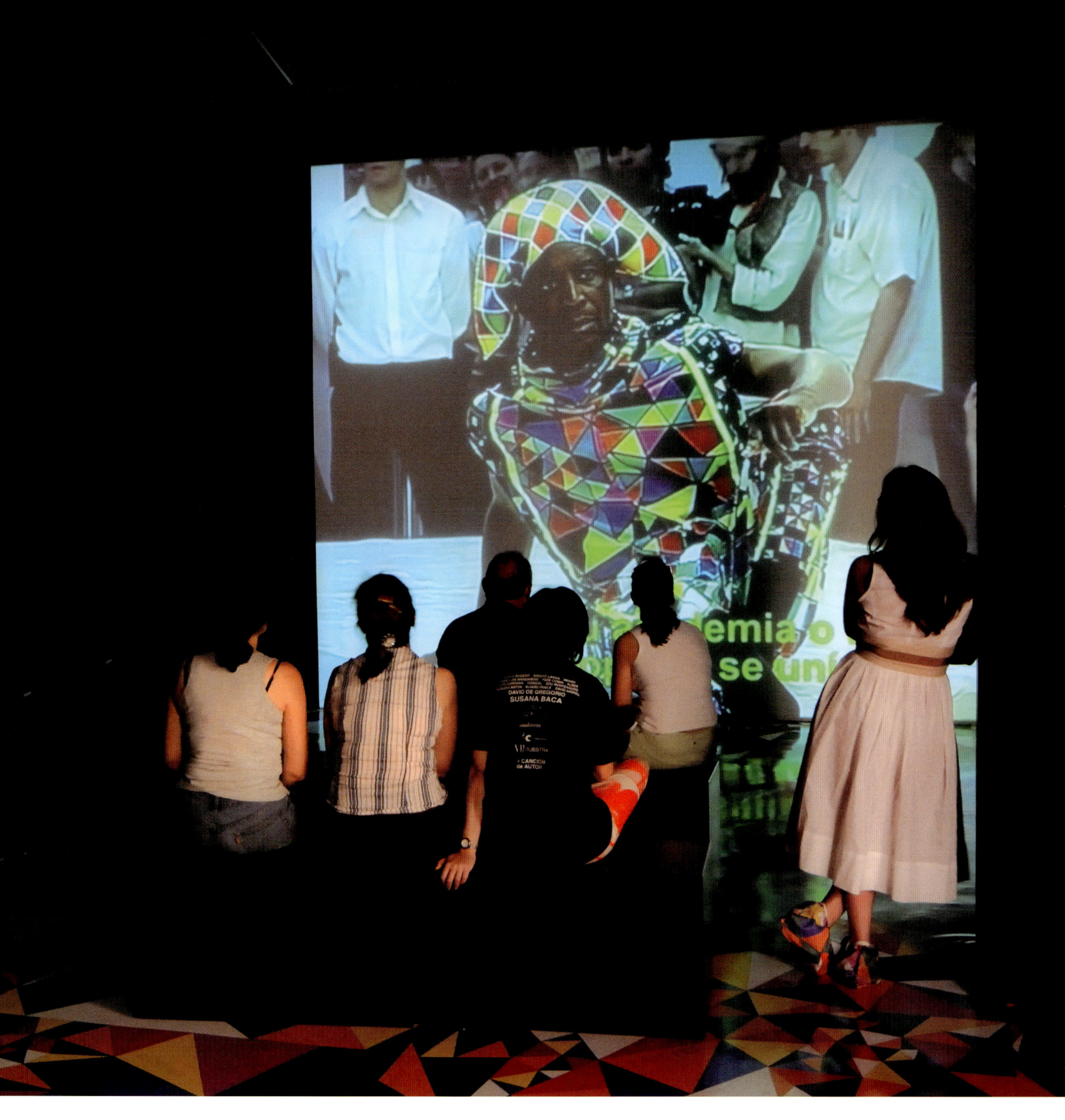

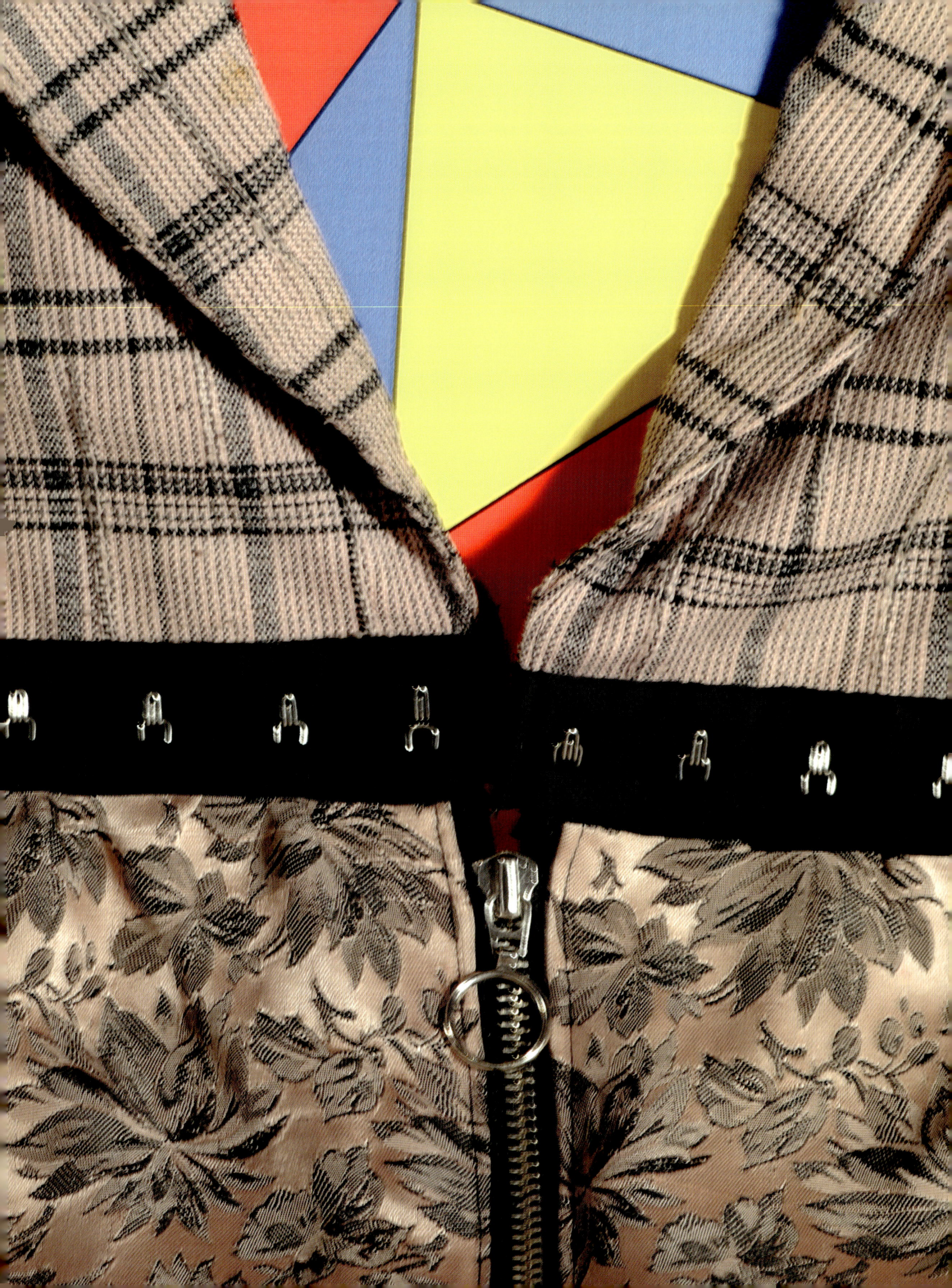

the miserable and the very rich, the complete idiot and the vivacious fool, the genius and the imbecile, the master and the slave, the emperor and the clown are joined? A monster certainly, but normal. What shadow must be cast aside, now, in order to reveal the point of juncture?

Harlequin-Hermaphrodite uses both hands; he is not just ambidextrous but a completed left-hander. You could see this clearly; when he undressed, his capes twirling on both sides, he was adroit even on the left. The charms of childhood combined with the wrinkles proper to the old made one wonder about his age: adolescent or dotard? But above all, when the skin and flesh appeared, the whole world discovered his mixed origin: mulatto, half-caste, Eurasian, hybrid in general, and on what grounds? Quadroon, octoroon? And if he was not playing the kind, even as comedy, one would have the urge to say bastard or mongrel, crossbreed. Mixed blood, mestizo or mestiza, diluted.

What could the current, tattooed, ambidextrous monster, hermaphrodite and half-breed, make us see now under his skin? Yes, flesh and blood. Science speaks of organs, functions, cells, and molecules, to admit finally that it's been a long time since life has been spoken of in laboratories, but it never says flesh, which, very precisely, designates the mixture of muscles and blood, skin and hairs, bones, nerves, and diverse functions, which thus mixes what the relevant disciplines analyze. Life throws the dice or plays cards. Harlequin discovers, in the end, his flesh. Combined, the mixed flesh and blood of Harlequin are still quite likely to be taken for a harlequin coat.

Quite some time ago, a number of spectators left the room, tired of the failed dramatic moment, irritated with this turn from comedy to tragedy, having come to laugh and been disappointed at having to think. Some, doubtless specialists in their fields, had even understood, on their own, that each portion of their knowledge also looks like Harlequin's coat, because each works at the intersection or the interference of many other disciplines and, sometimes, of almost all of them. In this way, their academy or the encyclopedia formally joined commedia dell'arte.

Now then, when everybody has his back turned, and the oil lamps were giving signs of flickering out, and it seemed that this evening the improvisation had ended up being a flop, someone suddenly called out, as if something new were playing in a place where everything had, that evening, been a repetition, so that the public as a whole turned back as one, all looking toward the stage, violently illuminated by the dying fires of the footlights: "Pierrot! Pierrot!" the audience cried, *"Pierrot Lunaire!"*

In the very same spot where the Emperor of the Moon had stood was a dazzling, incandescent mass, more clear than pale, more transparent than wan, lilylike, snowy, candid, pure and virginal, all white.

"Pierrot! Pierrot!" cried the fools again, as the curtain fell.

As they filed out, they were asking: "How can the thousand hues of an odd medley of colors be reduced to their white summation?"

"Just as the body," the learned responded, "assimilates and retains the various differences experienced during travel and returns home a half-breed of new gestures and other customs, dissolved in the body's attitudes and functions to the point that it believes that as far as it is concerned nothing has changed, so the secular miracle of tolerance, of the benevolent neutrality welcomes, in peace, just as many apprenticeships in order to make the liberty of invention, thus of thought, spring forth from them."

TRANSLATED BY SHEILA FARIA GLASER
AND WILLIAM PAULSON

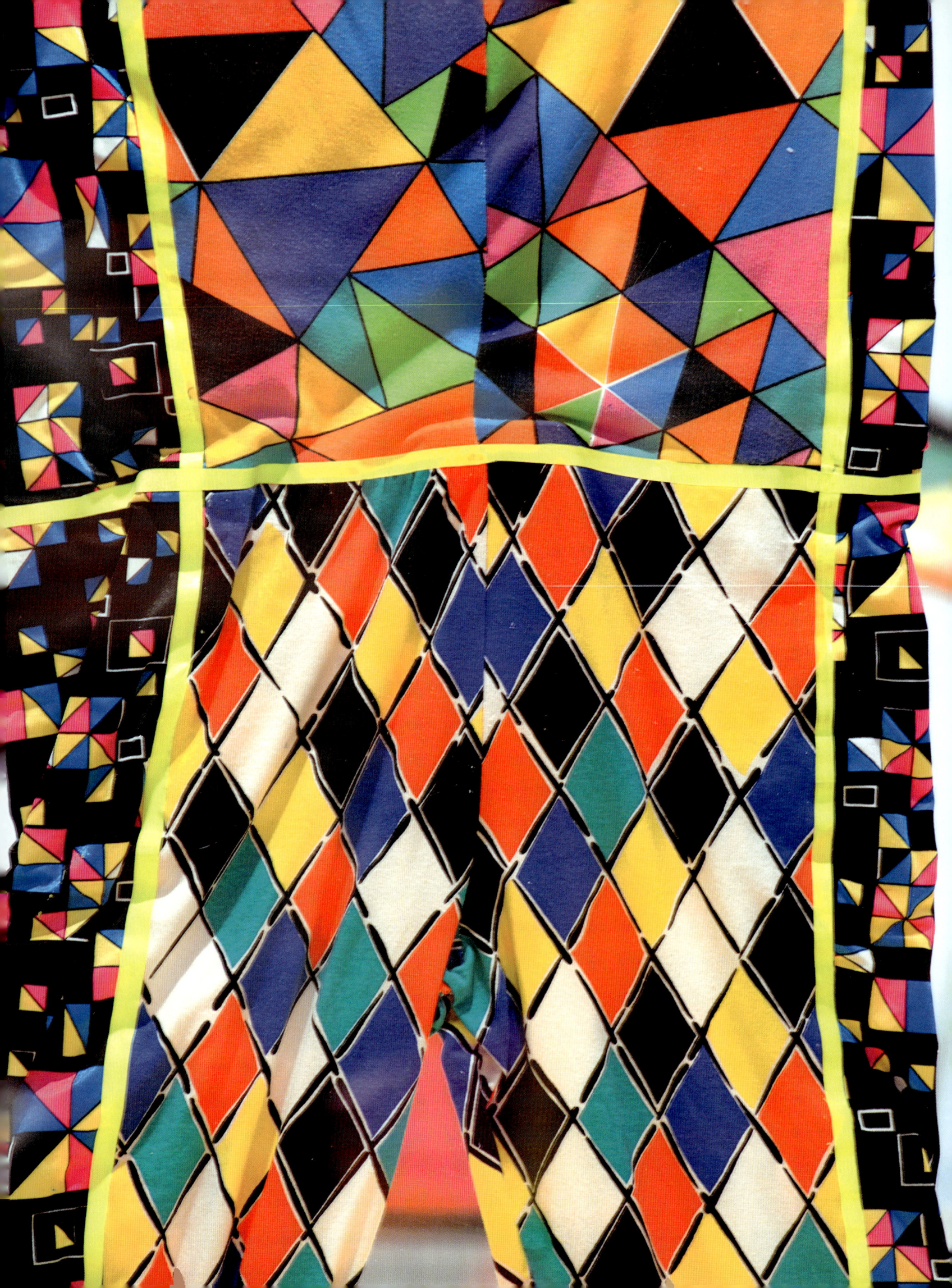

FASHIONING HYBRIDITY

RHONDA K. GARELICK

The stage should be invaded by these chairs, this crowd of present absences. . . . After a certain point the chairs no longer represent fixed characters. . . . They take on their own life.

—Eugène Ionesco, "Notes on *The Chairs*"

IN HIS ABSURDIST PLAY *les chaises* [*the chairs*], Eugène Ionesco uses empty chairs to conjure a crowd of spectral characters that the audience never sees but with whom Ionesco's two protagonists, played by actual actors, converse throughout the play. The chairs stand in dramatically for bodies, existing as purely theatrical characters, devoid of actors and costumes. The play forces spectators to acknowledge their own agency in the construction of performed identities, to see that identities exist dialogically, through language and social interaction. By the end, we lose our certainty of which characters exist in the flesh and which have been projected into existence by our desires and imagination.

In "Suture, Hybridization, Recycling" ORLAN seems to tip her hat to Ionesco, building her exhibition partially upon a circle of empty chairs, in a large-scale theatrical installation interrogating the parameters of selfhood. The exhibition raises some of the same questions investigated by Ionesco: How is identity performed? What renders us recognizable? Where or how, beneath our many layers of culturally tailored roles, do we exist? For over forty years, ORLAN has dared us to rethink our most basic assumptions about beauty, religion, art history, sexuality, and, ultimately, about the stability of the self. "Il faut toujours se méfier de la personne qu'on était" (One must always mistrust the person one was),[1] she has said—an apt credo for an artist who has spent a lifetime redesigning her persona, as well as years refashioning her actual physical being. With "Suture, Hybridization, Recycling" she now investigates even more deeply the frontier between self and other.

Situating herself within multiple genres at the same time, ORLAN sees her work as rhizomatic, borrowing the Deleuzean term; and the present exhibition powerfully demonstrates this quality. Here, in a highly collaborative endeavor, ORLAN literally and figuratively weaves together strands borrowed from biogenetics, fashion, design, philosophy, photography, and Renaissance performance history—specifically the commedia dell'arte tradition, from which she borrows the "Harlequin's coat," whose multicolored patchwork costume provides a motif at once visual and metaphorical.

This is not the first time that ORLAN has turned to the commedia dell'arte's Harlequin character for inspiration. In "Omniprésences" of 1993, the seventh and last of her surgery-performances, the artist kept a tubular harlequin hat perched atop her head throughout the procedure, while the medical team wore matching outfits of the same colorful pattern designed by Issey Miyake. Furthermore, during that surgery, ORLAN read aloud from a short text, "Laïcité" [Secularism], the preface to Michel Serres's *The Troubadour of Knowledge*. "Laïcité" is something of a philosophical prose poem by Serres, in which he posits the Harlequin as an avatar of human freedom and radical otherness, as a figure of profound epistemological daring. In Serres's text, the Harlequin is a grave yet fanciful figure, a performer whose being conjures the possibility of infinite identities coexisting. A futuristic, nearly science-fictional character, Serres's Harlequin (the Emperor of the Moon, who is just back from "inspecting his lunar properties") also evokes the ancient, hybrid creatures of Greek mythology: "Monstre? Sphinx, bête et fille; centaure, mâle et cheval; licorne, chimère, corps composite et mélangé."[2] "Laïcité" is a favorite text of ORLAN's and while it will not be read aloud this time, its title can be found imprinted within the colored Harlequin lozenges of the linoleum; and its spirit infuses the entire exhibition.

Serres's version of the Harlequin clearly attracts ORLAN. In her 2007 installation *Le Manteau de l'Arlequin*, she returned to the Harlequin motif, this time extending the patchwork or collage concept of his costume from the level of textile to that of the biological cell, recalling the science-fiction resonance of Serres's protagonist. Working with the scientists of SymbioticA—the collaborative art and science research laboratory at the University of Western Australia in Perth—ORLAN succeeded in creating a "Harlequin coat" composed partly of tissue from her own biopsied skin cells (excised in a diamond-shaped lozenge from her groin during a videotaped procedure, displayed as part of this exhibition), cultured in a bioreactor along with cells from diverse other organisms, including an aborted fetus of African origin, a marsupial, and a lactating human breast.

Petri dishes containing these co-cultured cells were then embedded within the diamond-patterned Perspex acrylic material of the Harlequin costume, while the entirety was lit by filmically projected images of living and dead cells. The coat is here again on display, standing up in its transparent case.

An artwork partially born in a laboratory, the Harlequin's coat, with its co-cultured cells, represents the product of an alternative, artificial version of cellular interaction, even while some of its constitutive elements evoke the components of more "natural" biological processes: ORLAN's groin-area skin cells, the lactating breast, and fetal cells all gesture toward the sites and products of human conception and pregnancy, for example. The marsupial cells (from a fat-tailed dunnart) introduce the presence of these rare animals whose females carry offspring inside their own bodies (in their pouches) even after giving birth, in a kind of inversion of gestation in which the inside becomes the outside.

These once-living cells, conjoined in a latter-day Ovidian process at Perth, now form but one layer of the current exhibition. They serve as a biogenetic translation of the patchwork motifs visible—designed by ORLAN—on the gallery floor and walls, in the hybridized garments that fuse ORLAN's personal wardrobe with new creations by designer davidelfin, and in the Philippe Starck "ghost" chairs, which are upholstered with cushions constructed of these hybrid garments (and out of some of which protrude "limbs" covered with the harlequin pattern. In other words, the entire exhibition is "harlequinized"; that is, ORLAN has designed it so that each individual object displays hybridity, and each element of said hybridity can in turn be further dismantled into its own composite, collage-like elements in a harlequinesque *mise-en-abîme*.[3] Like the Russian *matroucka* dolls, whose bodies open to reveal ever smaller versions of themselves nesting within, this exhibition, for all its apparent diversity of media and reference, retains the powerful running motif of harlequinized, multivalent entities at every level from the tiniest cells (invisible to our eyes) to the fabrics and chairs sewn and upholstered together into what ORLAN sees as modified Duchampian ready-mades.

Such a strong, recognizable signature motif is in keeping with the original spirit of the Harlequin, the comic theatrical figure born of the commedia dell'arte tradition of the sixteenth century. The genre of the commedia relied upon a series of stock characters with known, exaggerated personalities (Pantalone, the old man; il Dottore, the charlatan; il Capitano, the ladies' man; etc.), which could be endlessly recombined into different, improvised plot lines. While the actors varied and the stories changed, the characters—and their costumes—did not. Within the commedia dell'arte, then, the fictional characters remained the stable point of reference, irrespective of which actors played the parts. Theatrical identity and costumes determined the identities perceived by the audience, not the "real" individuals who inhabited them. Of all the consistent, yet fictional characters, Harlequin or "Arlecchino" was the most beloved and has enjoyed the greatest cultural longevity, for reasons quite pertinent to this exhibition.

According to the commedia's ongoing narrative, Harlequin worked (in most versions) for Dottore, a man so miserly that he obliged his servant to wear a coat of humble rags sewn together in patchwork fashion—this was the origin of the distinctive costume that later grew more refined and stylized. The Harlequin figured among the first clowns in the commedia and eventually rose to become the chief character of its stable of *zanni* or comic servant roles. Beginning as a simple buffoon, Harlequin developed into a clever and acrobatic leading player around whom entire sketches were built. He owed his popularity to the complexity of his character, for Harlequin was at once a light-hearted clown who danced and joked, and a sly, cunning trickster known for his wit, philosophy, and for the aura of disturbing magic that seemed to surround him. In addition to his colorful suit, in his earliest incarnation the Harlequin wore a chinstrap of coarse black hair and a black half-mask that covered his eyes and gave him a slightly demonic mien. These accoutrements hinted at the Harlequin's connection to the supernatural, as well as to his mixed-race identity, for the character was originally meant to suggest a black African man—an association that, at the time, connoted dangerous, even deadly powers. While he eventually lost the mask and facial hair, lessening his apparent racial difference, the Harlequin's basic costume remained consistent, as did his association with the underworld and its attendant mystical forces.[4]

For over four hundred years this suggestion of magic has intrigued artists of every stripe who continue to reinterpret the Harlequin motif. Modernists in particular were drawn to this trickster hero. Degas, Cézanne, and Picasso all painted versions of the Harlequin; Apollinaire devoted poems to him; and Meyerhold saw in him a progenitor of his own superhuman, biomechanical stage creatures: "Harlequin is a foolish simpleton, a sly servant yet seeming always to be a joker. But look, what is hidden

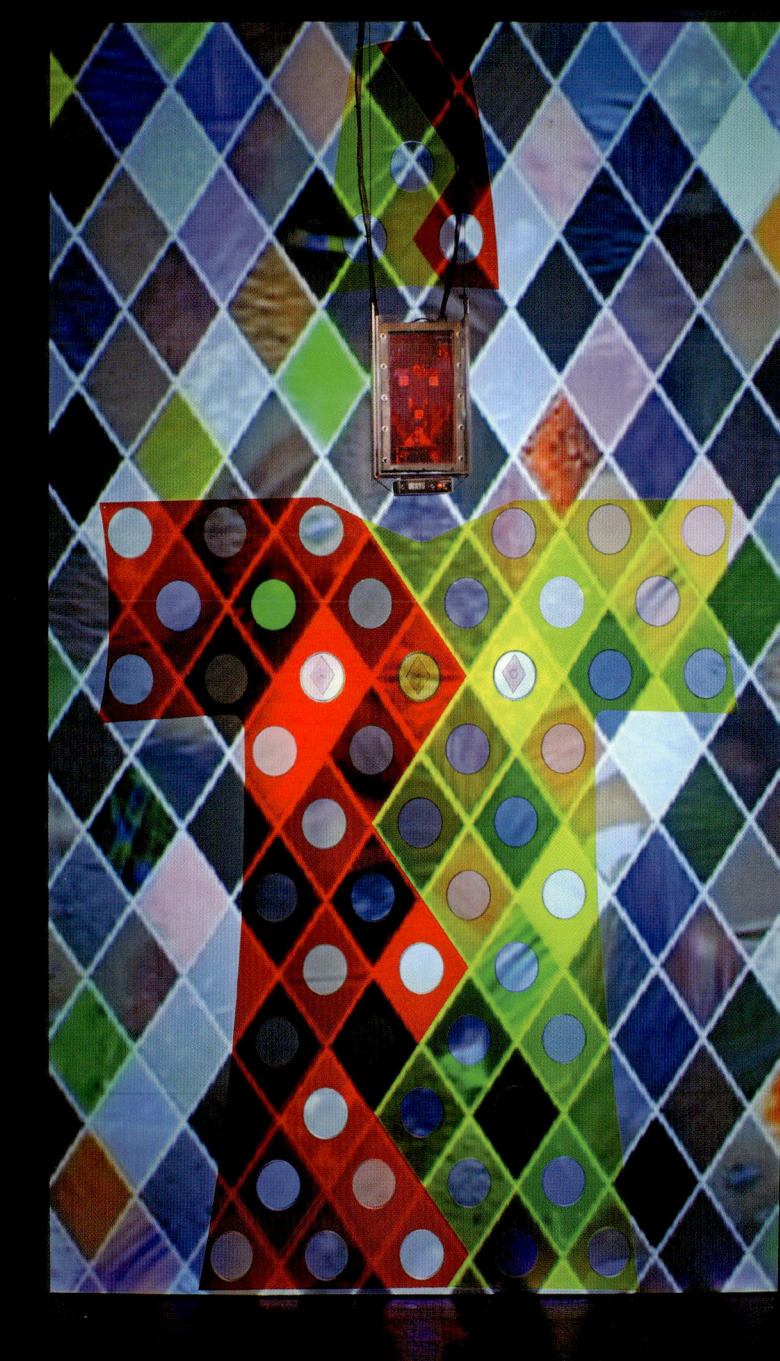

Harlequin Coat, bioreactor, cells, video projection, plexiglass sculpture, Casino Luxembourg, Luxembourg, 2009

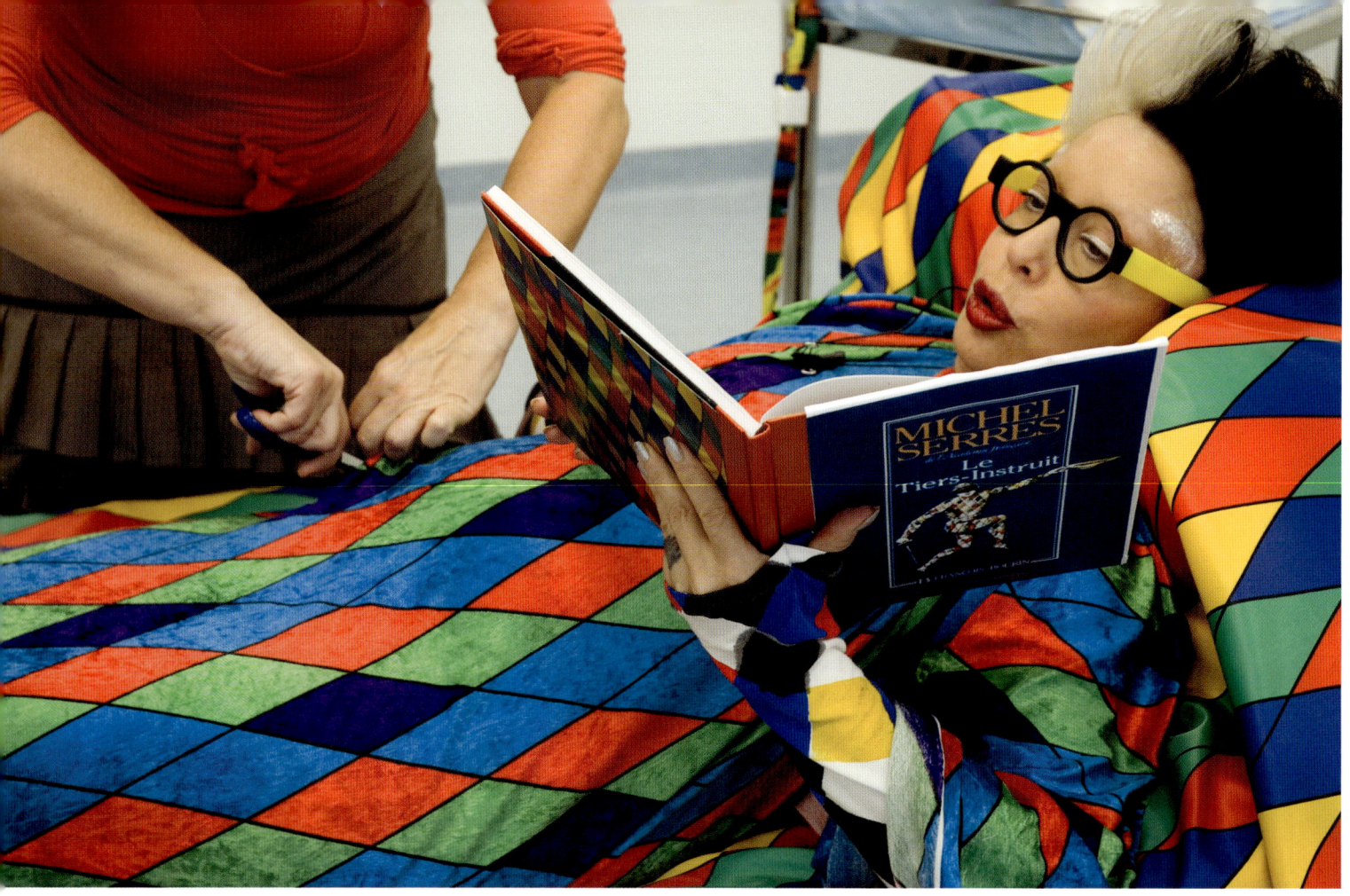

behind his mask? Harlequin the all powerful magician, the enchanter, the wizard. Harlequin, the representative of infernal forces."[5]

Harlequin, then, embodies contradictions: he incarnates a supremely recognizable, almost trademark-like identity, retaining his look and appeal over centuries. But this identity relies upon multiple, shifting personae. In his landmark study, *Portrait de l'artiste en saltimbanque*, Jean Starobinski teases out this very paradox: "The harlequins . . . [are] neither male nor female. . . . Hybrid beasts, [they] possess the awareness of the half-gods of Egypt. . . . [T]he Harlequin's supernatural power derives from his familiarity with the realm of death. . . . [D]rawing heaven nearer to earth, Harlequin supernaturally unites that which nature has separated. . . . All true clowns come from another space, another universe: his entrance must be a crossing of the limits of the real. . . . [H]e must appear to us as a ghost [*un revenant*]."[6]

ORLAN has chosen to share the paradox of the Harlequin. Like him, she performs her identity via a mutating series of varied racial, sexual, and historical sources. As her Self-Hybridization Series makes particularly clear, ORLAN's recognizability, like the Harlequin's, resides in her theatrical persona, and not within any kind of "authentic" flesh-and-blood self lying beneath it. When we contemplate ORLAN's myriad hybrid photographs of herself, we see the borrowed features of African, American Indian, or Pre-Colombian physiognomy and statuary, to be sure. Sometimes we see an ambiguity of gender. But just as clearly we see ORLAN, or rather the character of ORLAN, as she continually redesigns it over time.

Someone who crosses this many boundaries necessarily dismantles, even rips apart, our most reassuring assumptions about identity.[7] Such a process can be very unsettling, as Starobinski suggests when he likens the harlequin to a ghost or *revenant*, a creature both alive and dead, present and absent. In this exhibition, the Harlequin Coat, standing upright yet bodiless, has a ghostly quality. Presiding silently over the gallery, the coat delineates a human figure but, like a ghost, lacks all bodily substance. The chairs, grouped conversationally around the coat, share its curious immateriality for they are of course Philippe Starck's famous "ghost" chairs. Starck's chairs telegraph equally their historical and contemporary resonances. Their silhouettes replicate that of their eighteenth-century ancestors; but being constructed entirely of transparent plastic, they are unmistakably modern. These chairs are *revenants*, time travelers from the court of Louis XV, colorless shadows of their former ornate selves. Like the Harlequin, whose identity resides in his costume not what lies beneath, the chairs acquire their colorful depth from the exterior, from their cushions, and, implicitly, from the several signtures that they bear. As

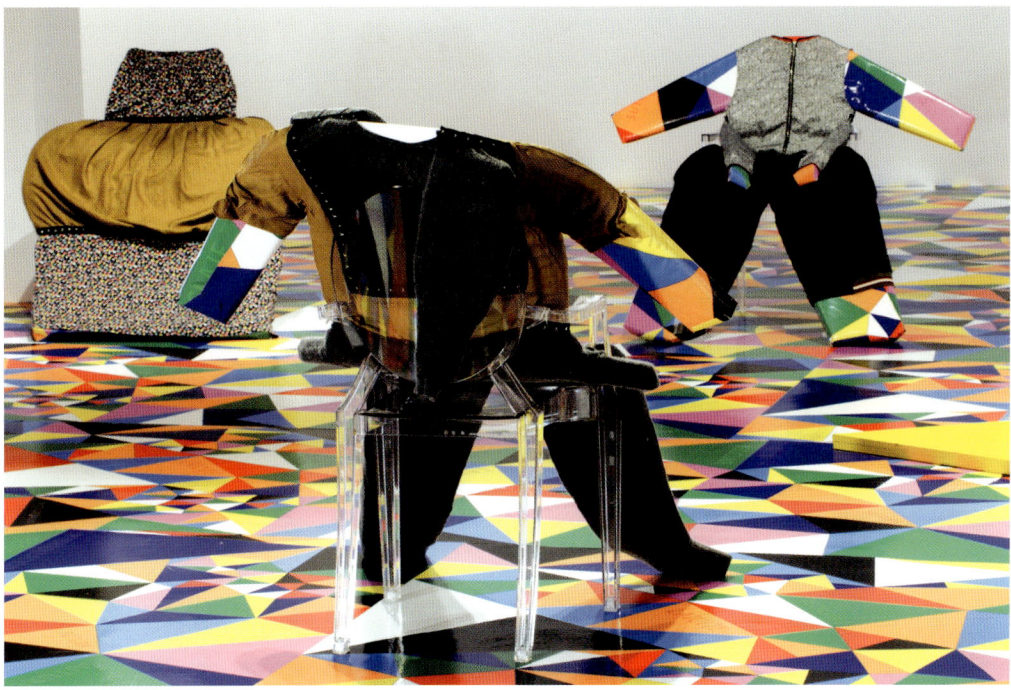

furniture-ghosts, they are "signed" historically by their association, with the Baroque.[8] They bear equally the signature of their famous designer, Philippe Starck, whose name has itself become a famous brand connoting luxury, newness, and the glamorous series of international hotels whose posh interiors he has designed.[9] And the chairs now sport two additional signatures: ORLAN's and that of celebrated Spanish couturier davidelfin, who here merges his own designs with elements of ORLAN's wardrobe, creating the hybridized, recycled clothing-upholstery covering.

When we sit upon these reupholstered ghost chairs, we sign the chairs again—with our bodies, impressing ourselves temporarily upon the fabric. The process is reciprocal: the chairs sign us as well; we merge with these objects just as our feet—in the borrowed harlequin slippers we receive at the door—merge with the patterned floor beneath them.

Our limbs mingle with those harlequin-patterned, prosthesis-like limbs that emerge from the clothes. We are now hybrid creatures too, subsumed for a time by the multilayered process set in motion by the exhibition. ORLAN insists upon this communality, upon the social, welcoming nature of the experience, reminding us that we pull up a chair in order to "talk, communicate, exchange, and meet." She points out that the hybridized garments attenuate the hard plastic of the ghost chairs, making them softer and more

welcoming: "the cushions caress the body, offer pleasure, relaxation, easy conversation."[10]

Yet as we enjoy the social, vibrant, even democratic contact implied by the chairs, we cannot escape their connotation of lack, of absence, even death. The first absence of course resides in the chair's self-declared "spectrality," their resistance to their own materiality, their association with ghosts—spirits of the departed. Even the garment-cushions have a slightly uncanny quality, for seated there in different positions, granted three-dimensionality by the foam stuffing within, they can be mistaken for lifeless, headless bodies, vestiges perhaps of interlocutors past. Those several "limbs" that are covered with harlequin-patterned fabric suggest the presence of a fragmented Harlequin body beneath the cushions, a layer of costume beneath the costume. This uncanniness finds its echo in the photographs circling the gallery's upper walls in a frieze. In this series a woman turns away from us, denying us her face, the typical marker of identity, while displaying a collection of hybridized garments—or perhaps

Biopsy, The Harlequin Coat, Perth University, Australia, 2007. Surgery-performance. Photograph by Tony Nathan.

Suture, Hibridization, Recycling: ORLAN + davidelfin, installation, Espacio AV, Murcia, Spain.

replacing her personal identity with that of the clothes—yet another move that recalls the Harlequin, the purely theatrical being who lives only in the realm of costume and attitude, never personal biography. This mysterious fashion model who seems to fly around the perimeter of the gallery ceiling evokes a surrealist frisson familiar from the works of Magritte, for example, who often painted figures of deliberately obscured identity, figures seen only from behind, or with faces veiled.

Looking at the many relationships here, we see a series of gaps never fully closed: between the cushions and the chairs, at the seams of the various garments sewn together, between the Plexiglas coat and the Petri dishes embedded within, and between the very cells within these dishes, there remains, perpetually, a distance to be bridged. We recall the first word of this exhibition's title, "suture," the Lacanian term that "names the relation of the subject to the chain of its discourse . . . [figuring] there as the element which is lacking, in the form of a stand-in," in the words of Jacques-Alain Miller.[11]

For Lacan, the subject's passage into the symbolic order effects a disruption, a gap or lack that subtends the constitution of the self in and through language. As Joan Copjec has written of suturing in relation to representation: *"The failure of representation produces rather than disrupts identity.* That missing part which representation . . . cuts off is the absence around which the subject weaves its fantasies."[12] As Copjec makes clear, such suturing of a void or wound is necessarily a creative, productive act in the face of absence. ORLAN has created a large-scale performance of and as this productive suturing, via the cushions that lend color and depth to "ghost" chairs, through the garments sewn and the cells co-cultured. ORLAN's own multivalent, multiply sutured (in the surgical sense) image remains unseen here. While her face (or various permutations of it) often figures prominently in her work, in this case, ORLAN has chosen to subsume her image entirely into the enchained, signifying processes here, into the collaborative works on display. She is visible only as one signature among many. "We are all playing together. . . . There are no great heroes here."[13]

The final gap that ORLAN negotiates here may be the most daunting, that between the animate and inanimate worlds. In her creation of these slightly macabre assemblages ("modified ready-mades," as she calls them) and her weaving of the Harlequin's coat, ORLAN has made chairs and clothing—inanimate objects—seem to come alive. She has dramatized a series of oscillations, a va-et-vient between biology and design, between science and fashion; and she has given us a role, too. We enter this space and for a time we meld into our surroundings. In their harlequin slippers, our feet disappear into the harlequin floor; our bodies mingle with these human-shaped cushions. It's a luxurious feeling for we are touched by the glamorous aura that attends the contributions of couturier davidelfin and of Philippe Starck. But let us recall that the Harlequin's coat was once just a meager garment, composed of rags stitched together. Over time, as his character gained power and magical connotations, the coat too metamorphosed into something sleeker and more finished. The Harlequin's coat, then, owes something of its dazzling colors and clean lines to the character's transformative magic.

Such magic persists today. The commercial seductions of haute couture and upscale design find their roots in ancient magic, in the world of the supernatural where everyday objects can acquire unusual powers. As Pierre Bourdieu has written, "What makes the value, the magic of the designer label [*la griffe*] is the collusion of all the agents of the system of production of sacred goods. This collusion is, of course, perfectly unconscious."[14]

It is fitting to end with Bourdieu's reminder of the connection between sacred objects and luxury products, for as we have noted, this exhibition draws inspiration from Michel Serres's text "Laïcité," which serves as an introduction to his treatise on secular education, *The Troubadour of Knowledge* [*Le Tiers-Instruit*]. The word "laïcité" explicitly raises the question of religion only to countermand it, a move that ORLAN frequently makes in her own work. In recasting herself as Saint ORLAN, for example, in her reinterpretations of sacred objects such as crucifixes or the shrouds of saints, or in her fabrication of reliquaries containing her surgically removed flesh or tissue, she has repeatedly borrowed and subverted the rituals and lexicon of the Catholic church for her own feminist, critical, and highly secular ends.

The sacred objects here are not overtly religious; they find their provenance in the commercial realm of luxury goods—the realm Bourdieu so clearly links to ancient magic and religion. Harlequin-like, ORLAN has made a patchwork of these objects, unsettling and hybridizing their functional identities, and by extension, the identities of those who visit the installation and sit temporarily upon these chairs.

Biopsy, The Harlequin Coat,
Perth University, Australia,
2007. Surgery-performance.
Photograph by Tony Nathan.

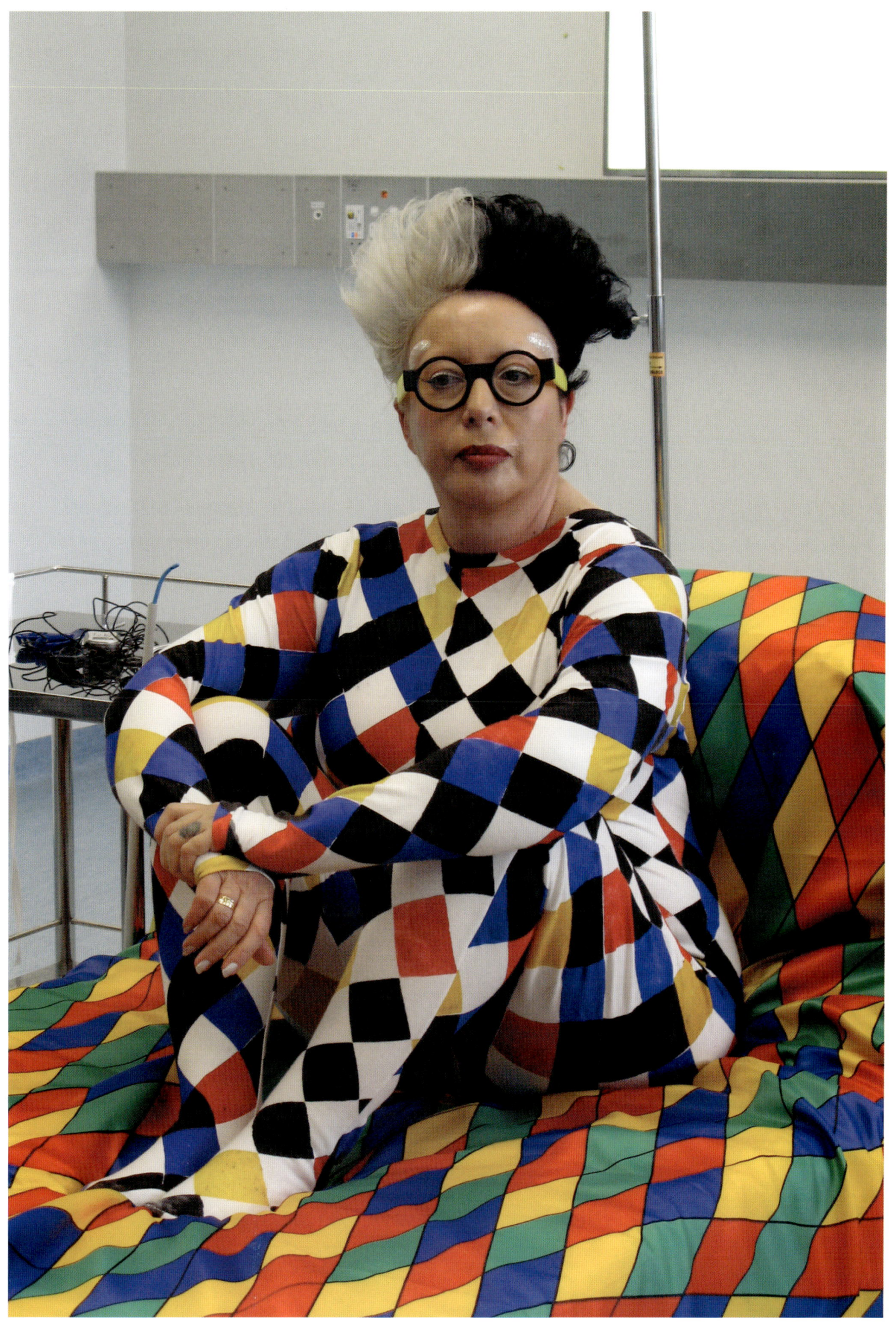

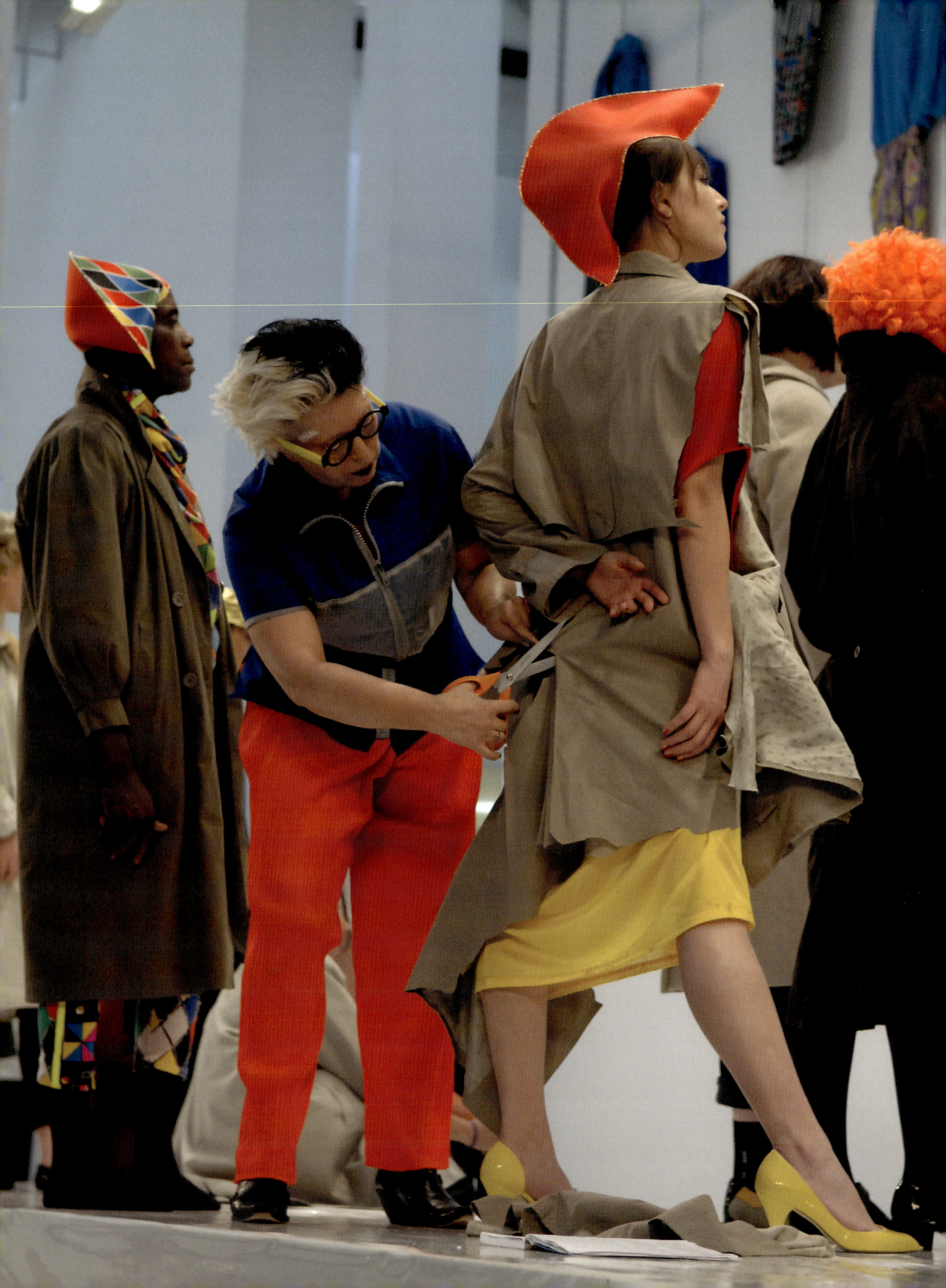

One might recall here the ancient rituals conducted in worship of Dionysus, in which participants sought to achieve trancelike ecstasy, subsuming their individual identities in order to merge with and through the god.[15]

Here, from within the arena of the modern sacred —the art gallery and the world of luxury goods— ORLAN has staged a large-scale, theatrical ritual that dares to resemble a Dionysian ritual, only in this case the central figure is the Harlequin who has no divine status (and inspires none of the bloodlust or cannibalism associated with Dionysus).

ORLAN's staging of ecstatic merging is entirely secular and rigorously egalitarian. As we put on the harlequin slippers and sit in the harlequin chairs, we are not worshippers ("no great heroes here") but active participants. We enter the Harlequin's permeable character and he enters us, and we are haunted by the void or lack that underlies all attempts to define one's self. We are faced with the impossibility of fixed identities. While disturbing, however, this impossibility comes to us in a playful, mischievous way, via the spirit of the Harlequin, the mysterious clown who roams yet among us.

NOTES

Epigraph: Eugène Ionesco, "Notes on *The Chairs*," in *The Chairs*, trans. Martin Crimp (London: Faber and Faber, 1997), 59–60. Originally published in French by Gallimard in 1958.

1. Private conversation with the artist, Los Angeles, December 26, 2006.

2. Michel Serres, "Laïcité," in *Le Tiers-Instruit* (Paris: F. Bourin-Julliard, 1994), 15.

3. This sequential, auto-regressive structure resembles Lacan's concept of the constantly sliding signifying chain, which he describes as "rings in a necklace that is a ring in another necklace made of rings" [anneaux dont le collier se scelle dans l'anneau d'un autre collier fait d'anneaux]. Jacques Lacan, "L'insistence de la lettre dans l'inconscient," 259. The foregrounding of upholstery here furthers this exhibition's Lacanian underpinnings by calling to mind Lacan's metaphor of the "points de capiton"—the anchoring points or "upholstery buttons"—representing attachment points between signifiers, moments which halt the otherwise constant sliding movement [glissement] of signification, giving the illusion of stable meaning.

4. "[I]t must be repeated that fundamentally Harlequin remained the same . . . and that he is recognizable in all his guises." Allardyce Nicoll, *The World of the Harlequin* (Cambridge: Cambridge University Press), 70. See also Robert Henke, *Performance and Literature in the Commedia dell'Arte* (Cambridge: Cambridge University Press, 2002).

5. Quoted in C. Moody, "Vsevolod Meyerhold and the *Commedia dell'arte*," *Modern Language Review* 73, no. 4 (October 1975): 866.

6. Jean Starobinski, *Portrait de l'artiste en saltimbanque* (Geneva: Albert Skira, 1970; Paris: Gallimard, 2004), 100–101. My translation.

7. In her performance installation at her 2007 retrospective at Saint-Étienne's Museum of Modern Art performance, ORLAN literalized her motif of ripping apart assumptions. She appeared onstage with her face and body completely encased in a vast black cocoon-like garment that she proceeded to cut open with scissors, finally tearing apart the fabric with her hands and stepping out from it dressed in a multicolored patchwork garment, thereby staging her own autochthonous rebirth.

8. ORLAN's oeuvre has long been in dialogue with the Baroque period, as we see in her Reincarnation of Saint ORLAN series, which reinterprets the classically draped figures of Bernini, particularly his *Ecstasy of Saint Theresa*.

9. These include the Royalton in New York, the Mondrian in Los Angeles, the Delano in Miami Beach, the Saint Martins Lane in London, and Le Meurice in Paris.

10. ORLAN, "Libre Parole," 1.

11. Jacques-Alain Miller, "Suture (Elements of the Logic of the Signifier)," trans. Jacqueline Rose, *Screen* 18, no. 4 (1977–78): 25–26. This essay was originally published in French in *Cahiers pour l'analyse* 1 (Winter 1966).

12. Joan Copjec, "Cutting Up," *Between Feminism and Psychoanalysis*, ed. Teresa Brennan (London: Routledge, 1989), 242.

13. Private conversation with the artist, May 30, 2008.

14. Pierre Bourdieu, *Sociology in Question*, trans. Richard Nice (London: SAGE, 1993), 133 and ff. This is a translation of *Questions de sociologie* (Paris: Minuit, 1984).

15. My thanks to Professor Richard Halpern of Johns Hopkins University for his keen observation regarding the worship of Dionysus.

"Secularism/Suture"
Performance, 2007.
Museum of Modern Art
of Saint-Étienne, France.

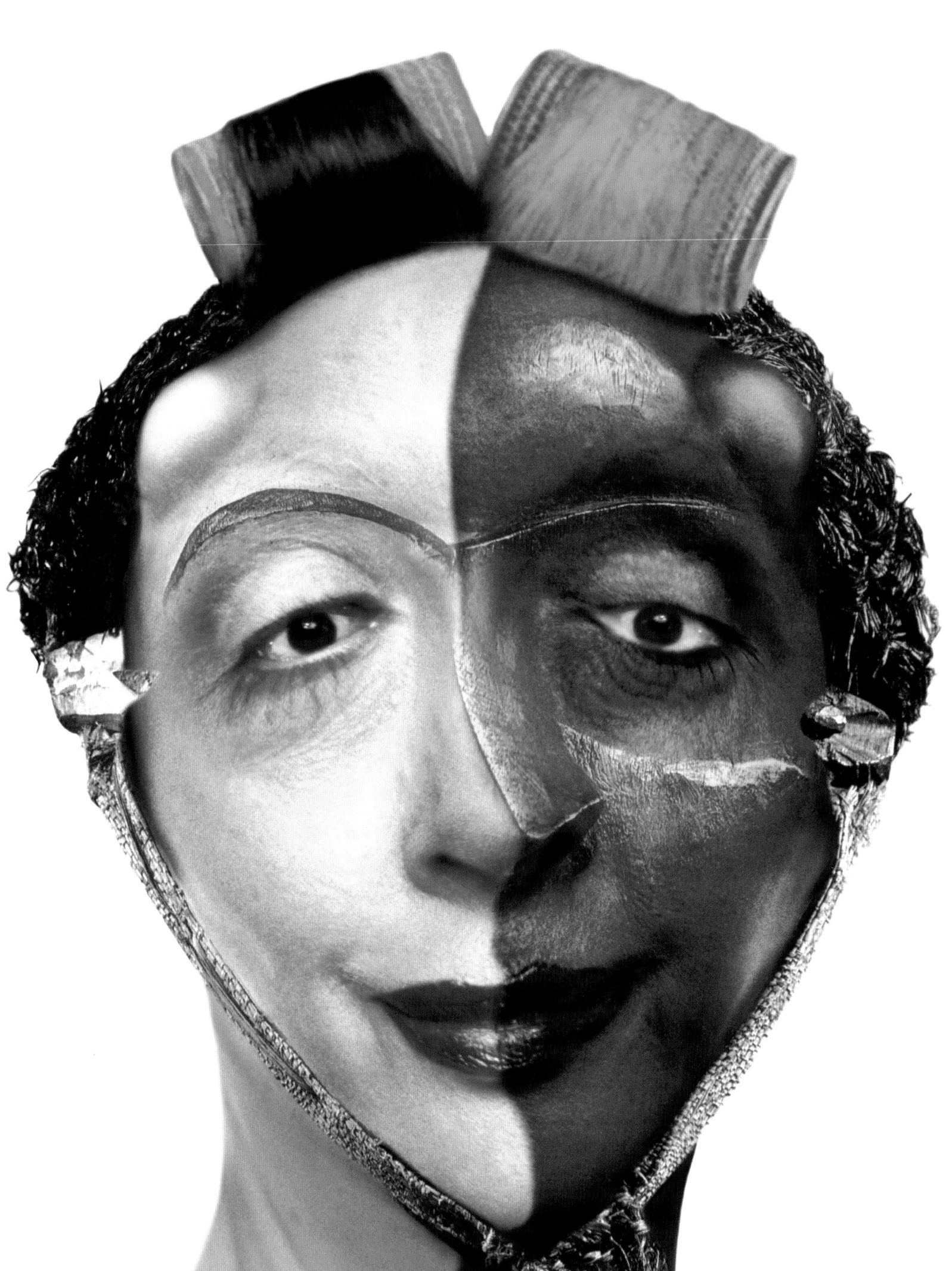

ORLAN AND THE CRITIQUE OF MULTICULTURALISM

JORGE DANIEL VENECIANO

I feel an artistic responsibility to speak, to interrogate
my time, while inscribing myself against it.

—ORLAN, *Transgression/Transfiguration*

IN THE *HARLEQUIN COAT* installation, ORLAN introduces an assembly of harlequin proxies—for herself and for us. Positioned as chairs in oval distribution, they invite us into a means of public discourse—a forum. In its performance of democratic hospitality, the work summons its requisite idea of secularism, and thus invokes the agonistic tension inherent to multicultural societies. ORLAN's is, in this democratic light, a discursive and critical art form.

The Harlequin motif and its exemplar text—Michel Serres's fable on secularism,[1] reprinted in this volume—have been present in earlier work as a counter-symbol in critiquing ideas of purity and national integrity in matters of cultural difference—ideas that have also structured multiculturalism, our present topic. Notions of cultural difference act as boundaries: they operate by exclusion. The excluded is what we suppress about ourselves as well as about others. These boundaries are not simply national, ethnic, or cultural. They are of the mind and of lifelong inculcations that, heaped up over time like stones in a wall, segregate the imagination from empathy. They are ideological boundaries. Dividing lines, drawn of ancient beliefs, tend to delineate for us the difference between what is civilized—the *we*—and what is barbaric—the *they*. Such conceptual boundaries provide the rationale for designating regions where domestication will be necessary—*there*—and regions to be protected from infiltration—*here*. Ideological boundaries precede and anticipate the geopolitical borders established on their behalf and the great walls that articulate them in stone and mortar.

In question in ORLAN's work is the singularity of identity—a singularity and unity applying to each of us and forged under the pressure of social norms. Her work performs a type of reading: a critique of the sign of woman, beauty, religion, civilization, even human, as so many blinders ever narrowing the singularity of identity and constricting the freedom

Refiguration Self-Hybridization, African Series: "Half-black half-white Mbangu Mask and Face of Euro–Saint-Étienne Woman with Curlers," 2003. Digital photograph, color print, 125 cm. x 156 cm. Collection of Jean-Michel and Pastri Beurdeley, Fonds regional d'Art Contemporain, Ile-de-France, France.

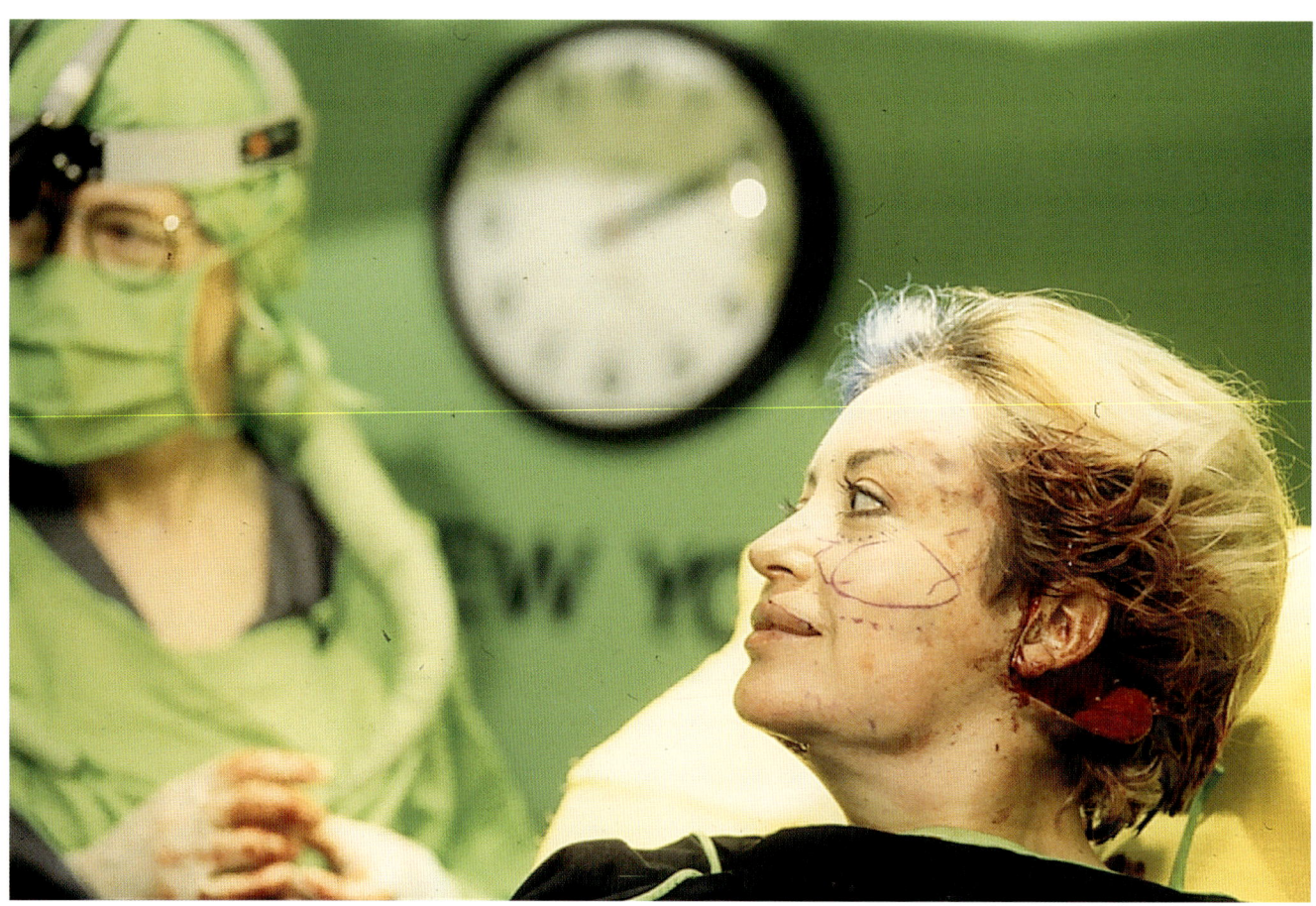

of thinking we might otherwise want to exercise. Of these discursive pressures, ORLAN writes,

> You speak of identities, I am not for definite identity, but in fact I am for nomadic, mutant, shifting, differing identities. It's here, it seems to me, that our era inscribes itself. We are in a prison from which we should perpetually be trying to remove the barriers, but we aren't yet able to sufficiently succeed.[2]

ORLAN set this problematic for herself, for her artistic career, beginning in the 1960s. If we accept her challenge to the pressures exerted by Western art and societies, we can extend it to model a critique of Western multiculturalism's own exerted pressures.

Through her surgical performances of the early 1990s, ORLAN demonstrated the violence that underscores and underwrites the Western strictures of beauty, especially in contemporary consumer societies, where aesthetic surgery renders plastic one's relationship to beauty and identity. In having altered her visage to mimic specific features of iconic female figures in Western art history, ORLAN has performed a visual exposé of such standards, illuminating the degree of violence requisite to the achievement of its mimesis.

Even the notion of "Western" art or culture is already corrupt with the violence of *internal* historical distinctions, before so-called non-Western exclusions can be imagined and conducted in its name. The history of European ethnic and cultural violence has to be overlooked in order to speak of Western culture. The internal distinctions are twofold: differences within historical moments and differences across historical periods. Standards of excellence are carved out along these two axes, leaving behind the shards and clippings of alternate and forsaken standards of excellence—what comes back to haunt the canons as multiculturalism.

THE HARLEQUINS OF MULTICULTURALISM

I would truly wish the body to be a costume—
something that is not definitive.
—ORLAN, *Suture/Hybridisation/Recycling*

To accommodate rather than suppress social differences, a form of neutrality needs to be implemented: a form of tolerance called "secularism." Michel Serres's parable on secularism concludes with such a lesson: "Just as the body . . . assimilates and retains the various differences experienced during travel and returns home a half-breed of new gestures and

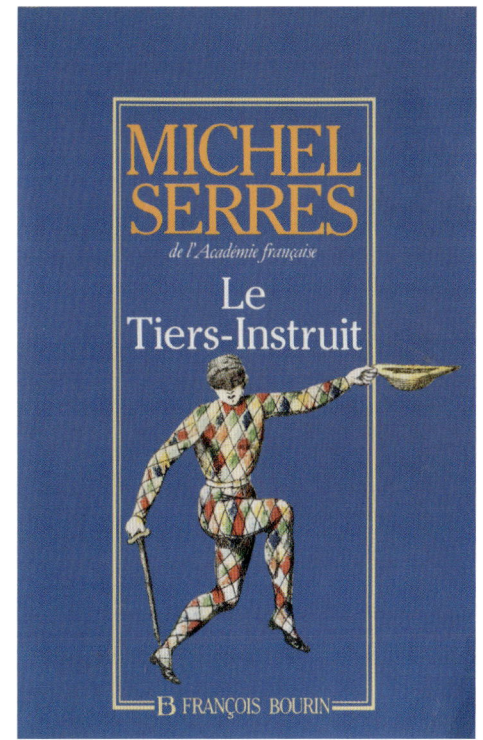

other customs, . . . the secular miracle of tolerance, of benevolent neutrality welcomes, in peace, just as many apprenticeships in order to make the liberty of invention, thus of thought, spring forth from them."[3] Though the story of the Harlequin king in Serres's parable is written as an allegory of secularism, it serves also as a cautionary tale of multiculturalism. Both secularism and multiculturalism subtend strongly in ORLAN's work.

When the Harlequin emperor (used interchangeably with "king") reports on his lunar travels at the beginning of the story, "the public is hoping for wondrous eccentricities."[4] However, he professes that in his travels "everything is just as it is here, identical in every way to what one can see ordinarily on the terraqueous globe. Except that the degrees of grandeur and beauty change. Disappointed, the audience cannot believe its ears: elsewhere must surely be different." But to the Harlequin, there is "Nothing new under the sun or on the moon."

The presumption that surfaces in the Serres parable is that difference pertains to what lies elsewhere, and that difference, thereby, must arrive from elsewhere. Claiming to find sameness elsewhere, as the Harlequin emperor does, must surely be evidence of blindness or fraudulence on his part. Either the eye recognizes difference or the motives withhold it. The

Smiling with pleasure, seventh surgery-performance, titled Omniprésence, New York, November 21, 1993. Cibachrome in diasec mount, 165 cm. x 110 cm. Edition of seven plus one. Photograph by Vlamir Sichov. LACMA Collection, Los Angeles.

Le Tiers-Instruit (*The Troubadour of Knowledge*) by Michel Serres, (Paris: François Bourin, 1991)

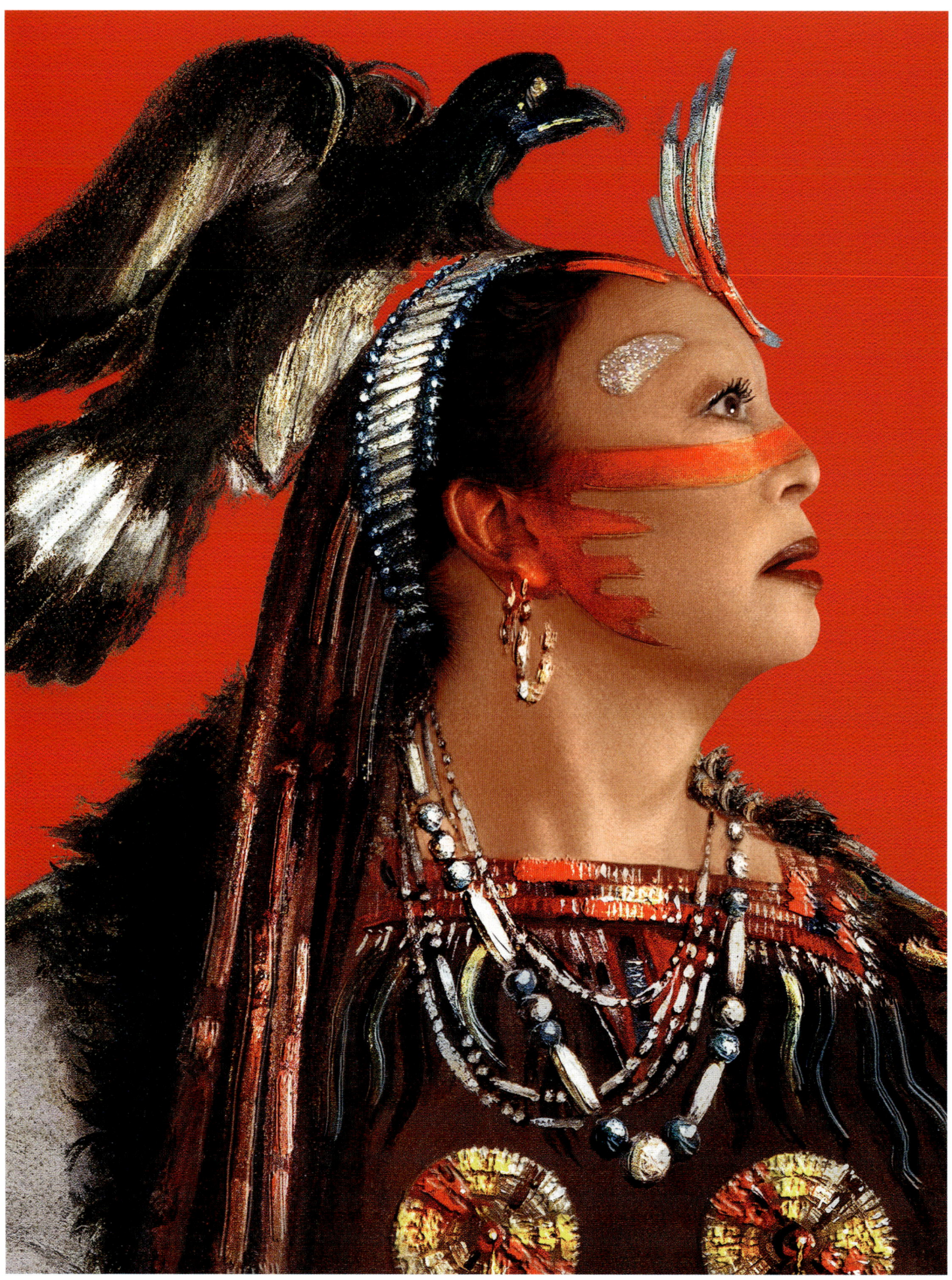

narrator explains, "Whether royal or imperial, whoever wields power, in fact, never encounters in space anything other than obedience to his power, thus his law: power does not move. . . . Thus reason never discovers, beneath its feet, anything but its own rule."[5]

The parable interweaves power and reason, exchanging the second for the first, telling us thereby that the power of reason limits itself to seeing its own imperial grounding. Reason cannot see beyond its own structuring, beyond itself—as Kant's First Critique argues. Reason thinks of the world in its own prescribed terms, its own royal red carpet. Crucially, however, the parable introduces the discourse of imperial power in relation to its multicultural expectations of difference, "grandeur and beauty."

The idea of a Harlequin emperor or king, already an oxymoron, conflates two opposites: ruler and servant, lord and bondsman. Hence the parable is already inscribed in the title of the principle character: one who is unaware of the roles he shares with another, or of the dependence one's identity has on the Other.

POSTING ORLAN

What are the social, political, religious, cultural pressures that imprint themselves on our flesh, in our body, and in particular in that of women, which we try to make over.

—ORLAN, *Transgression/Transfiguration*

In the three Self-Hybridization Series (1998–2006), ORLAN comingles features of her face with historical and ethnographic depictions of African, American Indian, and Mesoamerican subjects and artifacts. By inserting herself in the visual space of the colonized Other, the space of representation, ORLAN implicates herself in the colonialist dialectic. Her position is not a simple given: representing a French national vis-à-vis a colonial subject. Her work in hybridized portraiture must be read through the discourse of postcolonial responses to colonial authority.

By "postcolonial" we should understand the term to signify more than simply what comes after colonial independence. That meaning risks giving a false impression that the processes of colonialism are past, spent, or in remission. Instead, postcolonialism may be said to begin with "the discourse of oppositionality, which colonialism brings into being."[6] Colonialism, that is, invites the thinking of its own limits. As imposing authority, it provokes a critical attitude and resistance counter to its own interests. Colonial power, Homi Bhabha tells us, manifests itself in and through the forces of resistance it engenders.[7] Yet, oppositional gestures as such tend to dress themselves in the language of the conqueror—therein muddying the waters of so-called resistance, complicating it with a pinch or more of complicity.

The historical bind between colonial authority and subject has been much studied in numerous disciplines. Typically in these studies the authority is European and the subject non-Western. We find precisely this subject pas de deux at work in the Self-Hybridization Series, where ORLAN, a modern French woman, cultural heir to the legacy of French colonialism, meets the subjects of colonized lands: African, American Indian, and Mesoamerican. This encounter takes place, initially, in the world of the archive, not the geopolitical world of postcolonial relations. The images into which she introduces herself are culled from her research in North American and European archives and galleries. Nevertheless, archival logic tends to follow the imperial logic of world culture classifications (fine art and tribal art, for example).

It may seem at first, from a favorable perspective in postcolonial studies, that ORLAN could compare to Western authors who paint sympathetic narratives of colonial subjects—an important literary role historically, to be sure. That role, however, would best compare to the task of an artist like George Catlin, who, for instance, painted honorific portraits of various and numerous North American "Indians."[8] ORLAN does something strikingly different. Her work combines feminist and postmodern strategies that critically test the limits of our beliefs in the representational power of images and deny our tendency to naturalize representation. Catlin relied on such tendencies when he insisted on the veracity and authenticity (over the construction) of his painted portraits and scenes. ORLAN, in contrast, inserts herself—or disperses herself, depending on how one chooses to read her work—in self-consciously fictive fashion *into* the subject of colonial desire; trained, for example, on the exoticness of American Indian personal style that people in Catlin's day, as well as our own, want to see.

Within the fictive scope and technique of digitally enhanced portraiture—the scope of the Self-Hybridization Series—ORLAN insinuates herself

Refiguration Self-Hybridization, American Indian Series #17: "Painted portrait of Pa-ris-ka-róo-pa, Two Crows, A Group Chief, with photographic portrait of ORLAN," 2006. Digital photograph, 124.4 cm. x 152.4 cm. Musée du Nouveau Monde, La Rochelle, France.

into a relationship fraught with historical implication. With the dual-faced composites, she recreates therein an *ambivalence* similar to that which is inherent to colonial power and is productive of hybridization—a relationship into which she self-consciously intervenes. "The ambivalence," writes Homi Bhabha, "at the source of traditional discourses on authority enables a form of subversion, founded on the undecidability that turns the discursive conditions of dominance into the grounds of intervention."[9] In Bhabha's terms, hybridity names a strategic reversal implied in the discursive process of domination itself: it "represents that ambivalent 'turn' of the discriminated subject into the terrifying, exorbitant object of paranoid classification—a disturbing questioning of the images and presences of authority."[10] With her hybridized portraits ORLAN performs a cultural contamination, the sort of thing upon which colonial power relies for its authority—the threat of adulteration. In that regard, as with any resistance to power, her work could be considered also complicit in justifying colonial power, confirming its own sense of legitimation.

ORLAN's advance on postcolonial strategies of hybridization, however, is to deploy them from the relative subject position of authority, as colonial stand-in. Working from the standpoint of Western privilege and historical colonial power, she forces a split between what should pass as authoritative and original (Western culture, represented in the face of a French woman) and the repeated recounting of that authority through difference and mimicry of the original (through the iterative fusing of non-Western cultural elements to the same French face). "Hybridity," Bhabha explains, "is a problematic of colonial representation and individuation that reverses the effects of the colonialist disavowal [of its subject's authority], so that other 'denied' knowledges enter upon the dominant discourse and estrange the basis of its authority—its rules of recognition. . . . Hybridity reverses the *formal* process of disavowal so that the violent dislocation of the act of colonization becomes the conditionality of colonial discourse."[11]

If ORLAN's Self-Hybridizations dredge up the problematic of colonial representation, if they raise the specter of an old discomfort, they do so because they tap a source of ongoing disavowal, and test its reversibility in the postcolonial discourse of critical visual culture. Boundaries of power are besieged by the scene/seen of the Other. The uncertain and uncontainable nature of the hybrid terrorizes authority with its mimicry, mockery, and monstrosity.

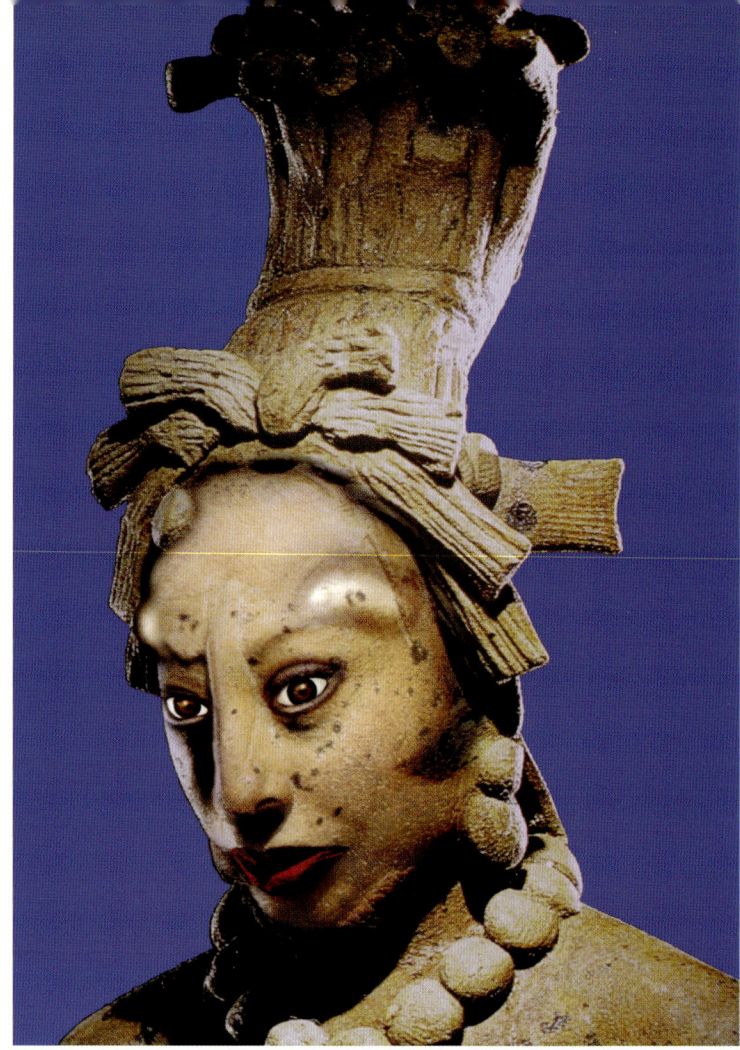

THE CRITIQUE OF MULTICULTURALISM

I have students, Koreans, Chinese, Arabs, who absolutely want to work with the materials of their countries, with their own origins, with their villages. I respect this, and I understand that it would be very difficult to be an immigrant or a refugee. But I can't help thinking that this attachment to origins is strange in an era when we live in continual flux.

—ORLAN, *Transgression/Transfiguration*

Beneath the mask of multiculturalism is a face of apprehension. Multiculturalism springs from the fount of cultural plurality and diversity. It arises as a need to accommodate that plurality and diversity which stem from the legacy of colonial history, its market expansionism, and the civilizing mission that tries to legitimize it. The tension abiding in multicultural efforts is expressed as an ambivalence over the relative success of colonialism's civilizing mission: that is, whether civilization is sufficiently served in its absorption by multicultural (read, neo-colonial) subjects and whether it is sufficiently distinct from their assimilation of it. Multiculturalism is the articulation of this neocolonial ambivalence: preserving civilization's distinction in the face of barbarism's attempt to mimic it.

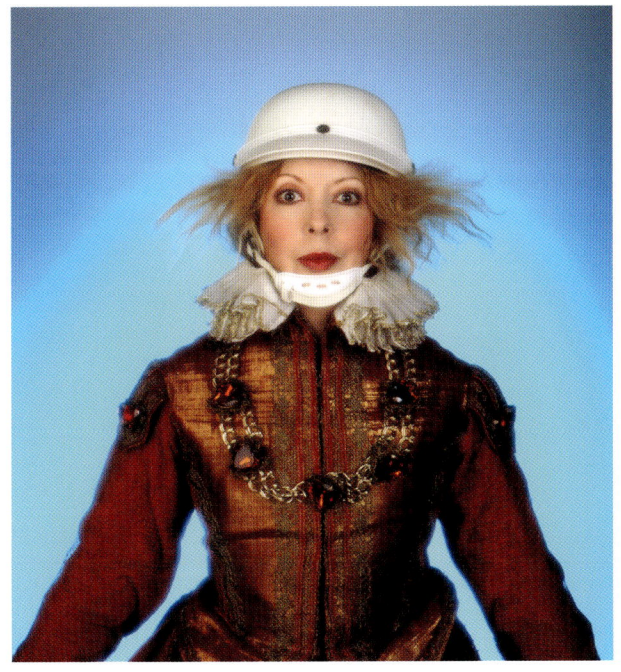 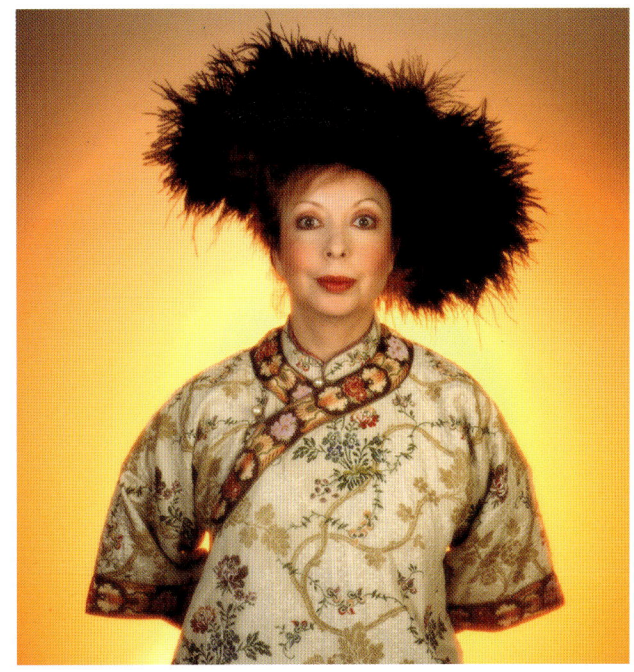

The heyday of multiculturalism, some like to think, was in the 1980s and early '90s. Made possible in the United States after the various civil rights movements, it meant increasing inclusiveness for women and ethnic minorities. Sharing space in cultural venues became a possibility if not always a practice—an annual exploration if not an ongoing one.

Multiculturalism arose in other Western nations as well. What these nations share is a history of colonial or imperial expansion. The "minorities" present in these countries arrive there not as hordes at the gate but as those petitioned in historical encounters and economic exchanges, whether trading for goods, labor, or humans. Western societies create new "minorities" at home as they create new markets abroad—the price and benefit of free trade.

If colonial or imperial expansion creates the conditions that multiculturalism has to redress, then surely multiculturalism has a history longer than that of the past few decades. The Ottomans must have had this problem too, as must have the Romans and Greeks and Hittites before them. The Hittites not only had to worry about the Egyptian Empire below them but also the new peoples in the Assyrian colonies, the Hattians, with their foreign language and with whom they had to negotiate. These crucial ethnic encounters were also of 1980s multiculturalism—BCE. The

Indo-European languages we speak today might be otherwise had the multicultural wars of the 1980s taken a different turn in the Hittite Kingdom. The time of multiculturalism, we must recognize, has no origin.

Imperial expansion is not the only stage for the emergence of multiculturalism. Simply trading with the people downriver constitutes an economic and cultural exchange because cultural intermingling takes place in such exchanges. Multiculturalism must be recognized as having crept into the corners of human history from places where history was never written. For that reason it has infiltrated our societies over time in ways we can no longer even identify. It is extrahistorical and unconscious. There is no society today—if there has ever been—that is not multicultural. The difference today comes with the use of the new term "multicultural," which acknowledges and welcomes difference—to some extent.

OPPOSITE: *Refiguration Self-Hybridization, Pre-Columbian Series #28*, 1998. Cibachrome, 100 cm. x 150 cm. and 60 cm. x 90 cm. Collection of Michel Rein, courtesy of the Michel Rein Gallery, Paris.

Donkey skin. To escape the realm of the father, one must change one's skin, 1990. Wool costumes. Color photographs by Pascal Victor. Courtesy of the Michel Rein Gallery, Paris.

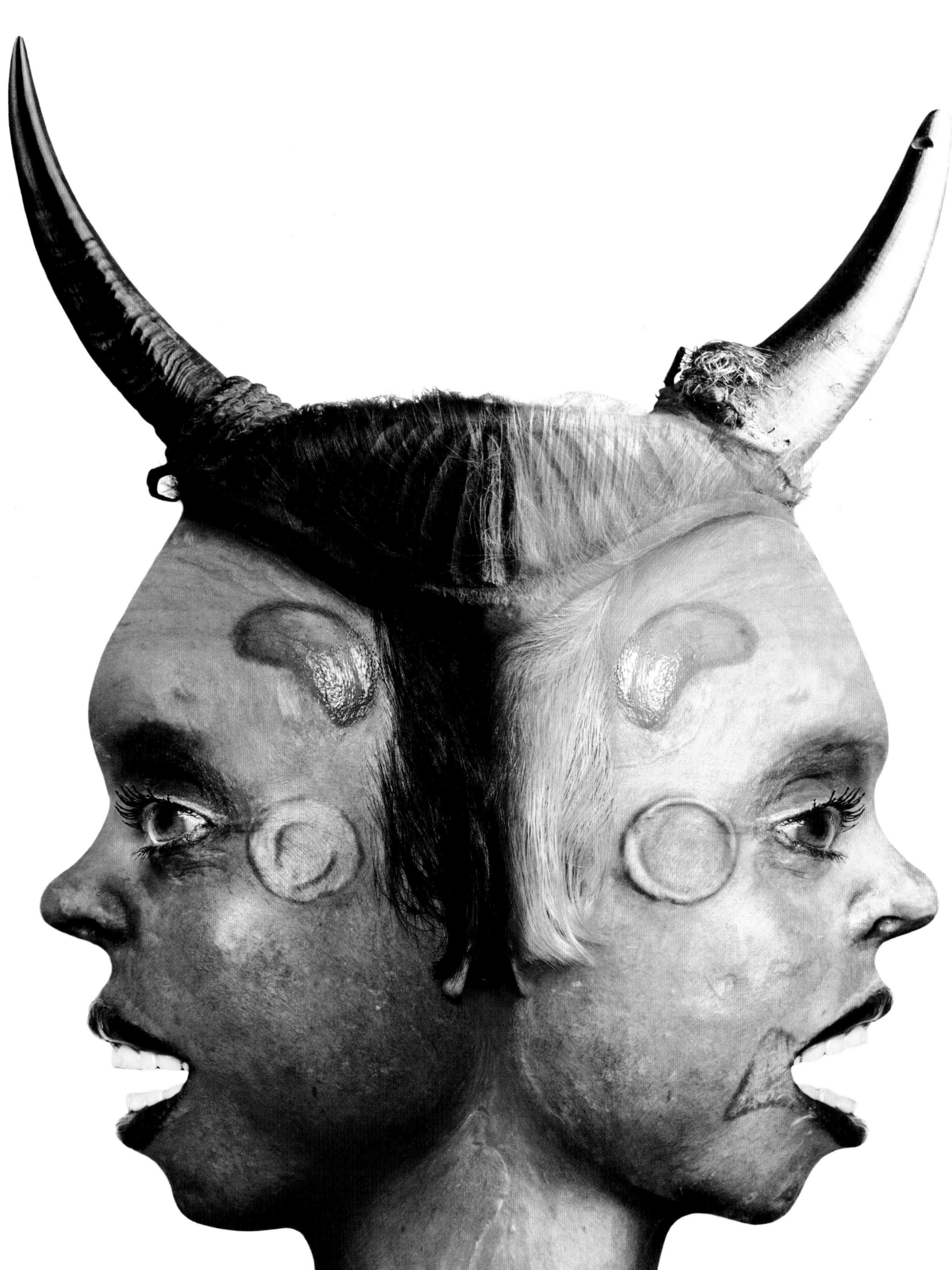

We have never been pure as nations, ethnic groups, or tribes. This is the secret underlying the work of ORLAN. The same holds true for the individual. The Same was never the same after it met the Other. And it never didn't meet the Other. So the Same was never really the Same. ORLAN's work makes manifest this latent and quizzical truth.

Nevertheless, in multiculturalism there remains —however well intentioned the gesture toward inclusionism—an element of noblesse oblige in offering space for inclusion: in structuring the relation between the included and the includer, between guest and host, this structure reminds them whose home they're in. ORLAN's Self-Hybridization Series resists this consequential arrogance by subsuming her image as guest to that of a host figure. By taking up residence in the physiognomy of the Other, she relinquishes the arrogance of multicultural liberalism. However, she trades it for the conceit of the artist: taking liberties where others can't. To critique the structure of multiculturalism from the vantage point of critical art, we must read ORLAN as double agent.

THE JANUS FACE OF EMPIRE

Cybernaut of my own faces, representations, nomadic, moving, without frenzy, without discrimination.
—ORLAN, *ORLAN: Carnal Art*

There is always a doubleness to working with others, always a risk taken if not calculated: a simultaneous attempt at distancing and absorbing the Other. The doubleness always inflicts the Self, not just the artist (in the case of ORLAN) who dares criticism. It involves the interior problematic of *facing the exterior*. Our point of interface with the outside world, for those of us who see the world, is the face. What strikes us most from the outer world is the face of another, according to Emmanuel Levinas, a postwar philosopher of ethics.[12] In the face of another we feel the alterity of ourselves—the general mystery of otherness in the Self.

ORLAN's hybridized portraits have a Janus quality to them in suggesting the cohabitation of contrary faces. Janus is an ancient Roman god of gates and doorways and, hence, is symbolic of beginnings and endings. He could look back and see the past, look forward and see the future. For these reasons he represents middle ground between young and old, pastoral and urban, and, in its generalized sense, between barbarism and civilization. This figure of liminality, of being between what is interior—civilization—and exterior—barbarism—indicates to us the extent to which imperial power was inscribed in the Janus symbol, a symbol of imperial ambivalence.

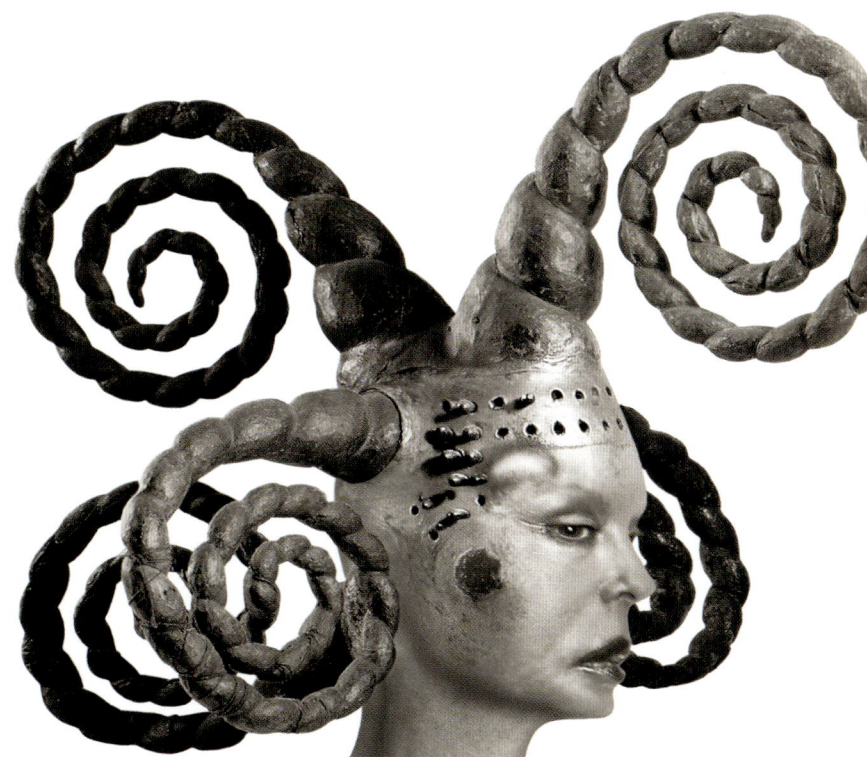

Refiguration Self-Hybridization, African Series: "Ekoi Janus Mask, Nigeria with Face of Euro-Forezian Woman," 2003. Digital photograph, color print, 124 cm. x 156 cm. Courtesy of the Michel Rein Gallery, Paris.

Refiguration Self-Hybridization, African Series: "Ancient Crest of Ejagham Nigeria Dance and Face of Euro–Saint-Étienne Woman," 2000. Digital photograph, color print, 125 cm. x 156 cm. Collection of Nadia and Cyrille Caudet, courtesy of the Michel Rein Gallery, Paris.

Gods and myths exist to resolve cultural contradictions. In that regard Janus, in his two-faced representation, is not a very subtle construction, but he gets the job done. Imperial power conscripts cultural iconography. In its more subtle operation, Janus relegates otherness to elsewhere: barbarity to the borders, age and youth to the offing. These moments of relegation reconstitute the integrity and sovereignty of imperial authority. Here, it confirms, is civilization. The function extends to the subjects of imperial power, reenacting the founding moment of the subject's own sovereignty as Self and same. ORLAN's hybridized images reverse the founding moments of relegation with those of integration, not in harmonious unity but in disfiguring cacophony. The Self is no longer the same. ORLAN's hybrids turn the Janus faces into each other, forcing them to see what they are constitutionally unable to see. Associating the Janus with ORLAN's work also reveals for us our subtext: art as the art of imperial power.

To the extent that the face functions as a visual trope of identity—all photo IDs rely on this function—the function of identity will suffer rupture with the disruption of the face that would be recognized. These are unsettling matters in the practice of modern law as much as in art history, both of which rely on proper identification and judgment to assign and safeguard human and property rights. This is to say, ORLAN's self-portraits symbolically and necessarily *deface* the law as much as art history. Their Gorgonic presence poses a menace to the gaze of authority.

THE LACK OF ORLAN

Being myself a woman, I think that it was important to risk stepping out of these constraints [feminine mannerisms] or at least to designate them.
—ORLAN, *Transgression/Transfiguration*

In seeing the faces of others, we see with desire what we wish to be and not be, and what we wish to possess and dispossess. In wishing, we express desire—to be or posses what we are not or have not. Those desires that are distinctly our own, that define us so to speak, also mark the absences around which our desires are organized and around which we therefore organize ourselves. This is one way to think about what psychoanalytic theory calls the "lack" at the very core of our being. It is the ghost of the Other that haunts our daily being and desires and provides us motivations with which we play our roles in life.

Interestingly and provocatively, ORLAN's work does not, in liberal fashion, entertain dialogue with the Other, nor does it practice the simple inclusiveness of multiculturalism. In her hybridization series

the artist, as self-representational subject, assumes the gambit of *inhabiting* the Other—of occupying the space and time of the Other. We have diametrical ways of reading this gambit. If we inflect the cheerful term of "inhabiting" with the darker association of "occupying" cultural space and identity, ORLAN's maneuver of engagement may be read as guarding colonial power and authority. If, on the other hand, the inflection is directed toward the submissive term of "surrendering *to*" the cultural space and identity of the Other, then the gambit looks like a gesture of postcolonial recognition, negotiation, or even resignation.

It is critically important here to point out that the direction which the inflected reading takes cannot be confirmed by the artist, neither by her good or ill intentions nor by her true or false testimony. We steer the inflection with the discourses we bring to bear on the reading. The political conscience of the artist is not on trial in the deliberation of our reading. Our deliberations, however, do reveal something about our own predispositions in reading. The political conscience we may be tempted to infer from a given work of art may include a transferential projection of our own conscience. Certainly we, as ORLAN's critics, expose ourselves in reading and writing.

With ORLAN's hybridizations, we get a perfect in-betweenity of the ethno-cultural identities that force us to make a judgment about the work. It dares us to judge because it places character in question—*character* in the sense of subject characterization and of the ethics of artistic practice. This daringness is what it means for art to provoke. The judgment we make may be about the work in question, but the choice of judgment will be about the chooser. The choice opens itself to be read—to be indicative of the chooser's investments culturally, politically, and aesthetically, that is, discursively. These are matters for ORLAN's critics to consider.

To begin with, ORLAN's hybrid images are not cross-ethnic but cross-categorical. She does not mix her photographic image with that of individuals of other ethnic groups, but with images of artifacts: statuettes, bas reliefs, drawings, masks, and paintings representing cultural styles of other ethnic groups. Nevertheless, her work relies on physiognomy and its semblances as emblematic of cultural difference.

*Sculpture of Folds.
Documentary study no. 1,
no. 2, 2002. Sculpture
in bubble wrap. FRAC,
Pays de la Loire, France.*

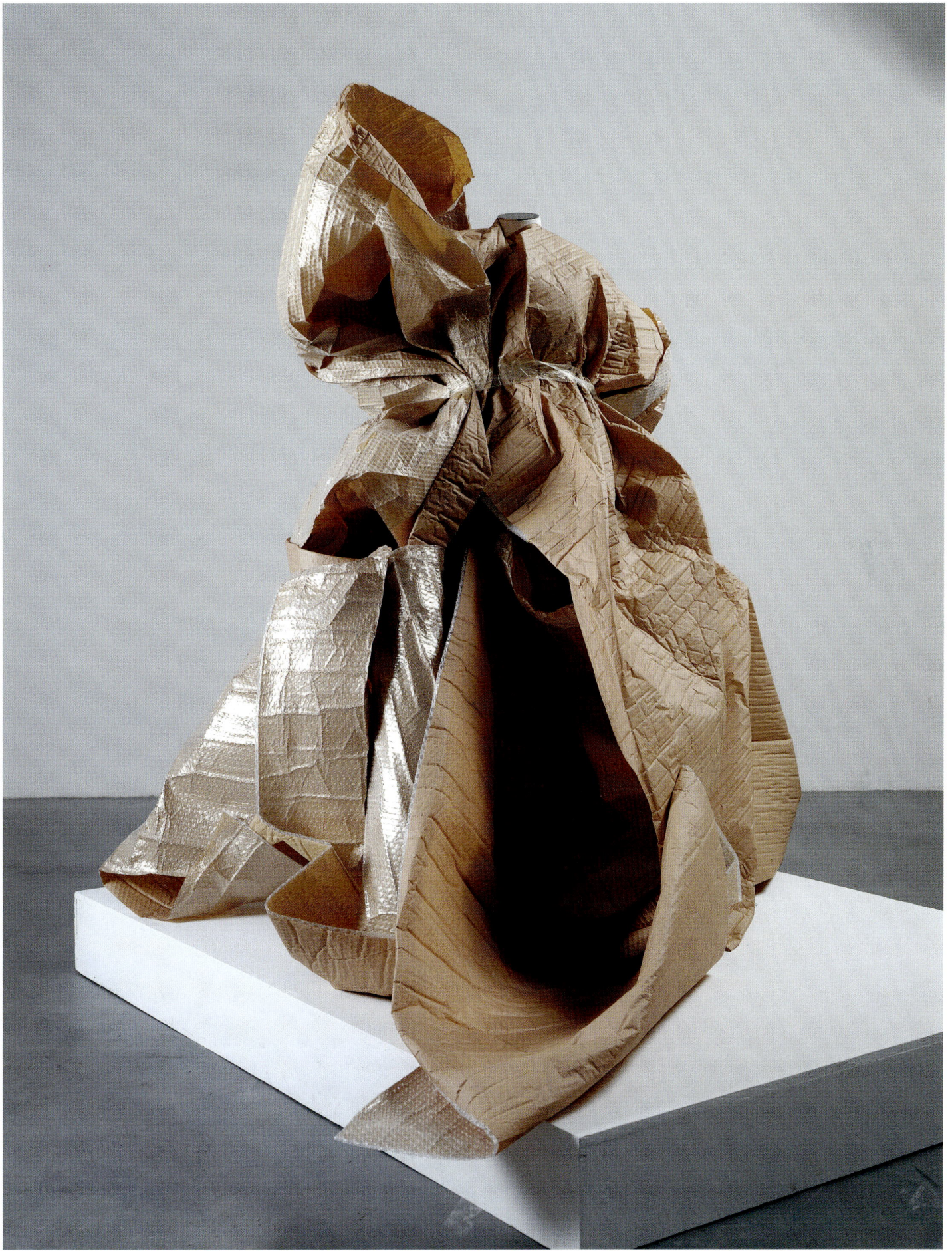

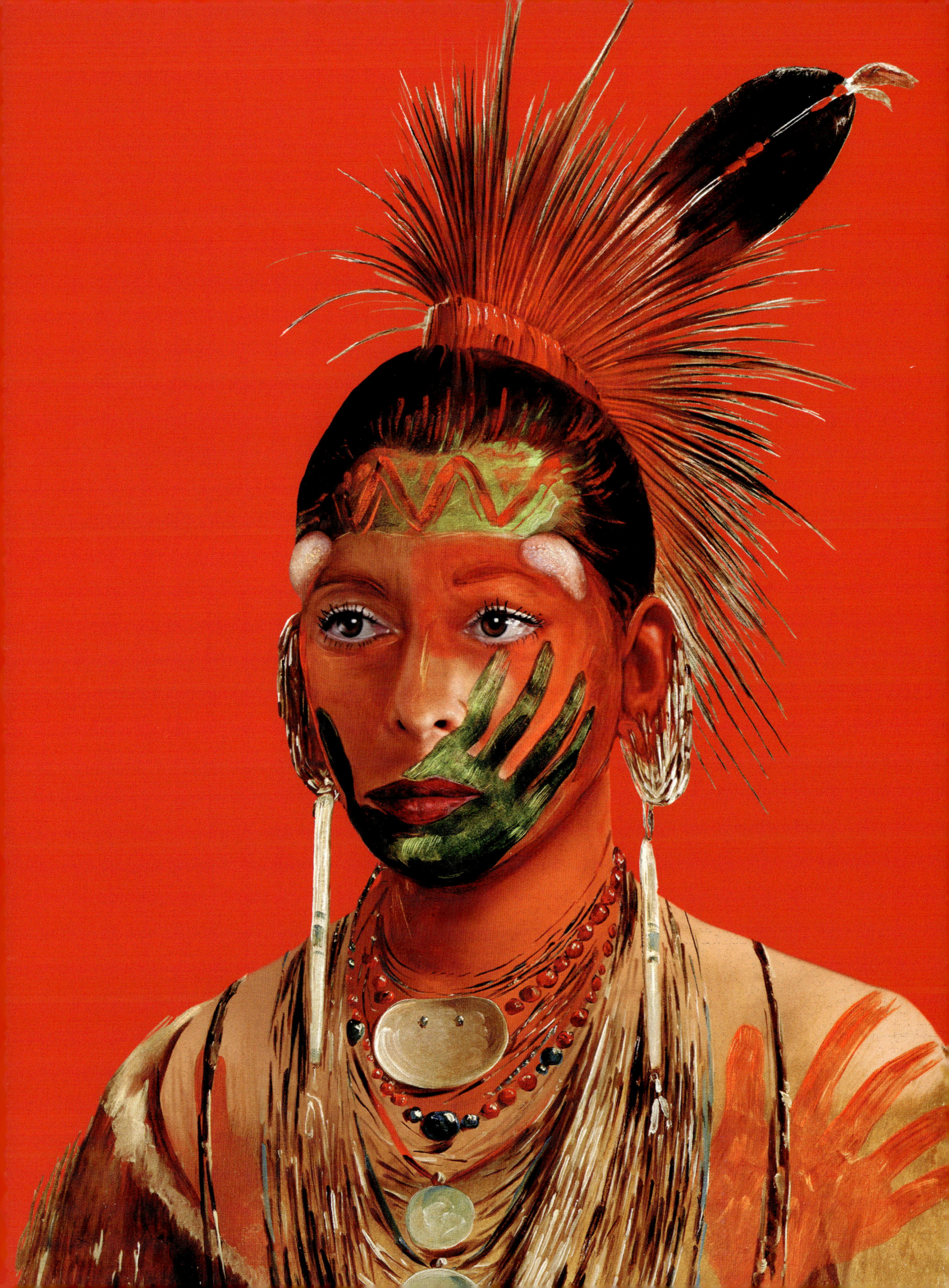

Hence, we see in her work the performance of ethnic and cultural miscegenation. As such, ORLAN's hybridized images allow her to generate semblances of foreign bodies and fabulous chimaeras. Via this method of digital montage she renders herself inhabiting the foreignness of the Other, the face of otherness, alienating herself from her Self. She performs a dialectic of negation but without *aufhebung*—without cancelation and elevation or transcendence—a reading of Hegel's dialectic. Instead, the effect compares to that of a hall of mirrors, of semblances without exhaustion or end, reiteratable, without a fixed or placeable subject or matrix. Identity in ORLAN's work becomes iterable and viral as much as virtual. It spreads from portrait to portrait, host to host, and eludes containment. It overcomes quarantine, circumscription. It writes itself into the host visages of others, becoming art-historical graffiti, a Duchampian intrusion into sanctified aesthetic texts: a mark, like a penciled mustache on a reproduction of an icon.

The dispersal of identity in iteration, however, cannot be counted as dispersal if all traces of ORLAN disappear. There has to be a sign marking the dispersion at work. The catch seems to be that one cannot lose one's identity entirely, or the loss would not register as such or be recognizable as a loss. Without some retention of the identifying source, loss cannot exist. Thus a paradox: no loss is complete without its incompletion, which is the function of the trace. But the paradox can be turned on its head to instruct us on the nature of identity's ascent, as well as its decline—identity's coalescence, as well as its dispersal. Identification cannot occur as a process without an essential lack of identity to command or warrant the coalescence of the identificatory efforts: the enunciative acts of identifying oneself or someone else. At the heart of an identity, the result of a process of identification, is an essential lack at its core, upon whose contingency identity revolves.

By working in a highly contested terrain and thereby subjecting her work to criticism, as appropriationist for example, she draws out those lines of defense dependent on ethnic and cultural authenticity, reliant, that is, upon a neo-essentialism. ORLAN's work is neither guilty nor innocent in the operation or charge of cultural appropriation. It is, instead, effective in provoking cultural willfulness and ideology, in ferreting out our emotional investment in cultural authenticity and purity of origin and destiny, whether Western or not. Reading the effectivity it produces becomes our task.

In the American Indian series, for example, ORLAN inserts herself in the patriarchal role of chief, in the ceremonial appurtenances of male leaders, warriors, and authorities. No Native women are depicted in this tradition of authoritative portraiture. When George Catlin paints Native women subjects, he classifies them as wife or daughter of a chief, or as "a pretty girl" or "a beautiful girl." In each case, they are subject to male authority or man's objectifying gaze of desire. To assume the feathers of the chief as one's own, to assume the phallus of chiefdom, is an impertinent act, a breach of the sign of woman in traditional societies, Western and Native.

The symbolic role of the chief in Catlin's ethnographic portrayals is that of father, of the group as well as of the family. In French psychoanalytic theory, this symbolic register is associated with order—and the "laws," customs, or rules that condition our sense of social order—pointedly called the *nom du père*, or (in the) *name of the father*, which is an allusion to the gendered privilege of the lawgiver as well as to Catholicism's deployment of "fatherly" authority. ORLAN's gesture is to wrest the phallus, "the name of the father," as law of the representer (Catlin) and as the *other* law of the represented (Native chief) and inscribe it with the sign of woman, their mutual Other. These exercises in representation compare to political exercises: parliamentary law of representation, for example, as a redirection or proxy for power and authority from the many to the few.

The power to balance contradictions if not to resolve them, the capacity to conflate opposites and collapse binaries, is a power that artists and poets have exercised widely and historically. In this conciliatory mode, this indirect and playful means of balancing tensional forces, art exercises what is at the same time a political power: an aesthetic faculty for executing détente and reconciliation, which are useful faculties for democratic living.

GHOSTING ORLAN

ORLAN presents her self-hybridizations as a confederation of signifiers. The subject fancied in the digital images is a composite of signifiers and traces. If we look carefully at the implication of such images, rather than the images themselves, we come to "see" the work of suture. Not something visible but conceptual as an implication: the discernment she offers is that *all* faces, even and especially those not

Refiguration Self-Hybridization, American Indian Series #3: "Painted portrait of Wash-Ka-Mon-Ya, Rapid Dancer, A Warrior, with a photographic portrait of ORLAN," 2005. Digital photograph, 124.4 cm. x 154.4 cm. National Archives of Contemporary Art, Paris.

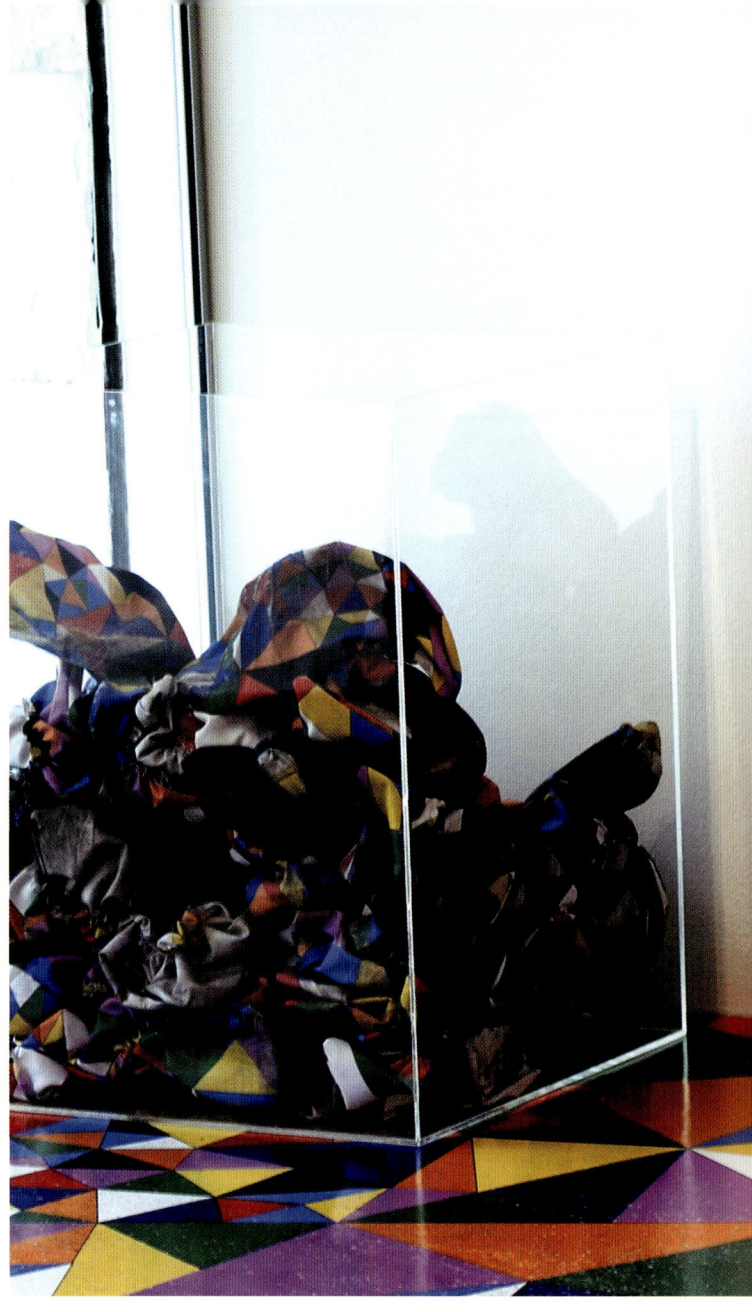

altered in representation by digital or surgical technology, are likewise composites of signifying elements that we call noses, eyes, lips, brows, and so forth. We are all Frankensteinian collages. Each of us monstrous as assemblages—if only we could see the sutures. Their invisibility safeguards our comeliness—saving face, cleaning up our act in the patchwork performance of self. In ORLAN's words, "I make images of mutant beings whose presence is thinkable in a future civilization that would not put the same pressures on bodies as we do today; such a future civilization could therefore integrate these beings as possible and sexually acceptable, and beautiful."[13]

ORLAN's notion of identity compares to the accumulation of skins, or outer garments, by which we become identifiable, iterative, and confusing. The cape of the Harlequin came to have this function in Michel Serres's parable. ORLAN's explorations in

the *Harlequin Coat* installation extend logically from the Self-Hybridization Series. In those series, exteriorizing the plane of attention to the surface of the face has the effect of abandoning the interior, which is found lacking. The essential lack constituting the subject is honored in the evacuation of the artist's self-representation from the *Harlequin Coat* installation. A coat, an outer surface, remains. Ironically, the ghost chairs of Louis XV by Philippe Starck in the installation may be more revealing of the artist, a greater gesture in exposing the evanescence of the artist, than the portraits involving aspects of her face.

In this ironic reversal of gesture, identity itself becomes the "in-between" moment of hybridity and harlequinicity rather than the sameness of Self. That in-betweenity of emerging identity, in the case of the artist, is transfigured as a sign, a signature that holds the works together, a suturing agency named ORLAN.

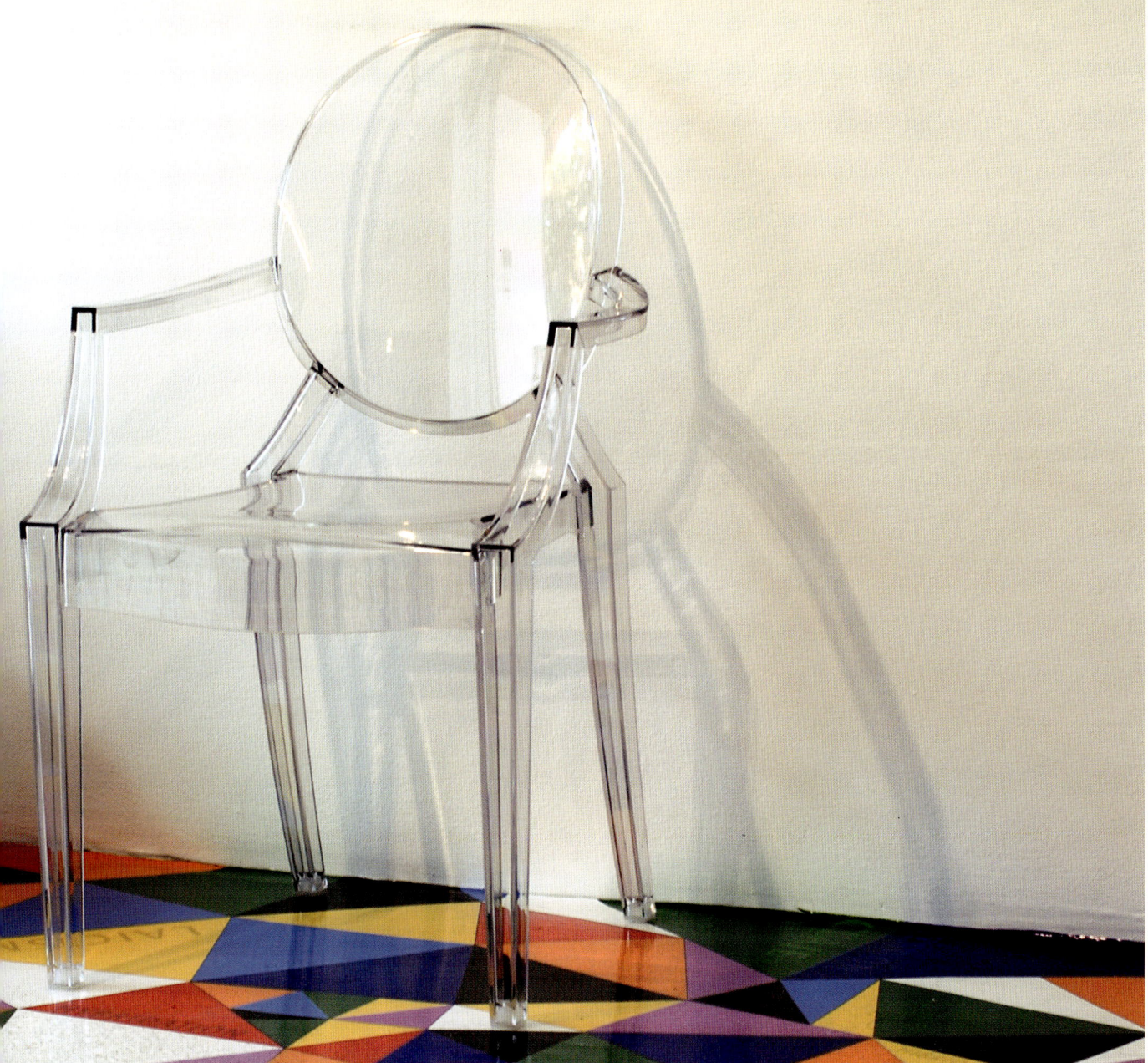

NOTES

Epigraphs: ORLAN, *Transgression/Transfiguration: A Conversation between ORLAN and Paul Virilio* (La Rochelle, France: l'une & l'autre, 2009), n.p.; ORLAN, *Suture/Hybridisation/Recycling*, ed. Isabel Tejeda (Murcia, Spain: Espacio AV, 2008), 141; *ORLAN: Carnal Art* (Paris: Flammarion, 2004), 167.

1. Michel Serres, "Preface," *The Troubadour of Knowledge*, trans. Sheila Faria Glaser with William Paulson (Ann Arbor: University of Michigan Press, 1997), xiii–xvii.

2. C. Jill O'Bryan, *Carnal Art: ORLAN's Refacing* (Minneapolis: University of Minnesota Press, 2005), 141.

3. Serres, "Preface," xvii.

4. Serres, "Preface," xiii.

5. Serres, "Preface," xiii.

6. Bill Ashcroft, Gareth Griffiths, and Helen Tiffin, eds., *The Post-Colonial Studies Reader* (London: Routledge, 1995), 117.

7. See the interview with Homi K. Bhabha in this volume.

8. In so doing, Catlin became increasingly critical of the imperial power that was enacting a form of what today we would call "ethnic cleansing."

9. Homi K. Bhabha, *The Location of Culture* (London: Routledge, 1994), 112.

10. Bhabha, *Location of Culture*, 113.

11. Bhabha, *Location of Culture*, 114.

12. The face plays a key role in the ethical philosophy of Emmanuel Levinas. Since ethics develops the capacity for interrelationships, a responsiveness of self to others, it is the call of the Other, in the very presence of another's *face*, that structures exteriority and the sphere of community. The problem of developing community enjoins the problematic of ethics.

13. ORLAN, *Refiguration Self-Hybridations: Série Précolombienne* (Paris: Dante, 2001), 50.

Suture, Hibridization, Recycling: ORLAN + davidelfin, installation, Espacio AV, Murcia, Spain.

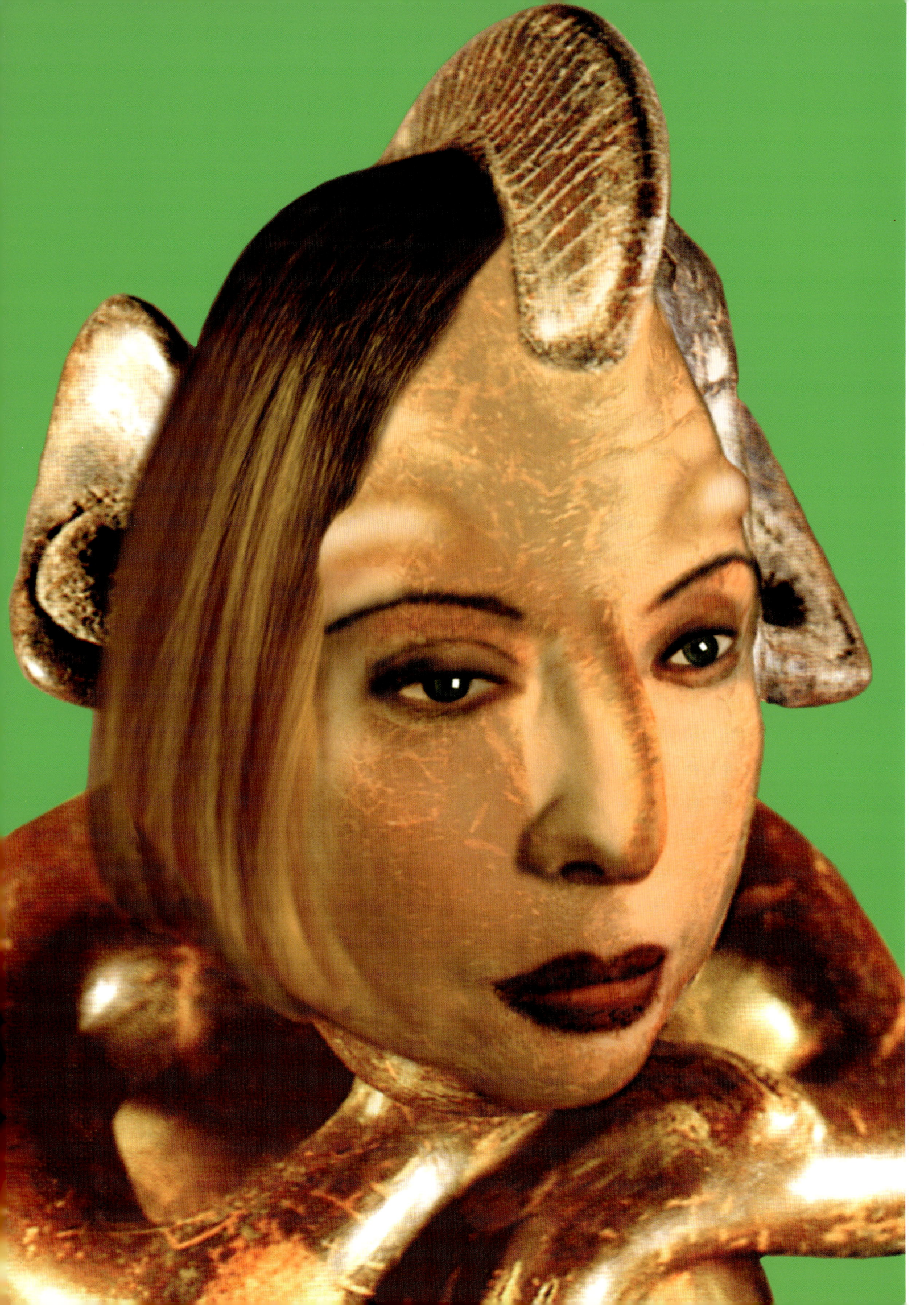

ORLAN AND THE TERMS OF WORK

AN INTERVIEW

HOMI K. BHABHA AND JORGE DANIEL VENECIANO

Homi K. Bhabha: First of all, I'd like to thank you very much for thinking of me for your show on ORLAN. It's not a thought I had; it's the thought that you've invoked and implanted, and I think it could be a very productive one. So I want to thank you for your creative suggestion.

Jorge Daniel Veneciano: Well, I'm glad you see why I invited you to respond to ORLAN's work. I think — certainly on the level of terminology — there's a great coincidence of terms that you and she have been interested in and which you've been writing about for some time. The invitation really suggests itself. One of the key terms, for instance, is "hybridity," and its derivations, "hybridization" and so on. Before we get to the Harlequin Coat project, I'd like to talk a little bit about the Self-Hybridization Series that precede it[1] and to ask you about the terms and conditions of "hybridity" involved in this project. I'll start with something from your own terminology. You've written about cultural difference and its articulation as productive of what you call "in-between" space, specifically for elaborating strategies of selfhood, identity, *innovative sides of collaboration* — I stress that one — as well as *contestation* — I stress both of those. Do the Self-Hybridization Series create or articulate an "in-between" space, as you conceive it?

Bhabha: Yes. I think so. Hybridization produces a kind of interstitial supplementarity: a whole set of identifications *and* objectifications that belong to neither one of the more recognizable sites involved in the confrontation or negotiation of differences. Hybridization is in a way like a camouflage. There are things that you recognize and things that you don't. There are things that are figures, forms of figurations, and then there are disfigurations. So, in this, even as I speak, even in the syntax of my sentence, you can see the emergence of an interstitial space, an "in-between" space. When I say that there are things you recognize and things you don't recognize, that's not bipolarity, that's not about two things. That is about a moment of transition, a moment between things. Hybridization is, in a sig-

Refiguration Self-Hybridization, Pre-Columbian Series #30, 1998. Cibachrome, 100 cm. x 150 cm. and 60 cm. x 90 cm. Collection of Michel Rein, courtesy of the Michel Rein Gallery, Paris.

nificant sense, a space from which you take the measure of the in-between. It's not some defined space. It's actually a process or a practice—a form of transition, a movement. That's what it is. And ORLAN has also talked about the process or effect of suturing as being a kind of transition. And, in a way, her entire art practice, or we might call it her life practice or her body practice, has been a lifelong set of transitions. Transition without an end. Transition without teleology. It is not, as far as I can tell, the work of transformation. But it's a work of trying, in a way, to hold in suspension and tension all the dialectical processes that occur in transition—all the contradictory, problematic moments of transition—to try and each time hold them at a standstill. I'm referring back to Walter Benjamin's notion of the image as dialectic at a standstill. Not that it's actually static, but it's the representation of a complex set of dialectical elements that become visible as a constellation and that initiate a process of transition, as we were talking about. You can see that in ORLAN's art where the work continually talks about transition, but often by taking on poses, the actual poses, which are in a way very fixed in a kind of baroque way. And I think that's where the issue of hybridization as producing the in-betweenity, this imminent in-betweenity—that process which I talk about in my work—I think, has a real resonance for ORLAN.

Veneciano: There occurred to me to be two senses of this in-betweenness stemming from your work that might apply to ORLAN. One is certainly, as you say, in the trajectory of her lifework as the subject in question. But the other, if you think about the images represented in these Self-Hybridization digital photographs, that's a very different entity from the kind of subject that you write about as *emerging*. So I'm wondering in what sense there is an emergence here—and I can see how that might apply to the colonial subjects that you've written about. How, and this is my challenge to you, how does this transition apply, if it does at all, to these crafted figures in the digital images?

Bhabha: Let's look at one.

Veneciano: Okay, how about this one here [see page 34]. It's from the Pre-Columbian series, and it appears to incorporate decorative and ritual elements of statuary that could be Mayan.

Bhabha: Well, first of all, there is the pre-Columbian sculptural phrase, so to speak. So when you look at it, it rings a bell—for somebody like me, who is by no means a specialist or has an extensive knowledge of pre-Columbian art except at the level of visual recognition. And so, optically, visually, you can tell; it gives you a sense of recognition. And

that is not only by what one might call the sculptural statuary: the way the body is presented or, indeed, the gold surface or the gilded surface of the work, but also the way in which the eyes have a look as if there is a sort of endless distance, which you often get in Mayan sculpture. The eyes are angled in such a way that they're inscrutable, and you never know what they're looking at or what they're looking through or what they are looking *for*. So I think you have all that. But then, at the same time you have recognizable elements of the ORLAN *visage*, if I might put it that way?

Veneciano: Yes, good.

Bhabha: And then you have the rather contemporary hairstyle, and, of course, you have totemic elements surrounding the figure. So, there is a continued contestation of images—you know, what is emerging, what is residual, what in a way belongs to the past and what belongs to the present. The work is a continual negotiation of time and form. And, in a way, the Mayan sculptural statuary, if you like—that Mayan monumentality—is present as a static yet trembling presence in the work. And then there is the ORLAN face, which is also striving to make its representational mark. I think it's very much a work of emergence. And, you know, by "emergence" one should not think of something new. Emergence is a constellation. Or emergence is a reconstellation, a *reconstitution*, where the anteriority—be it an origin or primordial identity—is always a mystery or an enigma. That's what emergence is. It's something incubational, as [Antonio] Gramsci once put it. Something which confounds time-as-presence just as, indeed, this particular image—this digital image—does, because it has the enigma of time written all over it in the contestation between the Mayan art and ORLAN's relentless migrations and refigurations of "me."

Veneciano: A couple of things come to mind here. The question of the sort of "visibility" of separate elements, which you've described in this one piece, may speak to the problem of suture in the piece—a problematic ORLAN raises in her field of terminology. And it appears that ORLAN wants to maintain a non-totalizing sense of suture, the representation of which becomes the subject of, well, representation—where otherwise invisible seams are now represented. I know that's a literalization of the Lacanian concept, but what are your thoughts in terms of the visualization of suture as possibly disrupting its function, through an image like this?

Bhabha: It's very interesting to think about the problem of suture. You know, when I read ORLAN's views on suture, I thought back to my own work on hybridization and suture. I remember insisting on

the *cut* or the *graft* in the suturing process as having to be a representational mark. I mean, she says
that the mark of suture should be visible. I don't
think I'd dwell so much on visibility or depend so
much on visibility. But I remember thinking that
the process of hybridization requires the moments
of articulation or grafting not to be covered over.
So I didn't explicitly say it had to be visual. I
didn't say that these cuts should be revealed, but I
remember thinking that they should be *registered*.
They should be inscriptively registered. Now,
when I think about it, in response to ORLAN and
her statements, I feel more sure than ever that
to want the suturing seam to be visible is not the
right way to go because if it is visible, and if the
reason for its visibility is that there should not be
any illusion or allusion to wholeness, then I think
the argument fails on its own grounds. Because
the stitching or the seam, if you insist on its visibility, satisfies the scopophilia. It satisfies the eyes'
desire for a visible object. It is an object there for
the eye. It might irritate it, but it satisfies it. It may
signify what is *not* whole—the fragment—but the
visibility of the suture is a fixity of time.

Veneciano: If I may, I would say that it may be
ORLAN's intention to redirect the scopophilia
from the unity of a wholeness she's trying to avoid
by fixing our gaze, our regard, on this seam. And—

Bhabha: But by fixing our gaze on the seam, even if
the object that you are fixing your eye on is nothing more than a liminal border or a suturing seam,
it is still something that satisfies the desire of the
eye. It does not elude it.

Veneciano: Whereas in Lacanian suture, that is invisible. It's not something that is satisfied by a direct
gaze. In fact, suture must work behind the gaze,
not before it.

Bhabha: It is not something that a direct gaze can rest
itself on. If you think about it, if the subject *knows*,
visually, what the suture is, if indeed the suture is
that kind of object that can be the object of visibility, then where is the unconscious? The subject,
with the gaze fixed on the suture, is the subject
aligned and oriented. What does the suture do?
It does not allow the subject to know from where
she or he speaks and therefore does not allow the
subject to know who or what is being identified.
So, the whole issue of identification is so wrapped
up with this kind of double knowledge of knowing
there's suturing but not knowing when and where
the suturing happens.

Veneciano: I don't disagree, of course. But I've led us
into talking about two different series of ORLAN's
work at this point. We started with the Self-Hybridization Series, and now we're talking about, as

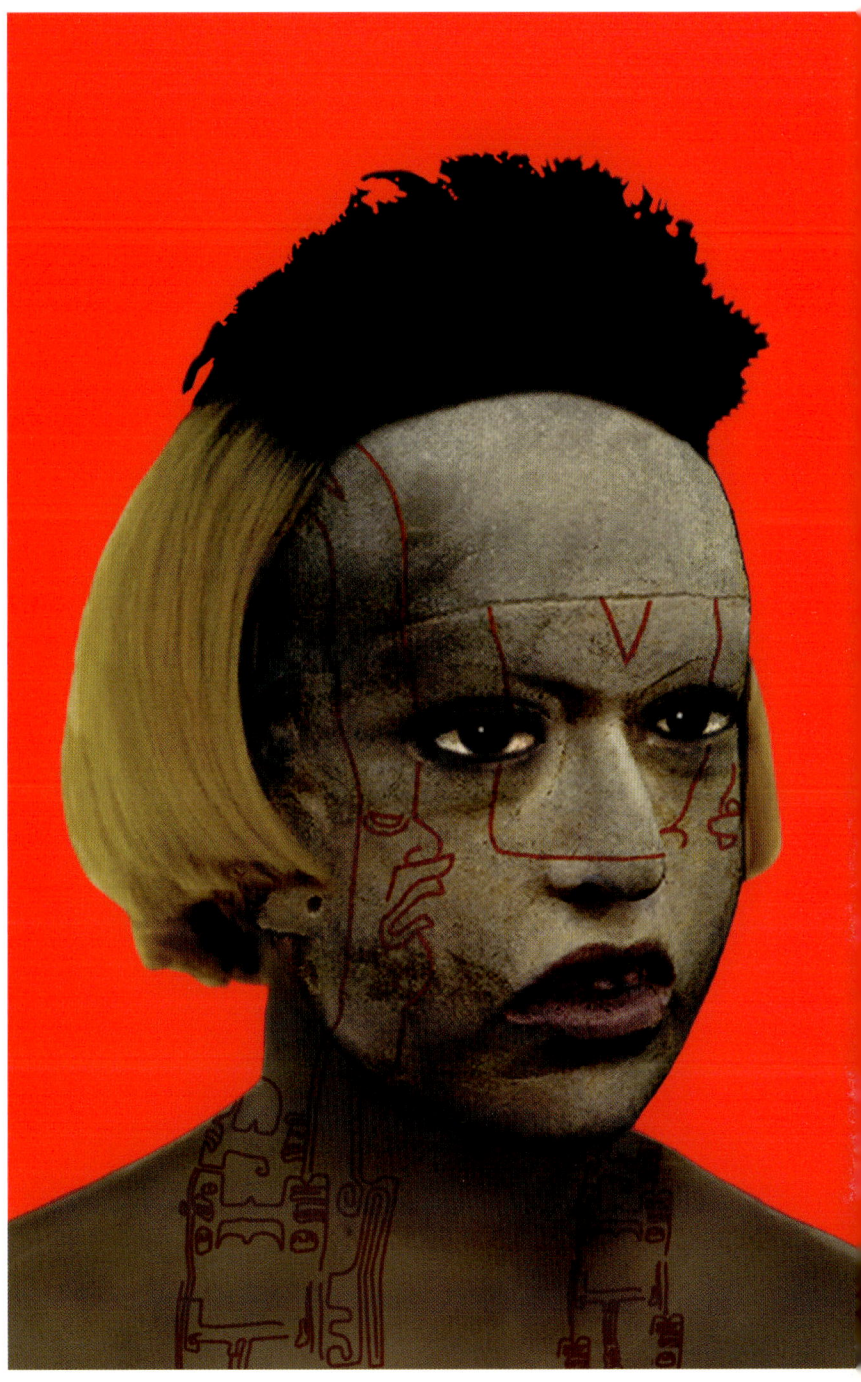

*Refiguration Self-Hybridization,
Pre-Columbian Series #1*, 1998.
Cibachrome, 100 cm. x 150 cm.
and 60 cm. x 90 cm. Collection
of Michel Rein, courtesy of
the Michel Rein Gallery, Paris.

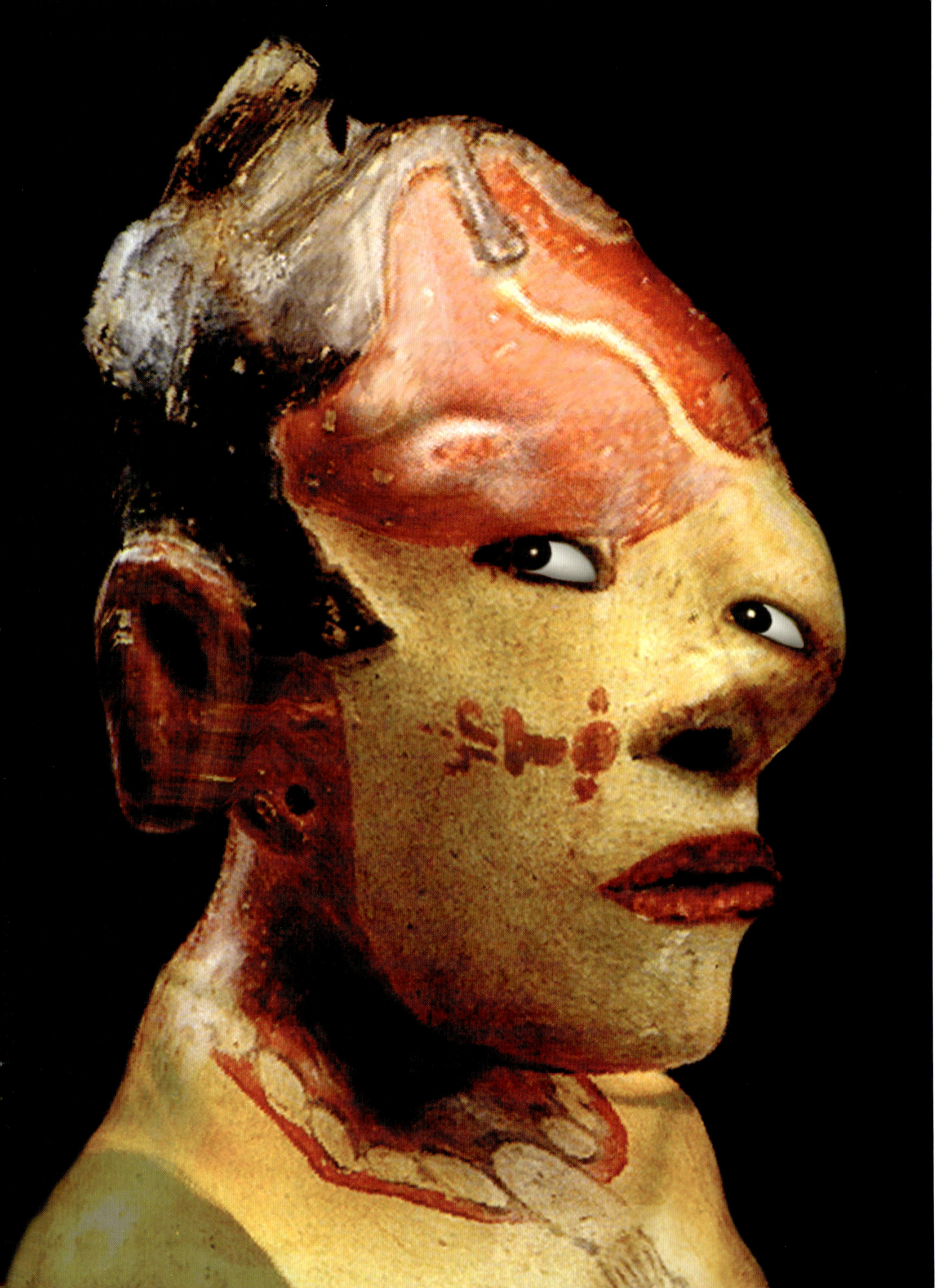

well, the Harlequin Coat project, where in fact the subject is completely dissolved and what remains are, well, the remnants/raiment: the clothing that stands in for the subject. And so, it's almost as though the suture that is symbolized, illustrated, in the Harlequin Coat project becomes the substitute for this subject of representation in the Self-Hybridization Series, where the suture is not visible in the same way, not illustrated in the same way, but is inferred—the very modality of the suture. So I'm wondering if that shift from subject with seamless suturing to marking the visibility of suture without subject makes a difference. Or is it still an illustration?

Bhabha: What's interesting is whether the artist can actually fix your eye or your gaze on the suture even if she really wants that to happen. That, I think, is the real issue, even in works, these digital works, where you can see the suture. The point is that the eye cannot settle on the suture. What the suture does is to keep moving the eyes in a fibrillation. That's the point. Even the artist who conceptually wants the eye to fall on the suture will not allow the eye to fall on the suture. And to take the dissolving of the body where all you have are the vestments, well what's interesting there is that the body disappears, right? But the vestments hold something. Just like when you get up from this leather armchair, the seat will still hold, in a negative way, the impress of your body, of your volume, of your weight. So, oddly enough, what you have in those works is not a disappearance of the body but the prosthesis of the body. The body is a prosthetic. And that, in a way, makes it even more uncanny, or more complex as a *form* or as an identification.

Veneciano: Perfect. That was an excellent observation on the supplement of the body. Coming back to the question of what an artist strives to do in a work, that always poses a problem because we have options as writers about art, as curators of exhibitions, and there is a choice to make, which is between what can be "read" or brought to bear in a work of art versus what an artist claims on behalf of the work. My preference is usually to *read* work, and less so to read artists' statements.

Bhabha: I agree with you.

Veneciano: I want to come back to something you said earlier about the Self-Hybridization Series.

Refiguration Self-Hybridization, Pre-Columbian Series #4, 1998. Cibachrome, 100 cm. x 150 cm. and 60 cm. x 90 cm. Collection of Michel Rein, courtesy of the Michel Rein Gallery, Paris.

You used a couple of Lacanian terms in addition to "suture": one term is "camouflage," and another you've used is "mimicry." I'm wondering if you have a sense for how these terms might apply specifically within the signifying function of the Self-Hybridization Series.

Bhabha: Yes, I think that both terms actually apply very well. Let's look at another image from the Self-Hybridization so that we have a range of illustrations in our text.

Veneciano: This is a wild one. Do you see what it says there?

Bhabha: It says "*Défiguration-refiguration.*" That's what I'm talking about. "*Self-hybridation préco-lombienne no. 4* (1998). Digital treatment. Cibachrome" [*see page 38*].

Veneciano: And there's something even monstrous about this particular piece and—

Bhabha: Well, it's hugely monstrous. So, here again, I think you've introduced this piece just at the right time: after I talked about both the prosthetic body and the fibrillation where there is suture. Now, I think something quite fascinating is happening with digitality, which allows you to manipulate the image more or less as you want to. And, in manipulating it, there is very little sign—unless you want to leave it there—of the suturing. You can Photoshop it; you can do whatever you like with it. You can change it. So here, in what looks formally like a kind of pre-Columbian cast of a face, you have a whole set of disfigurations. The eyes in particular, the way they're disaligned, the forehead, and so on. Then there are, of course, some markings, which seem to re-create the illusion of being more traditional, the traditional markings of a pre-Columbian ritual. But I think what is happening here in the *Défiguration-refiguration* in relation to what we talked about, as the in-betweenness, is that the defiguration of this face and the whole figure has a kind of fetal look. In a way—particularly with everything above the eyes—it looks to me either like a fetus or like the effect is almost of the kind of soft tissue that ORLAN spends so long getting rid of or manipulating. And it seems to me to be a kind of a bricolage of these various elements of her practice.

Veneciano: Yes. This one especially is, to me, reminiscent of a Picasso, in piecing together a patchwork of facial features in a decidedly disorderly way.

Bhabha: Yes, particularly with this projecting eye, which reaches outside the picture plane—and also outside the profile—and the nose. These eyes here are very interesting. This is why I said "almost fetal," because this projection almost looks as if it is a kind of humanoid thing in itself, a distorted

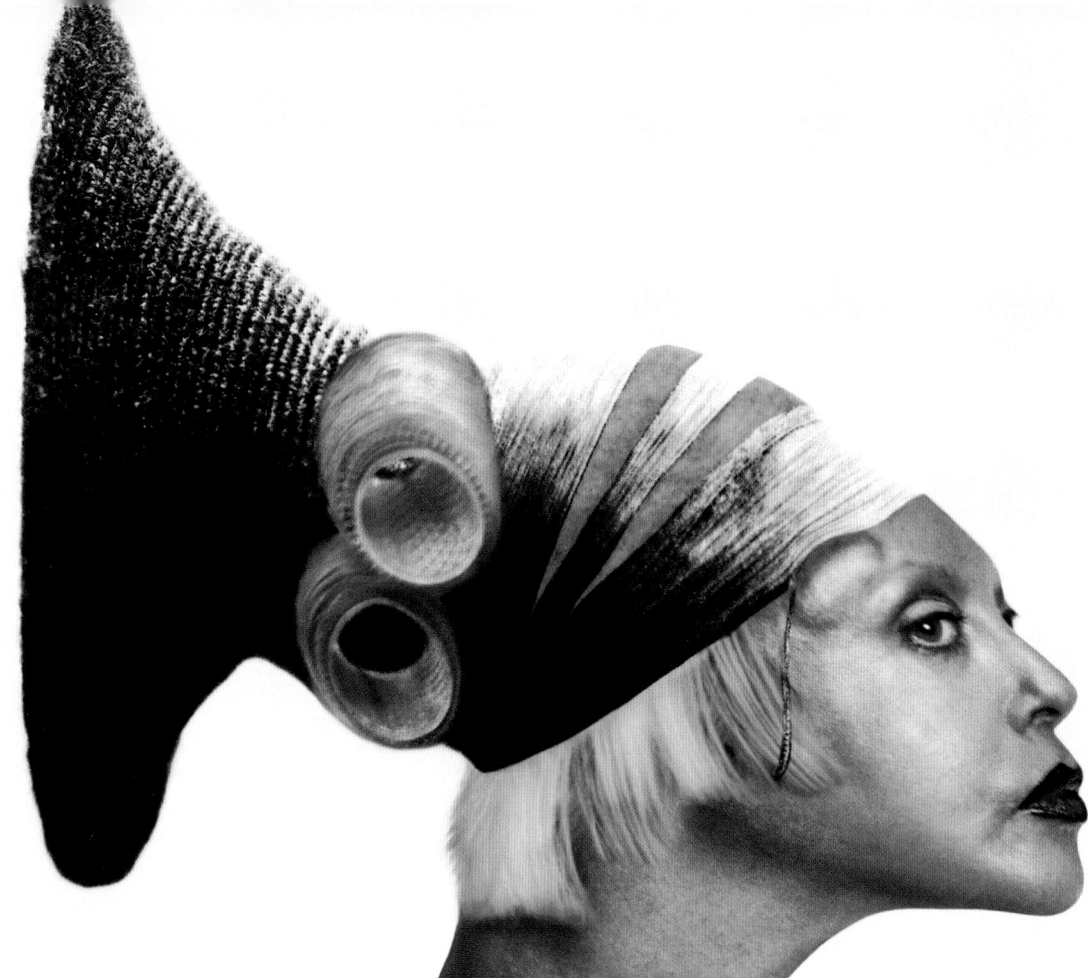

humanoid figure. The eye and this nose, this cavity. So, in a funny way, what gives it that Picasso-like character is the way in which there's a flattening of the image so that the other side of the face, the curvature of the face, is actually flattened out and put on the same plane.

Veneciano: Yes. I want to ask you, thinking of Picasso and of ORLAN's series now, which, as you know, is a blending of her western European French visage with pre-Columbian figures and statuary—an aesthetics of another time, another world—now in combination. She does this as well with West African imagery and masks, as did Picasso, crucially, with *Les Demoiselles d'Avignon*. Is there a sense here in ORLAN of reworking or rethinking that colonial relationship and its legacy between the French and the African colony, as figured in the African masks that come to France through colonial trade? In terms now different from Picasso's, is there a recovery from Picasso? Is there a *cause*,

essentially, here that is empowering, to the opposite extent that Picasso's project was objectifying? [*Silent pause.*] And that could be more my issue than yours. But I offer it to you for your thoughts.

Bhabha: You know, I think here we would have to talk about something like an artist's style: style not simply as the formation of a work, style not merely as a kind of an artist's pose, but style much more as a signature of an artist. And it seems to me that the use of the African mask or pre-Columbian—what should we call it—the pre-Columbian *disposition* is different with ORLAN because her practice has been, from the start, a kind of resistance to the givenness of the body or any cultural boundary. So, for her, introjecting a cultural influence or projecting a cultural influence is not playing with the Other's otherness. It is very much a way of revising or extending or reconstituting or collaging or bricolaging as a first-order principal. Different from Picasso. I mean, it's because in the modernist tradition, *in some way*, the African mask, or the *Africanité*, was *appropriated* and exoticized. We had that big debate about primitivism—was it in the early nineties?

Veneciano: In the mid to late eighties, after the MoMA show "*Primitivism*" *in 20th Century Art: Affinities*.

Bhabha: Exactly. But I think the premises are different with ORLAN because, for ORLAN, there is no normativity. This whole practice is a resistance against naturalization and normativity. So, the Afri-

Refiguration Self-Hybridization, African Series: "Profile of Mangbetu Woman and Profile of Euro–Saint-Étienne Woman," 2001. Digital photograph, color print, 125 cm. x 156 cm. Courtesy of ORLAN.

Refiguration Self-Hybridization, African Series: "Giraffe Woman Ndebelé Variant Nguni Zimbabwe and Face of Euro-Parisian Woman," 2002. Digital photograph, color print, 125 cm. x 156 cm. Fonds regional d'Art Contemporain, Ile-de-France, France.

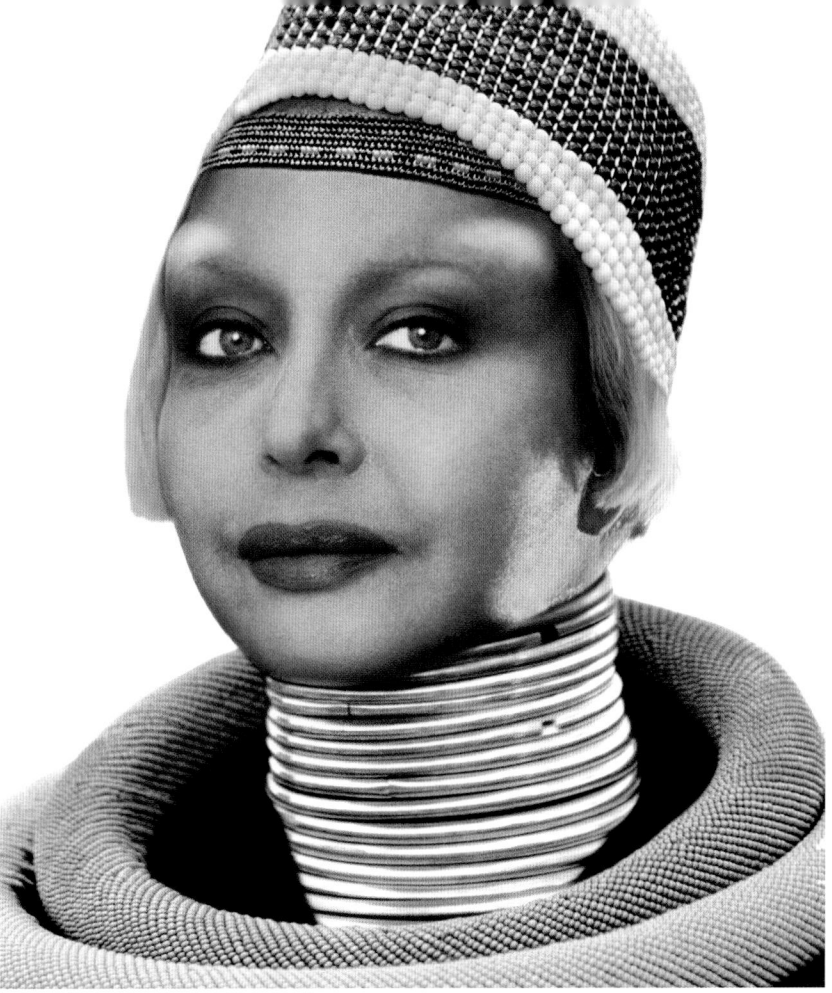

can influence or the pre-Columbian is not about otherness. It's about alterity. And I think it is not often recognized that there is a huge difference between the two.

Veneciano: Would you explain it?

Bhabha: In my view, at least, or in my vocabulary, *otherness*, whether it is something that is rejected or something that is invited *in* as an act of hospitality, is a process by which some alignment of the subject and the Other is maintained or negotiated. *Alterity*, on the other hand, throws all kinds of identification into a crisis from which you have to recover. I mean, alterity is like the unconscious. It is neither same nor different. The unconscious is not simply an agency that is different from conscious life. The unconscious is the shock of a contingent event that throws you in a completely other place from which you then recover, reconstitute yourself—fragmented, split, projected—however you want to put it. And I think there's a difference between otherness and alterity.

Veneciano: Does ORLAN's work manifest or invoke alterity in this series? And how so?

Bhabha: ORLAN's attempt in this series is to invoke alterity—the complete unsettledness of the whole question of sameness and difference. Here, I think, there is a deep ambivalence and a deep ambiguity, which is why in this case she calls it *Défiguration-refiguration*, a *ceaseless* repetition; something that

eludes sight and sense. And going in that way, from disfiguring or *de*-figuring to figuring, ORLAN is emphasizing the *transitional* temporality of figuration itself.

Veneciano: Does part of the provocation in ORLAN, this figuration toward alterity, concern the essential lack of subject? If there's a depth that you talked about, it's a depth without end because there is no bottom. I don't think of this as signifying in the usual sense, because digital imaging is unlike photography, which has a matrix—if we think of photography as producing an indexical register. This, however, has no matrix that produces this image. So in that sense, it is playing on a depth without end because there is nothing to which it refers; there is no ultimate signification. It is a sign without a signified, or waiting for one.

Bhabha: But all signs have a moment where there is a huge gap between the signifier and the signified. All of them. And that moment is the moment in which the sign is not yet part of a system and you're waiting for the systematicity. So if I say "cat," right, there is a huge gap until I say either, "This is my cat, Fido," or I say, "It's raining cats and dogs." So, there is always that moment that seems like cessation of signification but is, in fact, the transitional moment in which the signifier becomes a sign.

Veneciano: Composed of traces, yes. But the new context that you're insisting on, what makes a sign *work*

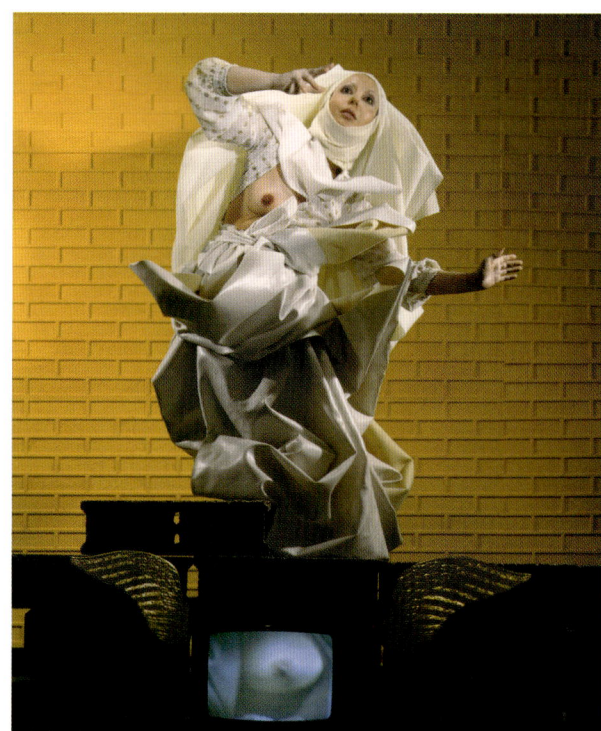

as such, I think that's the moment that ORLAN brings us to with a series like this: a moment of ambivalence and uncertainty. And it is up to those of us who look at it, who write about it, think about it, to invent, create a context—what I earlier called *reading* a work of art.

Bhabha: Well, absolutely. There's an element of the pre-Columbian as a trace or thread. There's an element of a particular kind of body art that ORLAN represents. There's a trace of performance, but there is also ritual, whether or not you call it performance art. There's body scarification and body decoration of a more tribal or more religious kind, whether it's one god or another. So, in my view, it's overfull of signification. It's brimming with it to the extent that it becomes difficult to read.

Veneciano: What you're describing is a patchwork of traces or signifying elements. What I had in mind was a ghostly center, as abyssal. Let me ask a different question. Are these elements composed by ORLAN in a constructive contradiction, and is that what Benjamin has in mind with this dialectical moment "standing still"? Is this a moment of contradiction staging emergence?

Bhabha: You know, here I think there is something like a moment of contradiction. But to say it's a moment of contradiction is not to credit fully the aesthetics of suture on which it's built. I think it's a different kind of contradiction. It's a moment of configuring through disfiguring. That's the process. It is a configuration of traces of elements of cultural seams. But it is a process of doing that through this particular kind of composition: this digital composition where the suturing seams completely flow into each other so that you can't really even see the axes of identification. They keep changing the figure itself. You know, this reminds me of pottery made by potters who are really not good at it or who want to make weirdly shaped pots. There are distortions in the form of the pot, which create distorted forms of scale so that one element of the pot is completely out of scale with the other. That is the effect of the work on me.

Veneciano: That's compatible I believe with ORLAN's feminist sensitivities in thinking of this as a kind of vessel function. Hélène Cixous, you know, the feminine has the capacity to encompass the Other—as Isabel Tejeda reminds us. [*Her essay appears in this volume.*] I was also thinking of Walt Whitman in terms of contradiction: "I am large, I contain multitudes."

Bhabha: Yes, exactly.

Skai and Sky video. Assumption of the White virgin showing her second breast against a backdrop of yellow bricks or, ORLAN on video monitor no. 2, 1983. Cibachrome over aluminum, 160 cm. x 120 cm., edition of three. Photograph by Jean-Paul Lefret. Courtesy of the Michel Rein Gallery, Paris.

Skai and Sky video. Assumption of the Black virgin with winged foot on video monitor no. 9, 1983. Cibachrome over aluminum, 160 cm. x 120 cm., edition of three. Photograph by Jean-Paul Lefret. Courtesy of the Michel Rein Gallery, Paris.

Donkey skin. To escape the realm of the father, one must change one's skin, 1990. Wool costume. Color photograph by Pascal Victor. Courtesy of the Michel Rein Gallery, Paris.

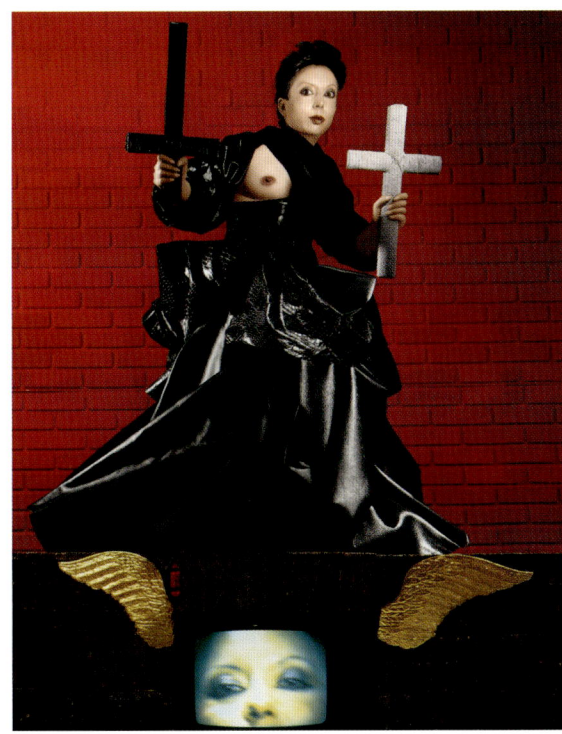 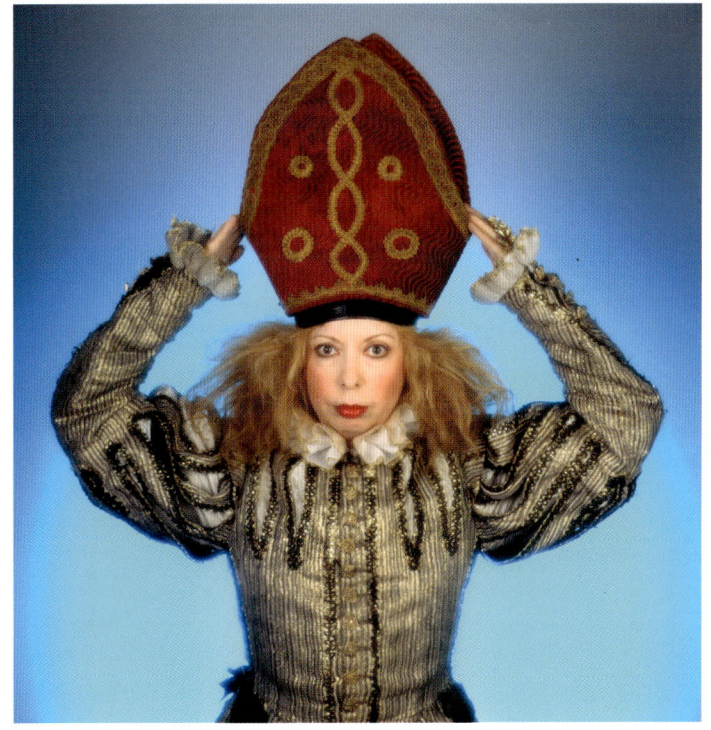

Veneciano: Let's switch now to the Harlequin Coat. Can we talk a little about the preface from Michel Serres's book *The Troubadour of Knowledge*, which appears in the Murcia catalog?[2] There are questions of multiculturalism, and also hybridity, that come up. I know these are problematic terms, and they have been so in your writing as well. One thing that the catalog does not feature at the beginning of that preface is the heading "Secularism," which does appear in the English translation of Serres's book.[3] Serres uses the French term "Laïcité," which ORLAN sees as specific to the history of French education, its particular separation from the Catholic church, and therefore as distinct from what we might think of as secularism. I know that the English term has been a highly charged word for you, in your writing. Do you want to offer a precaution about the use of the term "secularism"? You may not have thought about the term in reading this . . .

Bhabha: Except at the end, on the way he talks about toleration. You know, I think we're in a very unforgiving moment historically. Where the emergence of schools of fundamentalism are so strong that you think you can only deal with them by affirming stronger and stronger the liberal secularist beliefs and ideals. And I know why that is so, and you know why that is so. And it's an immediate response for many of us. Not all of us, but many of us. And then there is the thought that maybe our sense of the secular was so all-encompassing, so totalizing, that we have pushed religious fundamentalisms, Christian, Hindu, Muslim into the corner from which they now speak. So it's very much a double take. I

don't know what this has to do with Michel Serres, probably nothing. But it does seem to me that it's a very important issue in our time now, and one that frames much of what we do and think and that somehow all that was compellingly superstitious in secularism has been washed out of it, and it has become a kind of rationalist, instrumentalist ideal. After all, so much of secularism today is about proceduralism—you know, democratic procedures. I'm not telling you if they're right or wrong. I'm just saying this is the way you have to proceed if you want to live together. If groups want to live together, well, you know, so as long as we have toleration, and we have some laws that people follow and some civic practices that they follow, then they can all do their own thing. And yet we know that every time there is a problem—racial, ethnic, whatever, call it what you like—a problem around the distributions of difference in our society, the problem doesn't present itself as the problem of proceduralism. And the resolution to it is not also a problem of proceduralism.

The real issue becomes the fact that differences are continually seeping into each other and becoming unrecognizable, that the proximity of difference is the real problem of alterity, as I mentioned before. After all, think about the destruction and desecration of sites and peoples, the destruction of people and the desecration of sites. The German Jews were highly assimilated, so highly assimilated that what became the problem was assimilation. If you think about India, you think about the great Ayodhya mosque, which was also a place where both Hindus and Muslims for hundreds of years worshipped but became the great symbol of the rise in Hindu nationalism when people swarmed on this building and broke it down brick by brick, literally. There couldn't have been a fuller demonstration of the public will of a certain community when they literally swarmed on it, hundreds of thousands of people, and broke it down. What was really threatening was the proximity of difference there, not some kind of procedural "hold your peace." It was the actual intersection, the deep intimacy of difference. And that seems, to me, a lesson both for secularists and obviously for fundamentalists. For secularists, it's a lesson because there is something in that process of what I'm calling "the intimacy of difference" that allows you to constitute your life with different kinds of belief so that there might be certain forms of superstition, there might be certain forms of emotional or affective anxiety. You're a secularist; you're a rationalist. Yet there are other forces at play that may contradict that, and the openness to that, I think, has reduced itself. And it's at that point that one almost feels that certain secular rationalist practices have created the monster that they feared. And now there is a monster, but the monstrosity is, in a funny way, on both sides.

Veneciano: I'm curious: does proximity of difference render it something like invisible, so long as there's no crisis, to the gaze of power? Does it become inconsequential to the position of power, as in the Michel Serres text, when the Harlequin emperor seems oblivious to differences he may have encountered in his lunar travels?

Bhabha: Well, here I have "Power" scribbled on my little sticky on the page of the Serres text. I have a different understanding of power and difference. Or power *in* difference. Or difference in power. I have a different view of it. Michel Serres says, "whether royal or imperial, whoever wields power, in fact, never encounters in space anything other than obedience to his power, thus his law: power does not move. When it does, it strides on a red carpet. Thus reason never discovers, beneath its feet, anything but its own rule." Now, all my work, as you probably know, would rise up in protest at that pronouncement because at every level, conceptual or historical or affective or imaginative, power never simply strides the red carpet. Power is always anxious. And the anxiety of power is, of course, about the loss of power. But, it's not just simply about the loss of power. The anxiety of power is the result of the way in which power functions. And here I want to introduce another term to describe the exercise, the anxious exercise of power. And this term is "authority." So power, in order to create a representation of itself as empowered, has, in a way, to atten-

uate itself. It's only where power can be seen to overpower something that is resisting it, that power is power.

That's why you have the crazy system in a totalitarian state where the population is completely beaten down. You have more policemen and more soldiers on the street than any other place. What does that tell you about power? Even at its most powerful mode, in a totalitarian state, there is a heavy presence of the police, in the broadest Foucauldian sense, but also of soldiers, which tells you that power is always living in fear of resistance. But I would say something other than that; that's historical. And again—just to carry on for a minute— it's because totalitarian states need to be seen to be powerful, that even totalitarian states will say they have a human rights commission, that they have an ombudsman. They will always have to. These may be complete puppet things, but they have to because if they don't have that, they have power but no authority. And power and authority is a two-part dance. But for power to know that it is powerful, it always has to have some resistance. For power to actually have that resistance, which it needs for itself, it's a problem of its autoimmunity, in a way. For it to have that, it has to play a game at the edge. It always has to slightly allow its power to be fragile or to be fractured in order to be able close up again and show that it is powerful. So we must never forget that power is always attenuated in its search for authority. There is this moment of contingency in power where the opposition to power has some possibility of making an intervention. There may be historical reasons why there is nobody that can actually take advantage of that moment. Political parties have been destroyed; individual acts of heroism are impossible. There are no resistant groups because they have been gunned down. But the fact that you have this continual armed protection even of the most powerful is a sign that in the political imaginary of power there has to be the opposition to power, otherwise power is not power. And therefore I am really at odds with what Michel Serres writes in the preface [to *The Troubadour of Knowledge*].

Veneciano: I took that passage that you read about power in terms of finding the red carpet being rolled out as a portrayal of a symptom, of a *disavowal* of the kind of power dynamic that you're talking about. So I don't see it as Michel Serres's point but as an allegorical point that's being made there. Nevertheless, you're point stands.

Bhabha: What is power if anything other than obedience to its power? I'm saying that all power is predicated on disobedience.

Veneciano: Right. I just didn't take the narrator's claim

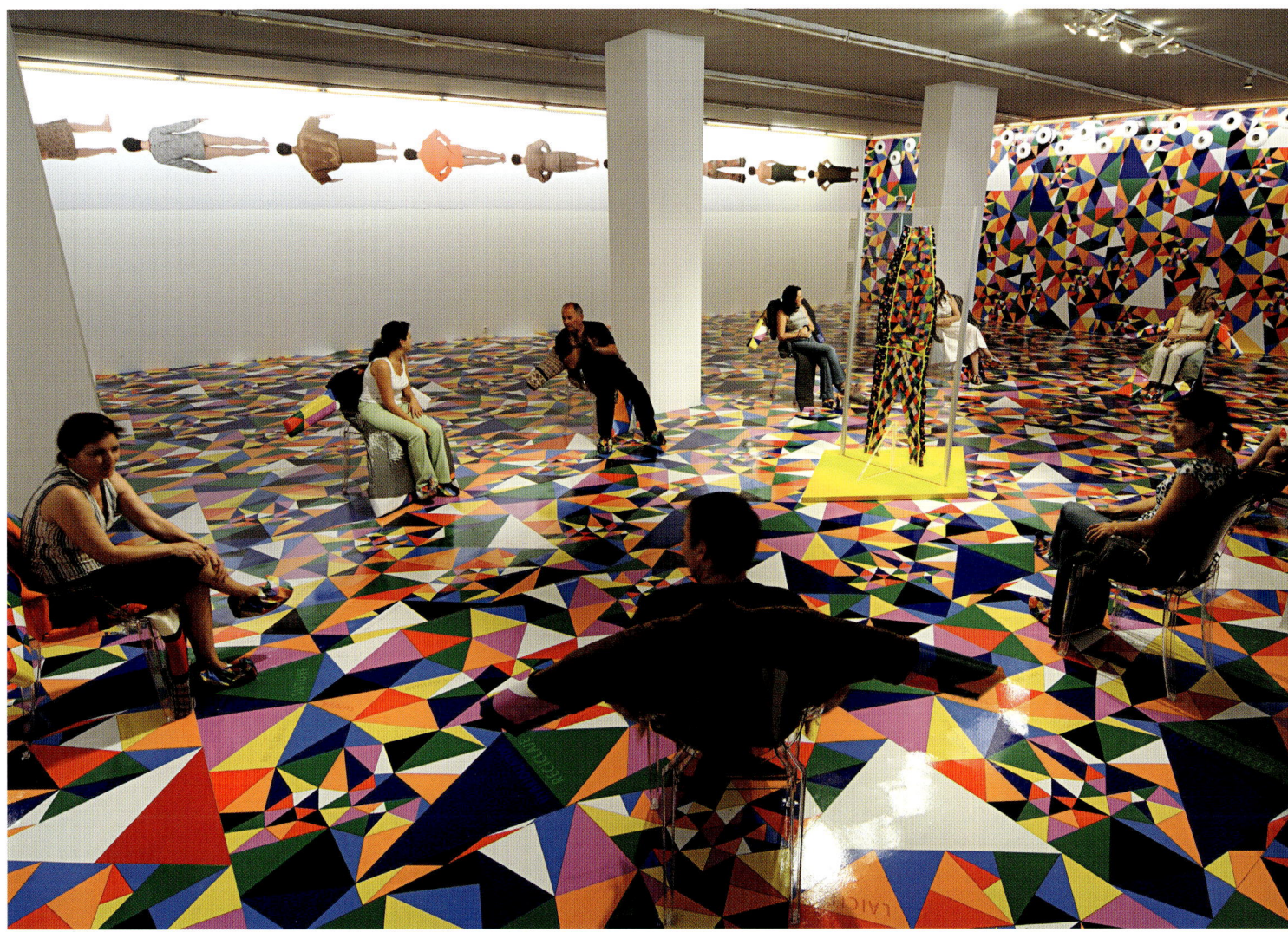

as Michel Serres's point, but as an allegorical point of power's disavowal of its own mechanism, which you reject. Your counterstatement reminds us that that's an impossibility. And, for me, within the allegory of secularism that Serres portrays there, it's a way of trying to understand the self-justifying shortsightedness of the Harlequin emperor.

Bhabha: Okay, I understand.

Veneciano: Your explication of power is most useful in this context. Well, coming back to the point about secularism, there is a note in the text about the Harlequin being multiple and diverse, undulating and plural. Is that a reason for this parable, if that's what it is, on the subject of secularism? Is it the need to make space for this kind of multiplicity?

Bhabha: Well, you said something that is more interesting or more significant for what I want to say than you know. It's significant in itself, what you said, but for my own purposes you said something you couldn't possibly know that this is what I'm about to say. You used a phrase "make space." And the reason why I've always been skeptical of the lan-

guage of pluralism, of a certain kind of pluralism, is that the assumption is that in a pluralistic world there is always space enough and time, in the best circumstances, for people to live beside each other, as neighbors. The assumption always has been that if there's lots of space, then there's not a problem. And if there's lots of time, you know, people need time to get used to each other, people need time to appreciate each other. The more I think about it, the more I think it's got nothing to do with that. To put it very simply, people have lived in ghetto-like circumstances—disadvantaged people, of course. People with great wealth, very wealthy Palestinians, and very wealthy Jews, or very wealthy *Zionists*—I shouldn't say *Jews*—but very wealthy Palestinians and very wealthy Zionists, they may not eat together, but I'm sure there are many, many expen-

Suture, Hibridization, Recycling: ORLAN + davidelfin, installation, Espacio AV, Murcia, Spain.

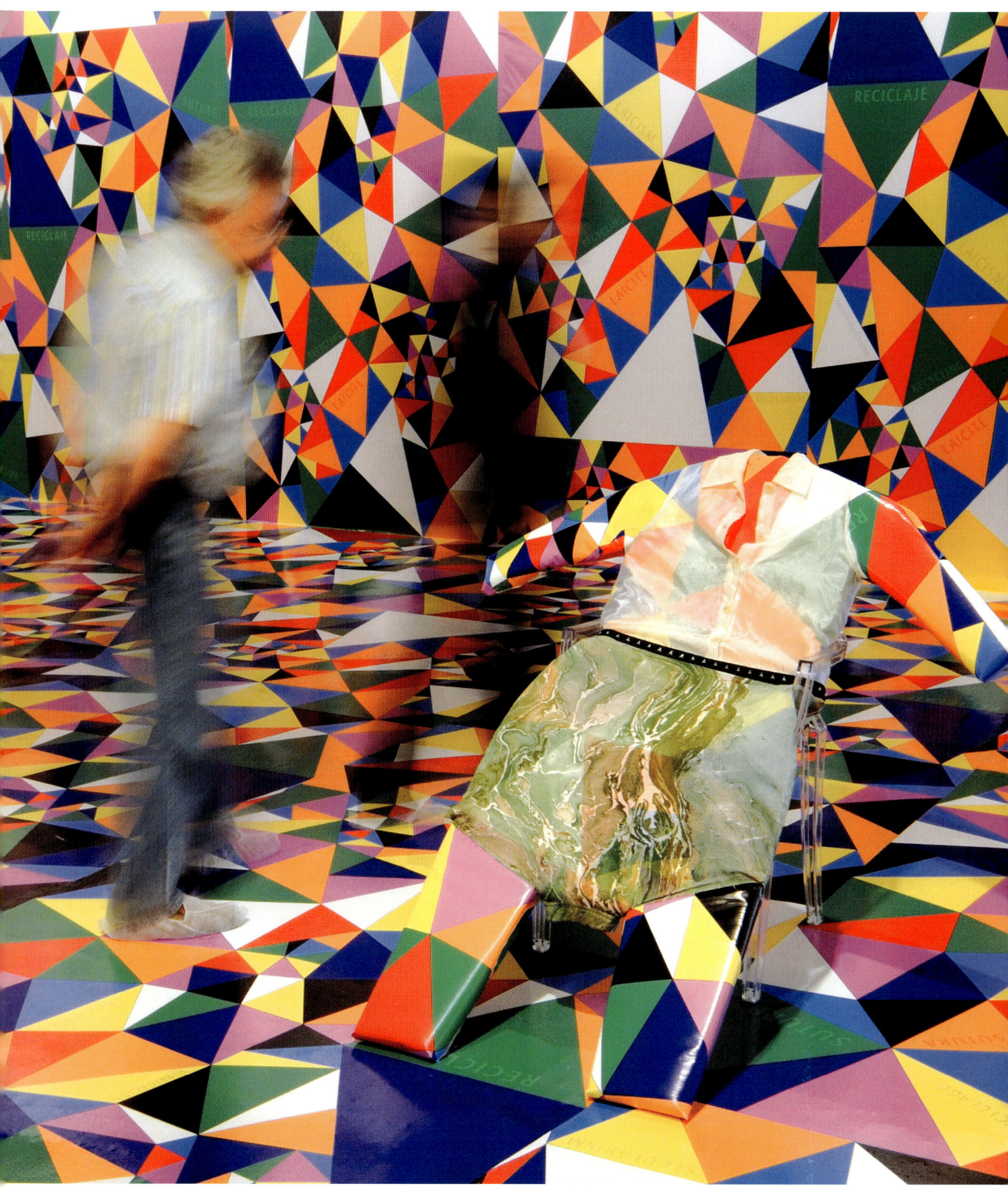

sive New York condos, Manhattan condos, or Boston townhouses where people live next to each other with great wealth, and there's never an issue.

I'm saying that when we want to understand what is at the heart of racial or an ethnic conflict, we've got to rid ourselves of this idea of pluralism, which always assumes that had there been time enough and space, we could work this problem out. Because what happens in these moments, I feel, has got nothing to do with diversity and everything to do with the construction of difference. Hindus and Muslims will live in very, very closely configured areas—maybe separate, but very closely configured. So closely that for their daily lives—I'm thinking of Bombay here—they will continually have to crisscross each other's territories, buy fruit from each other, buy goods from each other; you know, the metaphor of the market is brimming, and everyone is happy. Then something happens. It's a political issue; it's an international issue. But at the point at which conflict begins to happen, diversity will save nobody. The knowledge of diversity will save nobody because what becomes configured at that point is a sort of phobic object. So that, in the world of pluralism and diversity, people wear saris—women wear saris and walk around the street every day. On the same street, in a moment of racial tension, it is the sari that becomes a new kind of border. It is infused with a new semiosis. The sari becomes the sight of aggression, exclusion, paranoia, bestiality. That same textile, that same vestment that two months before was just part of, you know, *other* people's clothes, suddenly becomes infused. So the issue really is: What are the circumstances and what are the conditions of turning something into a destructive or destroying difference? That's the point.

Veneciano: You're speaking to the problem, maybe the impossibility, of democracy.

Bhabha: No, I'm not speaking to the problem of the impossibility of democracy. I'm speaking to the problem *of* democracy. The problem *of* democracy, in which whole areas of the human condition are somehow excluded from the language of politics and the language of policy. And this is the area of affectivity, the area of the imagination, the area of the psyche, the area of a kind of emotional intelligence or a lack of emotional intelligence. This whole area, democracy has never found an adequate, or rarely finds an adequate, language to deal with. Therefore, all the 9/11 reports will say that whether we believe in failed states or whether we don't believe in failed states. Whatever it is, humiliation, or people feeling humiliated, particularly from poor underdeveloped countries or from

the margins of wealthy countries, *humiliation* has something to do with the mentality of contemporary terrorism. Everybody will agree to that. I don't think anybody has disagreed. Some people will say the hopelessness is because, you know, these societies are inherently hopeless. Some people will say they are politically hopeless. Whatever. Some people say they're hopeless, therefore they have to be Christianized. Then they will see hope. But nobody will take anything other than an instrumentalist policy-oriented notion of humiliation. There is humiliation, yes: "Well that's because they don't have American-style markets and democracy. What they need is more schools, more this, more that—they will not be humiliated." People don't understand that the time or the temporality of, yes, political and psychic trauma, psychic abuse, political neglect, has a very different time scheme in creating action and effects than the way in which policy wonks talk about political disasters or political solutions. The whole *time* of the psyche, the *time* of affectivity, the time of the link between the affectivity and history, the time it has taken to produce an explosive solution, the time that it will take to get out of it is completely different from the time of resolution that policy people think you need for these matters.

Veneciano: Your words and your tone suggest that what you're talking about is, in fact, a neglect that needs to be paid attention to. I mean, democracy is deliberative, so it's the other side of this—it's the unconscious—that is not addressed. But, if I use that model, there is no democratic procedural sense in which those needs could ever be satisfied.

Bhabha: Now, I knew you were going to say that. You're absolutely right to pose the very large question: How to make the unconscious into something which is democratically productive? And which would mean that you would have to instrumentalize that part of the human psyche that is most un-instrumentalizable. I mean, the reason why it is important, even as a concept, is that you cannot instrumentalize its element. It is contingent, it is disruptive, it is interruptive. But I do think that, whereas it cannot wholly be inserted into democratic theory, there are elements of the *effects* of the unconscious that those who draw up policies and those who think about the political lives of communities and the public good, should be more aware of. And therefore I think not that all of society should be made to lie on a couch, but what I

Suture, Hibridization, Recycling:
ORLAN + davidelfin, installation,
Espacio AV, Murcia, Spain.

HOMI K. BHABHA AND JORGE DANIEL VENECIANO

do think is important is that, for instance, the notion of the will of the people, the people's will, which is such an enlightenment idea, has to be recast and rethought.

Most important of all, people have to realize those who construct the law or conventions or declarations or proposals or policies, they have to, I think, realize that there is a mode of symbolic action that human beings are capable of. Which may run counter to the idea that everybody acts on the basis of the enlightened self-interest. That enlightened self (and I underline *self*-interest) may actually lead people into problematic and perverse positions, not because they do not believe in freedom or equality, but because they feel that their circumstances are so constrained that what they see as their acts of freedom or their acts of autonomy are actually acts that may eventually imprison them even deeper. It is this kind of, not irrationality, but the non-rational — the affective — and I think this goes back to our discussion about secularism, which should be taken with a deadly seriousness in democratic discourse. And there is no reason why that should not be the case. So just to take one example, which comes to mind now: in a way, it was Ghandi's espousal of a non-rational notion of *satyagraha*, or non-violent action, that allowed Indian independence. Whatever else you think about Ghandi, and there are many views, it allowed Indian independence to gain its measure of success. But it was a kind of appeal to the non-rational. The rational thing would have been to have had resistance — well, of course, there were resistance movements — to have mobilized the country, in a way. But that was not his motive. He knew that what was expected of him, rationally, was a much more virulent, physical resistance. So he responded to that by letting the body go limp, by creating a vacuum where a punch is expected.

Veneciano: That's what I meant about the impossibility of democracy: acknowledging a limit, where democracy requires a supplement. If its response can only ever be deliberative, it is constructed to treat a symptom — a rational response. The example you gave is not of an exercise of democratic power or resistance to power, but, importantly, what you said about this is that it's a symbolic act that can appeal to the non-rational in a democratic society, or what should be its "sense" of democratic justice.

Bhabha: That's right. And I think that is important. The strength of human rights does not depend on whether or not they are supported by law. The fact that human rights, for instance, opens up more and more democratic demands and more and more constituencies for those demands is based on the fact that it is the *symbolic* nature of right that makes people feel they have a right, even when they have no law telling them they have a right. Even when they have the world telling them that they have no rights. That symbolic aspect, of course, we need to embellish much more, enrich that concept much more, which we can't do in this discussion. But it is that that is most important.

Veneciano: Allow me to offer you a contemporary example of what you're talking about: Barack Obama. He was awarded a Nobel Peace Prize, but not for having accomplished anything —

Bhabha: [*Simultaneously*] — anything, but for being something.

Veneciano: — but for offering symbolic hope, which is what his campaign and its success were all about.

Bhabha: Exactly. I completely agree with that. Absolutely.

Veneciano: Agreement and hope, good symbolic notes on which to end for now. Thank you.

CAMBRIDGE, MASSACHUSETTS, OCTOBER 23, 2009

Refiguration Self-Hybridization, Pre-Columbian Series #2, 1998. Cibachrome, 100 cm. x 150 cm. and 60 cm. x 90 cm. Collection of Michel Rein, courtesy of the Michel Rein Gallery, Paris.

NOTES

1. *Pre-Columbian: Refiguration Self-Hybridization*, 1998; *African Self-Hybridization*, 2002; *American Indian Self-Hybridization*, 2005.

2. Isabel Tejeda, ed., *Suture/Hibridisation/Recycling: ORLAN + davidelfin* (Murcia, Spain: Espacio AV, 2008).

3. Michel Serres, "Preface," *The Troubadour of Knowledge*, trans. Sheila Faria Glaser with William Paulson (Ann Arbor: University of Michigan Press, 1997), xiii–xvii.

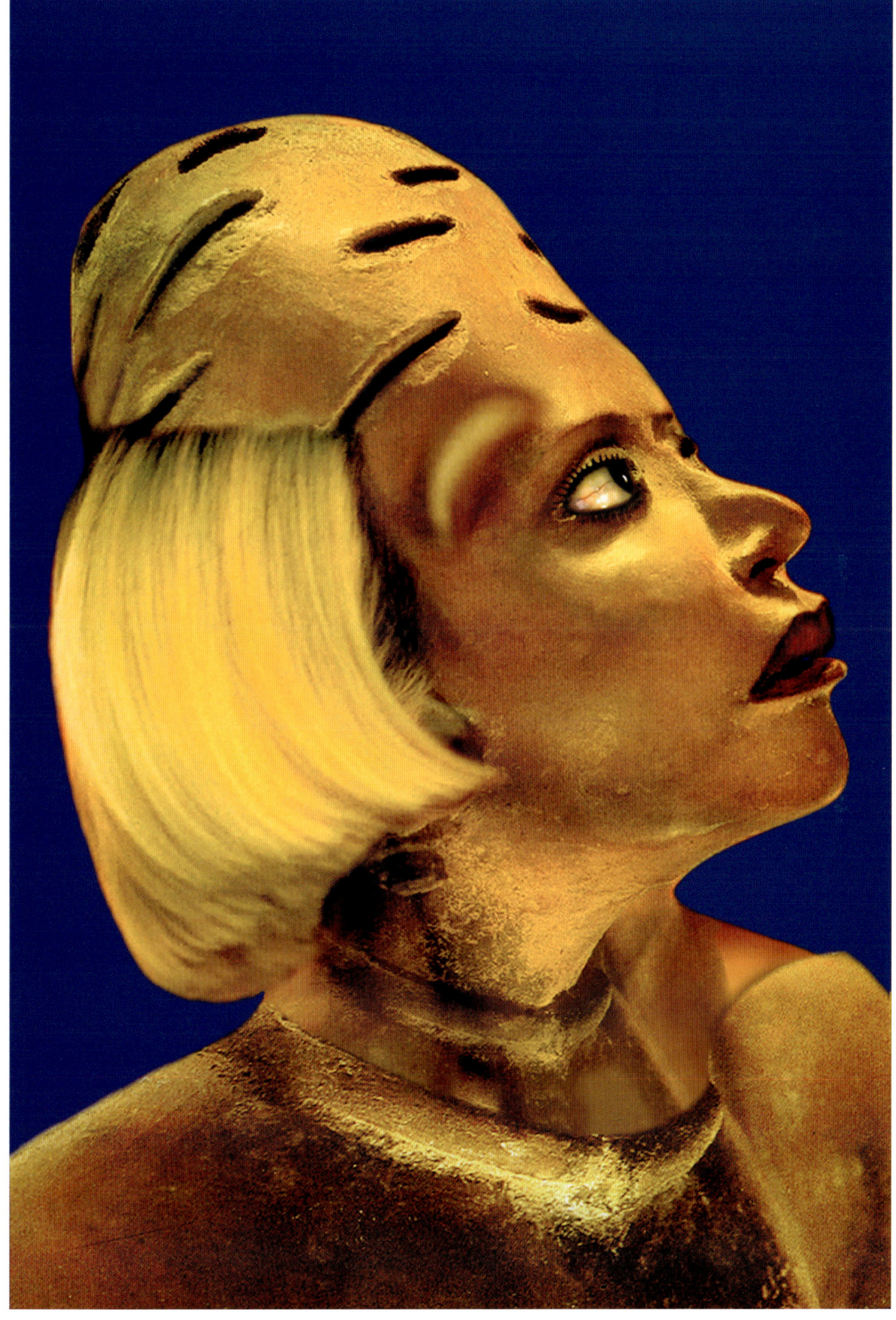

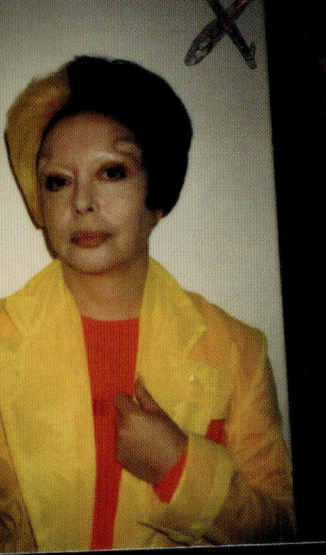
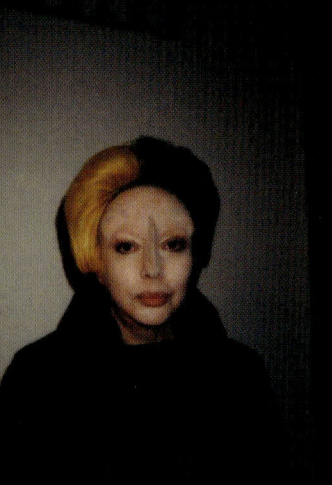
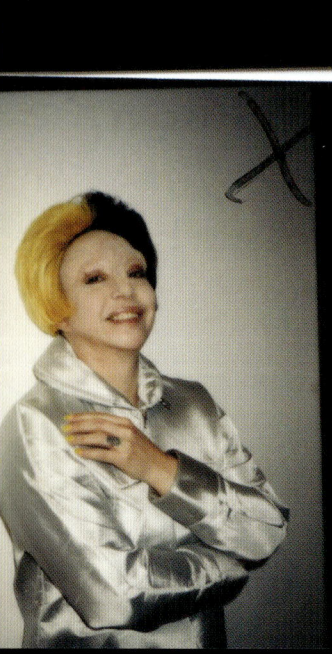
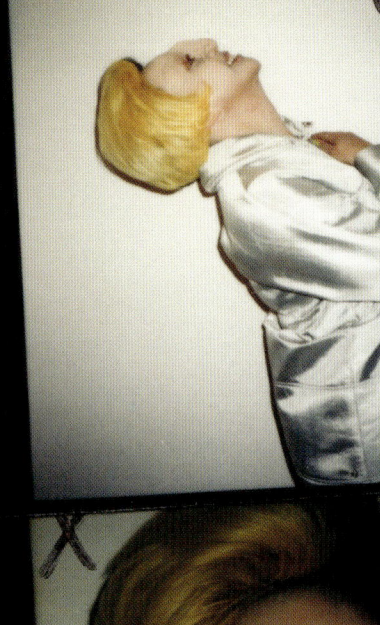
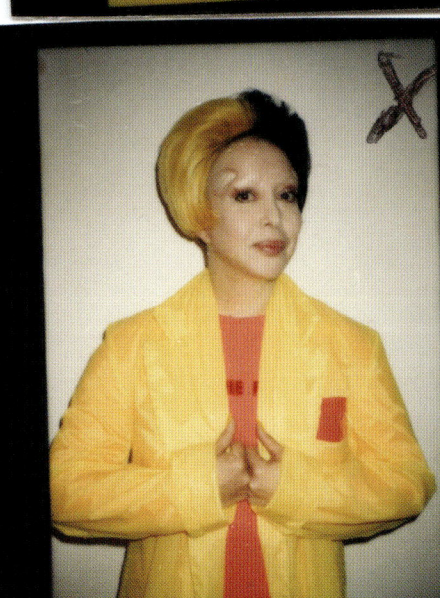
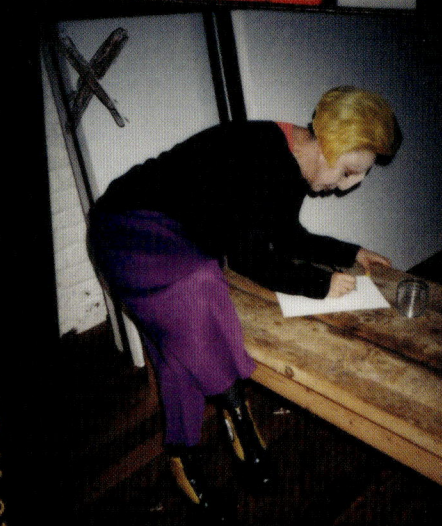
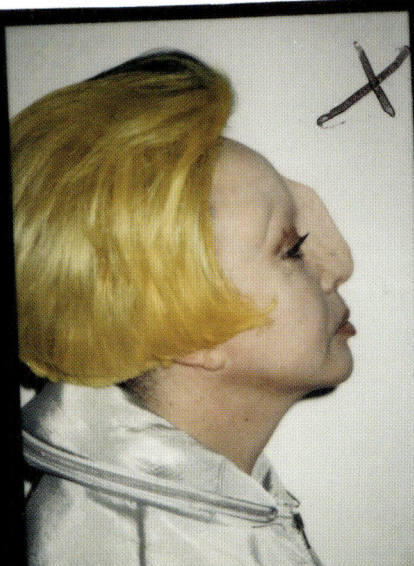

TRANSGRESSION/TRANSFIGURATION

ORLAN: When Annick Notter suggested that I exhibit in the Museum of the New World, which she is directing now, I immediately thought to join together the forces[1] present in La Rochelle for this "New World." It was an occasion to see you again, Paul Virilio, our last encounter having been now twenty years ago.

Paul Virilio: The New World, this is also what has just arrived! It is not simply the world beyond the Atlantic, it is the world of great closure, the ecology of the finished world, the world whose finiteness we are living, and which is at the same time a plenitude. It is therefore surprising to see that you are speaking of the New World of Columbus, and that in a way it is of course the new world of the end of the world: that is, the world of the end of geography. The world is perfectly spherical, and we run around it constantly. Google Earth was invented to allow us to see it practically in real time. That is also the new world.

I believe that what is interesting in our encounter is the rapport with the body, not only the animal body of man and woman, but also the territorial body reduced to nothingness by progress. I was speaking of this recently: the world is too small for progress. It is not only I who say this, it is ecology. In ecological practice, we would need three earths to continue to consume as we do. A world too small for short-term profit: the crisis is here. When Barack Obama tells us that a continual disaster is threatening us and it is not simply an economic crisis, he is daring to speak of this. The world is too small for ultra-rapid profit. The question touches on nihilism.

The world, is it too small for our project? Is this the apocalypse? Absolutely not! Au contraire! There is a passion in the new world that is the opposite of the nihilistic passion where everything is finished. We think of running away to other planets. The exobiologists tell us: we will find an exoplanet. We relaunch the colonial myth. I think that "New World" has for you as for us, a double meaning, both geographic and historic.

Now, to get to today's topic, many critics, basing themselves on a postcolonial analysis, see in the work

Photographs by Juergen Teller.

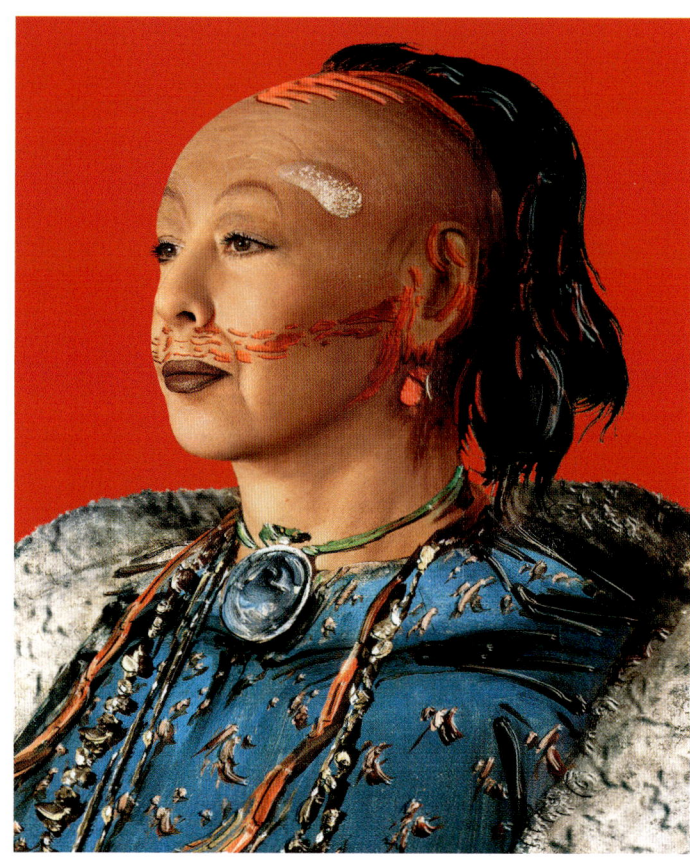

of ORLAN a colonialist attitude. In fact, they do not realize that they dehybridize the hybridizations as if they were unable even to conceive of what ORLAN has put in place in her works, she who makes room for the Other, who creates a halfway being, which is neither one thing nor the other.

ORLAN: At the Ecole de Beaux-Arts in Paris-Cergy, I have students, Koreans, Chinese, Arabs, who absolutely want to work with the materials of their countries, with their own origins, with their villages. I respect this, and I understand that it would be very difficult to be an immigrant or a refugee. But I can't help thinking that this attachment to origins is strange in an era when we live in continual flux, as much from a physical as from an intellectual point of view. It is as if all artists, born as I was in Saint-Étienne, were obliged to work with coal, or with *les Verts*, the soccer players so talked about, the "French Hunter," or with guns, when we are all citizens of the world. We all have the Internet, and we all travel in every direction. Is there an obligation to be authentic? This anachronistic attachment is not the only way to be authentic. It's absurd. I've been asking myself this question for a long time. Of course, if that works upon us, and if we are nothing but memories, there are those things that are obviously inherent to our origins. But we are also made of constitutive elements through the bias of

the Internet, through television, through our travels and encounters, which forge in part our consciousness of the world. There are so many other ramifications, networks, and inscriptions that enter into the flux, and which are not part of this rigidity to which we must absolutely refer!

Let us return to what you were saying about the problem of the body as a territory and its inability to be in sync with what is happening now—an "obsolete body" as we say along with Stelarc. We are made neither for speed nor for most of today's technologies in this new world. Ultimately, we mutate at the speed of cockroaches, while we conceive of high-performance instruments, supersonic vehicles, and high-tech prosthetics—the above and beyond. On the other hand, we must consider that we don't have one but several bodies, all of which are made of our own cells and our own programming: a baby does not resemble a teenager, or an old man, who often will not recognize himself, so much will he have changed. When the same bodies are exposed to cold, to hunger, or to illness or when they express themselves in joy, in pleasure, or in sex, they are once again extremely different bodies in their particular chemistry. The body on which we harp ceaselessly, our territory and our vehicle for a lifetime, is in fact a kind of fortress in which we are very ill at ease, not only with regard to what is hap-

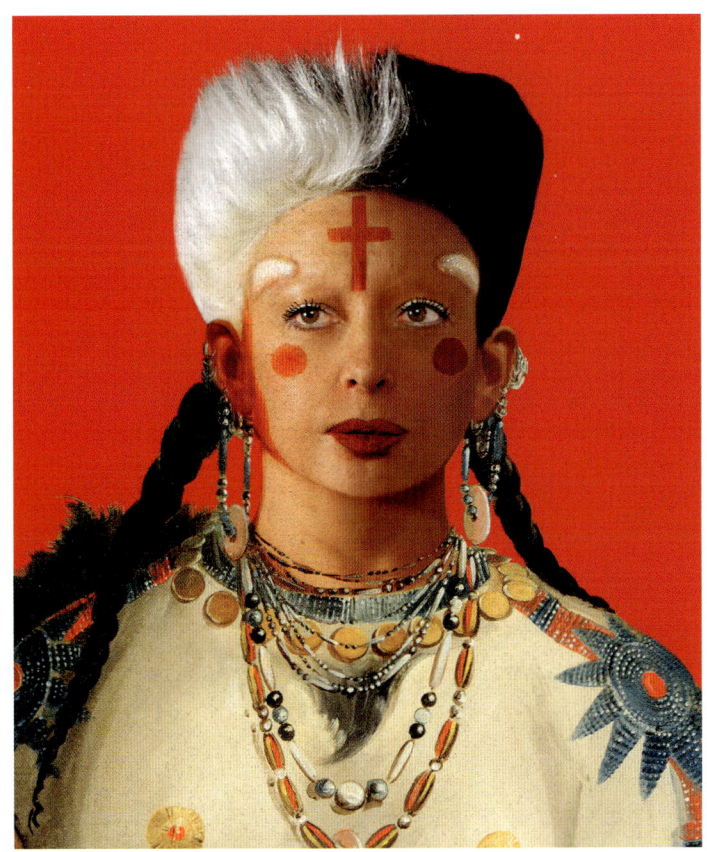 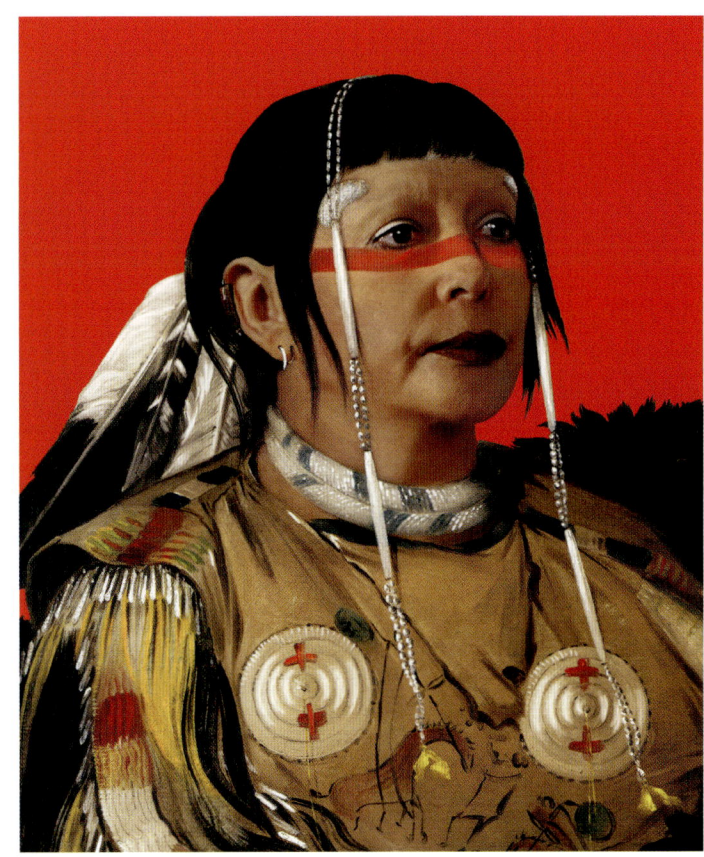

pening on the outside, but also, and more particularly, in the fact of being constrained by great speed and a geography that is closing in on us.

I have this problem with my body: if I travel to the other side of the world, I can do it, but that doesn't keep my body from becoming tired, sick. It loses its immunity because it is being agitated, discomfited by travel. We still live in the generality or the particularity of a situation, furnished with a body, which is not in sync with what we would like for it, or toward it or against it. It is sometimes a body helping us to think, sometimes a body that defies us, sometimes stopping us from advancing, or even a body that decides for "us," as if outside of us.

It is also for these reasons that I have developed a series of images of my body and of its representation in order to make new images with my works, not as a personal effort but to put it into perspective, to put it at a distance, as something understood in my way of thinking about art and my life, which sometimes

Refiguration-Self Hybridation, American Indian Series #14: "Painted portrait of Ah-ton-we-tuck, Cock Turkey repeating its prayer, with ORLAN's portrait," 2005. Digital photograph, 122.4 x 152.4cm.

Refiguration Self-Hybridization, American Indian Series #7: "Painted portrait of Tis-Se-Woo-Na-Tis, She Who Bathes with Her Knees, Wife of the Chief, with photographic portrait of ORLAN," 2005. Digital photograph, 124.4 cm. x 152.4 cm.

Refiguration Self-Hybridation, American Indian Series #18: "Painted portrait of Sha-Co-pay, The Six Plains Chief, with ORLAN's portrait," 2005. Digital photograph, 122.4 x 152.4 cm.

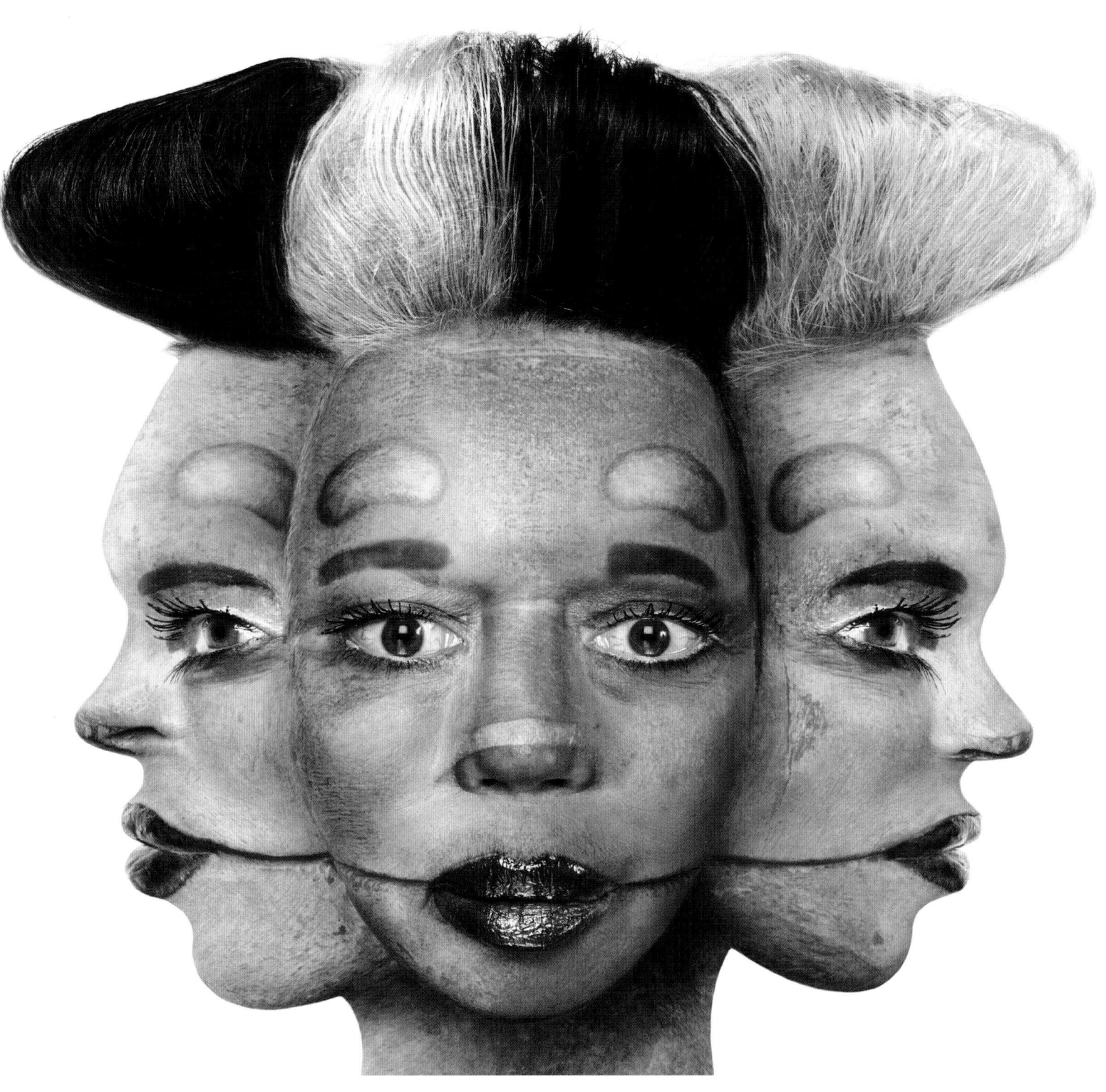

come together: the body as material, the art-matter of being, the sculpture of oneself and the invention of the self, the body as language, trying therefore to turn the Christian affirmation "the word made flesh" into "the flesh made Word."

I have tried to do this by hurling myself at the real and voluntarily employing the literality of performance and the violence done to the body—and in particular to female bodies. I have also developed a series around my image and my representation while thinking about nomadic, mutated, mobile, and different identities, following the flow of life and geography.

Virilio: In a certain sense, ORLAN illustrated what I was saying a while ago in an interview. Someone asked me the following question: "You say that the world is too small for progress, what is then the effect of this on the body? On the animal body? 'Animal' in the sense of animate, of course. On the social body?"

My response was this: You know, me, I am claustrophobic. The claustrophobe is someone who, enclosed in a room, feels as if he is in an armoire. Today we are enclosed in the world, the world is too small. We feel what the Ancients called "obsidional fever." You know that in states under siege, including La Rochelle, people came down after a while with a fever of enclosure. Obsidional fever is a real fever. He answered, "Sir, claustrophobia, it is of the body itself, not of the world." Facing the world, we are in an enclosure, but facing this enclosure, this last claustrophobia, is that of one's own body. The body is itself too small for its future. Not only too small for progress, the world is too small for progress and for instant profit, but our own body feels this smallness and therein is the physiological claustrophobia, an obsidional fever of one's own body that in a sense ORLAN has anticipated by mutating, by self-transfiguring. I use this religious term deliberately because in the works she initially created, she made reference to this sacred dimension, since transfiguration is a dimension of the body. It is not simply cosmetic, it is much more. I see in ORLAN a sort of preeminence [in French, *primate*], not to say a sort of primitive [in the sense of originary] of bodily claustrophobia.

ORLAN: Upon the claustrophobia of the body itself are inscribed other pressures that make us even more claustrophobic! These are the pressures of dominant ideologies, the constraints and influences of the moment one lives in, the place where one lives.

Virilio: It is the social body, the third body.

ORLAN: All my life I have worked on this very question. What is the status of the body in our society? What are the social, political, religious, cultural pressures that imprint themselves on our flesh, in our body, and in particular in that of women, which are heavily encoded. I have tried to escape these shackles and to kick society in the face by allowing myself to design other models, other ways of thinking or of seeing my bodies, my attitudes, and to be at a distance from those mannerisms called feminine. Being myself a woman, I think that it was important to risk stepping out of these constraints or at least to designate them. Of course, these are only attempts to move the bars of the cage, the body-cage, the geographic and social cage. But I believe that the fact of trying while showing that there could be other images, other ways for our era to imagine bodies, was really essential in light of new technologies and surgery, including plastic surgery, which is more and more common. To have recourse to surgery, whether plastic or otherwise, is not a natural thing, but, just as when one takes antibiotics in order not to die from an infection, it is a perfectly integrated, possible choice.

Virilio: There is more than one current phenomenon we must combat, and I don't think that ORLAN shares this perspective, and that is bioengineering, cloning, the techno-scientific mutation of bodies. ORLAN's interest is that of an artist. She is not a surgeon or an exobiologist—those who speak of life at the limits of death, of extreme viabilities. There is science's will to power, which absolutely revolts me because I remember that this was [Josef] Mengele's project! Whence his interest in twins, we must not forget.

What is interesting in what ORLAN has just said is that it is not about bioengineering, but about art, and there is a big difference. Industrializing life as we have industrialized death. The eugenicist project of the camps, it was only about eliminating bodies; it was the industrialization of life. *It was industrializing life, hence the interest in twins.* There is in ORLAN something, in my opinion, very original. Even if she has touched [altered] her body—it is art in this touch. It is not the forceps; it is not the scalpel; it is not chemotherapy, etc. There, this is what I can say about this extremeness, for we are in *outrance*.

ORLAN: Thank you for speaking of art, since sometimes observers note the phenomenon, the risk,

Refiguration Self-Hybridization, African Series: "Three-Headed Ogoni Mask, Nigeria and Mutant Face of Franco-European Woman," 2002. Digital photograph, color print, 125 cm. x 156 cm. Courtesy of the Michel Rein Gallery, Paris.

the scandal but forget about artistic questioning. Instead of seeing the moon, they look at the finger pointing it out. We never stop touching [altering] the body. That is part of surgery, transplants, genetics, when we replace a tooth, put in implants, replace a knee with a plastic one that works better than the one nature gave us. We alter the body all the time without the sky falling on our heads. Metamorphosis is an old myth, and in all eras many cultures have altered the body—through scarification, excision, circumcision, deforming the skull, incisions—under the pretext of religion, for membership in a group or tribal tradition. Throughout history we have wanted to make the body, and have fabricated the inhabitant of this body.

Linked to this, certain taboos are very anachronistic. Let us take, for example, that of pain. Human beings have suffered for millennia, without having the possibility even of taking an aspirin tablet for a simple headache or toothache! People sometimes exhibit my work with those of the New Primitives who use pain, and with other artists too, who through corporeal modification make themselves suffer in public. I understand why people associate me with this artistic current, but I am far from these rituals of self-torture. In my manifesto, *Carnal Art*, I say clearly that I do not believe in pain as redemption or purification, but I believe more in body-pleasure. The famous, "In pain shall you bring forth children," seems absurd to me in this age of the epidural. I have militated a great deal for medical staffs to dispense powerful painkillers to people who suffer.

Virilio: In this sense, all art is sacred, since we can question everything . . .

ORLAN: Even to desacralize what others sacralize. I am currently making cultures of my cells with other human and animal cells. In continuity with my Self-Hybridizations, created with digital photography, there is an important installation with macroprojections of living cells and a special bioreactor that keeps them alive. It is a way for me to ask the questions of our era, while using cutting-edge technology that fashions our time and our future, as you ask them yourself, whether at the Fondation Cartier [a contemporary art museum] or elsewhere, while making a record, but while trying also to find the right questions to ask together in order to be able to manage our times and what is happening, and what we imagine will happen. I feel an artistic responsibility to speak, to interrogate my time while inscribing myself precariously, while creating slippages. I produce therefore a sfumato between presentation and representation.

Virilio: Twenty years ago we parted on my reservations about your surgery project. You had spoken to me about it. I had told you—and I believe you were displeased by this—that I had reservations. These reservations remain. They are part of our dialogue. We cannot achieve consensus on this and it is very important that there are hot points in a dialogue. In the exhibition Native Land: Elsewhere Begins Here, at the Fondation Cartier, we also had important points of friction with Raymond Depardon. These disagreements are less those of persons than of City and Country. Dialogue is fundamental; if we said, "Oh well, okay, let's go on," in my opinion that would no longer be art.

ORLAN: Many people tried to dissuade me [from surgery]. My psychoanalyst, abandoning her reserve, warned me: "Do not do this." If I had announced to her, "I want to commit suicide," she would have said, "I have an opening tomorrow, come in and we'll talk." This is the reason why I wanted to meet you again at the Museum of the New World. I knew your reservations, and mine also on certain points, and particularly on several of your current positions, which surprise me. This does not prevent me from agreeing with you on other points or from respecting you as a person. I think you have the same attitude [toward me], and what is interesting are the dialogues, the exchanges, even if pointed.

I very much liked what you said about the idea of causing fear. Many people fear my work and even my person, and I feel this in a very strange manner. It is, however, often true. You can perhaps develop this argument since I don't know if it is true—nor what is the truth. But in any case, it's about taking risks, including that of being a pioneer and opening the path for others who follow.

Virilio: We are in an era when optimism is an obligation. It's extraordinary. We must be optimists! There is an interdiction on pessimism that I see personally. But there are others, there is the fact that truth is considered an offense. The simple truth, I am not saying the entire truth, but the act of truth or the word of truth is considered an aggression. I would even say a terrorism. I think that this is the case for many intellectuals in Europe. Not in America, because when I see the contacts that I have all over the world, I never feel this rejection before what they call my terrorism. I have been interested in the bunkers of the Second World War, therefore I am a fascist! I was interested in their side functions, therefore I was imbalanced. I am interested in speed, therefore I am a pessimist. This brings us together, we two, the violence of the true, let us not say the truth of the true. What ORLAN does is true since she bears the marks of it on her body. We can accuse ORLAN of many things but not of pretending. I do

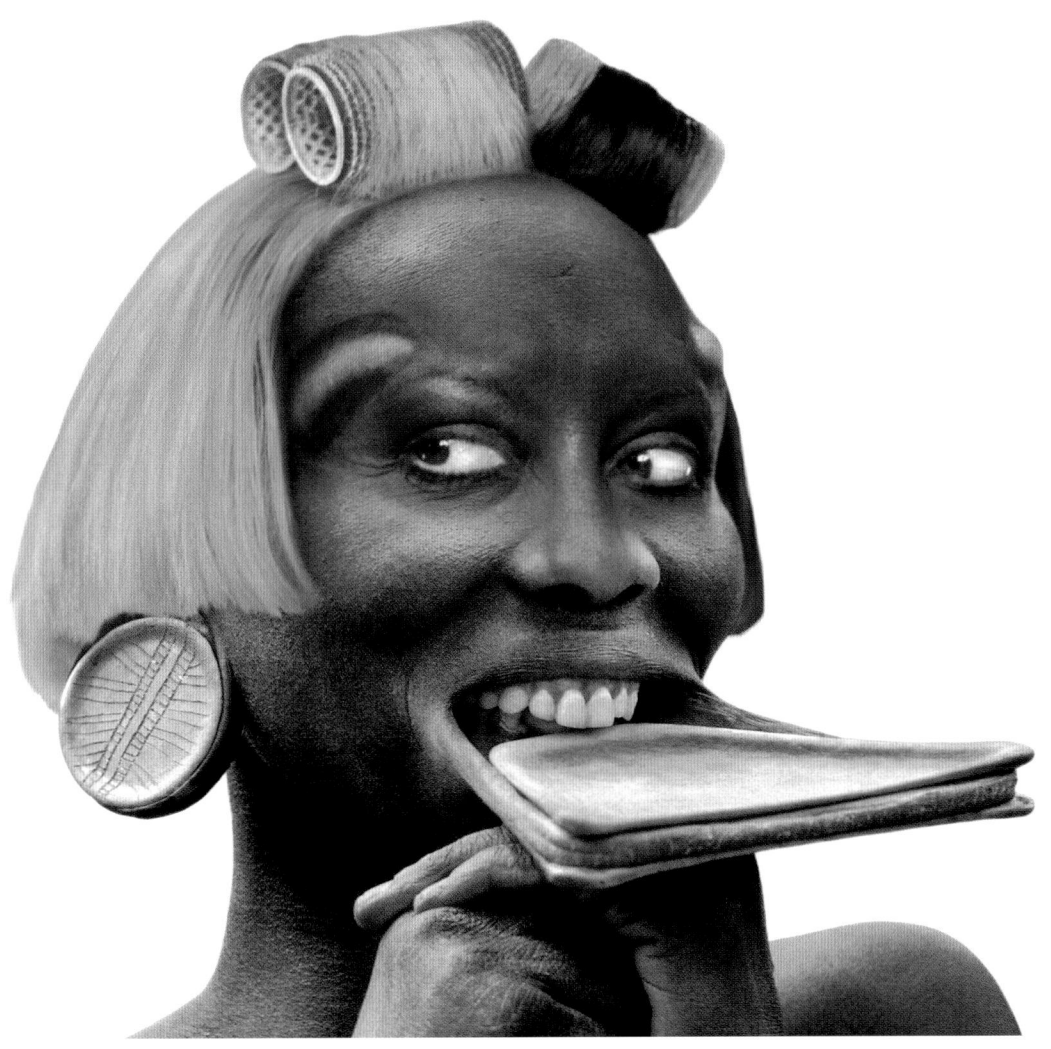

not pretend either; I am not a liar. When someone asks me to lie, I cross the street. I can't do it. It is not a virtue; it is a violence, the violence of the true.

ORLAN: We can also say this of me, and of the reactions I elicited when I used plastic surgery. The public thought that it was because I necessarily wanted to be more beautiful according to contemporary standards, which is totally the opposite of the message I wanted to transmit.

At the time of my performance-operation *Omnipresence*, simultaneously transmitted to the Georges Pompidou Center, the Sandra Gering Gallery in New York, and to the MacLuham Center in Toronto, people could watch me and ask me questions live. The operation was even on the *CBS Evening News*, since reporter Connie Chung was in the operating room. The program *Extreme Makeover* came out six months [after that operation]. I do not have the impression at all that anything I did had anything to do with this reality show. During my operation-performances, I do not submit—I orchestrate. In the O.R., I direct the photography, the video, the filming, I draw with my fingers and my blood. When the surgeon turned his back or when the lighting wasn't good, since in an O.R. one cannot control everything, I would say, "We are not getting good images, so we have to redo this or that gesture. The surgeon would redo the gesture or pretend to, in order to get the image. These videos were then edited, reframed, exhibited.

This distance and this deformation of the real, which permits the production of works of art, seem to me extremely salutary and vital. At the time of my surgical operations, the majority of people had extremely "epidermal" reactions. The images prevented them from thinking, from reflecting, whereas at the cinema, for example, we are accustomed to seeing very violent images, sometimes

Refiguration Self-Hybridization, African Series: "Surnas Woman with Lip Plug and Face of Euro–Saint-Étienne Woman with Curlers," 2003. Digital photograph, color print, 124 cm. x 156 cm. Collection of Michèle Barrière, courtesy of ORLAN.

where we must close our eyes for a few seconds. But we do not reject the director, the actor, or the film. Now with regard to my surgeries, people deem certain of my images to be between madness and the impossibility of seeing. I have shown images to which we are not accustomed and which, most of the time, render us blind and make us faint because we do not see the opening of the body. We look at the steering wheel, not the landscape in which we could talk. It's strange because ever since [Andreas] Vesalius, we have been opening bodies, showing them. We know what the machine is made of. [. . .]

Virilio: What strikes me is that there is an important moment in art, which is the portrait. It's the portraits of Fayoum, the portraits that are likenesses, which are not stylizations. These portraits of Fayoum and self-portraits, as much pictorial as photographic, are a very important moment in art, which interests me a lot. Now here, it seems to me that the art of ORLAN, this self-transfiguration—I use the word because I am thinking of Christ and of the Transfiguration—is a kind of self-portrait. The self-portrait, it's not simple; it's something unheard-of that was invented: likeness. It's fabulous when we think that among the Egyptians or elsewhere, and not only among iconoclasts, resemblance did not exist. There was a style, not to say a stylization, of the face, whatever it was, which replaced portraiture: the identity card.

They therefore invented self-portraiture as a personalization, and particularly that of the painter, since he was the first to condemn himself to this pictorial transfiguration. When we see the portraits of Rembrandt, we are obliged to think of this. I put the work of ORLAN in this tradition of self-portrait. It's important because self-portraiture has not finished its story. I believe that there is something fundamental played out here, and it is in the process of collapsing into the ID photo and even the biometric portrait.

There is a history of the art of landscapes, seascapes, still lifes, and the portrait that traverses art history through sculpture, painting, etc. ORLAN's work continues the self-portrait. The self-transfigurations prolong portraiture. Is there still *faciality* [*visagéité*] beyond normal resemblance?

If I say transfiguration it is because when Christ transfigures himself, it is not exhibitionism. He makes his self-portrait because we see him as a man. Most people said at the time, "Who is this guy? It seems he makes miracles, but he's a guy like any other. He looks like nothing!" You see, other than the Holy Shroud, there is no self-portrait. Then Christ did his self-portrait: that is called "the Transfiguration"—that is, the portrait of the Man-

God. No one had done his portrait, despite the myth of Veronica. But he did his self-portrait. In my opinion there is something religious in what ORLAN is doing. That is why I call this self-transfiguration.

ORLAN: So we cannot escape the Holy Face? "In a little while, you will not see me no more" [John 16:16]. I have created an installation based on this text, but you are right. There are successive self-portraits. I have figured my face, therefore created representation, therefore refiguring transfiguration. My goal has never been disfigurement or mutilation, but the "even more."

Virilio: But as for Saintly Faciality, Deleuze was telling me that with the invention of the close-up in cinema, the face became a landscape. That is, therefore, also a transfiguration.

ORLAN: For me, God is not a hypothesis for work or for life! But you do well to speak of Christ because, thanks to Christianity, we can make portraits and images, which is not the case in all religions. And I have benefited from that, we could almost say outrageously, beginning with the idea that I am unrepresentable, unfigurable—without taking myself for a goddess, of course! But I have always had the impression of feeling my way, of turning around all the possible images of myself, with what I have made up to now in my work, whether it be in photos, video, etc.

Regis Debray writes, "The divine, objects the iconoclast, is indescribable. This is why all images of him can be but 'pseudo' and not 'homo,' misleading and not likenesses. Spiritual and invisible then would be synonyms. It is this immortal couple that is broken by Christianity: revolution in Revelation." I think, thus, that any image of myself is pseudo, whether it is fleshly presence or verbal. All representation is insufficient, but not to create any is worse, like being without figuration, without image, without representation, and it is not the face or faciality that will save me.

What matters is to identify the possible images, to make them appear in stages, to push them out of me. I remain always surprised by the vision of what could be oneself and this material of being. Whatever images are produced, they are uncanny in Freud's sense.

Catholicism accepts multiple versions of the representations of Christ, virgins, saints—iconography

Refiguration Self-Hybridization, Pre-Columbian Series #32, 1998. Cibachrome, 100 cm. x 150 cm. and 60 cm. x 90 cm. Collection of Michel Rein, courtesy of the Michel Rein Gallery, Paris.

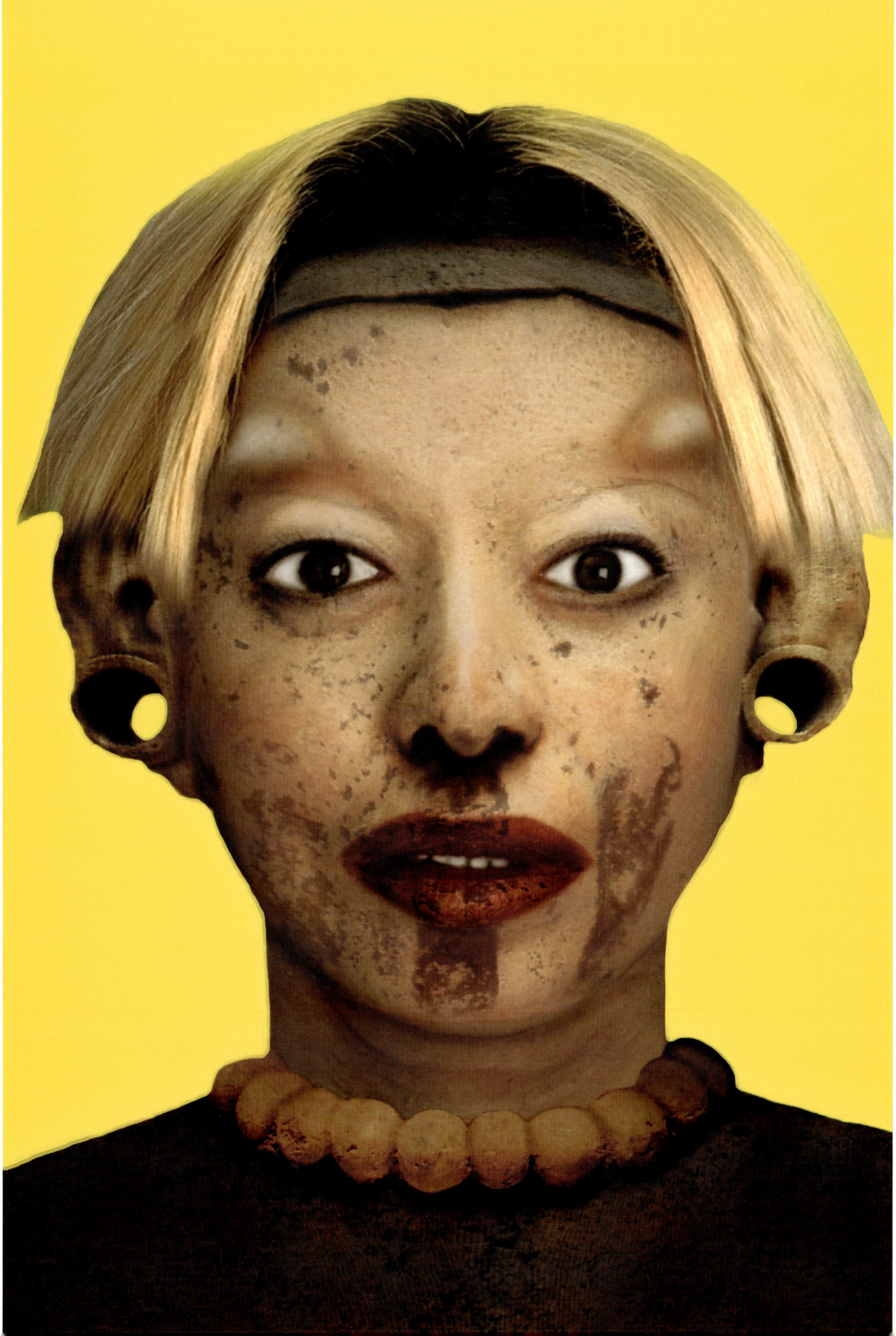

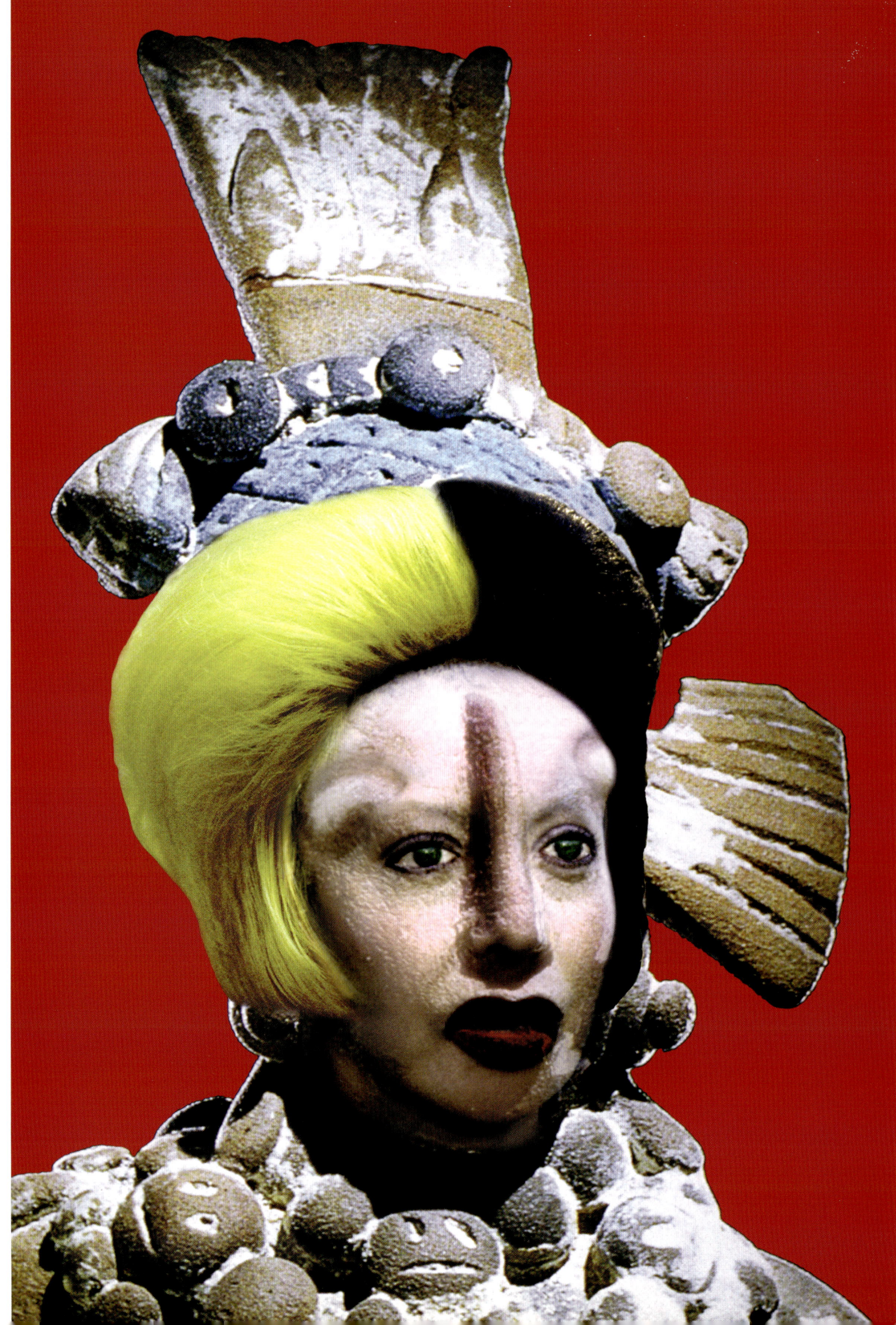

that permits an approach and lets us see something rather than nothing. To give oneself up to be seen, to make others believe that one can be seen through successive images, straw images, pseudo images. Like Adam and Lilith born from the mire and mud, throughout my work has been a stream of images, myriad photos, a hemorrhage, a charnel heap, a dysentery of images of myself that are just so many beginnings, proof of my incarnation from this common mud that I would call our "primordial soup." To work on my representation is better than nothing, but that does not represent me. In a certain sense, I am always elsewhere, in the unseizability of multitudes and the moments of these bodies that are only successive glimmers.

People often tell me that my process is very narcissistic and exhibitionist. That is fairly specific to the field of plastic arts, when an artist tries an approach to demonstrate what might be. It is also typical of a certain intolerance. On the other hand, when I don't know which great popular singer plays with his or her body, practically masturbates on stage, gives himself over entirely in front of twenty thousand spectators, no one says that is narcissistic, or too exhibitionistic, or disgusting, since finally the appetizer doesn't matter. It is the result that counts, if he produces something interesting. [. . .] Let us get back to the Self-Hybridizations and particularly to those that the museum in La Rochelle is exhibiting. And I would like to situate the pre-Colombian Self-Hybridizations. When I decided to organize my surgical performances, the principal idea was to make myself another image, to create new images of myself. It was about putting figuration, representation, on my face. It was not about mutilation but about a questioning of art. It was rather more about taking off a mask than about putting one on—to escape the obligation of wearing the face that one has been given. And who gave it to me? When? How? And why do I have eyes of this color, this kind of skin, etc.? Not having fashioned it myself, it therefore means very little to me. What interests me is how I can intervene, or how I can work, think, reflect, and put a bit of my social project or philosophy of life there where I can concretize them pictorially, or physically.

My attempt is founded, which is rarely said, on my culture, the one in which I evolved. It is the history of the Christian religion that for a long time has imprinted itself on our paintings and sculptures. I have cited it often, even if I don't know it very well, since I did not receive a religious education, my parents being libertarian, anarchists, nudists, esperantists, and anticlerical. The surgeries were therefore hinges between one culture that I

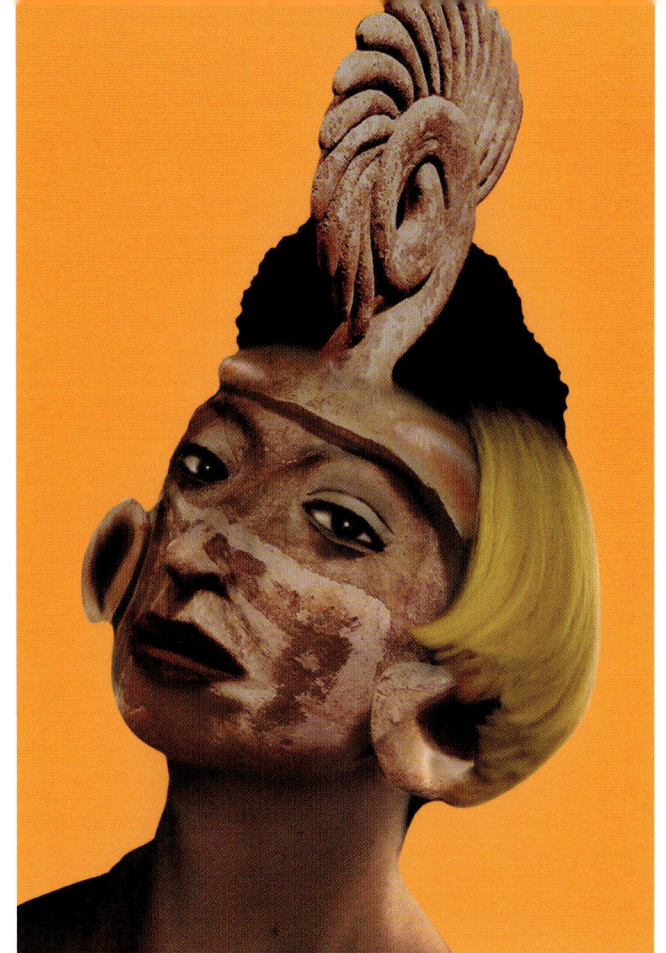

knew minimally, but which in a way constructed me and a part of me, the most conscious possible, where I wished to make room for other cultures, and for which I introduced, as in the period before my operations, the notion that I am not "I am" but "I are."

This type of *I*, even if it is not visible or legible, is for me really an illusion, something that does not exist, that exists only as a memory, created by all the territories I've traversed, by all the people of all origins that I've met, by all that I have heard, seized, read, either on the Internet or otherwise! And I told myself that beginning with this new image created in and by the material body, I could create new images using new referents.

I therefore entered into my postoperative phase, working on the pre-Colombians. I was fascinated by these civilizations, and I did research at the Anthropological Museum of Mexico in collaboration with their team. I took many photos and began this series of hybridizations, created with digital photography, of which the first referent was sculpture. Keeping the texture of stone or of clay, I, like a sculptor, conceived of all sorts of mutant beings, beginning with

Refiguration Self-Hybridization, Pre-Columbian Series #29 (OPPOSITE) and #5, 1998. Cibachrome, 100 cm. x 150 cm. and 60 cm. x 90 cm. Collection of Michel Rein, courtesy of the Michel Rein Gallery, Paris.

my face, supposedly representing the standards of beauty of my era, mixed with the standards of beauty of the pre-Colombian period. I then became interested in Africa—and I traveled a lot—and in Africans, who taught me a lot, and in ethnographic photography, which marks the imprint of the first times that people went to photograph the Other. This entire series is in black and white because it refers to silver-based photography of earlier [times], even though I worked also in digital. It is therefore both a hybridization of two civilizations and of traditional and computer photography.

The third series was created beginning with the paintings of American Indians. I was invited for a stay at the Getty Research Institute in Los Angeles. I asked myself what I could learn about the history of America and its history of art, without being false to myself. After long research at the Getty library, at the Smithsonian Museum of New York, and in Washington, I saw paintings by the American George Catlin, whom I did not know and who drew my attention with his extremely risky and passionate approach. In effect, he went into the American Indian tribes—before photography, before [Edward] Curtis—to paint with great respect the tribal chiefs dressed in their ceremonial regalia and makeup, as one would paint Louis XIV in all his majesty. These images went against the grain of his era, when the entire world thought these people were dirty, naked, uneducated, savage, and cruel. He gave them a magnificent image, which people criticize him for sometimes, arguing that he embellished reality. But when he visited an Indian chief, it was not about causing him difficulties or representing him badly! His entire story is very impressive, and I thought I could, with this legacy, give myself permission to resurrect these images, while mixing myself into them. It was of course a fairly extravagant project since women had neither the right to be chief nor to wear the necklace of bear claws or to paint a hand over their mouths, which was a symbol of young men who had killed an enemy with his own hands. The fact of "gluing" myself in began with respect to both the painter and the chiefs he represented, before they disappeared, while still conserving my critical distance regarding this culture, as I keep in regard to my own culture as well.

Globally it's about a work of hybridization between cultures, sculpture, silver-based photography, ethnography, painting, and digital photography. Each series begins with distinct referents. All my life I've wanted to break down barriers between generations, the prejudices about skin color, about the sexes, and notably about artistic practices. This

is not always perceived, since one cannot read immediately that my work is constructed in this manner, in these images, with this complexity.

Annick Notter: What is striking is that between these pre-Colombian, African, and American Indian Self-Hybridizations, you have always begun with civilizations and societies that the West has destroyed or colonized. Is this also a way of restoring equality? It is certainly not an accident that you have not chosen China or the Middle East, very proud and very self-aware.

ORLAN: Yes, absolutely. It has been an attempt to maintain the memory of these peoples who despite all, continue to exist. Recently, I had the pleasure of meeting a famous Cherokee artist, Jimmie Durham, whom I like a lot and who told me he loved my work, which touched me greatly and reassured me about my work, since I can now think that I have not said too many stupid things about "the Other." It is always delicate to use images that might shock those whom one is referring to.

Virilio: ORLAN illustrates Rimbaud's famous formulation, "Je est un autre."

ORLAN: "Je est UNE autre" [I am a female other]. And furthermore, "I ARE" rather than "I am."

Virilio: One important question at the heart of your work, I believe, concerns the mortal risk of losing your face, of losing faciality. Since the interest of the face, as Deleuze would say, is that it is a language, a life, a narrative. The face is a story, a landscape.

ORLAN: The face is in perpetual motion.

Virilio: Disfigurement—that is losing faciality. It's an infirmity without a name, beyond being blind or deaf. This is a big question in our era. I am surprised to see, for example, how much all young women look alike. There is something in that that frightens me: one might no longer recognize the woman one loves! It's horrendous! This reminds me of what Juliette Drouet said to Victor Hugo: "I am not beautiful, I am worse than that!" That is a wonderful remark.

Behind these questions of the face and disfigurement, there is worse, not worse in the sense of being repulsive, but worse because the person is gone—specifically because the face is gone. [. . .] I have never seen anyone who goes as far as you do toward the forbidden. It's true that it surprises me. ORLAN is at once known and misunderstood, which is worse! It's better to be simply unknown.

ORLAN: Misunderstood in what sense?

Virilio: The richness of what you do and what you have just said does not get transmitted in what is written about you.

ORLAN: That's true for most artists. People stop with

a single work or image, and the depth of the work or certain other periods of the artist's work are ignored. I think my work is very complex, and it's easy to reduce it to tabloid headlines. But distance and analysis are required, and not all spectators are capable of that.

Virilio: Yes, as you said to me when you arrived, "You have reservations, since they've written so many things about me that are false." Indeed, I think that what we've just been discussing goes to the heart of the question, and it's a big question. This is not a celebration!

ORLAN: Nonetheless, I am one of France's most recognized artists, in the street, here, anywhere I go in the world. The public comes up to me and asks me questions about my body, which I've turned into what I wanted, into a site of public debate. The misrecognition you speak of exists above all in relation to my surgery-performances, which indeed frightened people. But there are different moments in my life as an artist. I am a normal artist when I'm not in an operating room. Plastic surgery is not my hobby! I only worked with it between 1990 and 1993.

If you look at my work and the reception of my earlier and my postoperative work, you realize that works from these periods are at the moment very sought-after and selling quite a lot. Several museums, including the Centre Georges Pompidou, the FNAC, and the FRAC, have bought them. These pieces are traveling in the United States, and my new creations are also doing well on the market. What is polemical today are, above all, the surgeries and perhaps also the culturing of cells, just as, at the time, *The Kiss of the Artist* created a big scandal and got me illegally fired from my job, which also deprived me of my studio as well as all the works that were inside it. However, thirty years later that series [*The Kiss of the Artist*] has been bought by several institutions, and so there was a "happy ending."

TRANSLATED BY RHONDA K. GARELICK

NOTE

1. Referring to Paul Virilio, who resides in La Rochelle, France.

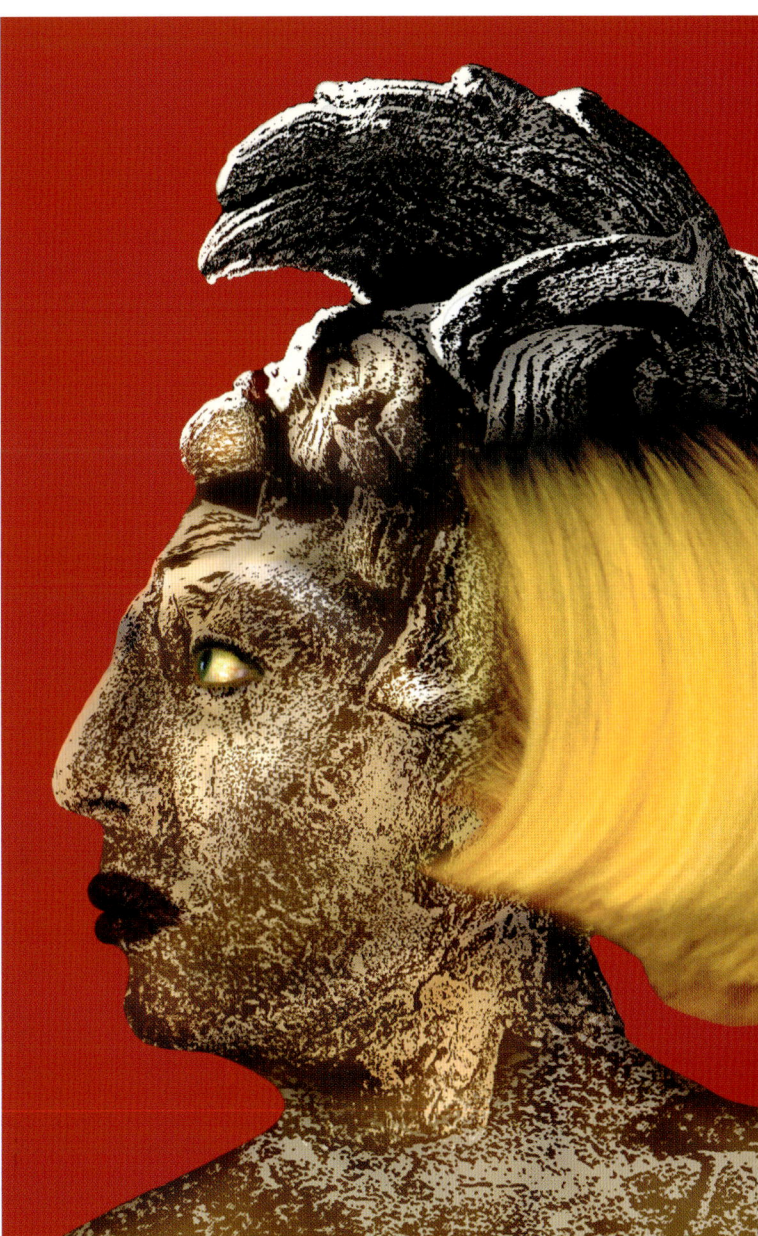

Refiguration Self-Hybridization, Pre-Columbian Series #18, 1998. Cibachrome, 100 cm. x 150 cm. and 60 cm. x 90 cm. Collection of Michel Rein, courtesy of the Michel Rein Gallery, Paris.

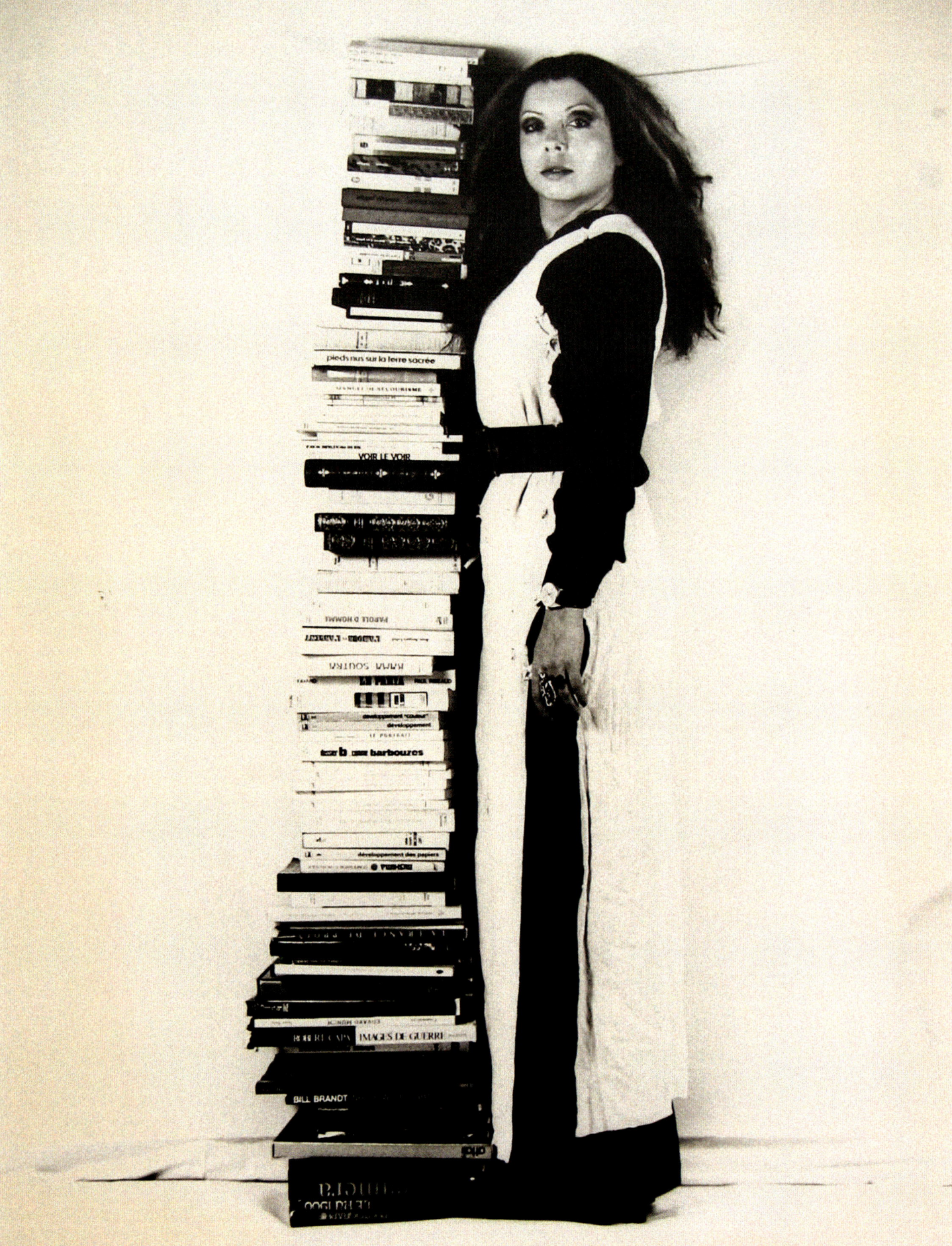

ORLAN, SUBJECT OMITTED

ATTIRE AS EPIDERMIS, EPIDERMIS AS ATTIRE

ISABEL TEJEDA

FASHION, ALONGSIDE TEXTILES and clothing in general, has run through the work of ORLAN since she started her creative career in the 1960s. Perhaps on account of the power and spectacular effect of her performance pieces from the 1990s—I am referring to the surgical operations upon her own body which transformed her appearance, her skin—the reading of her work both in the mass media and in critical writing has focused narrowly on these works, allowing them to eclipse others produced earlier, some of which have remained unknown until recently.[1] Some interpretations of ORLAN's work, furthermore, which are in fact patently incorrect both conceptually and contextually, continue to be repeated, perpetuating misunderstanding of her project.[2]

Performance as the basis of ORLAN's work has led to her body, or more precisely her face, the repository of identity, being its support and material. This practice in her career, however, has disappeared for the first time in the line of work that started with the artist's 2007 retrospective exhibition in the Museum of Saint-Étienne—her hometown—in which she began to collaborate with fashion designers.

Certainly as time goes on I have less desire to be present myself or, at least, not in the same way. I am present with my history and my clothes, but, except in the videos, my face is not. This is something really happy and liberating for me, because after a while you get tired of yourself, there's a wearing down, and although you could perfectly well carry on, the fact of not being there allows me to say things in a different way, to say different things and, consequently, to get beyond my usual frame of reference. I even thought of putting on this exhibition under a pseudonym, with another name, as if I were a new, younger artist who makes work with designers. I also think that the fact that my face is present, that my name is very well known, generates a strong pressure that means that there are things that I cannot do, because I know very well that they are waiting for me in that space and nowhere else, and that, in any case, how peo-

One ORLAN-body-in-books, 1979. Black and white photograph, one of a kind. MesuRage Performance. N.R.A. Gallery, Paris, France.

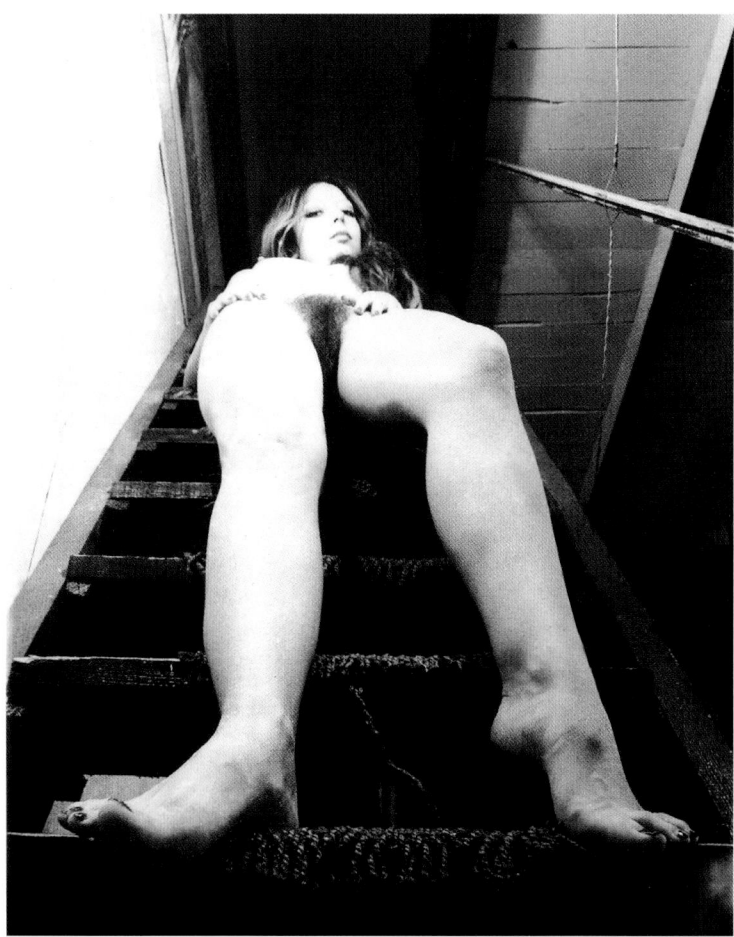

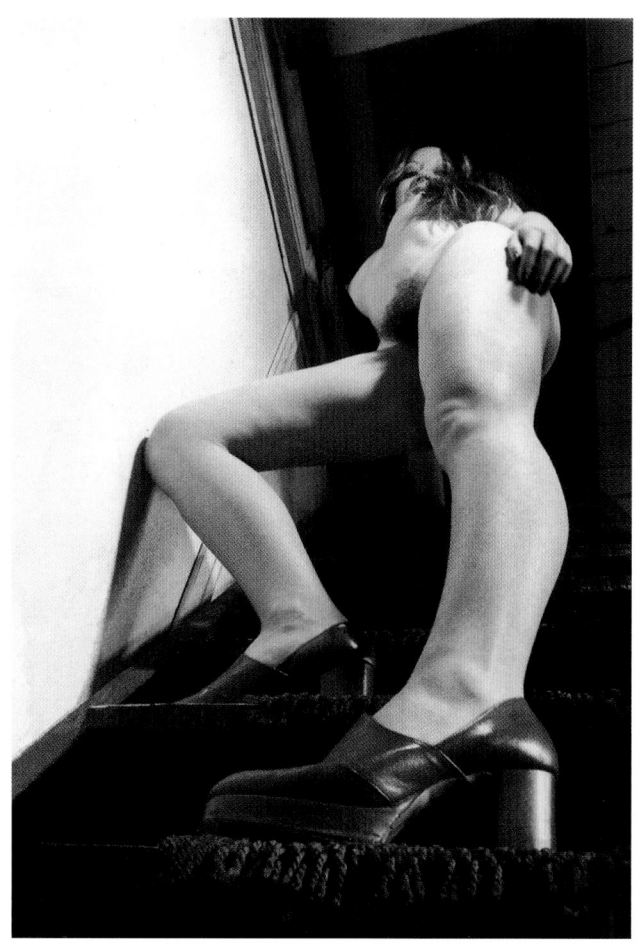

ple look at my work will be fabricated from every-thing I have shown before.[3]

In this sense, what appears to be a new chapter in ORLAN's career becomes a project in which the artist becomes an omitted subject paradoxically passing through a retrospective of her life, as represented by her own clothes. The project presents a trajectory of great conceptual and discursive coherence, in which some of her less celebrated works cast a new light not only on her latest work about recycling, hybridization, and fashion but also upon an under-analyzed concept that has nonetheless long been the backbone of her work: her constant, somewhat conflicted flirtation with clothing. ORLAN has consistently explored how fashion exerts social control over the body and over the construction of arche-types of beauty.[4] She detests this ethics and aesthet-ics of fashion, but at the same time is attracted by its possibilities, its subject matter.

> Before the surgical operations I was quite reti-cent about anything to do with the creativity of makers, designers, decorators, etc. I used to think that I was situated in the Arts with a capital "A," and that the rest were, let's say, minor arts. There

was a moment when looking back at what I had done in the past, I realized that there were things in my work which were in fact related to creativ-ity, to style, to decor: the decor of the operating room and my relationship with clothes, which is, we could say, a fetishistic and ambiguous relation-ship—I love to touch high-heeled shoes, I love shapes, certain clothes that I wear immediately give me new energy, they wash away stress, they make me stronger. I have become aware that it really is as if I had been working without knowing it on something related to style, decor, or the cre-ation of objects. When I questioned myself a bit more about these disciplines, I said to myself that they were like my SymbioticA Harlequin Coat, in which I tried to make cells of different origins and species cohabit: we might say that design, style, decoration, etc., would be different disciplines, but they would form part of a porous whole connected with contemporary art.[5]

I intend to analyze this latest work made by ORLAN and put it in context, despite its obvious formal dif-ferences, as another piece in the kaleidoscopic uni-verse of this artist.

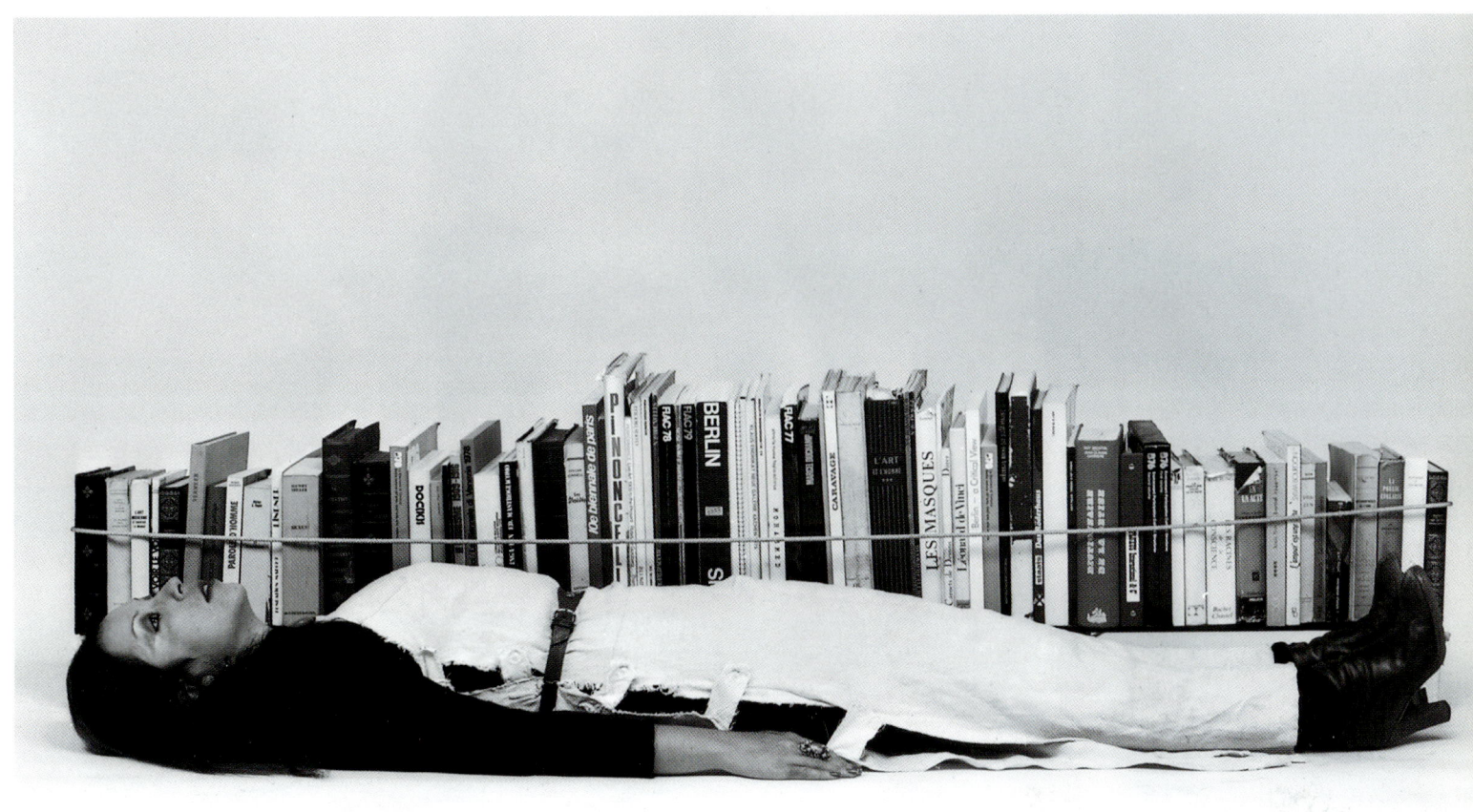

GOING DOWNSTAIRS . . . MEASURING THE WORLD GOING UP IN SOME SHOES

Beginning with her first performances and photographs in the 1960s, clothes have not been just an accessory to ORLAN's complex project of gutting the ego, exploring otherness, and interrogating the ownership of the body and the construction of feminine identity. Already in works like *Nu descendant l'escalier avec talons compensés* [Nude descending staircase in wedge heels] of 1967, the insolent, naked image of the artist photographed from below, offering a monstrously anamorphic reading of her body, was grounded on giant platform-heeled shoes, a fetishistic addition to the wardrobe representing Western feminine sexuality.[6] In *Un ORLAN-corps-de-livres* [ORLAN body-of-books], which took place on November 8, 1979 (Galerie N.R.A., Paris), the boots worn by ORLAN became part of her body, creating a fascinating tension between nature and what is accessory to it. In this performance, ORLAN invited the viewers, many of them artists, to bring with them to the gallery, a book that had played a crucial role in their own lives or creative practices. In this way, a line of books laid out on the floor was created, building a shelf whose length measured the

same distance as that between ORLAN's head and the base of the heel of her boots. ORLAN pledged to stay in the gallery night and day until she finished reading this collective library. Although there have been numerous analyses of this work, I would like to focus attention on her clothes and on her accessories as limbs or appendages to her body that fall into the same category as an arm or the head, and how these items have a substantial role in the interpretation of ORLAN's early works. The shoe was not only part of ORLAN's body as recipient of knowledge, an illustration traditionally reserved for men, but also, by extension, of her construction as a contemporary artist who measures the world with her body, plus its added parts. Set against "man as measure of the world" in the Renaissance tradition represented by Leonardo da Vinci in universal form—a naked man of pure nature rooted in humanist values—ORLAN confronted us with the physicality and irreducible otherness of her own femininity.

Nude descending the staircase, Low-angle shot with head, 1967. Black-and-white photograph, one of a kind.

Nude descending the staircase in wedge heels, 1967. Black-and-white photograph, one of a kind.

One ORLAN-body-of-books, 1979. Black-and-white photograph. N.R.A. Gallery, Paris.

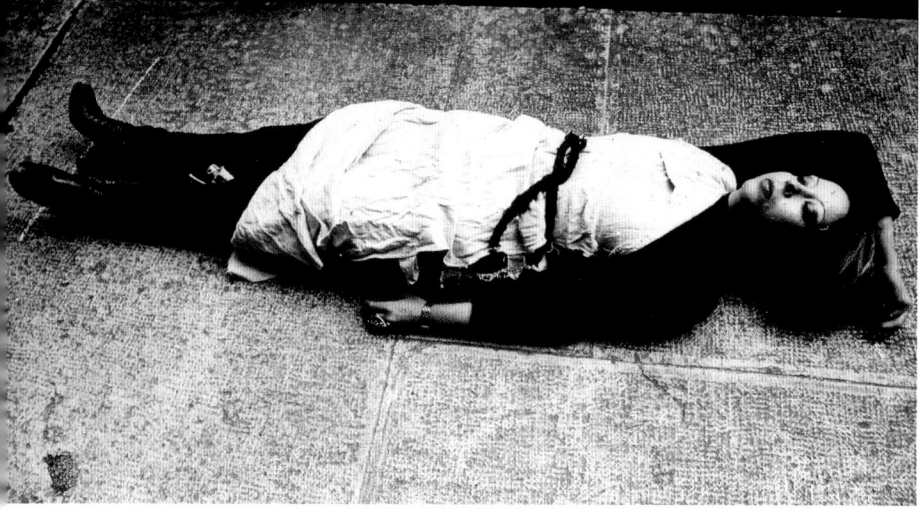

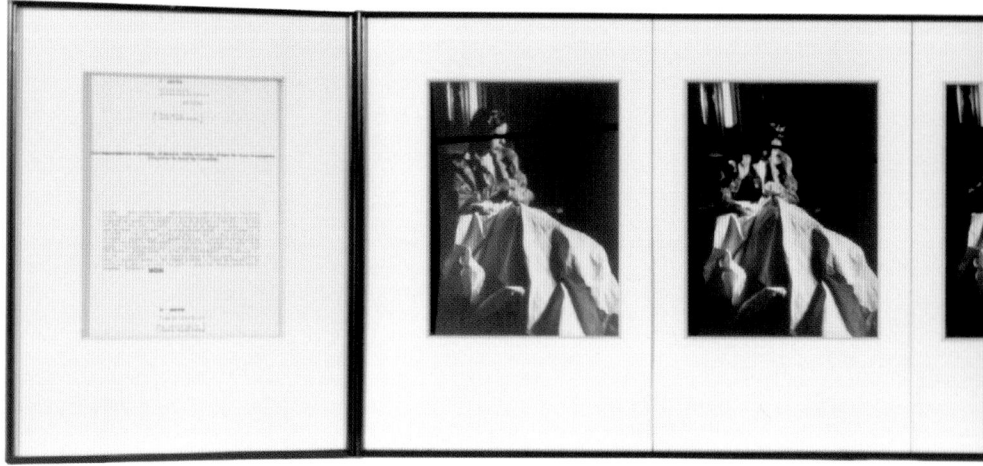

Her different hair, her made-up face, her clothing, and the height that high-heeled shoes confer on her refer to specific social and cultural circumstances. In this way, the accessories, the clothes, the socially accepted and appropriate femininity were part of the identity she presented of the body as a measure of the world.

This *MesuRage* [MeasureRage] of *Un ORLAN-corps-de-livres* was part of a project that was started in 1978 and completed in 1983, in which ORLAN —her body and her clothes—converted herself into a new unit of measurement of distinct urban spaces: an *ORLAN* as measure of everything. The clothes that the artist put on for those occasions were not chosen lightly, and it was not that ORLAN did not dress up as a performer but that her clothes were laden with moral significance and with memory, which are the other aspects that I would like to underline in her work.[7] Her dress was roughly made: there were tunics without hems, sewn without the need for any pattern, with straps that clumsily tied the sides together leaving a hole big enough to put her head through—a costume made with the rudimentary sewing skills of a child dressing up her dolls.[8] Nothing then of the glamorous design with

which, a decade later, she will dress up her operating theatre-stage and even her surgeon-actors. But the quoted reflection about memory to which I have referred is not found in the type of clothing made to simulate a pilgrim's tunic—Catholic iconography and rites of inspiration run through a large part of ORLAN's work—it is evident in the origin of the material with which they were made: sheets from the artist's trousseau.

The feminist maxim of those times, "the personal is political," wove together ORLAN's individual memory with the collective imagination of women—for many, summed up in that construct that they call "woman"—which was represented in this work by a text without writing (text means textile, as Barthes has reminded us): the blank page of ORLAN's trousseau sheets that lost their immaculate meaning with the bloodstain, the only sign in this unknown cartography, announcing a loss of virginity.[9] Preparing their trousseau was the fundamental work occupying the time of marriageable women— who resembled so many patient Penelopes—work which united them with their mothers in a bond of whispered confidences that, together with the sheets, were transmitted from generation to generation,

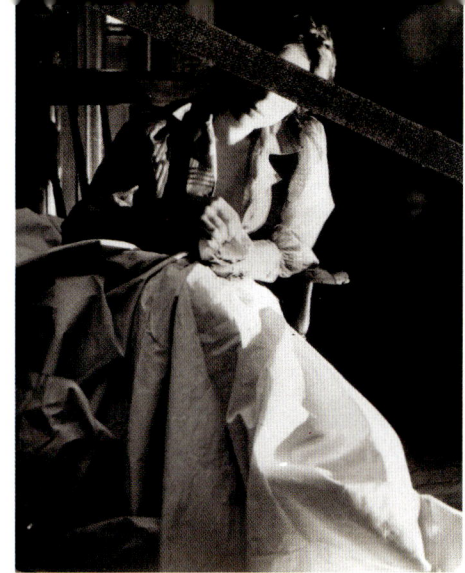

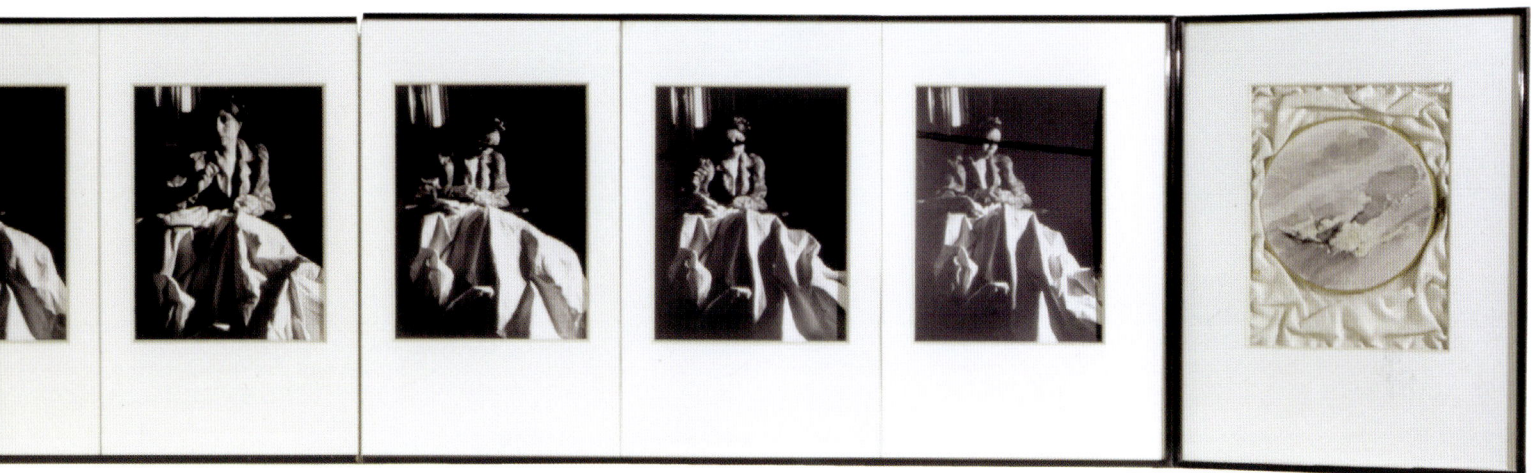

embroidered on sheets, tablecloths, and mats. Let us recall that the first tablecloths that girls embroidered were called symbolically in Spanish "you and I" (tu y yo)—wasting the time of teenagers who waited like sleeping beauties for the kiss of their savior-princes, who waited for the only time of imagined importance to them: the time that would be used up by their marriage.

ORLAN used her trousseau sheets for several performances and pieces from 1968 onward and which would carry on—sometimes materially, at other times merely referentially—in the important body of her work titled *The Triumph of the Baroque* (1974–1985/90). In the case of ORLAN it granted a critical and alternative use to this blank page with a single sign. In the work called *Plaisirs brodés. Étude documentaire no 1. Couture-Clair/Obscuro [Embroidered pleasures. Documentary study no. 1. Chiaroscuro couture]* of 1968, she imprinted the trousseau sheets time and again with marks that sullied the unpolluted fabric artistically and sexually. The marks were the semen stains left by her lovers, which were later outlined by embroidery that traced roughly and imperfectly around their silhouettes. Here ORLAN, as a single woman artist, affirmed her freedom to enjoy

feminine pleasure and sexual experience when she chose to—a freedom often forbidden to women. In opposition to the expected *petit point* embroidery of a married couple's initials on pillowcases and sheets, ORLAN shamelessly exhibited her choice to be both unmarried and sexually free—which were both fundamental rights claimed by the feminism of the 1960s and 1980s, along with the freedom to understand motherhood as a personal choice instead of an obligation.

In support of this idea ORLAN gave a performance in which she dressed herself up as a good girl from a bourgeois family: she wore a long suit with leg-of-mutton sleeves and wore her hair in long braids, attire in which the only discordant note was the extended low neckline which allowed a partial glimpse of her breasts. In this piece, which is preserved through a large series of photographs accom-

MesuRage of Institutions, 1979. Black-and-white photograph. Musée Saint-Pierre, Lyon, France.

Embroidered Pleasures. Documentary study no. 1, 1968, with detail. Seven black-and-white photographs, one of a kind, 260 cm. x 190 cm. National Archives of Contemporary Art, Paris.

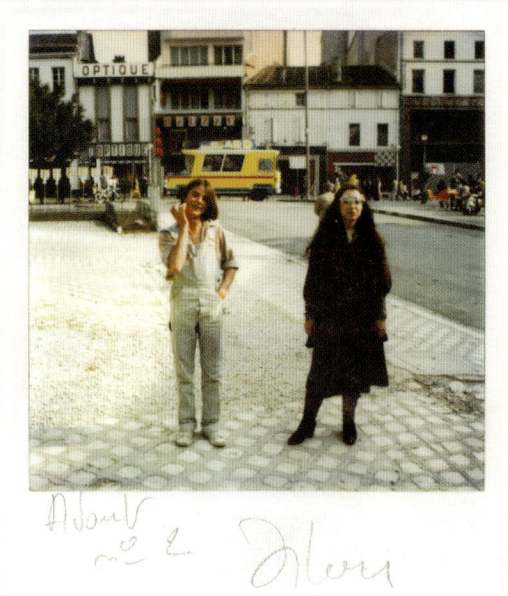

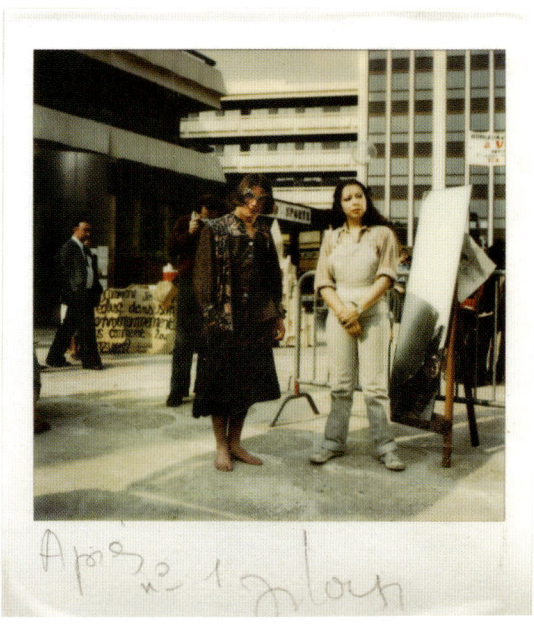

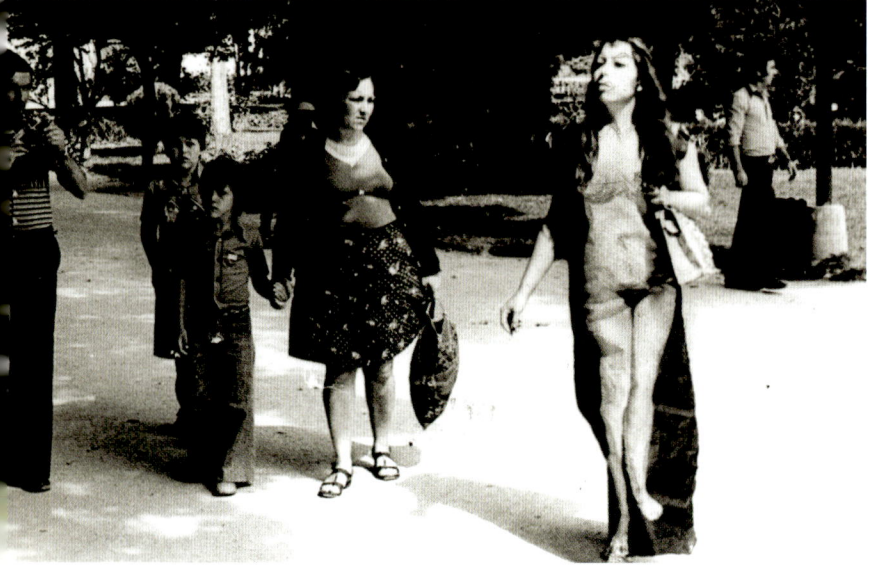

Dressed in Her Own Nudity,
1976–1977. Black-and-white
photograph, edition of seven
plus one. 10 cm. x 18 cm.
Courtesy of the artist.

Performance, Angoulême,
France, 1978. Polaroid
photographs for
documentation.

panied by a fragment of sheet on a stretcher frame and by a manifesto,[10] ORLAN embroidered the design in semen that her lovers had previously "painted."[11] The carnivalesque masquerade, fancy dress, and humor that accompanied these works of ORLAN were provocative declarations that women are not born but constructed, declarations that demonstrated her individual will, as had already been expressed by Simone de Beauvoir in *The Second Sex*.

While making a claim to the formal and conceptual possibilities of the languages traditionally considered as feminine and craft-based, as an alternative to those raised on a platform considered patriarchal—just as Barbara Kruger did in *Pattern and Decoration* or as Ghada Amer did—ORLAN used embroidery or sewing without skill to emphasize the identification between the silent, neat task of embroidery and the passive role of women in the private sphere of the family and home. Embroidery was therefore used parodically.

ORLAN has rejected on numerous occasions the links that have been made between her work and Body Art.[12] I consider that the connections which can be traced in her work are directed at the Duchampian sense of humor that passed through the Fluxus movement, relationships at first fortuitous and fruits of the libertarian cultural context of the 1960s.[13]

I have always tried to work with humor, with distancing, with sensuality, with, let's say, a certain optimism about life, about human beings. My work is imbued with the desire for communication, for rapprochement, for pleasure. Even in the surgical operations, everything I did in the

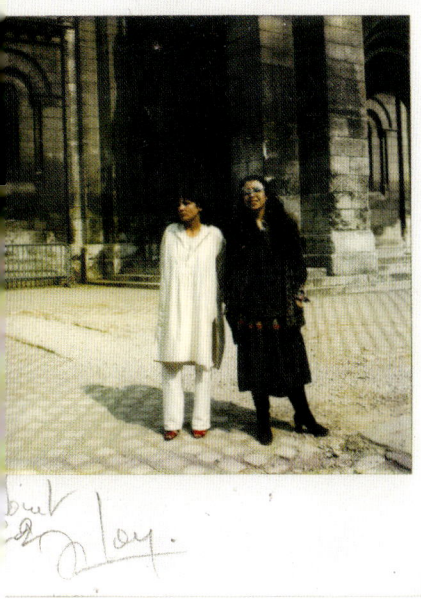 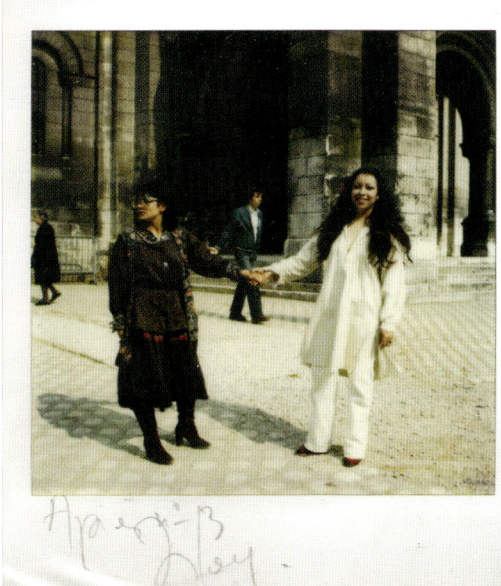 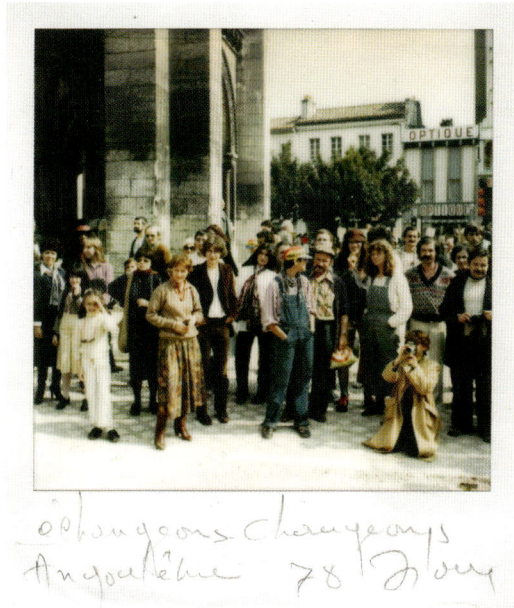

operating theatre was directed toward life, toward humor, there was nothing morbid about it, and the same with the shapes of the work. The very first thing that I wanted to get away from on getting into the operating theatre was aesthetic heaviness, always the same, which is a bit scary and so professional. That's why I endeavored to give the place some life, happiness, color, elements in creating performances, texts, etc., that contribute something and instill them with energy, life, pleasure, play, etc.—the opposite of what happens there usually.[14]

Robert Watts and George Maciunas, both of Fluxus, also made use of parody and play in their work, often employing clothing as vehicles of liberation via the construction of identity. Maciunas's work, *Venus de Milo apron* (ca. 1970), a cook's apron silkscreened with the torso of a Greco-Roman female sculpture, perversely updated trompe l'oeil and called into question the closed categories of masculine and feminine.[15] This work, which can be found in the Fluxus publications and versions of which can still be purchased in museum shops, clearly resembles ORLAN's performance, *S'habiller de sa propre nudité* [Dressed in her own nudity] (1976–77), in which she silkscreened a photograph of her own naked body onto a tunic sewn of her trousseau sheets. Dressed in this costume, ORLAN walked through the streets, creating the illusion that she was provocatively unclothed. This dressing and undressing, dressing up in her own nakedness or undressing through the baroque folds generated by the trousseau sheets, this revealing and hiding

through clothes, is a continual theme in the French artist's work.

We can see more clearly ORLAN's proximity to Fluxus and her strong divergence from Body Art by studying representative works about gender identity from each movement. First, I would like to refer to Maciunas's playful performance *Black & White* (1978), which made use of the costumes of his own wedding in order to question the notion of unique, untransferable identity. In this piece, the Fluxus artist photographed himself next to his wife, first in the wedding outfits that were socially assigned to both of them by their gender, and then having exchanged clothes, thus putting into question those same roles.[16] The second performance I will refer to is Marina Abramovic's exchange of identities with a prostitute from Amsterdam's red-light district in her *Marina Abramovic: 4 hour Amsterdam: Red Light District/ De Apple Gallery* (1975), in which she occupied the prostitute's display window for four hours while the prostitute opened Abramovic's exhibition.

Unlike other action artists who inflict harm upon their own bodies or those who relinquish their will to others, as in the Abramovic performance, ORLAN has never given any performance in which she might have lost control, caused collateral damage to her person, or which might have contained excessive pain or drama. In fact, she aligns herself more with post-Dadaist pretence—in the operations, sedated and without pain, ORLAN smiled at the camera, and she dressed all the participants in the operation glamorously, colorfully, while reading aloud from philosophical and literary texts.

With this in mind I would like to refer to a perfor-

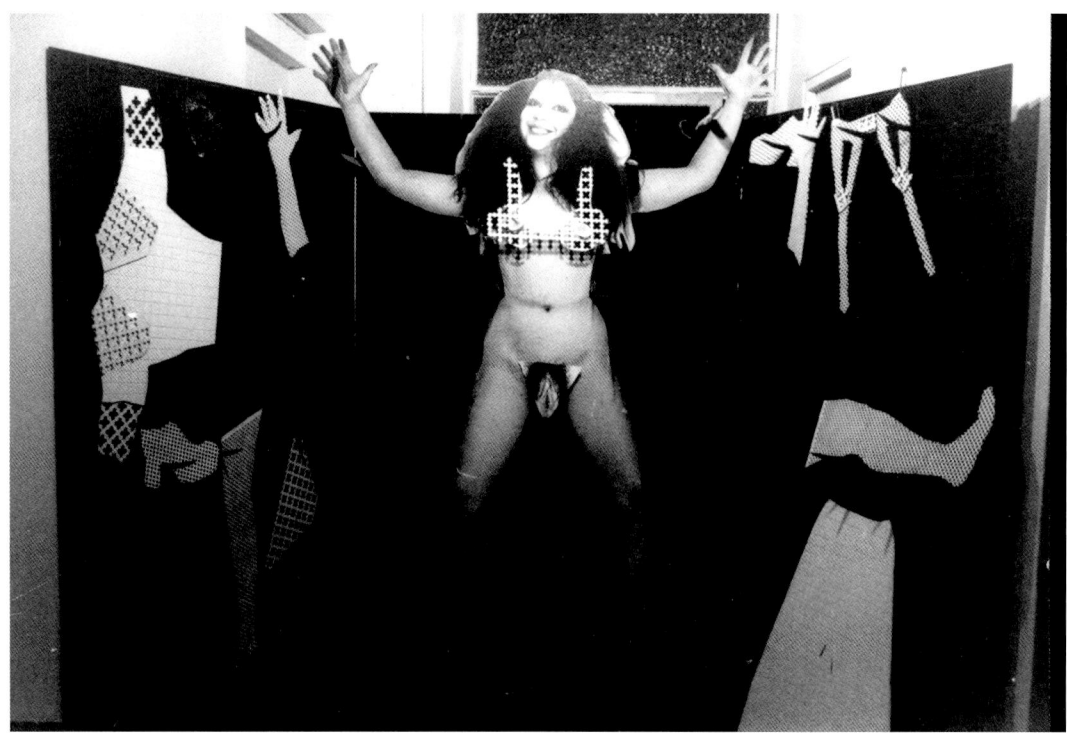

mance that, surprisingly, still remains unknown: a fresh, playful happening which took place in Angoulême in 1978 as part of a festival. In this performance, ORLAN worked with the idea of the transvestite and with the negation of a pure and unique identity, making plain that our social and gender identity is branded by the clothes we wear and that reconstructing our identity is possible if the container of the content is changed. The artist exchanged clothes inside a van with various passersby—people who voluntarily decided to participate in the game—and then they walked casually down the street in their borrowed clothes. This performance has been preserved thanks to some improvised documentary Polaroids showing the wearer of the clothes and ORLAN together before and after the garment exchange.[17] Both the sexuality inherent in the form of fancy dress and the conventions that our clothes confer emphasize fashion's role in the social construction of gender, permitting not only a game of multiple sexual identities but also a reconsideration of other concepts such as social class, age, or profession. Take, for example, the case of the young man whose own look of beret, smock, case, and portable easel was based on the archetypal model of the classic French "Montmartre" painter. When ORLAN and the young man exchanged their

outfits, it not only produced a situation of sexual ambiguity approaching the carnivalesque, it also required ORLAN, for the first time in her life, to don the official costume of "the artist," a concept she has dealt with in her interviews.[18]

In *Panoply or the Possessions of a Marriageable Girl* (1972–73), a title which makes literal reference to war armor (from the Greek "panoplia," meaning "arms" or "weapons"), ORLAN constructed a large pink mannequin mounted on wood, representing her own life-sized naked image, with the detail that her pubic hair was made with green plastic parsley.[19] The figure was hanging in midair, and the public could dress and undress it as if it were a cut-out doll, although the clothes were hung from a type of meat hook. Again, the game involved the participation of the public in a radically different way from the dramatic *Cut Piece* of the Japanese Fluxus artist Yoko Ono or the performance *Rhythm O* in the Studio Mona Gallery in Naples, which took Marina Abramovic's abdication of will to its ultimate extreme. The paradoxically feminine cuirasses and shields—tights, bra, suspenders, skirt, and so forth—armor-plated the representation of the artist but also could be used by the visitors, who could put the pieces on over their own bodies in an exchange of attributes—as ORLAN herself did in a performance cross-dressing as her-

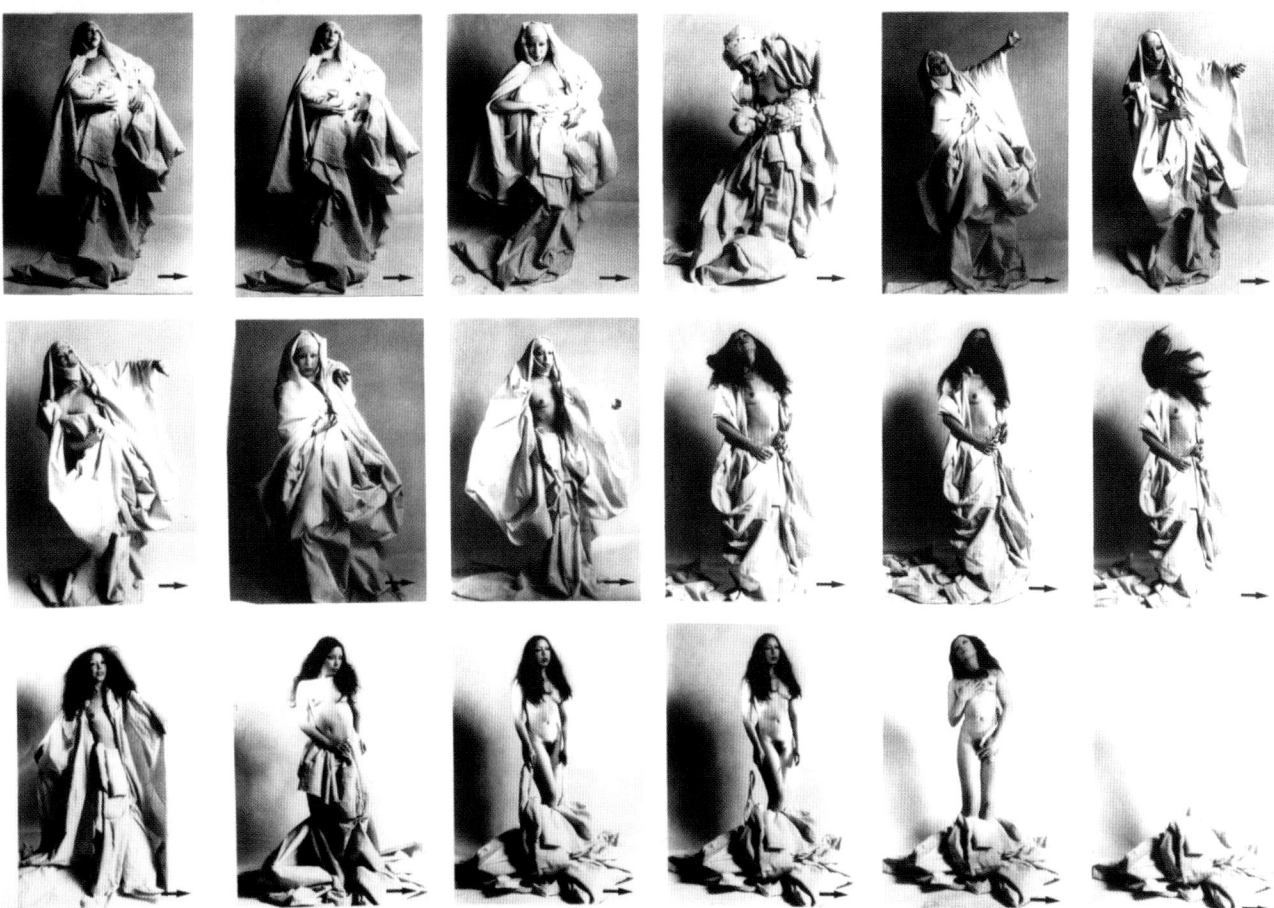

self.[20] This work is informed by the duality between reality and representation, between body and attributes, between the fictitious linked to play and the body as something physical and psychological existing underneath our clothes and skin.

Memory has always been critically significant in ORLAN's work. Present but barely emphasized, it has been discussed as a vehicle for certain constraining social assumptions about gender, social class, race, sexual choice, and so forth. Most striking is that, unlike *The Dead Class* by Tadeusz Kantor or certain works by Christian Boltanski, who both relate memory to death, ORLAN's work treats memory with a carnivalesque and Rabelaisian sense of humor. We can see her in her costume as a demure little girl embroidering her trousseau with the stains of her lovers; in this way she opens a new chapter in the silent history of women transmitted through the bed because, as ORLAN shows in a work like *Baiser de l'Artiste* [Kiss of the artist], there were only two possible roles that women could traditionally adopt: the positive—virgin and mother—and the negative—prostitute. She shakes up this Manichaeism by assuming both roles in the work noted above and also in *Strip-tease occasionel à l'aide des draps du trousseau* [Incidental striptease with the help of trousseau sheets] (1974–76) where she trans-

forms from a draped baroque virgin, inspired by Bernini's *Saint Teresa* with her ecstasy in worldly excess, to Botticelli's *Venus*, whose nudity has an iconic, art-historical dimension that renders its cultural nature perfectly clear. Again, her trousseau sheets serve to rewrite a different text, in this case that of an art history whose representations of the female body reflect assumptions that will again be made plain in *A poil/ sans poil* [Naked/hairless] (1978).[21] I refer to *Le Drapé le Baroque* [The draped the baroque], a series of performances and photographs of ORLAN dressing canvases with large folds that emphasize multiplicity in unity, followed by sculptures of folds now without bodies. These sculptures on some occasions were made with crude shears (*Robe sans corps. Sculpture de pli* [Dress without body. Sculpture of folds], 1983), while others, such as the ones she made for her first retrospective in the Frac des Pays de la Loire titled

Trap, pot, chain, and Panoply of the bride stripped bare, 1977. Life-sized, pink mannequin of ORLAN, wood, green plastic. Galerie NRA, Paris.

Incidental Striptease with Trousseau Sheets, 1974 (assembled into a single work in 1975). Eighteen black-and-white photographs on Canson, 44 cm. x 60 cm. Photographs by Jean-Paul Vacher, edition of seven. National Archives of Contemporary Art, Paris.

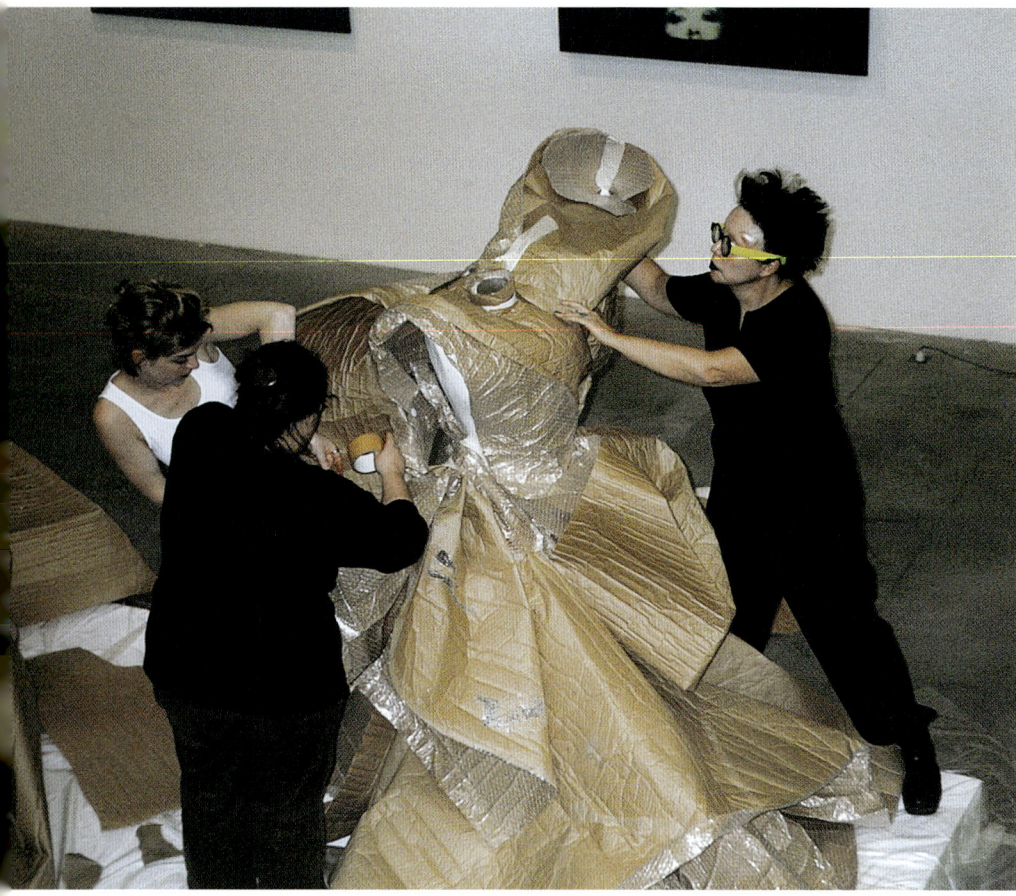

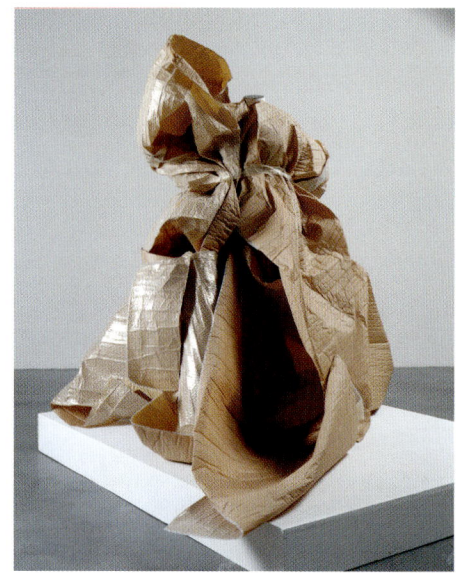

Sculpture Construction of Folds. Documentary study no. 1, no. 2, 2002. Sculpture in bubble wrap. FRAC, Pays de la Loire, France.

Sculpture of Folds. Documentary study no. 1, no. 2, 2002. Sculpture in bubble wrap. FRAC, Pays de la Loire, France.

Robe hibridée, 2008. Hybridized dress from ORLAN's wardrobe. ORLAN in collaboration with Agatha Ruiz de la Prada.

Eléments favoris [Favorite elements] and organized by Jean François Taddei, were made with bubble wrap (*Sculpture de plis-Étude documentaire no. 1, no. 2* [Sculpture of folds documentary study], 2002).

The fold doesn't hide the body, it is the material, whether sewn or not, which totally deforms the body. Often in these pieces we don't know any more where the body is and we find it again in the face, and again we find it eventually if there is a breast or hands, but the rest is totally transformed. All my dresses, the ones that I made all through my life and also those of my trousseau sheets, have disappeared: they were ephemeral sculptures. Jean François Taddei proposed that I remake those sculptures and told me that the Frac was committed to finding a solution to conserve them forever.

I made them like you make patterns. All my works of the baroque period are called documentary studies because they are exercises in drapery, form, volume. I made them neither with material, nor with the sheets from my trousseau, of which hardly any were left, but with what I had in the studio, with the packaging of the works which became the wrapping for a body that doesn't exist,

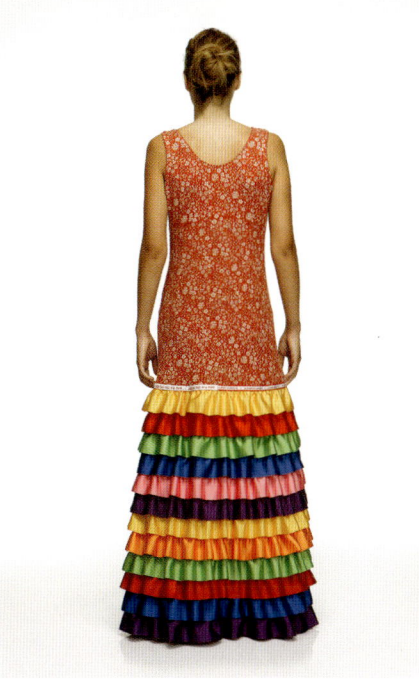 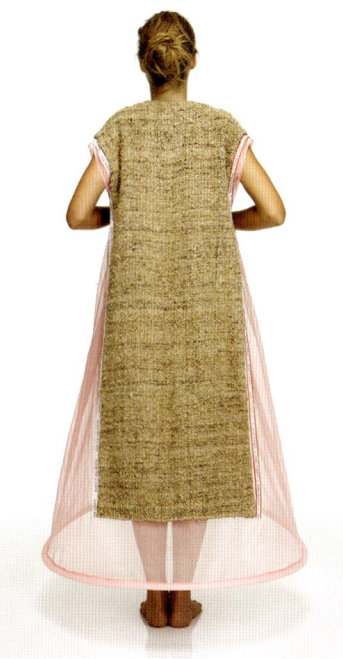 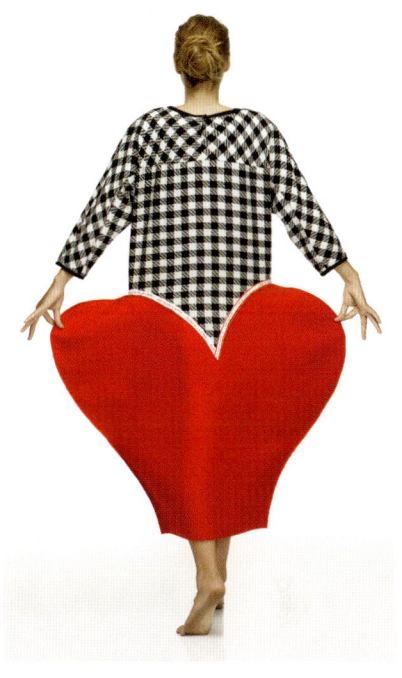

that is empty. It was very pleasurable to work with that paper, with plastic bubble wrap and Kraft paper, because the plastic absorbs the light and when well lit it shines brilliantly. Unfortunately the two dresses are in the Frac des Pays de la Loire and they haven't found a technique for conserving them. I am tired of yet again producing ephemeral things that just disappear.[22]

HYBRIDIZATION AND RECYCLING

As Hélène Cixous has observed, the feminine embodies the capacity to welcome the Other. In ORLAN's latest works, as in her Self-Hybridizations and the morphings and in her Angoulême performance of 1978, she does not speak exclusively of feminine identity and its construct. Although the place of enunciation is ORLAN's clothes, it is open to the concept of multiculturalism, which the artist started with her Self-Hybridizations and which had a biotechnological component in the work she made with Symbiot-icA in Australia.[23] Other antecedents of this direction in ORLAN's work include her collaborations with the French designer Maroussia Rebecq at the Museum of Saint-Étienne, with the Spanish couturiere Agatha Ruiz de la Prada, and also with the Spanish fashion

designer davidelfin—for an exhibition in the Espacio AV, Murcia, Spain—works which I shall now briefly analyze.

Coinciding with Le Récit, her retrospective in 2007 in the Museum of Saint-Étienne, the artist decided to hybridize her wardrobe, which she had accumulated from her adolescence up to the present. To do so, she collaborated with the designer Maroussia Rebecq. The clothes with various patterns and textures were constructed as hypostasis of the skin and within them hid snippets of social, cultural, and anatomical identity from various moments in the artist's life. It was the first time that ORLAN had made her private wardrobe public and converted it into a piece of art.

It is part of the game, it really amuses me going back over my images where you can see me with clothes that are just the ones that I have hybridized, that I have recycled and so on. Those clothes are something very intimate that have been part of me, totally. When I try them on, it feels quite strange now to be bringing back a whole epoch, some gestures, or a different essence and way of being, because when I make an inventory of all the clothes, I often try them on again.[24]

Her work then is defined by recycling, by hybridization, and the suture, clothes being her raw material. Her own body, her successive bodies as she likes to call them, which are the potential material in all her performances and previous pieces, become the fancy dress which the artist gets rid of again and again, representing the feminine as a masquerade. This is a metamorphosis of both physicality and identity, which confirms her particular revolution against consumerist society and which reminds us, constantly, that the norm is always illusory.

In this exhibition, ORLAN reinterprets the concept of the retrospective by creating a work which, by means of unwritten memory, traverses her whole creative life beginning with adolescence—she made her first works at the age of seventeen—up through the birthday that coincided with the show: her sixtieth.[25]

In the Saint-Étienne Modern Art Museum I wanted to make a new work for this exhibition and for my sixtieth birthday. Straightaway I thought of my wardrobe as something that carried my skin, my history, and at the same time just history, because the history of fashion is inscribed in clothes anyway, even those you might call normal, classical, and not necessarily by great designers. This is a sign of our times: flared trousers, miniskirts, shoulder pads, . . . so I said to myself this is really the moment to use this wardrobe for art and for it to become art, but that at the same time, it will integrate the fact that they were pieces that came from other people, from brand-name designers that are going to encounter each other, and that then they will be manipulated again with a reading that is of our time. So it will integrate art, style, decoration, and production.[26]

On the day of the opening in Saint-Étienne, ORLAN remained present in the gallery for a performance in which she read the preface to the French philosopher Michel Serres's book *Le Tiers-Instruit* [*The Troubadour of Knowledge*],[27] a short text devoted to secularism (or *laïcité*). A reading of this text also accompanied her last operation, which took place at SymbioticA in which skin cells were extracted from her and fused in a bioreactor with the cells of the aborted fetus of a black woman and also of a marsupial.[28] In Saint-Étienne, before the reading of the text, ORLAN appeared hidden under a black blanket/shroud which splendidly lay across the rows of the expectant public and which the artist pierced with a pair of scissors letting her eyes, nose, and head be shown little by little until the standardized tunic was rent, revealing ORLAN's brightly colored street clothes and her bicolored hair—half

white and half black. A grotesque catwalk of absurd models, dressed in outfits designed by Rebecq and derived from ORLAN's wardrobe and coiffed with carnival wigs and commedia dell'arte hats, stretched the tightrope between humor and seriousness in an artistic act which had fashion as one of its objectives.

The exhibition that, afterward, took place in the actual museum included some display devices for the clothes which connected these pieces to the display of the measuring outfits from the 1970s. Since completing the *MesuRages*, ORLAN exhibited each side of the tunic between two pieces of glass or Perspex as if they were in a laboratory slide or, better, in a giant reliquary.[29] Similar devices, only with a diamond-shaped support beneath them painted in several colors, were used in the Saint-Étienne project to conserve and display the dresses, one of which (made by Maroussia Rebecq with various fabrics printed with a harlequin pattern) presided over the center of the Espacio AV in Murcia, Spain.

After various measurements, the dresses were very worn out from the sun, from washing, etc. I showed those dresses, which are made in two pieces and have in fact a face and a back tied together by straps so that they can easily fit any body, in the exhibitions next to the dirty water from washing them, also in little labeled flasks sealed with wax. I encapsulated them in Perspex, which is really the same type of display that I used with Maroussia Rebecq.[30]

ORLAN's collaborative exhibition with Agatha Ruiz de la Prada, which took place at the Spanish designer's Paris studio, followed different work processes. Here, ORLAN's wardrobe was not used exclusively; only the concept of hybridization linked the artist's clothes with Ruiz de la Prada's designs. The suture, an aspect of great importance in this series of works and which had been underlined by Rebecq in Saint-Étienne with a shrill strip of phosphorescent yellow, in this case adopted a different formula: a label with the name of the designer and the brand "Le Baiser de l'Artiste" [The kiss of the artist]. The costumes were displayed as they would typically be in boutique windows, thus honoring the context in which this project was produced. They appeared hung on frames made from coat hangers that simulated bodies.[31]

For the next installation, which took place in Spain, ORLAN collaborated with davidelfin, a Spanish designer very close to contemporary art in his frequent use of references to creators such as Louise Bourgeois or Joseph Beuys.[32] For this recycling and hybridization with the artist's wardrobe, the designer chose the hook and eye as an ele-

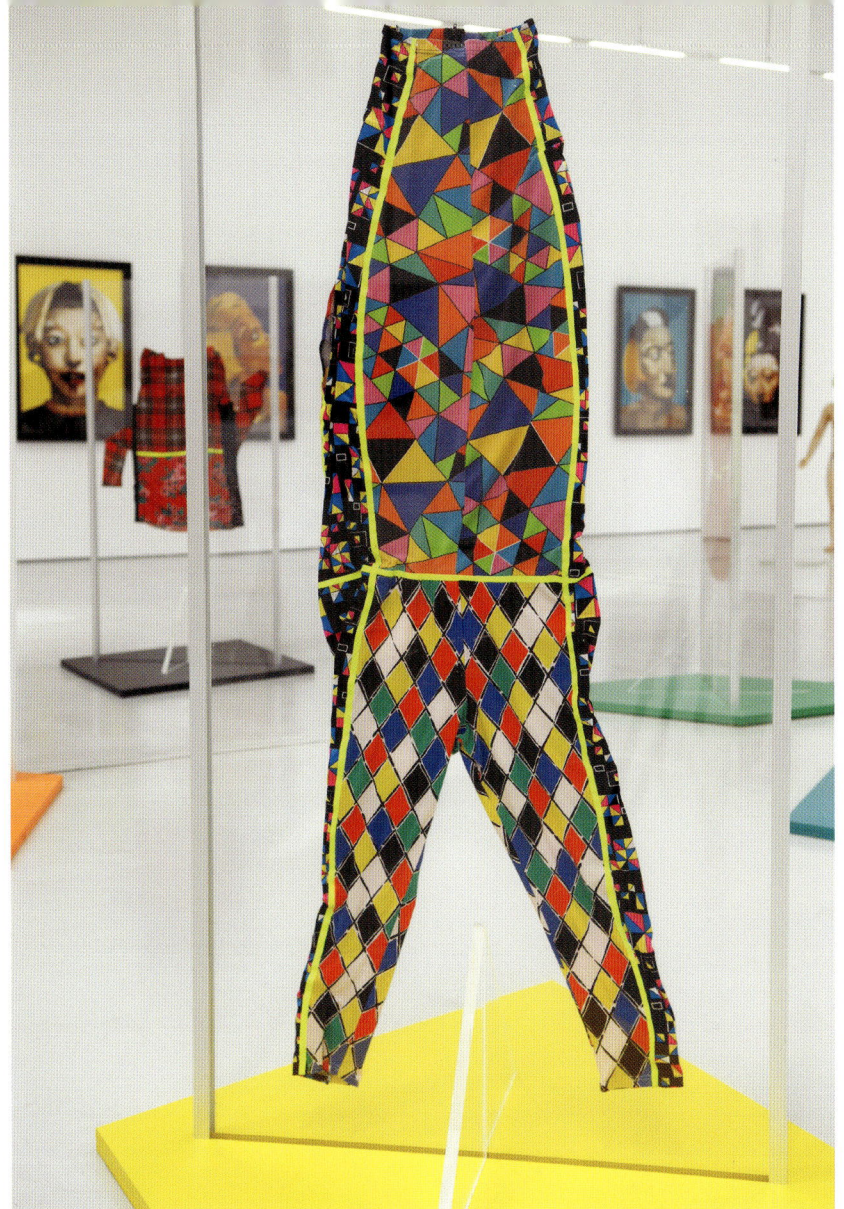

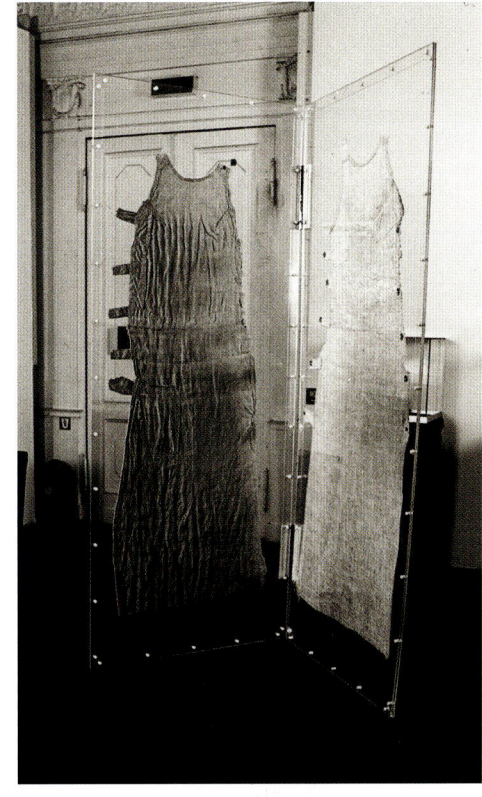

ment of suture, a piece of dressmaking which allows an aperture to be opened and closed at will. Thus, the aperture becomes a metaphorical encounter between different entities always susceptible to mutations, a product of endless hybridization, reversible in time.

ORLAN's clothing, hybridized by davidelfin, appeared as traces of bodies dressing or upholstering transparent Louis Ghost chairs by Philippe Starck. When the spectator sits down on the chairs, the clothes then serve as cushions, providing a sensation of comfort that is not usual in dressing up in somebody else's clothes, suggesting the concept of "the other in itself" and borrowing from the metaphor of the Harlequin as a figure of multiculturalism and secularism, as proposed by Michel Serres in his preface to *Le Tiers-Instruit*.

Michel Serres's text is, for me, like a manifesto. Really, I was not looking to actually illustrate it, but this text is so integrated with what I feel, and with what I think about our times that it really

The Harlequin Coat, 2007, in collaboration with Maroussia Rebecq (Andrea Crews), Musée d'Art Moderne of Saint-Étienne, France. Hybrid piece of cloth from ORLAN's wardrobe framed in plexiglass.

Mesu-Rage Dress, in the Method of the Artist Exhibition, 2004. Fabric between methacrylate sheets. Curator Régis Durand. National Center for Photography, Paris.

functions very well with everything I have done. This text is very interesting because it is a philosophical tale with a message that now is not only in the text but has infiltrated everything that is on show in the exhibition, everything that's been produced. Serres plays a principal role in this project. Harlequin plays a principal role.[33]

Around the perimeter of the gallery ran a photographic frieze depicting a model—seen only from the back, hence with no visible identity—dressed in the clothes used in this exhibition, both in their original state and as later hybridized. These images on the frieze were displayed horizontally to avoid the rhetoric of standardized fashion photography and its concept of beauty. ORLAN continues, then, in this new series of projects with the line followed by the Self-Hybridizations, which was the first exercise in accepting the "other in itself." Her work implies a protest against the pressures of "correct" physical archetypes, a reflection on the mutant body, and the cultural construction of identity in an unusual line of feminist critique that questions the pressure of social and cultural conventions on women's bodies. ORLAN continues to question traditional concepts of beauty and identity in a work begun in the mid-1960s, when the artist began interrogating the "status" of the feminine body in art history and in society.

ORLAN adds an interesting twist in this new project, since she has foregrounded one part of her biography that previously had remained intimate in the private sphere: her everyday clothes. However, her face and her body, which the French artist has typically converted into a public space, are now for the first time in decades kept hidden. Public and private meet again in her biography, they get mixed and interchanged. As she herself puts it, it is not the first time she has worked with memory—the images from art history that she has made use of are inscribed in all of us like a collective memory—yet it is true that once again ORLAN is returning to the intimate, which the trousseau sheets represented in her early works, and which on this occasion can be seen as a reversing or folding of time.

If in fashion the old comes back in the form of "retro" or "vintage," ORLAN rejects every type of evocation so as to construct the suture in a concrete biographical moment. In the materiality of the past, in the remains inscribed on the clothes, the line of suture constructs a "now." As ORLAN has observed, the suture is not a soldering but the visibility of two spaces and two time periods coming together, which is visibly underlined in each one of the projects that, up to now, she has mounted using her wardrobe. On the other hand, this visibility in the line of the suture lends a public character to a craft—sewing—which was private when encountered within the sphere of the traditionally feminine. It's not about manipulating the gaze—which stresses her idea of the secularism in which a body is not made in the image and likeness of a supreme entity—but about speaking of a changing body.

TRANSLATION BY TREVOR BURGESS
AND RHONDA K. GARELICK

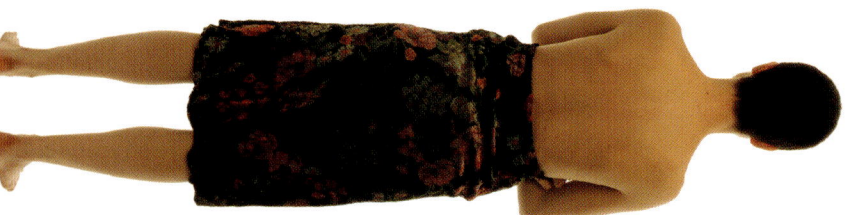

NOTES

1. Some of the pieces from the 1970s that I will analyze here, such as *Panoplie* (1972–1973) or the performance that took place in Angoulême in 1978, have not been seen since then and have remained in ORLAN's own archive. The artist generously gave me access to this documentation when I curated her exhibition Suture/Hybridisation/Recycling in the Espacio AV (Summer 2008). These images were published for the first time in the catalog that coincided with the show.

2. ORLAN forcefully rejects the commonplace view that her face, after the operations, has become a compendium of fragments of feminine representation in important pictures from art history: "Those responsible have been the communications media. After that everybody has copied them—even critics and art historians who are very honest have done so. It's an infernal machine which, really, ends up being very difficult to stop." (ORLAN, interview by the author at the artist's studio in Paris, August 2008).

3. ORLAN interview, 2008.

4. ORLAN has not only collaborated with designers, she has also influenced them. In this context I would point to the performance which the Belgian designer Walter Van Beirendonck

put on in the Boijmans Van Beuningen Museum, Rótterdam, in 1998 in homage to the artist. The models and spectators at the event put artificial cheeks on their foreheads at the time when ORLAN put on an Inca nose. Beirendonck made these declarations which crossed over the real and the artificial: "I think that the use of color in makeup is definitely passé. It has been totally exploited to the point of banality by the magazines. I am seeking something innovative, but also something that might be real." In *Believe, WVD & Wild and Lethal Trash!* Boijmans Van Beuningen Museum, Rótterdam, 1998.

5. ORLAN interview, 2008.

6. This photograph has a copy in which ORLAN appears without shoes, titled *Nu descendant l'escalier—contre-plongée avec tête*, also from 1967.

7. After measuring the cities dragging her body, ORLAN washed the dress and kept the dirty water in a transparent jar as a reliquary, the first of countless references to Catholic rituals and iconography so frequent in her work, especially the series called *The Triumph of the Baroque*.

8. The straps, as ORLAN herself has emphasized, allowed any type of body, whether small, large, old, young, fat, or thin, not just her own, to put on the tunics (ORLAN interview, 2008).

9. I have borrowed the concept of the "blank page" from the title of a short story by Isak Dinesen in which she tells of a supposed custom of the Portuguese royal family: after the marriage of a female member of the family, the sheet from the wedding night was hung from a palace balcony with a sign proclaiming "Virginem eam tenemos" (I declare she was virgin). The sheet was not washed nor was it ever used again, and it was framed in a nearby convent with a notice on which was written the name of the princess. However, among the row of sheets there was one, totally white and nameless, whose silence was more eloquent than the signs of all the rest.

10. ORLAN has tied her artistic practice to the tradition of the manifesto hallowed by the historical avant-gardes. Her entire practice and works count as a manifesto. The manifesto covering her current work is published under the title "Libre parole," in *Suture/Hybridisation/Recycling: ORLAN + davidelfin* (Murcia, Spain: Espacio AV, 2008), 10.

11. In fact, before the sexual use of these sheets, ORLAN had used them as canvases stretched on stretcher frames, which she had painted on. Although I have not found any critical references that I can quote, it is interesting to bring up Picasso's declarations that he associated his pictorial energy with that of his virile member, something which was later taken up by the American Abstract Expressionists, especially Pollock. The identification of painting with masculine discourse was also widely contested by the proto-feminist artistic manifestations of the 1960s—for instance the Japanese Fluxus artist Shigeko Kubota with her performance *Vagina painting*—and by the creative feminists of the following decades.

12. Self-knowledge, resistance to pain, physical danger, and ritual as formulae to approach the most primitive human states, concerns which run through the work of action artists at this time such as Rudolf Schwarzkogler, Marina Abramovic, Gina Pane, Stelarc, or Chris Burden, have nothing to do with ORLAN. Her actions up until the 1990s imply parody and not reality, pleasure and not pain. In the operations of the 1990s that ORLAN called *Carnal Art*, pain was eliminated by chemical means and sedatives; there was no interest in suffering. Her work was based on questioning the assumptions which restrict individual liberties and which create patterns of conduct or aesthetic and coercive behavioral archetypes.

13. This is a question which I put specifically to ORLAN: What were her points of reference in the 1960s? Obviously, one had to be Duchamp—witness her performance parody of *Nu descen-*

dant l'escalier—however, as she herself indicated, the artists who worked with these concerns did so in a fairly isolated way. She was in Saint-Étienne and as a seventeen-year-old lacked contacts, information, and references in general about contemporary art. ORLAN did not know the members of Fluxus until 1973 (ORLAN interview, 2008). On her relations with Fluxus, see *ORLAN: Carnal Art* (Paris: Éditions Flammarion, 2004), 248.

14. ORLAN interview, 2008.

15. George Maciunas credited these pieces to Ben Vautier in a letter quoted in Simon Anderson, "Fluxus Publicus," in *En l'esperit de Fluxus* (Barcelona, Spain: Fundació Antoni Tàpies, 1994), 40. Watts designed t-shirts and underwear. In the case of Maciunas I am speaking of the work *Venus de Milo Apron* (ca. 1970). Although Surrealism produced similar trompe l'oeil works, it is clear that its objectification of the female body is the opposite of the critical and deconstructive reading that began to be produced in the 1960s by Fluxus and the various artistic strands of feminism.

16. George Maciunas and Billie Hutching gave this performance in New York in 1978, making reference with the title to the colors of the clothes that the bride and groom customarily wear and that are assigned by gender.

17. This work came before the lecture ORLAN gave on the writings of Eugénie Lemoine-Luccioni.

18. See Eugenio Viola, "Entretien avec ORLAN," in *Le Récit* (Milan, Italy: Charta, Musée d'art Moderne de Saint-Étienne, 1997), 90.

19. With this work ORLAN anticipated the references to the absence of pubic hair in representations of the female nude in art history, which she criticized in works such as *A poil/sans poil*.

20. Although the piece and the performance that followed took place in France in the first half of the 1970s, it has been impossible to assign them to a specific date and place.

21. Note the relationship between these series and the critical reading of objectified representations of female bodies in the history of art and their invisibility as subjects in the work of collectives such as the Guerrilla Girls.

22. ORLAN interview, 2008.

23. SymbioticA is a group of Australian artists who have a laboratory specializing in skin culture at the University of Perth. While working on the project ORLAN also met Jens Hauser, a biotechnological art theorist.

24. ORLAN interview, 2008.

25. Birthdays appear to be dates on which ORLAN introduces innovations in her work. Her famous *Baiser de l'Artiste*, which took place at the FIAC in Paris, coincided with her twenty-fifth birthday.

26. ORLAN interview, 2008.

27. See pp. 10–12 in this volume.

28. Rhonda Garelick has written a thorough survey of the literary and theatrical evolution of the Harlequin figure in and the acceptance of its use as a metaphor for multiculturalism by Michel Serres, relating it to the work of the French artist (see Garelick's essay in this volume). ORLAN used the Serres text for the first time in her *Seventh Operation*.

29. In the presentations that were put on after the performances of *MesuRage*, the dirty water obtained from the ritual washing of the clothes was also displayed in glass jars inside display cabinets.

30. ORLAN interview, 2008.

31. This project took place in the designer's studio in rue Guénégaud from May 29 to June 21 during the show Art Saint Germain des Prés.

32. There are two other, in this case involuntary, collaborators in the Murcia project: Michel Serres and Philippe Starck.

33. ORLAN interview, 2008.

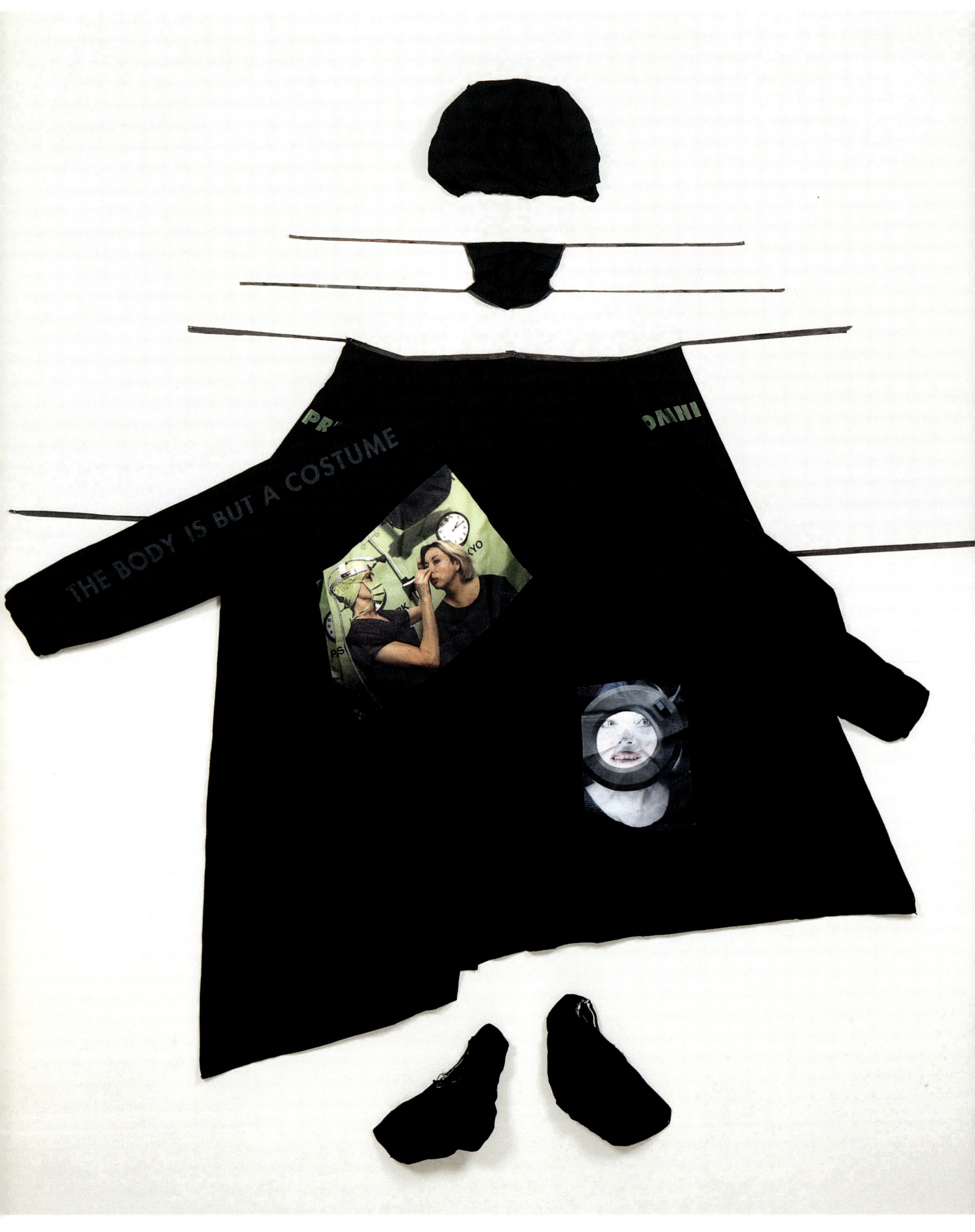

ORLAN, FORERUNNER OF TENDENCIES
LAN VU

ORLAN SAYS SHE DOESN'T BELIEVE in ghosts, but in the warmth of human exchange.

In an information age where Facebook and other social networking sites make the concept of identity fluid and transparent, ORLAN's work raises vital questions. What elements actually define one's persona? How much of it is real and how much is fabricated? Through avatars and profiles, we can now create online personalities. These are based on reflections of how we view ourselves rather than on factual reality.

ORLAN's work is the forerunner of this virtual identity movement. Years before the Internet became commonplace, she was reinventing herself in myriad ways. Her famed "plastic surgery performances" from 1990 to 1993 are extreme examples of this. Those performances were made to put features on her face that she liked very much.

Her latest exhibition, *Suture, Hybridization, Recycling,* delves further into hybridizations. Using decades worth of clothing collected throughout her artistic career, she and designer davidelfin recycle and reinvent these pieces into new garments. Thus each creation has its own identity, yet still retains traces of its past. The recycled garments are then turned into cushioned "ready-mades." They are placed onto Philippe Starck's polycarbonate Louis Ghost chairs, which are themselves a fusion of historical Louis XV design and modern minimalism.

The clothing, fastened by transparent plastic laces, sits on the chairs without bodies to fill them, making the chairs comfortable. ORLAN's face, usually so prevalent in her art, is not present. Instead she allows the clothing to tell its own intriguing narrative. Each detail and fragment of the garments recalls a memory from a particular era in ORLAN's life. She invites visitors to share in this intimate experience. By sitting on the chairs and engaging in the scene around them, they add part of their being to the setting, another layer to the hybridization.

Recycling and hybridizations are important concepts in the current fashion world. The textile industry is increasingly focused on developing new ways to

Incriminating Evidence. Costume from the seventh surgery-performance, 1993. Costume worn by translator, Sophy Thompson. Photograph by Bruno Scott.

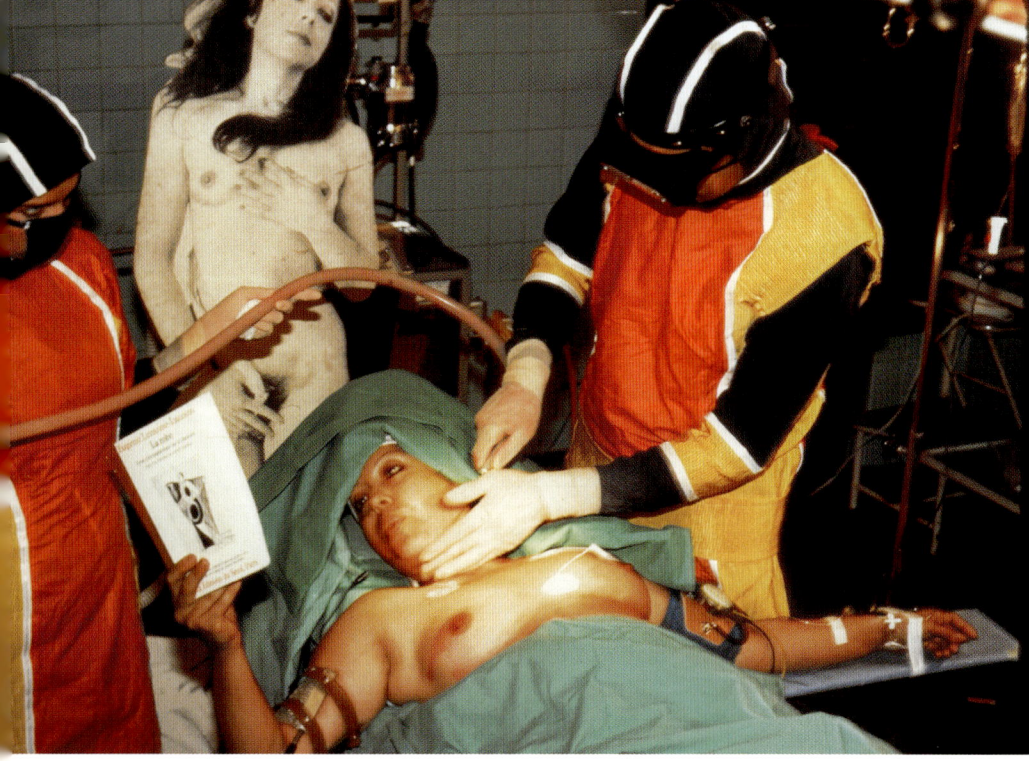

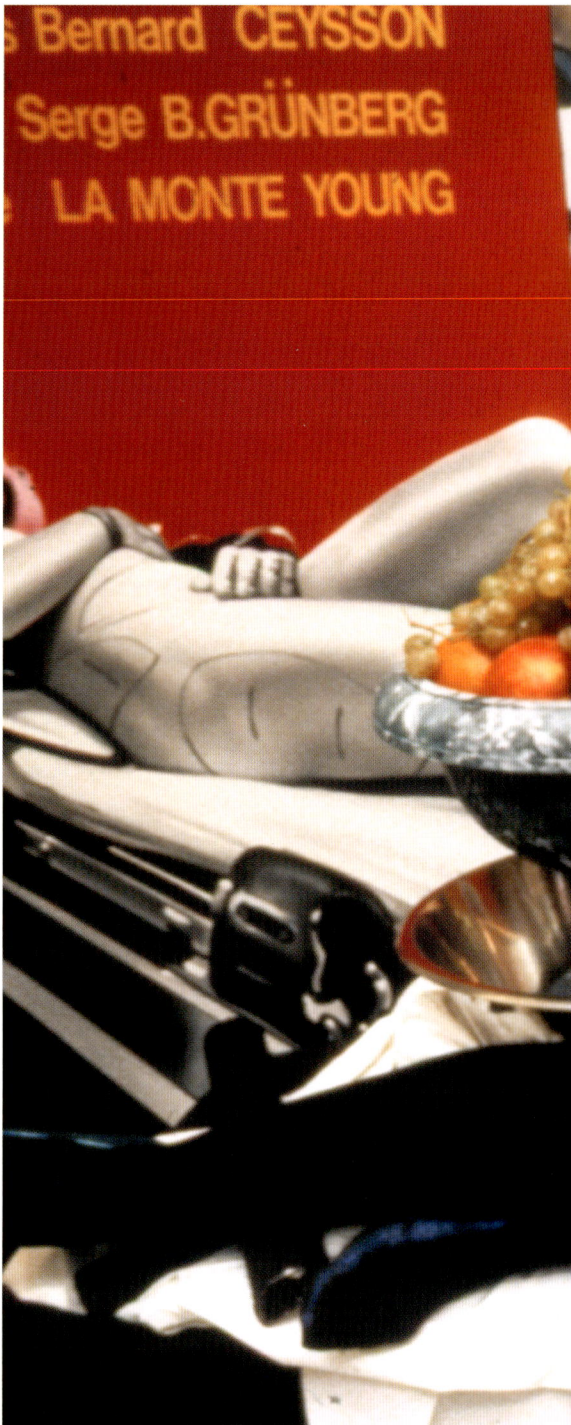

ORLAN reading Eugénie Lemoine-Luccioni's La Robe (The Dress), *July 1990. First surgery-performance. Cibachrome in diasec mount, 165 cm. x 110 cm. Designed by Charlotte Calberg. Paris.*

Reincarnation of Saint ORLAN or, New Images: ORLAN with dress by Franck Sorbier, July 6, 1993. 110 cm. x 165 cm. Fifth surgery-performance with Dr. Chérif Kamel Zaar, Paris.

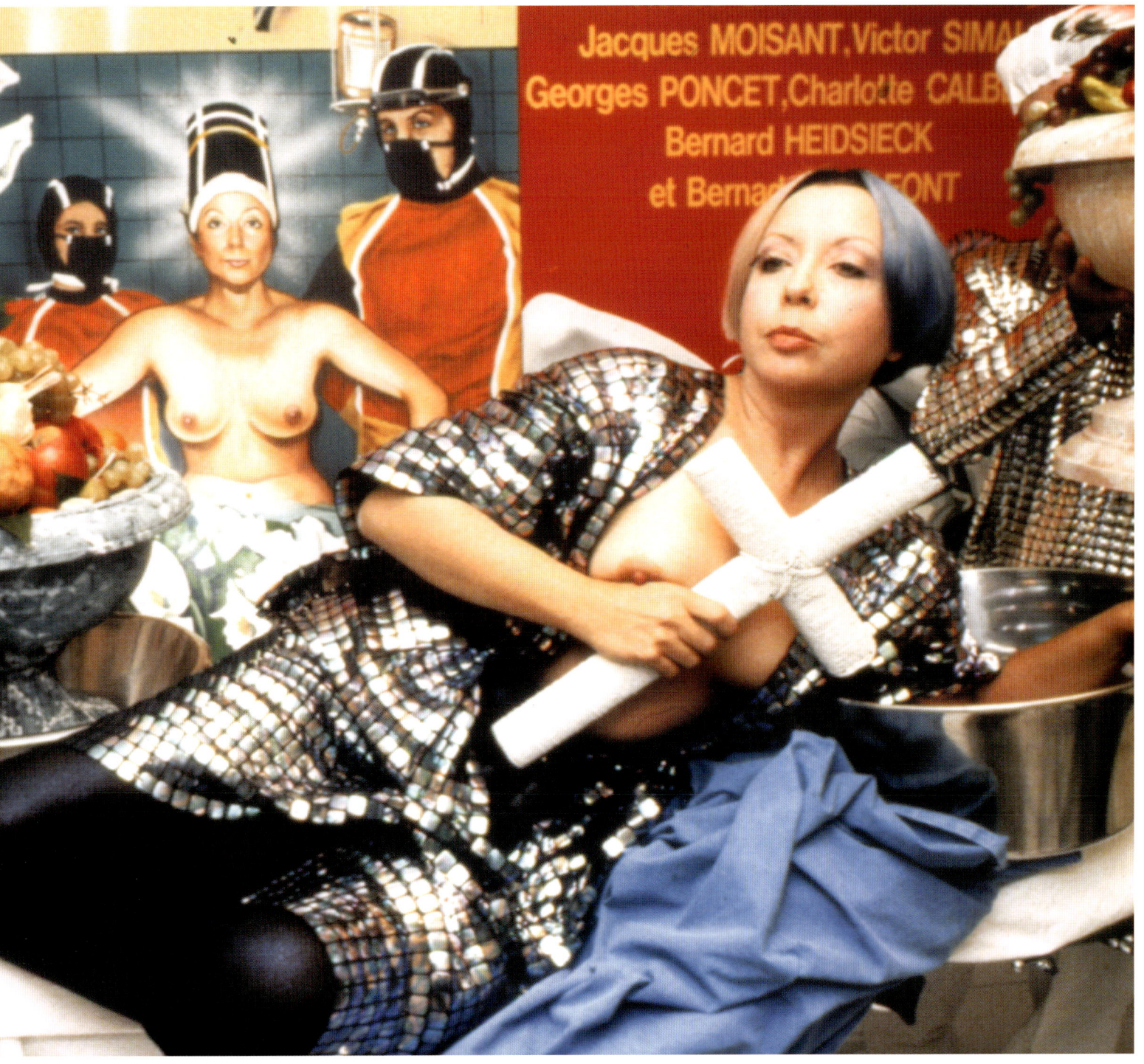

use recycled materials, such as making denim from recycled plastic water bottles. Recycling also applies to clothing silhouettes. Each decade has had a distinctive signature look. If flappers defined the 1920s and bohemians ruled the 1970s, then the 2000s are about recycling. Vintage clothing is widely popular, as women flock to secondhand stores and flea markets. Elements from past decades are combined in ever-changing juxtapositions. In a search for newness, this frenzied mix has come to define the signature style of the 2000s.

ORLAN also tackles the question of "signature" in this exhibition. Using Philippe Starck's chairs and

mixing her own name with davidelfin's, as she did with Maroussia Rebecq, Agatha Ruiz de la Prada, and others designers, she hybridizes her whole wardrobe.

ORLAN's work provides a unique bridge between art and fashion. Clothing is an important element within her work. In 1976 in Portugal, ORLAN "got dressed with her own nudity" for a performance where she wore a dress on which her naked body was printed. This idea was also taken up a year later by Vivienne Westwood and Malcolm McLaren.

For her December 1993 *Omniprésence* surgical operation, a team of New York designers and I created costumes for ORLAN, Dr. Marjorie Cramer, and the

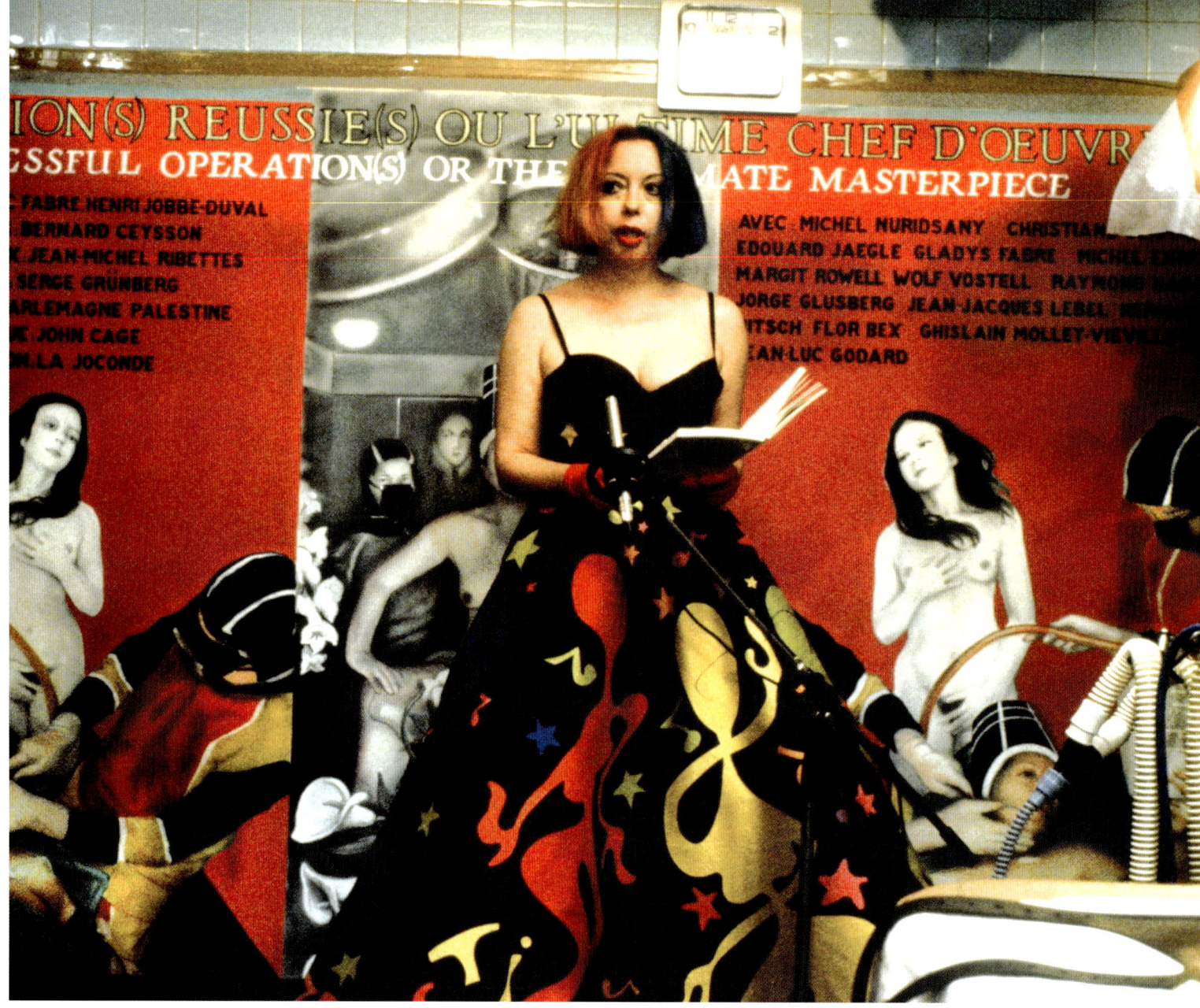

entire medical crew. Drawing from her work, we distorted the body through cotton padding in the form of bumps and tentacles. These appeared on the shoulders, stomach, and sides in striking color combinations such as yellow and chartreuse, red and black. The result had a graphic sci-fi edge, which interestingly resurfaced four years later on Paris runways.

Many designers, such as Jeremy Scott and Walter Van Beirendonck, declared that they were inspired by the work of ORLAN. For his winter 1998 collection, Van Beirendonck gave his models the same bumps as ORLAN. During the opening, the guests had false bumps and their true nose whereas ORLAN had a false nose but true bumps.

In 1997 Comme des Garçons, one of fashion's most avant-garde labels, presented its celebrated "lumps and bumps" spring/summer collection. It featured predominately tight tops and skirts that were swollen by goose down–filled lumps. This also led to a collaboration that same year with choreographer Merce Cunningham called "Scenario," in which Comme des Garçon's Rei Kawakubo continued the concept of surrealist lumps and distortions in his stage costumes. Such is the impact of ORLAN's work on the realms of international fashion and theater.

ORLAN pushes the boundaries of art, fashion, and technology. Powerful and flamboyant, her work continues to challenge our perceptions of beauty and identity, confronting us with our humanity in the face of a virtual world.

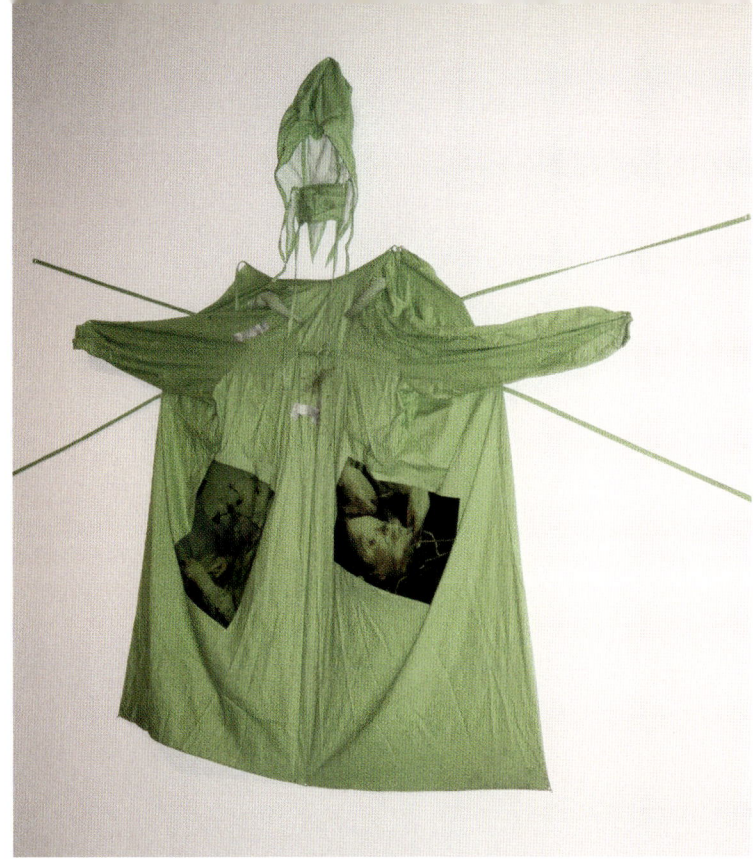

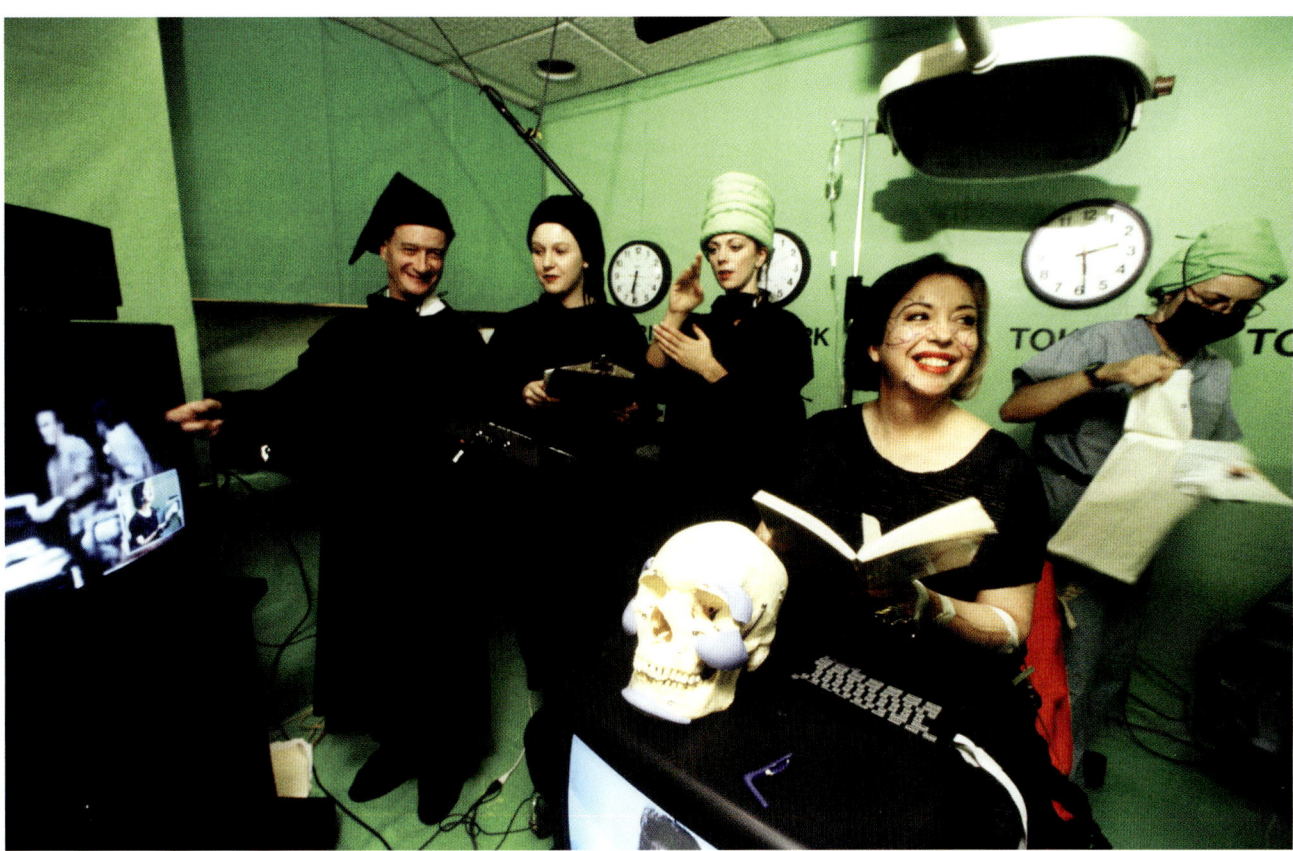

Reincarnation of Saint ORLAN or, Surgery-Performance, July 6, 1991. Color photograph. Dress by Paco Rabanne. Photograph by Alain Dohmé for Sipa-Press.

Green dress for the surgery-performance, 1993. Designed by Lan Vu and her team.

ORLAN reading La Robe (The Dress) *in the operating room before the seventh surgery-performance, titled* Omniprésence, New York, November 21, 1993. Cibachrome in diasec mount, 165 cm. x 110 cm., edition of seven plus one. Photograph by Vlamir Sichov.

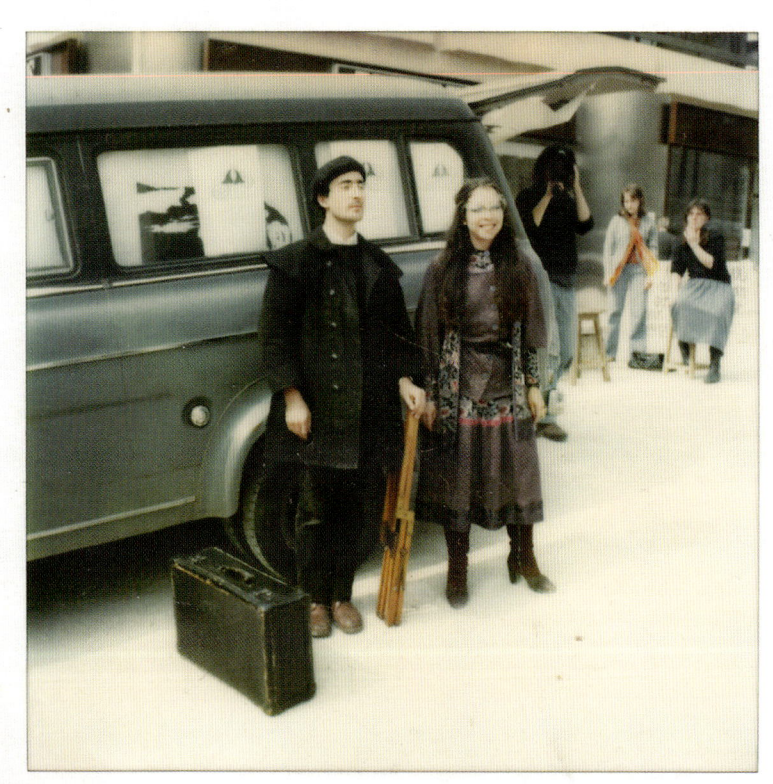

Avant

nº 3 *Alan*

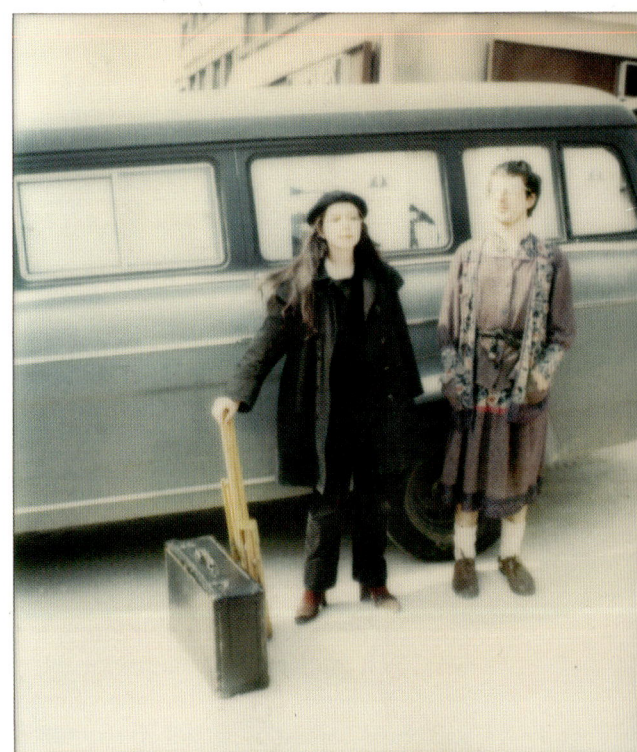

Après le *Alan*.

IN THE NAME OF ORLAN

ARTIST AS TEXT

JORGE DANIEL VENECIANO

"ORLAN," THE NAME, ANNOUNCES itself as something other than a name. Composed of capital letters it resembles an acronym, standing for what, we cannot be sure. It announces, suggestively, something other than an individual, who would otherwise warrant "a Christian name," especially for someone coming from France. Instead, it suggests the acronym of an enterprise—a corporation, cartel, or NGO; in any case, some form of concerted effort—rather than a person's name. This diversionary "name" or label turns out to work quite felicitously with the kind of art ORLAN produces, as we shall see, in which she renders herself a manufactured composite with a transnational mission.

By extension her name, as a stand-in for the composite nature of her work, suggests something about the individual as composite subject—not something we see in her work per se, but something we *read* through her work—the subject as corporation of functions and productions, as art and performance, in ORLAN's case, and in NGO fashion, working across national boundaries.

As an acronym, the name performs like a coded label, a nonsensical word standing for a string of words. In its appearance the acronym would stand not for a person but for a script, a second layer of language, text, and signifiers on the other side of which would lie the referent, placing the signified (the artist) at a farther remove from the name— not immediately present, as in a traditional "Christian" arrangement of names. If we reached toward the conclusion that there resides something vaguely anti-Christian in the acro-name, we wouldn't have far to reach.

ORLAN's name, as an artist's name, first appeared as "Orlan." At some point in the artist's series of transfigurations, her name changed to "ORLAN," moving from name-like word to the current label, brand, or sign—from identifying an individual to indicating a signifying function, the acronym. As "Orlan," the name itself speaks; it speaks in abbreviation, pointing us to different trajectories of inter-texts associated with it. As abbreviation, "Orlan"

Performance, Angoulême, France, 1978. Polaroid photographs for documentation.

provokes a little anxiety—the anxiety of uncertainty. It is an unfamiliar name, and it is the performance of abbreviation: the truncation of a familiar name, Orlando. "Orlan" amends "Orlando." The neutering of "Orlando" adds another layer to the sense of anxiety "Orlan" may provoke.

Though it may not have been the artist's intention in naming herself to neutralize the gendered name of "Orlando," it remains the consequence of her choice. And a telling consequence it is, for an artist known for crossing boundaries. Consider an intertext by the name of Victoria Mary "Vita" Sackville-West. The English author and poet Sackville-West liked to dress as a young man on her outings with novelist Violet Trefusis in France and other places in Europe.

Identity as a construct, we learn from Sackville-West's example, seems ready to entertain more extravagant liberties when traveling abroad than when staying at home. Home is the placeholder and anchor of identity. Abroad, *being* abroad, performs the physical displacement of identity and sites the terrain of difference, a terrain elsewhere from here. This was the expectation among the Harlequin king's audience in Michel Serres's preface to *The Troubadour of Knowledge* (reprinted in this volume): that difference resides in places away from home.

Like Sackville-West's, ORLAN's identity-trading performances in Angoulême, France, in 1978 included cross-dressing: trading clothes with male and female participants. "ORLAN in this case," writes Isabel Tejeda, "worked with the idea of the transvestite and with the negation of a pure and unique identity, making plain that to a large degree our social and gender identity is branded by the clothes we wear."[1]

Sackville-West, the woman who dressed as a young man when going out with her female lover, becomes an inspiration for Virginia Woolf. Sackville-West becomes "Orlando," a male character in Woolf's novel *Orlando*. So, we have a woman in life who, in fiction, becomes a man who, in the novel, gets transformed into a woman who falls in love with a man. If this dizzying sense of comedy sounds Elizabethan, it may be because it recalls Shakespeare's familiar set of comedic texts.

This is how intertextuality works. "Orlando," the name and role, provides the trace, implicating different texts. "Orlando," we now recall, names the male protagonist in Shakespeare's *As You Like It*. In the play's most titillating scene of gender-bending homoeroticism, Orlando meets a character named Ganymede, who is, in essence, a man (the Elizabethan actor) *performing* as Rosalind (a female char-

acter and Orlando's love), *disguised* as Ganymede (a male character), *pretending* to play, for the sake of *performing* love therapy, the part of Rosalind (again female) in a mock encounter of the lovers' relationship (a tertiary order of farce). The *performance* of gender identity in this scene replaces irredeemably any hope of returning to a place of grounding, a place of home, in the function of natural identity—character, gender, or otherwise. All are astir in the airy realm of the symbolic.

Orlando has nothing to do with ORLAN's work. Yet the intertext of *As You Like It* has everything to do with it. That identity, as such, and the very motivations that underlie and mark the internality of identity, can inhabit its opposite, be inflected with its opposite, *become* its opposite (in Woolf) and produce a felicity, even if a hysterical one, is the political message and political import of comedy. The hysterical felicity in recognizing or retrieving *the Other within* is the performance of a democratic politics—the performance of tolerance. Such is the type of comedy we find staged in ORLAN's Self-Hybridization Series and the *Harlequin Coat* installation.

In the United States "Orlando" names a city in Florida, home of the Magic (a professional basketball team), whose own nominal intertext resides nearby: the largest theme park of the uncanny, Disney World. According to its most popular legend, the city was named after Orlando Reeves, an army sentinel, who was felled by arrows in 1835 during the war against the Seminole nation. At the cost of his life, Reeves alerted his company (stationed there to protect incoming settlers) to an impending attack, saving his fellow soldiers from a nighttime ambush.[2] "Orlando"—Saint Sebastian–like as one imagines him riddled with arrows—gives a name to and preserves the honor of martyrdom in the spirit of expansionism beyond the thirteen colonies—a spirit reinstantiated from English colonialism to a mimetic American colonialism, which was then directed to southward and westward expansion. "Orlando," in this context, becomes a sobriquet of colonial authority under the new policy of Manifest Destiny, which assumed the United States' "inevitable" expansion over all indigenous nations on the continent.

"Orlando," the name, inscribes the sacrifice of life inherent to colonial history and the violence

Donkey skin. To escape the realm of the father, one must change one's skin, 1990. Color photographs by Pascal Victor. Courtesy of the Michel Rein Gallery, Paris.

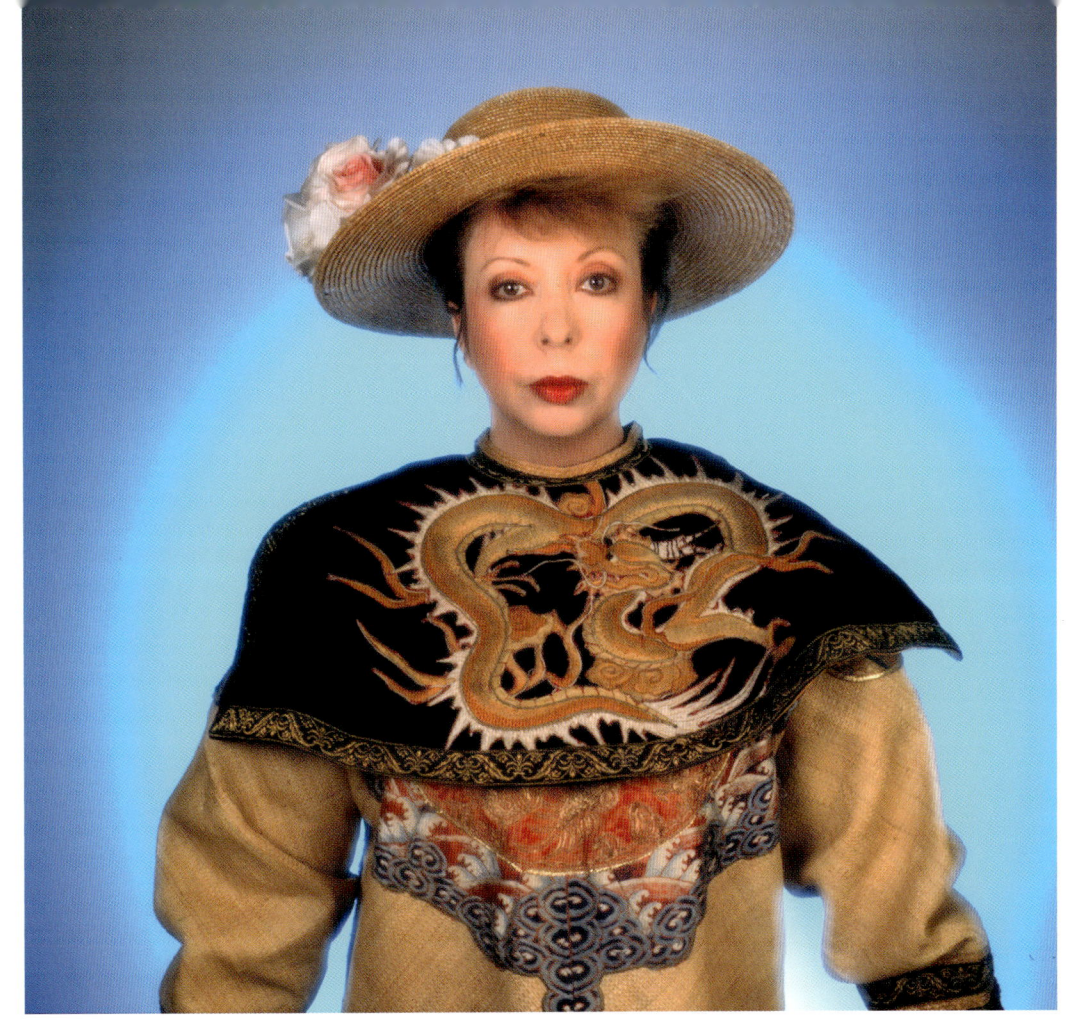

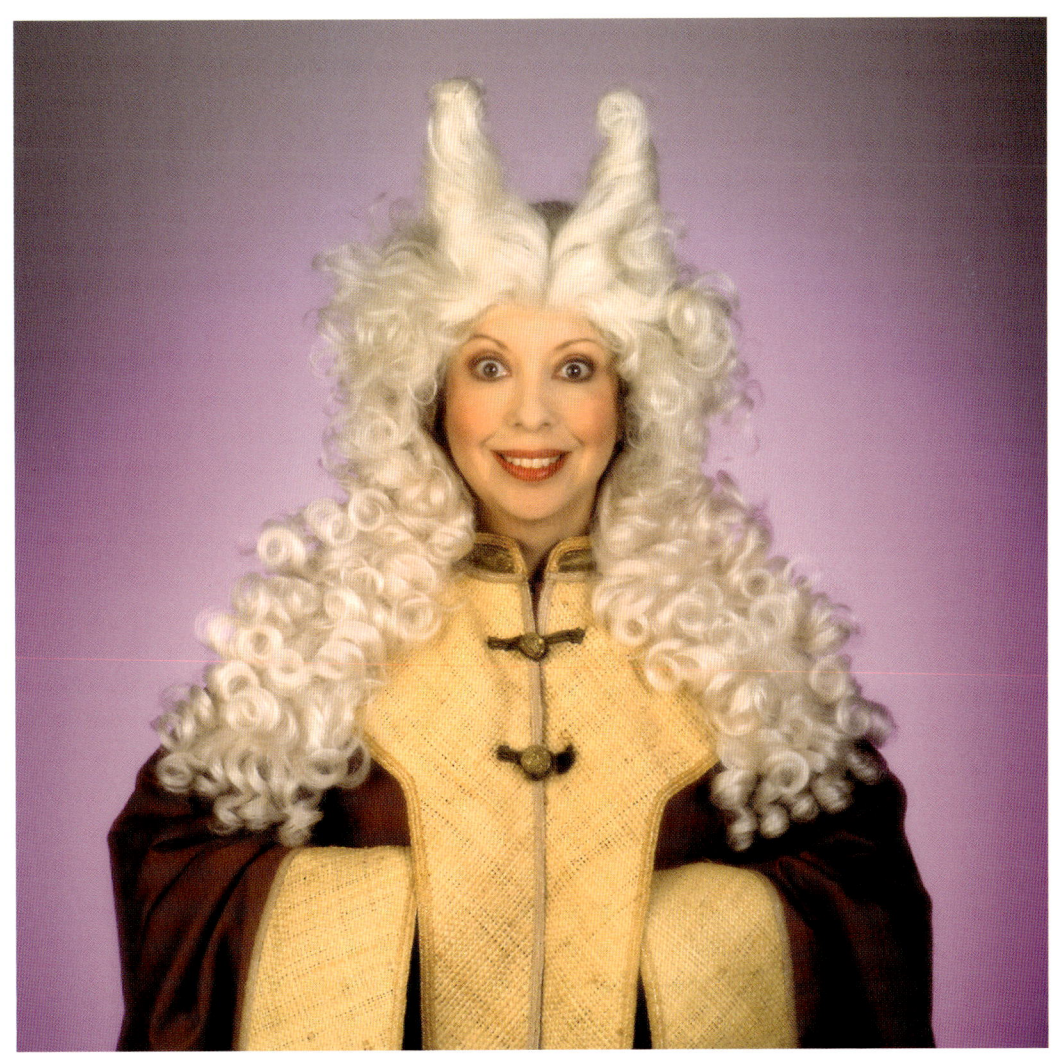

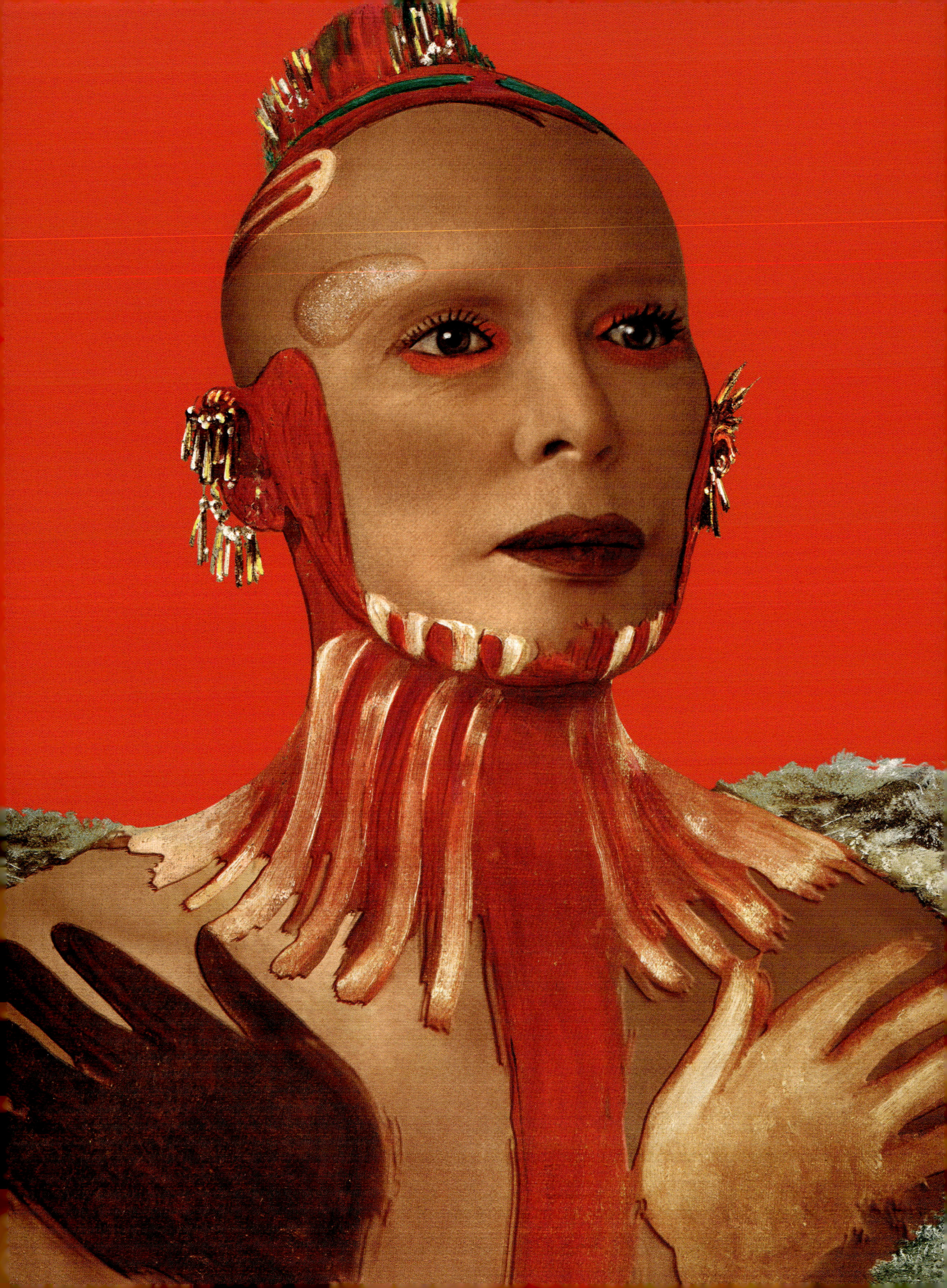

that underlies and underwrites "settlement," the making of home. As founding myth or primal scene of colonial genesis, Orlando unlocks the relationship of difference that founds a city. Identity emerges from difference, from antagonisms (wars) maintained to preserve difference, in order to preserve an ideal of purity and to promote the conquest of the pure over the impure.

These issues map the terrain of ORLAN's work. In her recorded performances as Saint Orlan (a masculine-gendered saint), for example, ORLAN parodies this sense of martyrdom, associated, however, with a different expansionism: that of the Catholic church, over what she feels is its own colonial subject—woman. To the issue of American expansionism, ORLAN has inserted herself into George Catlin's American Indian portraits, which cover a wide range of subjects from Great Plains Indians to the Seminoles implicated in Orlando.

ORLAN's work has nothing to do with Orlando, Florida, and, again, everything to do with it. Her work implies a world—her work contains a world —not specifically Orlando but the broader historical, political world that subsumes it. One could go on, and one should, not simply to avoid ghettoizing the neighborhood of art criticism, but to demonstrate how culture overdetermines its productions, overinscribes its messages and messengers.[3] Another famous martyr, for example, from French Catholic culture and history—ORLAN's erstwhile focus— is Roland, Charlemagne's nephew. "Orlando" is Italian for "Roland," as in the *Chanson de Roland*.

The character of ORLAN's work in anti-martyrdom stands diametrically opposed to the Holy Wars, which pitted Christians against Muslims, and the militarism of religion and masculinity that characterize *The Song of Roland*.

"Orlan" subsists within the discourses of "Orlando," performing as a response through the traces of a name. In these various guises, "Orlando" names the return of the repressed, the eruption of another will, identity, gender, or religion. "Orlan," on the other hand, admits alterity. It names an openness to the Other, even as an ethical politics of sexuality—a permission of reinfiltration, inhabiting and inhabited by the Other.

Because the artist's name is chosen, not given by birth, it should not surprise us that her name bears witness to the similarity of motivating forces behind choices in her work, as in her name. In fact, the trajectory of ORLAN's entire career is summed up in the name she invented for herself. The name is an invention of hers, suited thereby to the work of reinventing the artist herself. As it changes from name-like appearance (lowercase) to acronym-like label (uppercase), the transfiguration of the name maps her movement from self-decentering subject to self-evanescing signifier. It is performative in producing numerous effects, including the de-Christianizing textualization of her name, the acronym. It performs an operation of gender criticism, neutering the masculine name "Orlando," thereby performing the very act, symbolically, that is feared most about feminism. It is therefore hyper-feminist, "ORLAN."

Refiguration Self-Hybridization, American Indian Series #16: "Painted portrait of Wée-Sheet, Sturgeon-Head, A Fox Warrior, with photographic portrait of ORLAN," 2006. Digital photograph, 124.4 cm. x 152.4 cm.

NOTES

1. Isabel Tejeda, ed., *Suture/Hybridisation/Recycling: ORLAN + davidelfin* (Murcia: Espacio AV, 2008), 126.
2. "City of Orlando's History," http://www.cityoforlando.net/cityclerk/history.htm.
3. The name ORLAN invites wider speculation than can be explored here. We find, for example, homophones in "Orlane," a French cosmetics company, and "Orlon," a trademark acrylic fiber. These two alone are enormously apropos of ORLAN's work.

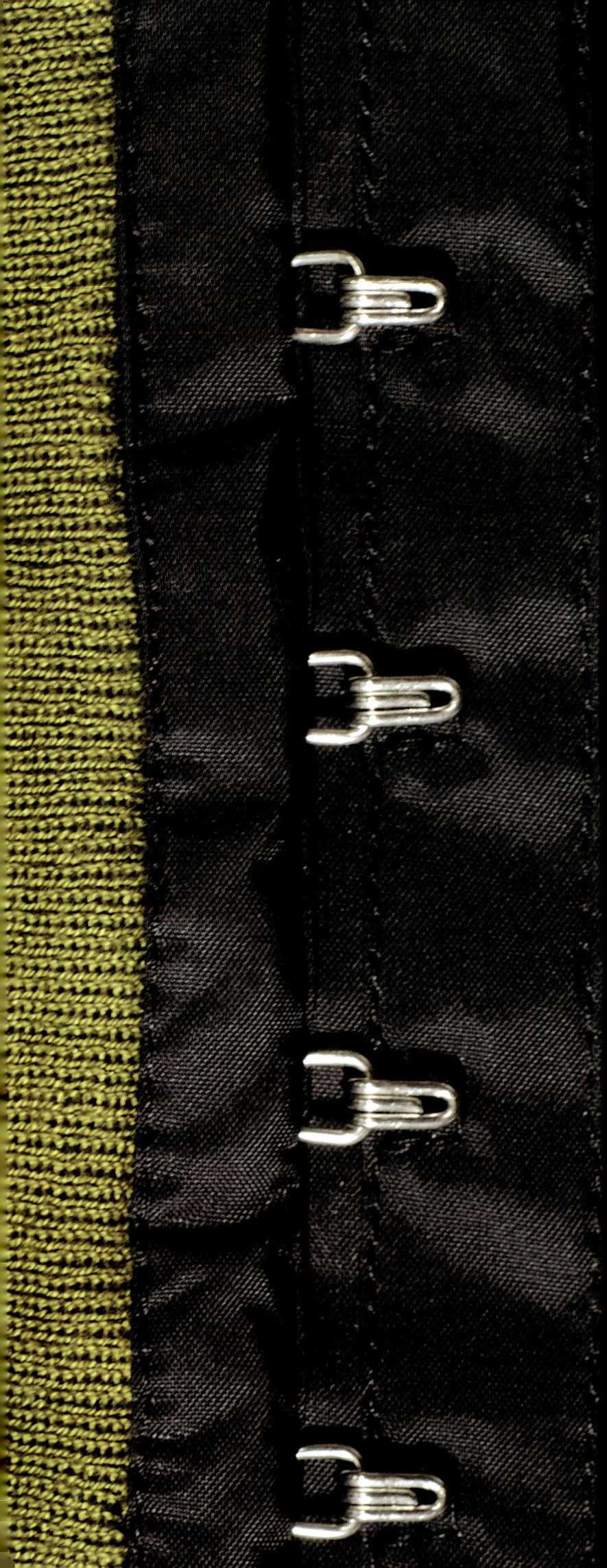

SUTURE

I begin with the psychoanalyst Jacques-Alain Miller's definition of suture as a kind of ghost of totality, tying together things that cannot be joined. This idea of suture has been taken up in cinematic theory by Kaja Silverman, also a psychoanalyst. She analyses how the viewer creates the suture between her desire, her own projection, the images she perceives, those she doesn't see, and those that carry more emotions, and so on. In the end the viewer forms a whole from something that is not exactly what exists. She has fabricated something new. It is a system of unconscious fusion. When I became interested in self-hybridization, in the Other, and in particular in non-Western cultures, I asked myself what I was constructing with my personal images and with the ones that derive from other referents. In short, what was I trying to assemble? This idea inhabits my hybridized wardrobe, recycled: what must the suture be, by which I mean the scar of the materials that overlap each other and fabricate a kind of total and complete unity. I have to stress that the idea of total fusion appears to me extremely dangerous, and that, both in my digital photos and in the work with my wardrobe, I wanted the suture to be shown, and I wanted the two entities that I worked with to have the ability to emerge separately and be seen. I didn't want them to be in a total fusion-confusion. I wanted the place where it all happens to be seen, a place of passing, of transition, that is not really a bridge, but at the same time could be one, since the relationship with the Other is always very difficult: the Other is the Other; to fuse into the Other is pathological. I like very much to tell people, "this is what I do, this is how I operate" so they might know what is happening. I don't want to make them believe in something; I want them to know something. I want the demonstration of two differences to take place and that they get closer by being conscious of the difficulties of such an encounter.

have inscribed hybridization in reality, since I attempted to hybridize my own cells. For the time being, at the level of laboratory technique, we are feeling our way, we are babbling, which implies that there is no real possibility of a fusion between cells of different provenance. I got interested in working with a laboratory and with the current technology of the latest biological research, something thrilling that is happening in our times. What I did with SymbioticA in Australia is not really hybridization but symbolic, a straining toward hybridization in that co-cultivation of my cells with those of another species and those of a black woman. I should make it clear, I do not desire fusion; what we were doing was to put a living cell alongside another that we also kept alive: they were co-cultivated, not a mixture of the nuclei joined together.

RECYCLING

We recycle every day, we group plastics on one side, bottles on the other . . . it is a thought of our times, indispensable for the survival of the world, just like turning off the tap so it does not drip; a thought to slow down a hyper-consumerism that is taking us toward every possible catastrophe. We can be systems of saving resources if we make do with what we have and if we see how we can reuse what we have. I have conserved all my clothes, which on occasion has created storage problems, nuisance, and excess. There is always the possibility of giving them away—I have given away a lot—or of selling them—I have also done that on occasions—but I have kept most of them to make art rather than buying other materials, as I regard them like a second skin. So since recycling, shopping secondhand, and so forth, are practices inherent in our times—and they are becoming more so—I wanted to adopt this idea as well.

It is understood that effectively the word "I" lies outside reality. In place of saying "I am," we ought to say "I are." In French "I are" means absolutely nothing, but it does demonstrate that "I" is not alone, that in the "we are" of that "I" exists all the thought of others, the memory of others, and at the same time the context in which we live, its system of references, its networks. In French "I are" is at once the art of being in the midst of variety, and a sum: various things that are joined and generate a sum of things. For a long time I have worked in collaboration. In addition to working with designers, I have collaborated with choreographers, with people working in sound, cinema, and video, with an architect . . . recently with stylists: Maroussia Rebecq, davidelfin, Agatha Ruiz de la Prada, and with many others in my surgical operations. To work with somebody is never easy, because the other is the Other. In any case, as in the digital self-hybridizations, it is accepting the Other as itself and allowing it space. That place, nonetheless, could be momentary, where we can create a piece of work which, although it is part of a personal concept, is put together with someone who brings to it something one would never have thought of alone. This compares to my digital images: there are two images, two identities, and a third entity is fabricated which is not only the sum of the first and second, but something more. So, for me, collaborating is very, very important so that I might avoid working only with what is comfortable, with preconceived ideas, in their framework. I have always wanted to break out not only of frameworks in general but also from my own frameworks, because I know very well that from a certain point onward, we get comfortable in the systems we have constructed. That's why, if we work with others, we accept being uncomfortable again and we are obliged to think differently, as well as more quickly, to imagine what we are going to produce together. How, suddenly, another imagination for creating this thing is generated, "between two."

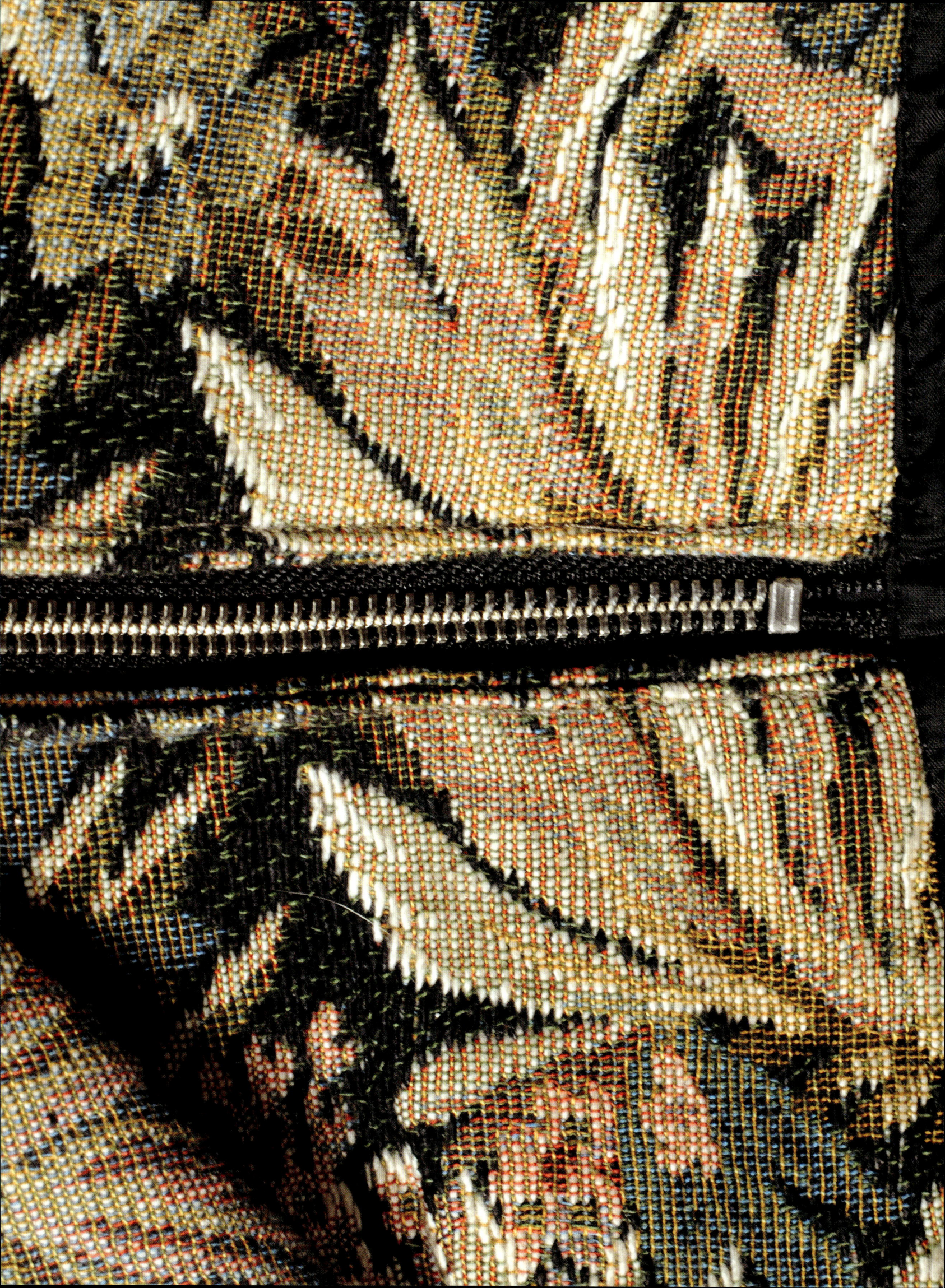

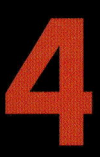 QUESTIONS TO davidelfin

SUTURE

To hybridize ORLAN's clothes, I decided to use the hooks and eyes as a means of joining [material] because it allowed me a form of fastening that is not definitive and the possibility of creating multiple mutations in clothes from different decades, mixing up textiles and time. Turning in all directions, new placement, new order. A wardrobe that generates activity, that moves away from calmness, and comes near to the term "nomad," which the artist used on several occasions during our conversations.

HYBRIDIZATION

Sum, experiment, ambiguity, exquisite corpse, or how we "tear apart" with our gaze. In this case mixture, not fusion.

RECYCLING

I started in fashion recycling military clothes. On them I found names, grease marks, patches. I am interested in traces, the memory they hold. What's more, nowadays recycling is something of vital importance. I care for the world that I belong to, in which I find my family and everything that I love. I am concerned about the Earth's mistreatment, creating a lot of my collection out of organic cotton.

COLLABORATION

Riches. It separates us from the ideology we are familiar with, delivers us to the world and helps us accept differences. Individualism is nothing more than another form of poverty. Feeding the ego is not productive.

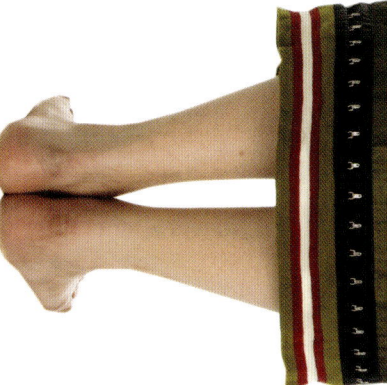
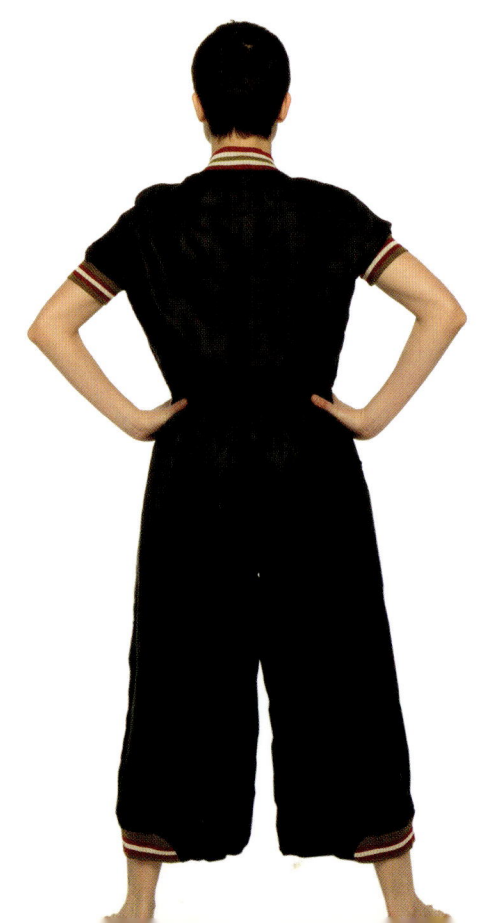

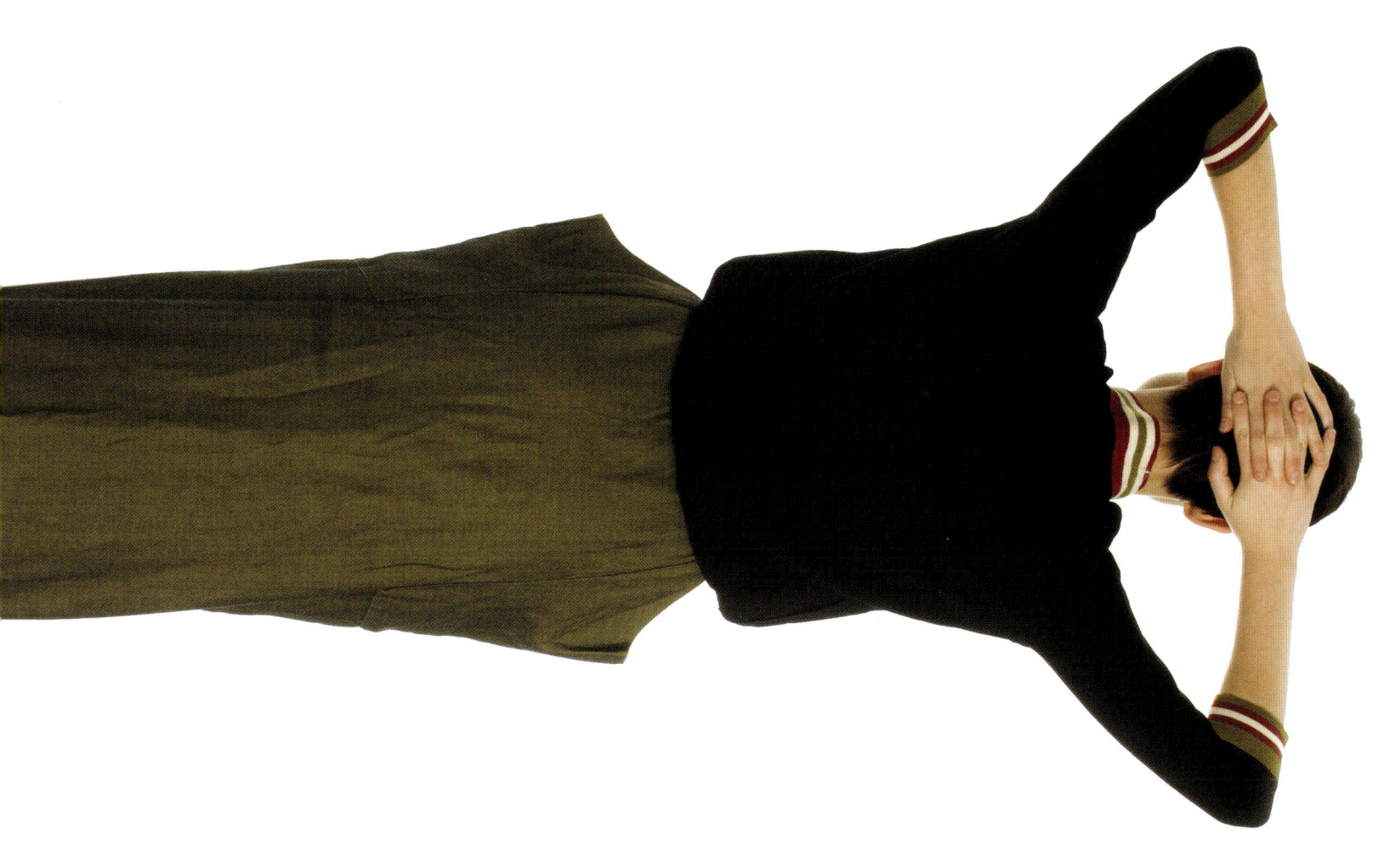

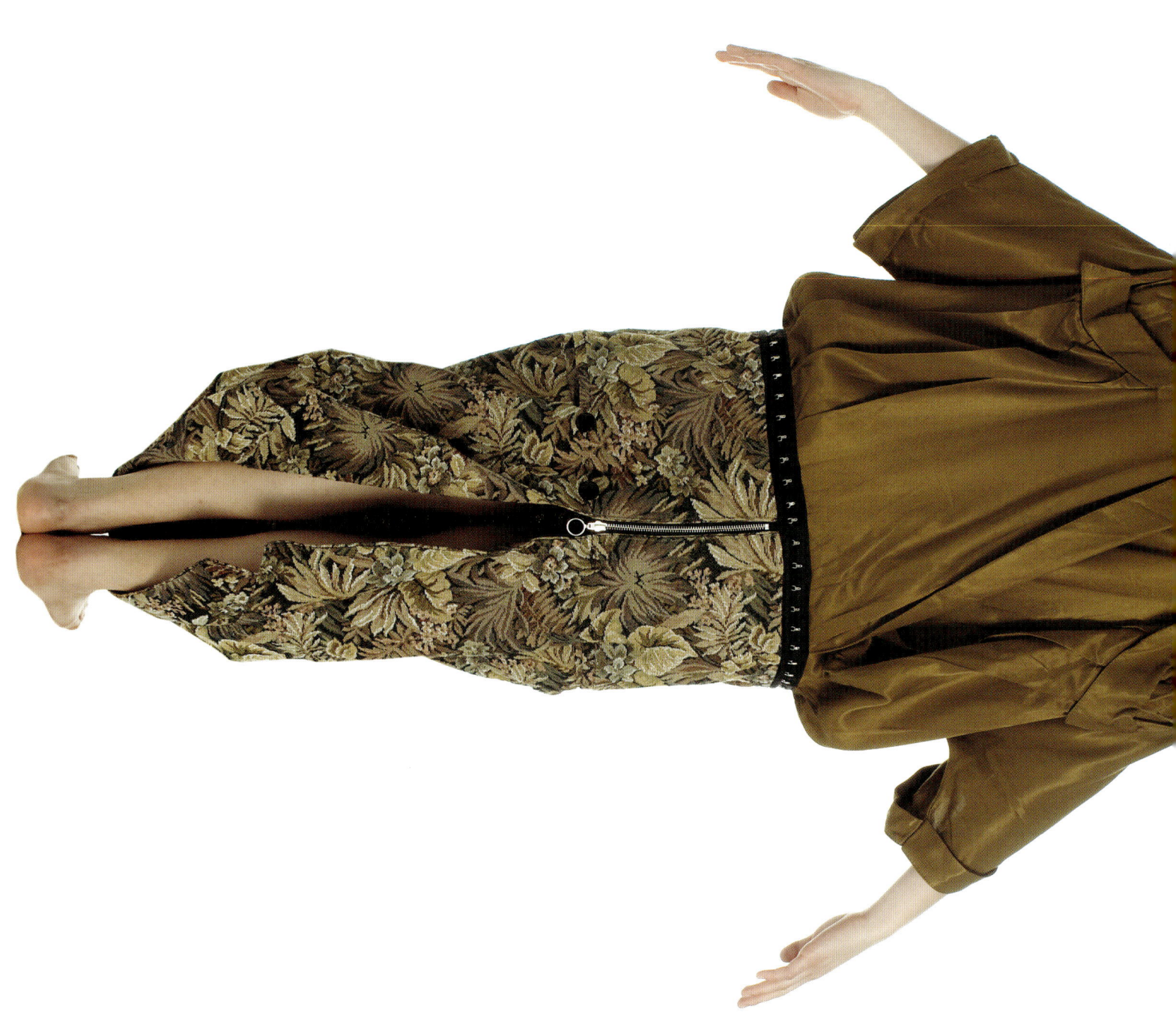

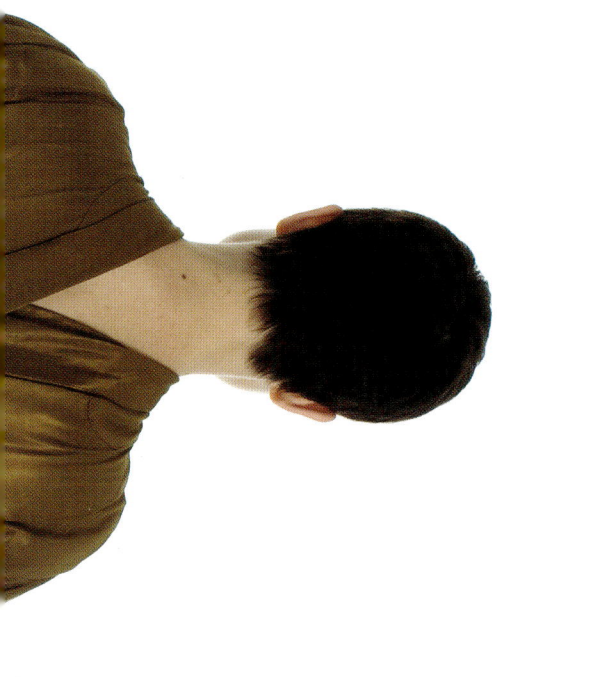
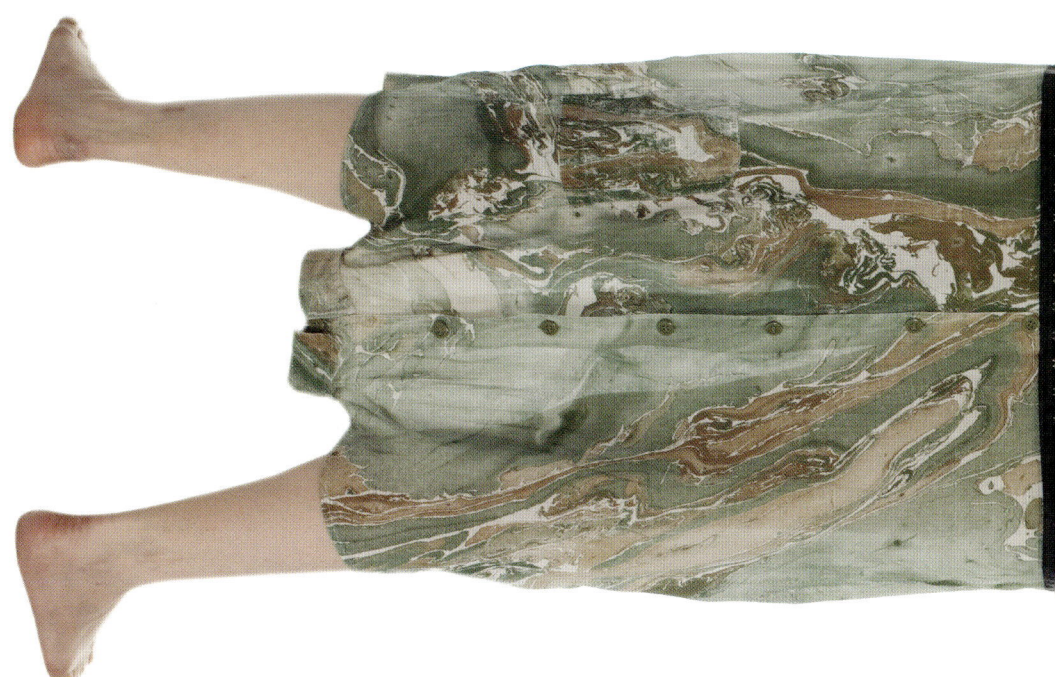
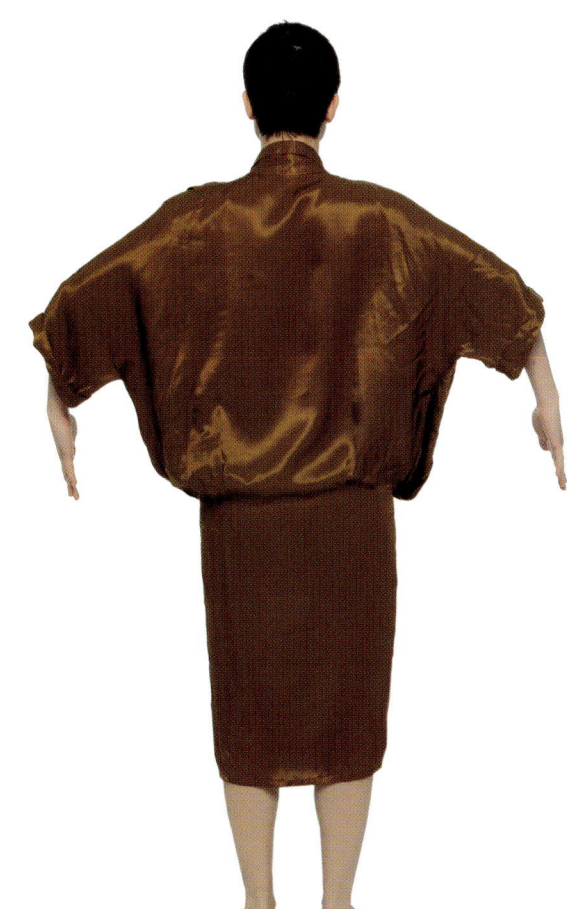

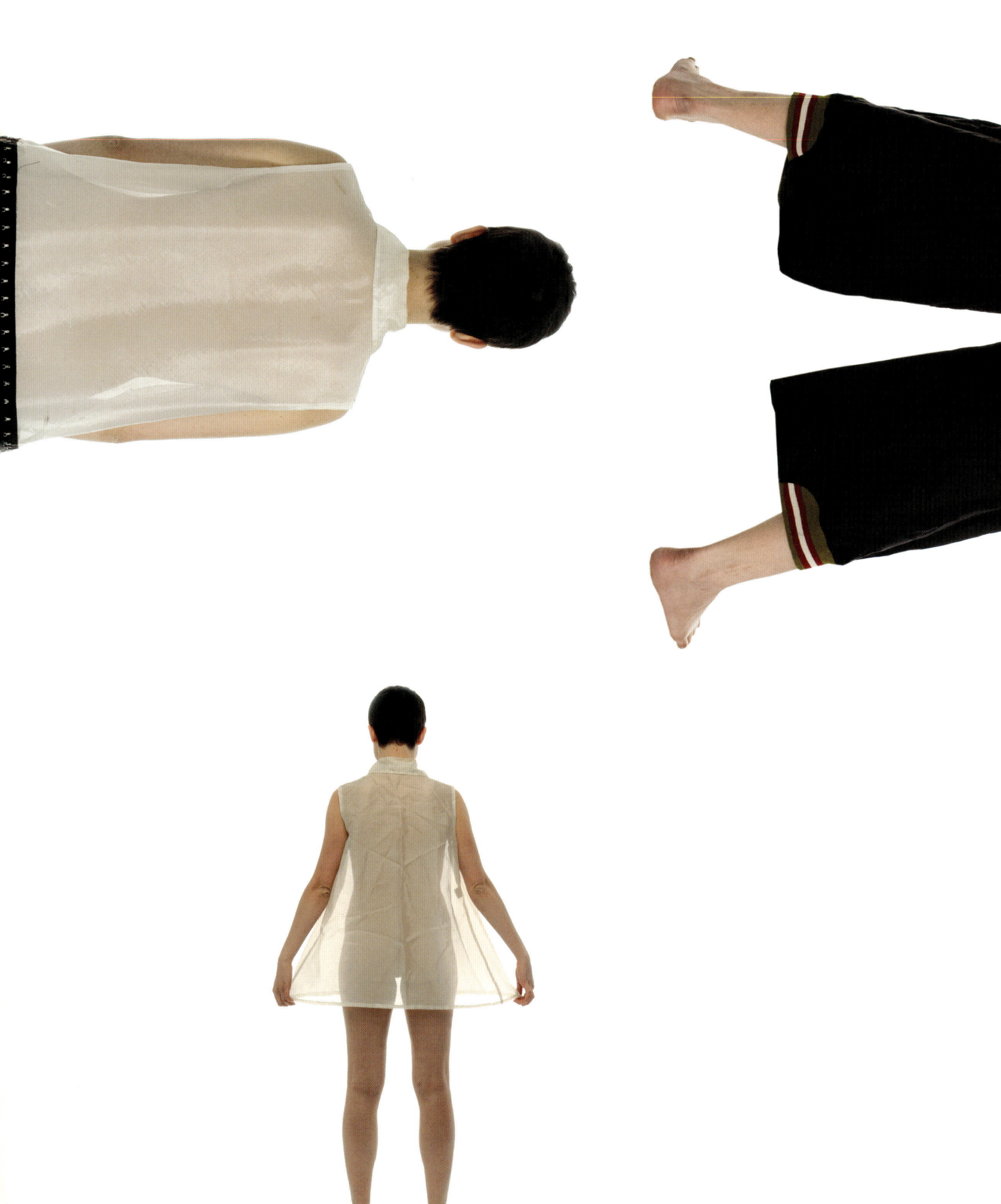

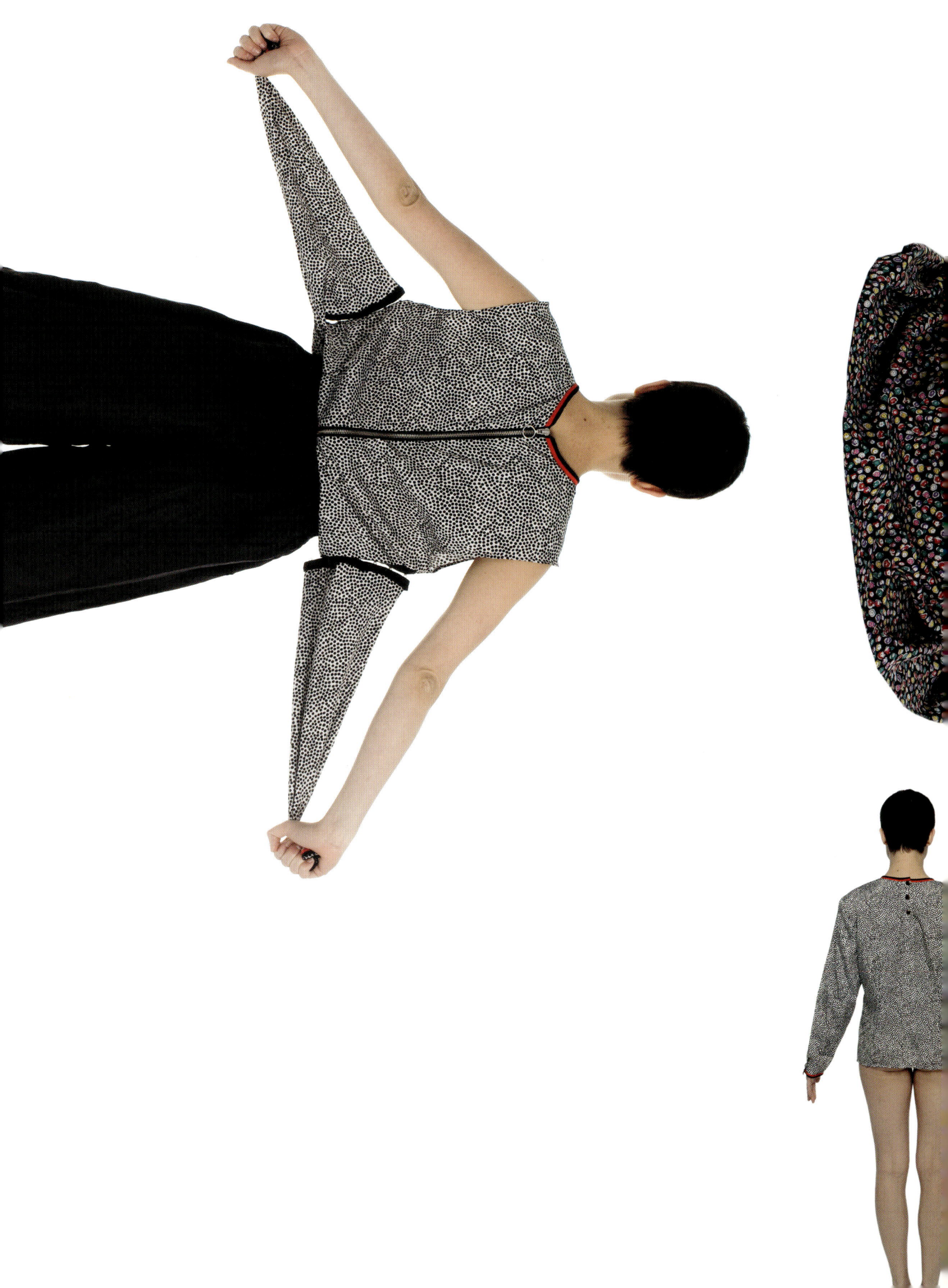

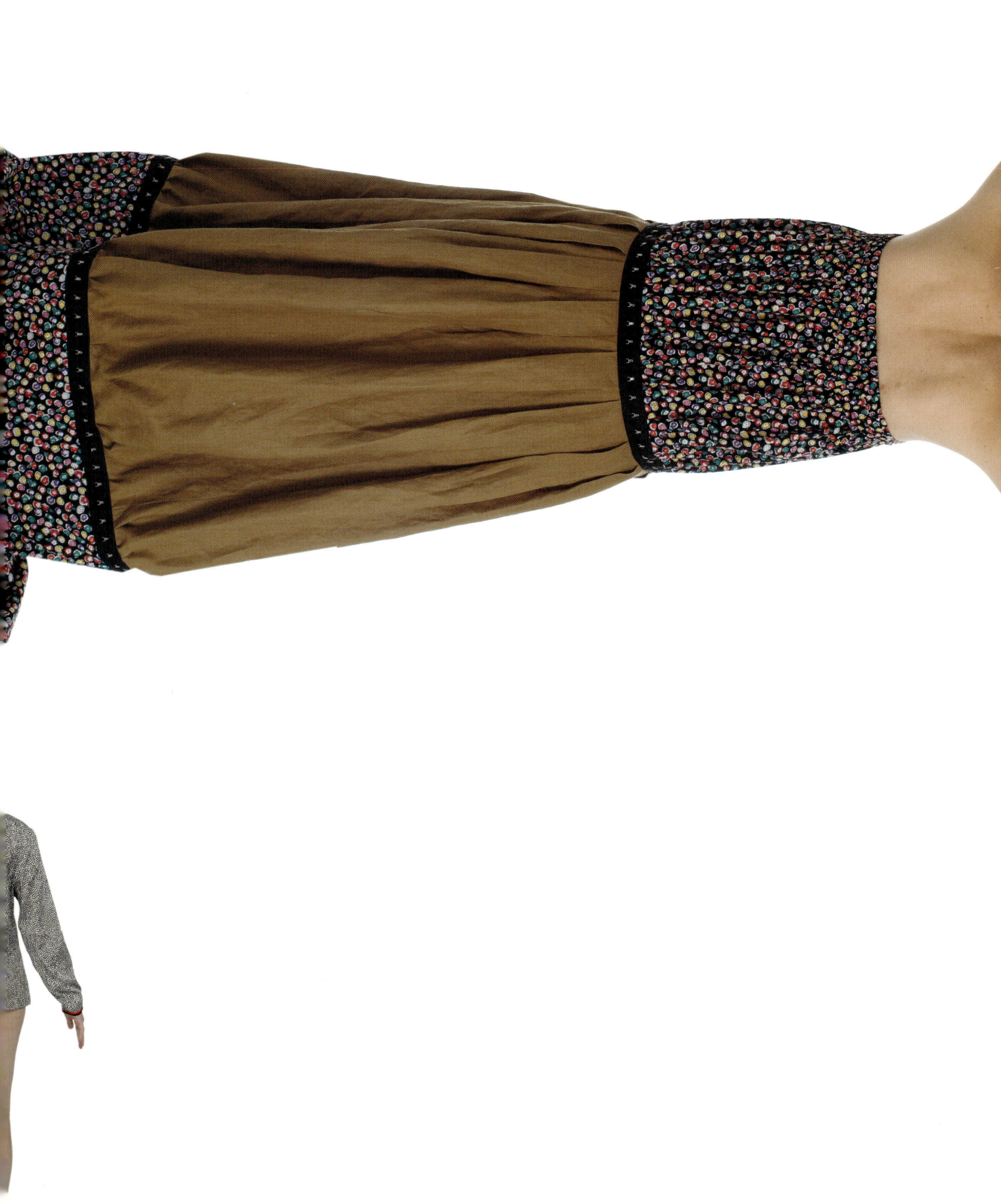

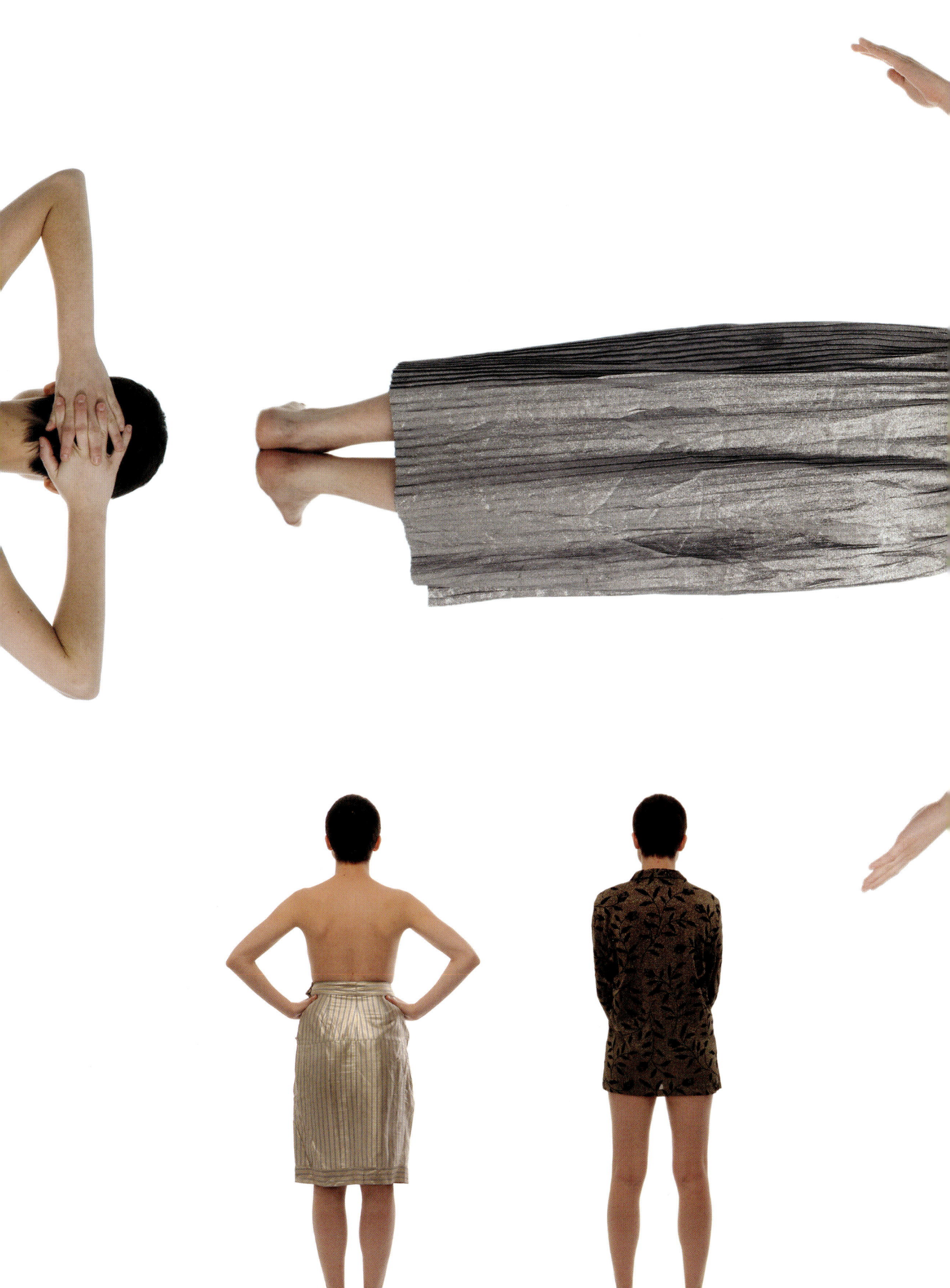

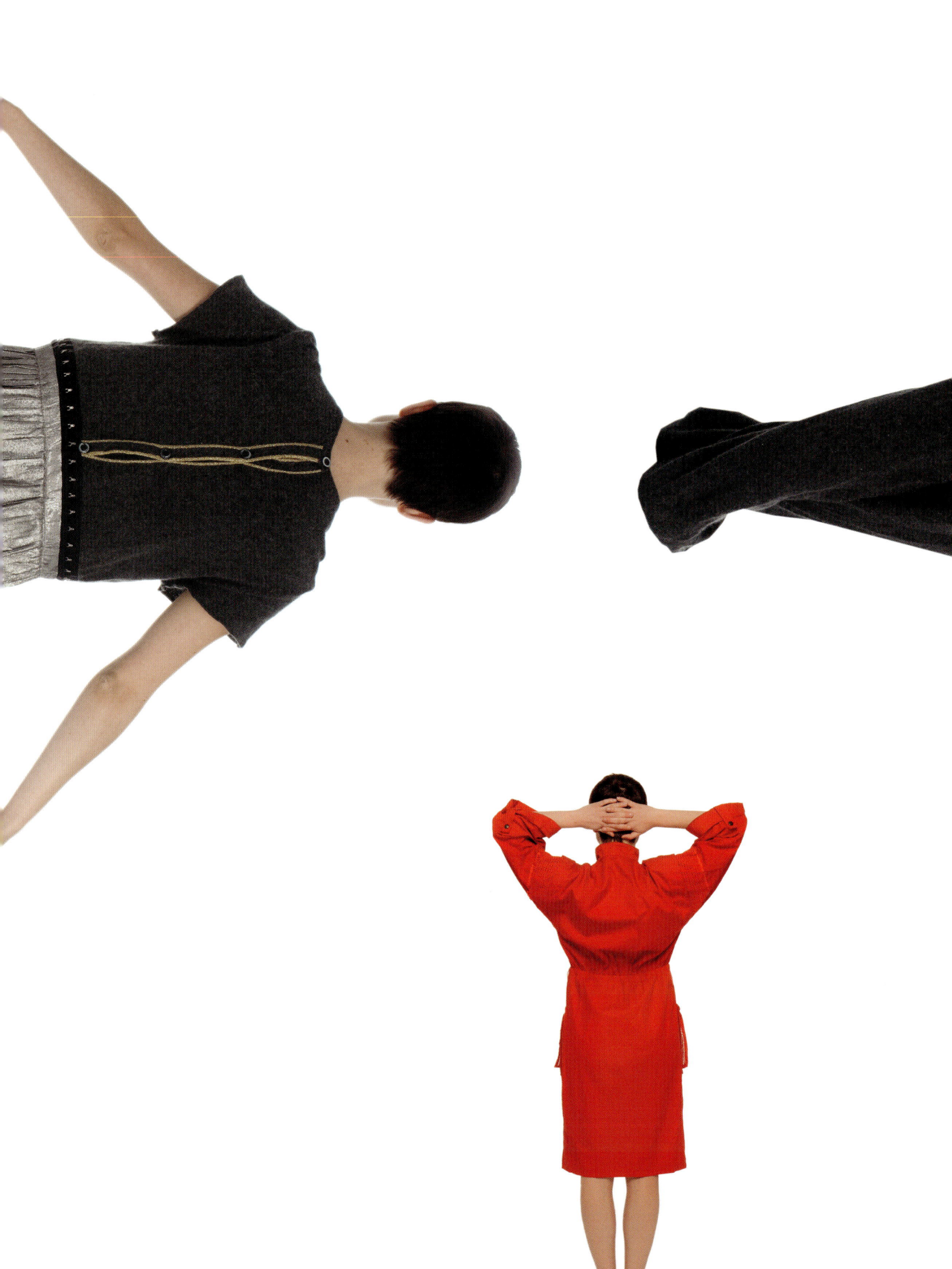

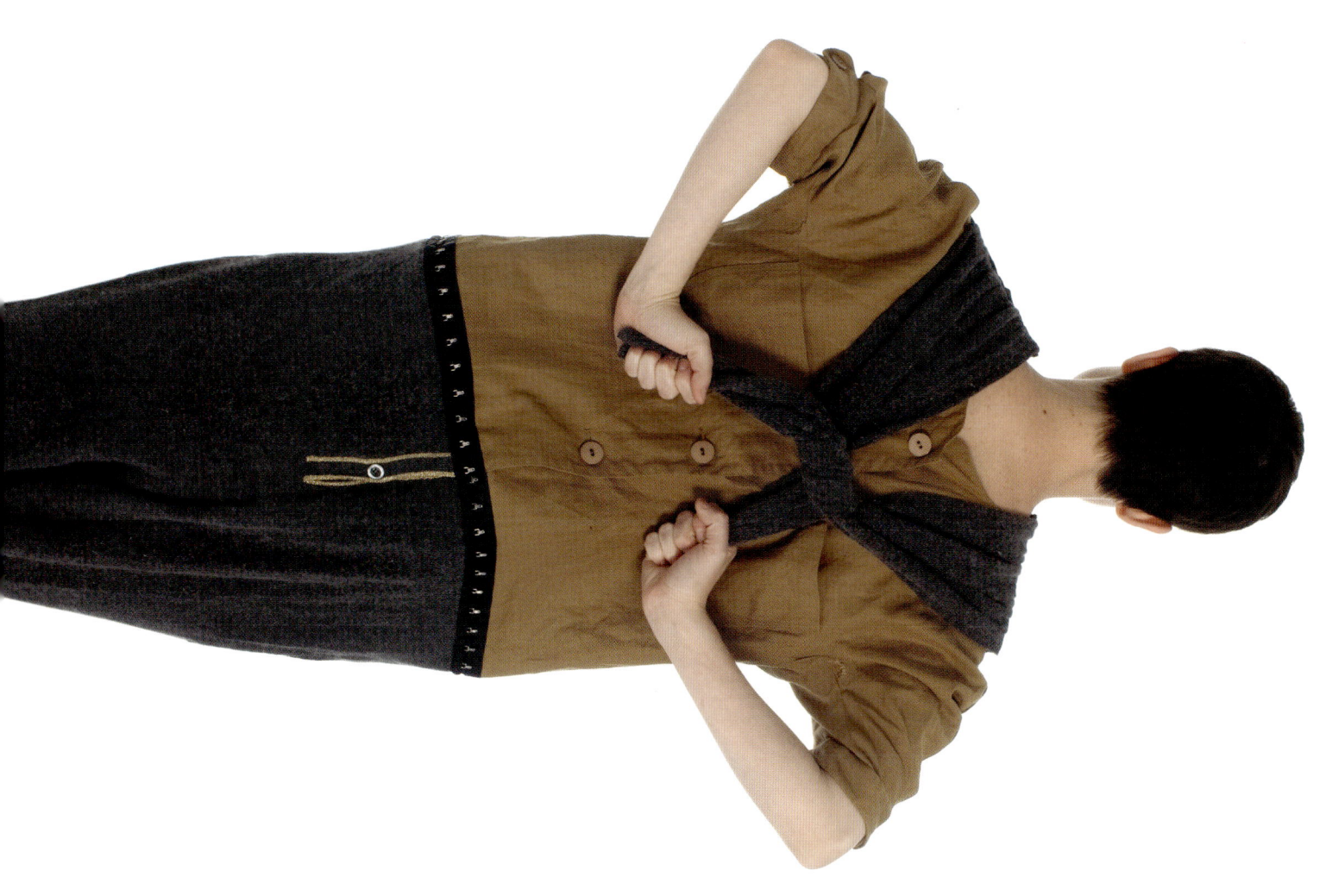

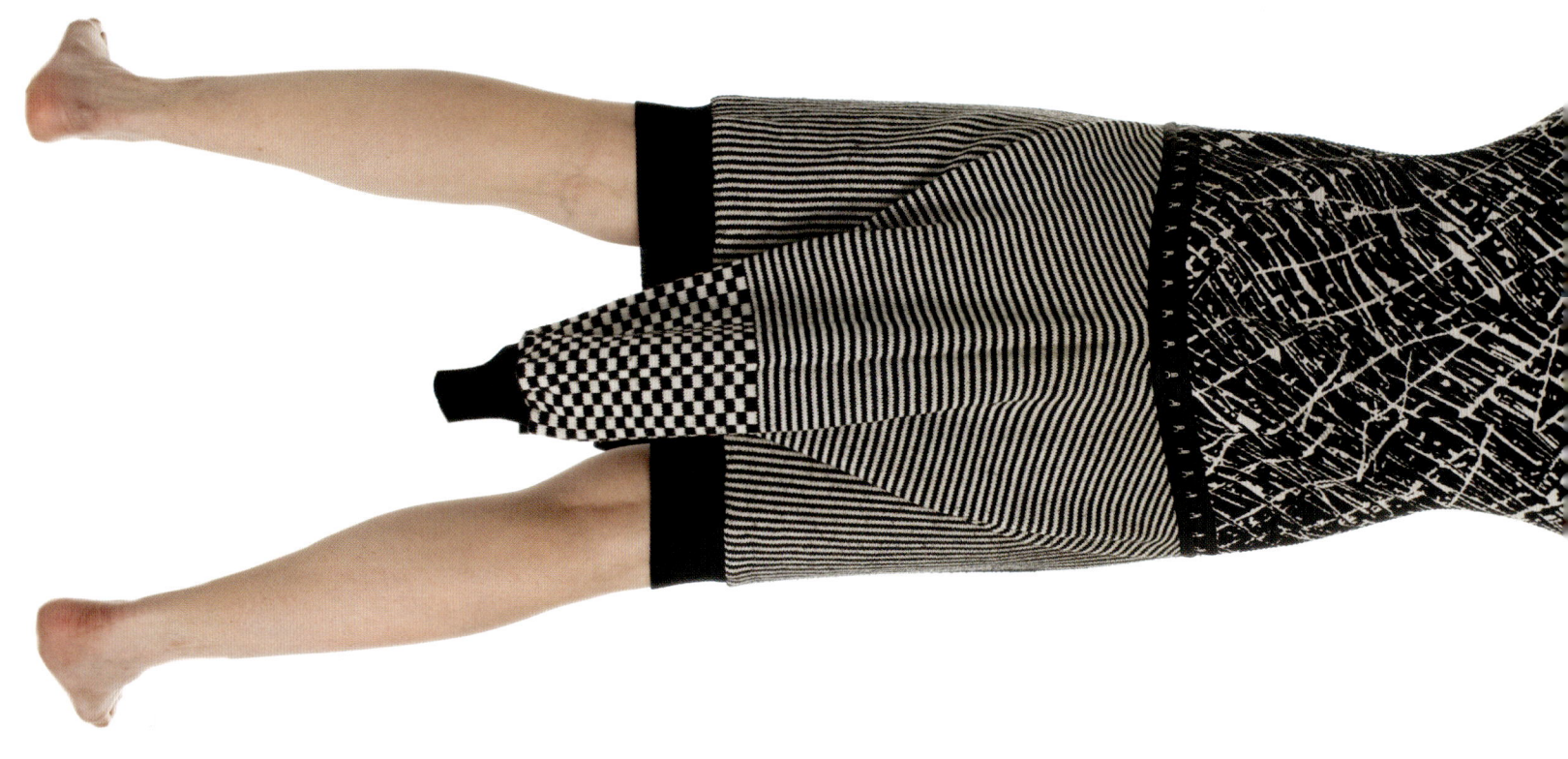

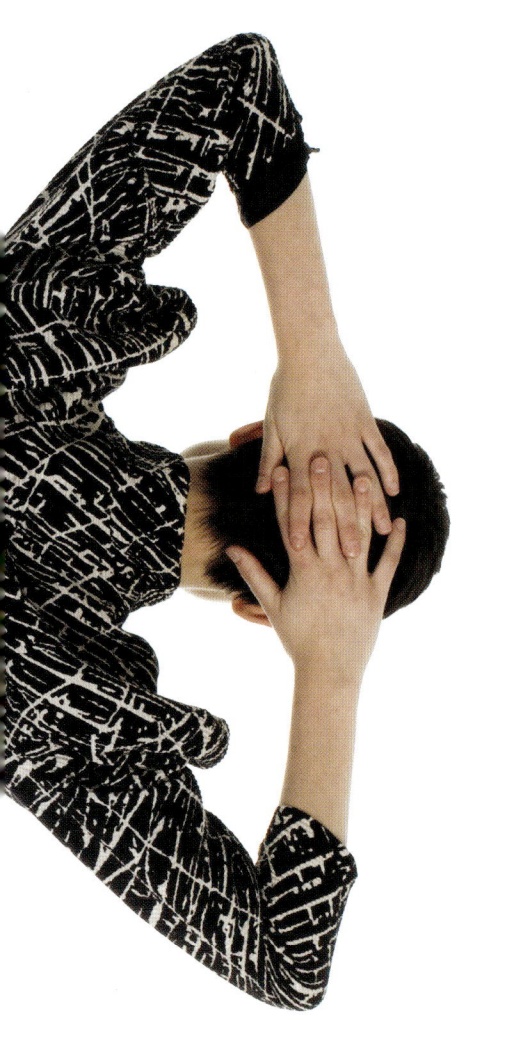
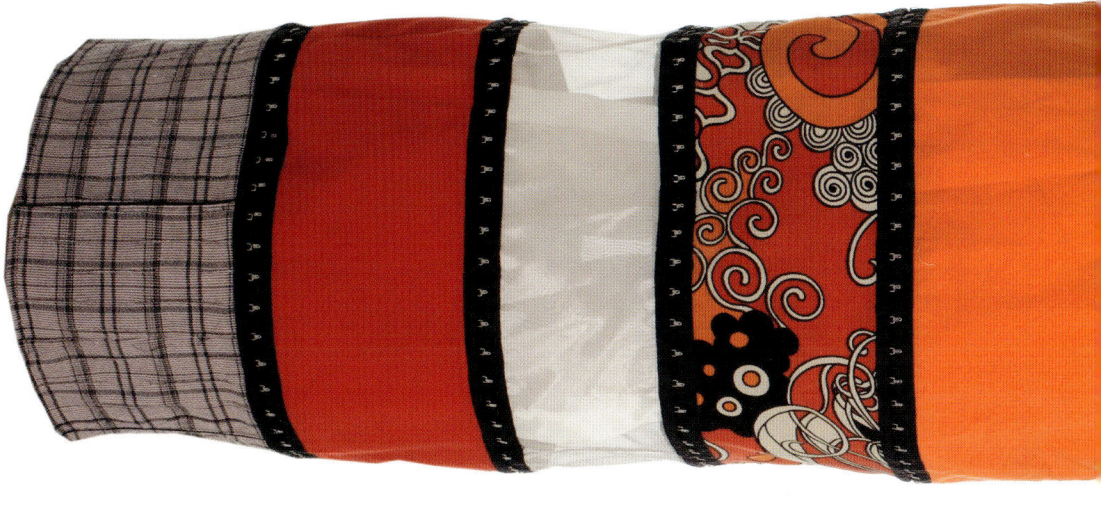
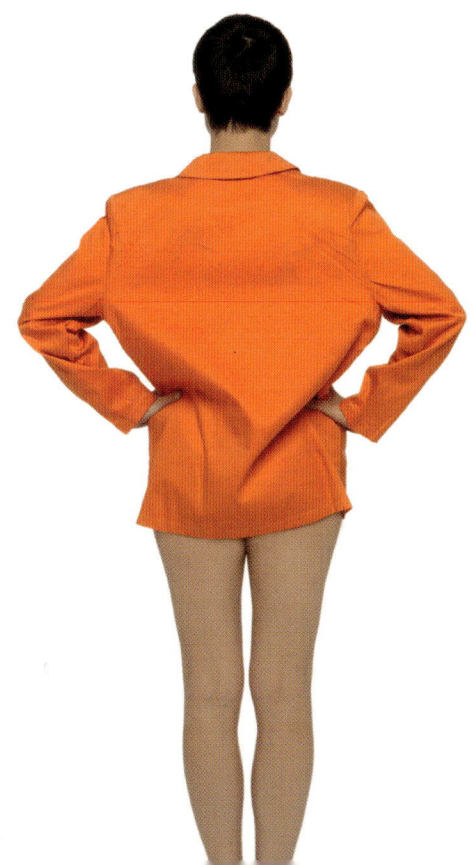

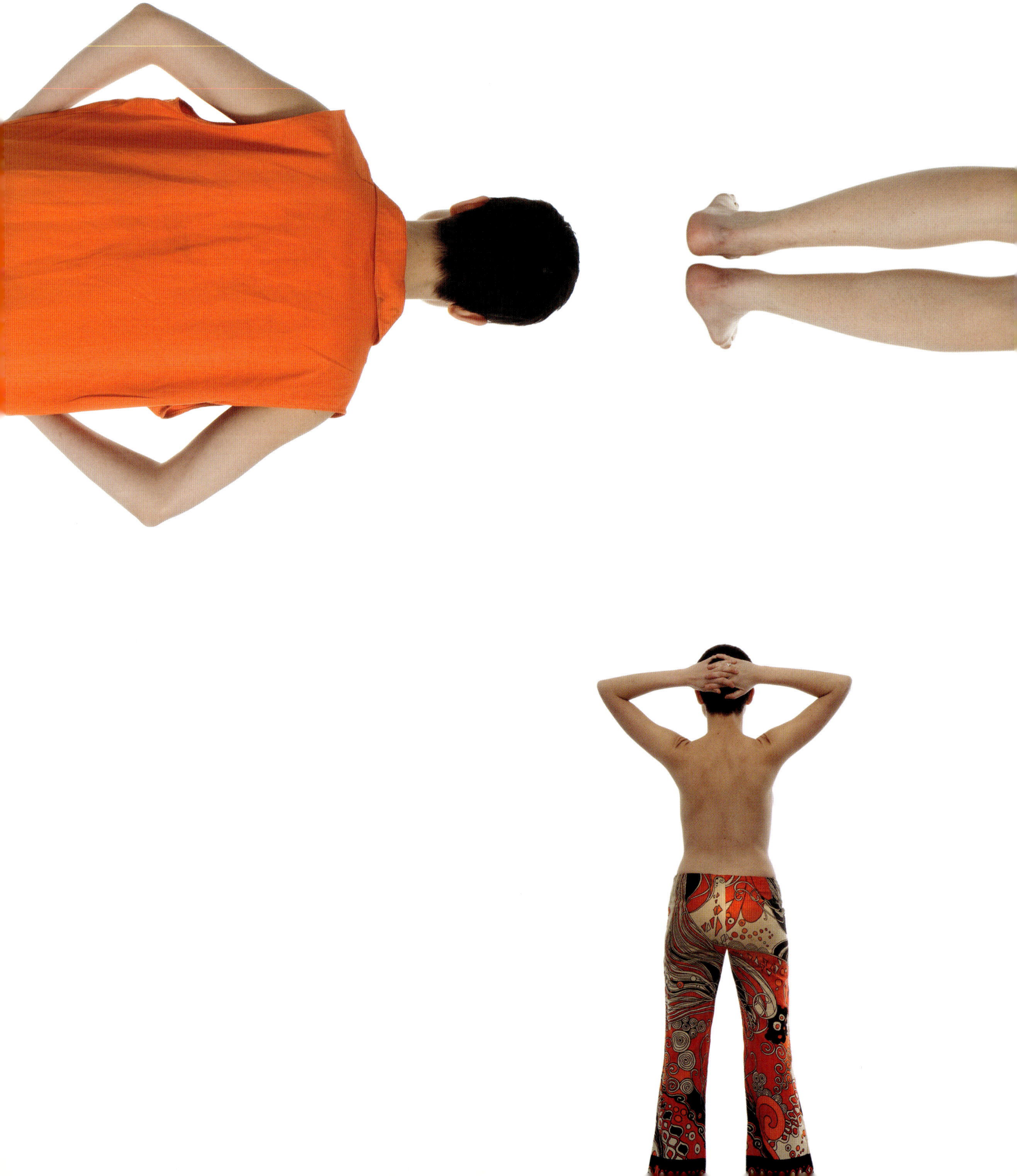

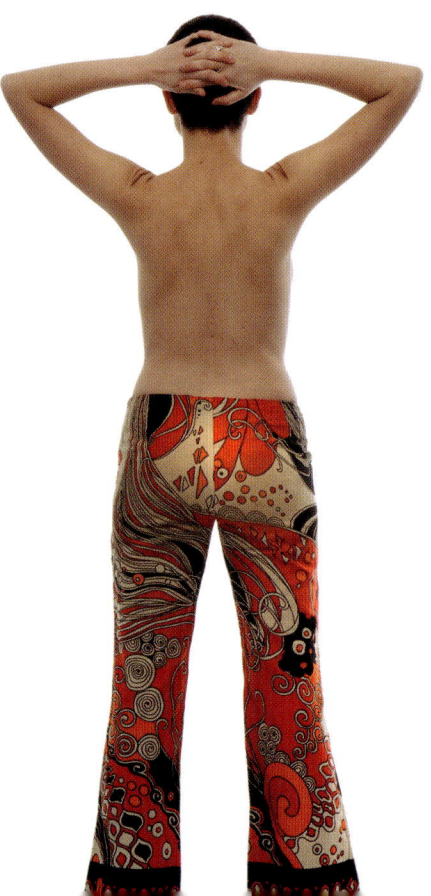

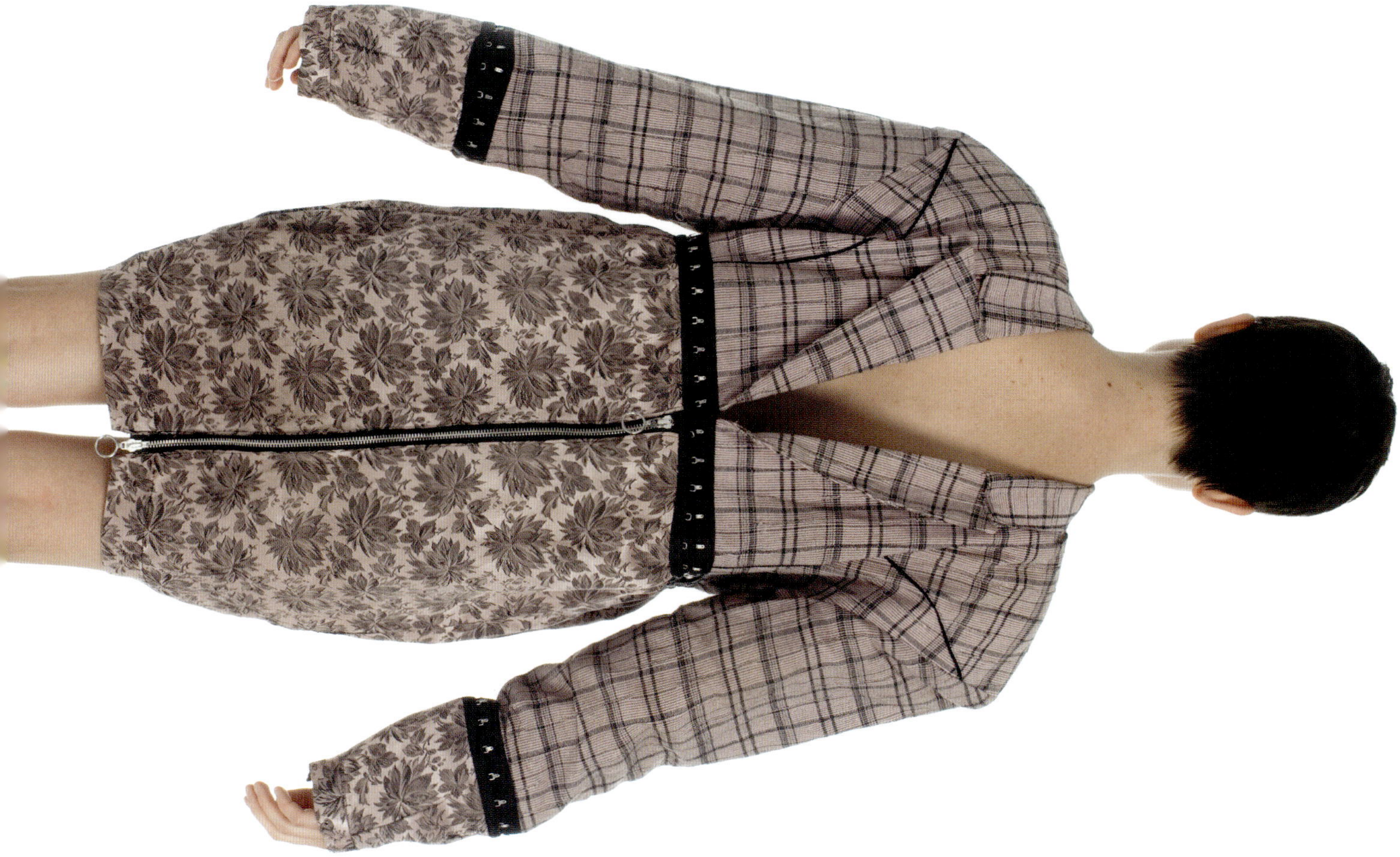

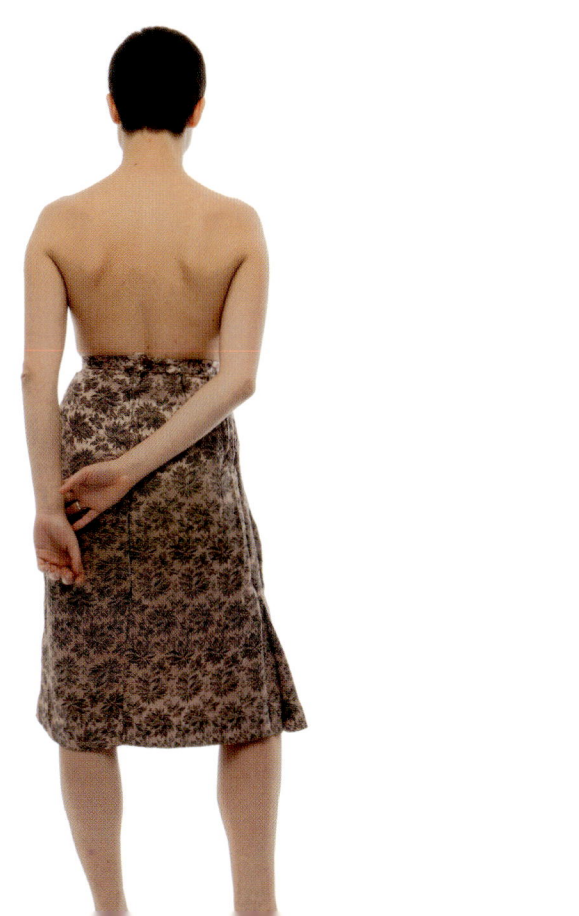

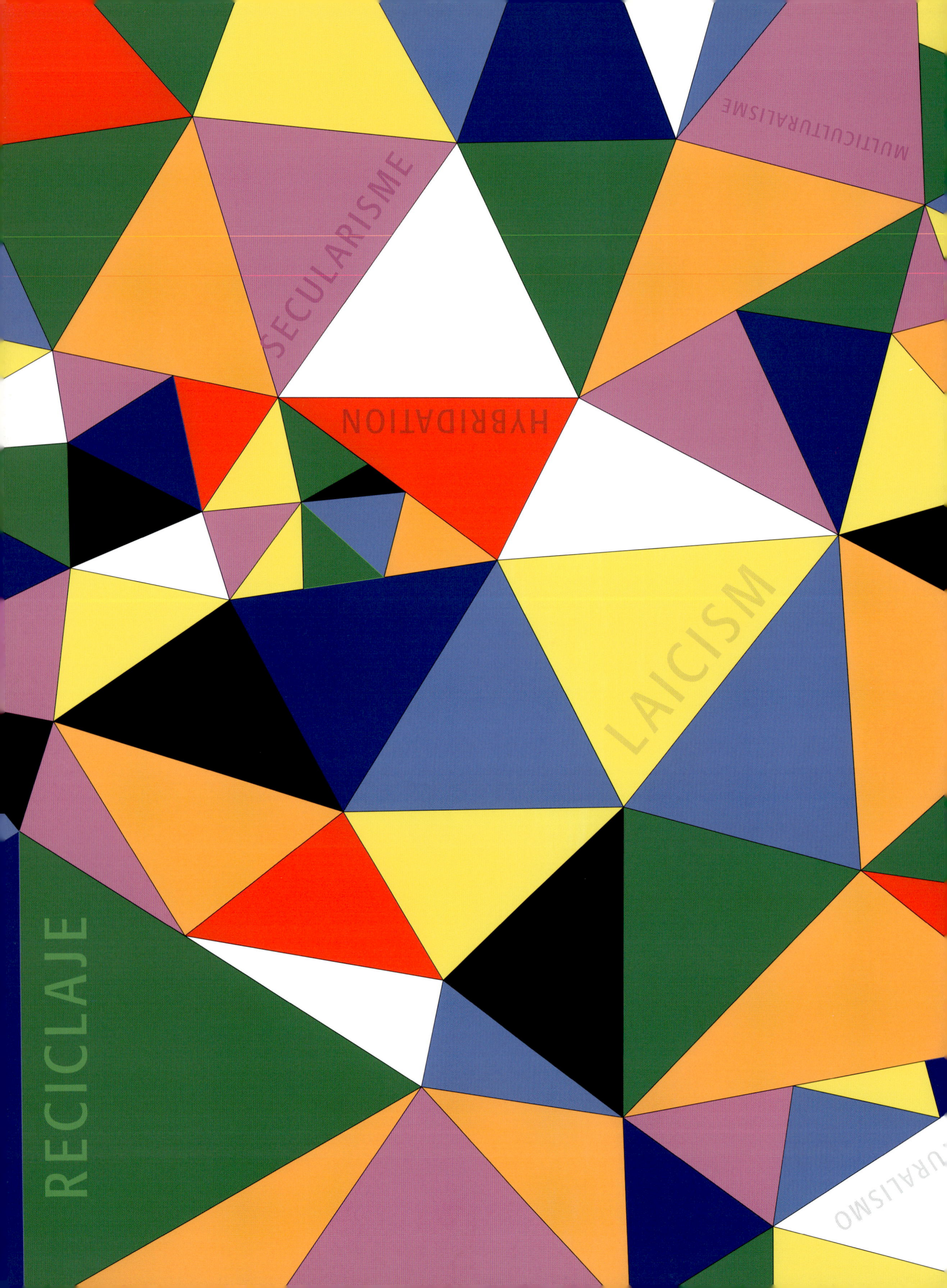

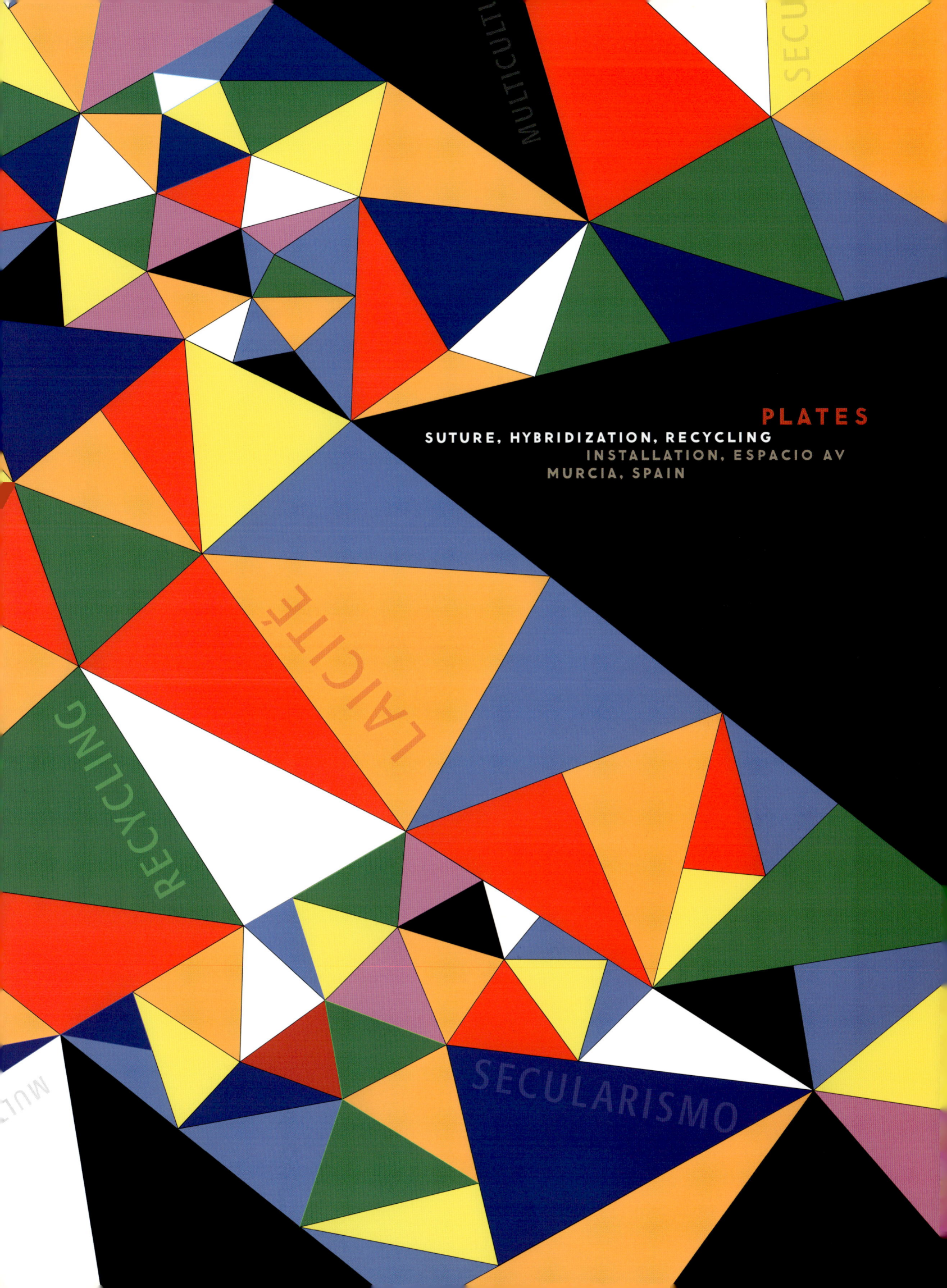

PLATES

SUTURE, HYBRIDIZATION, RECYCLING
INSTALLATION, ESPACIO AV
MURCIA, SPAIN

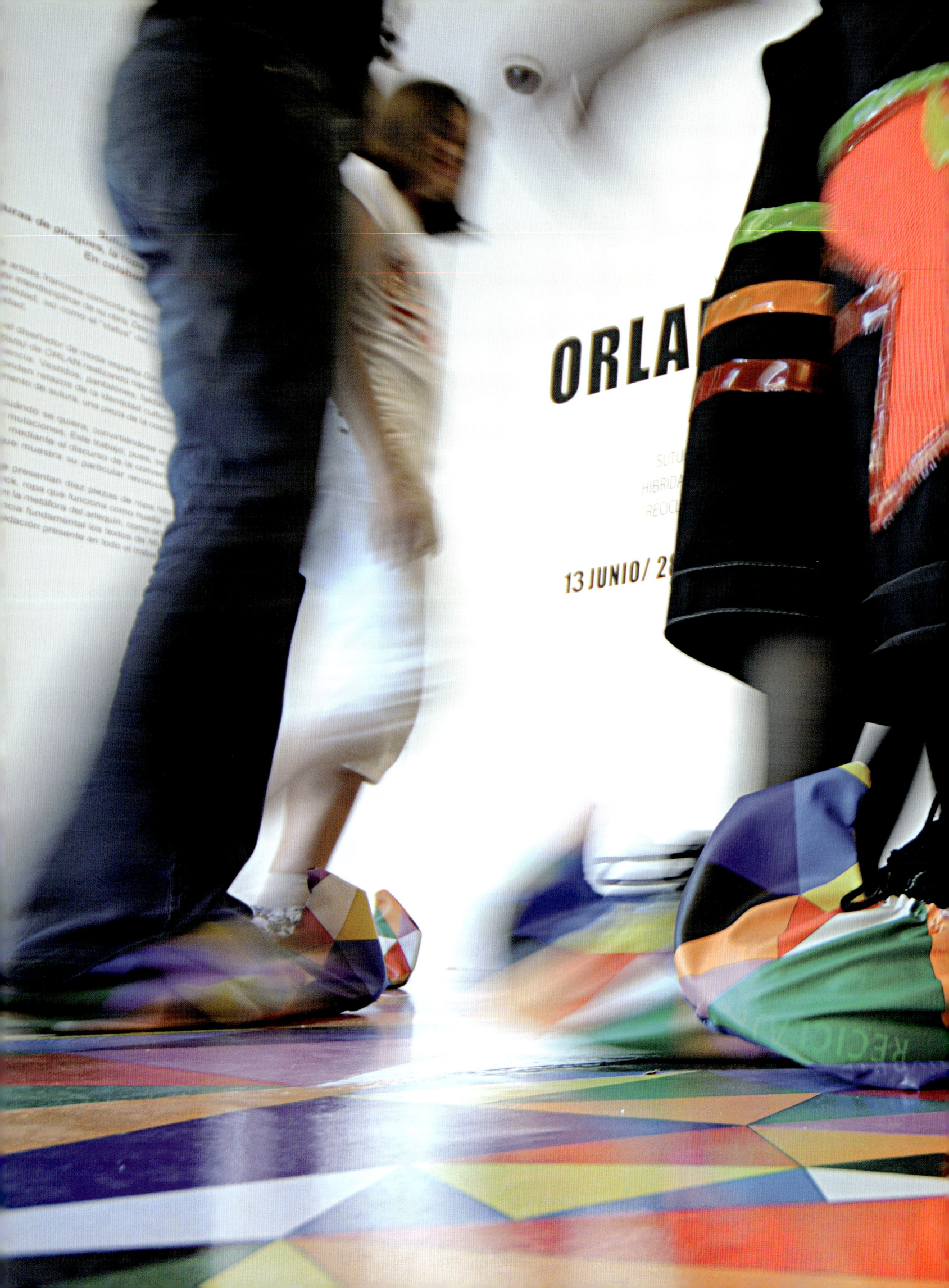

ORLA

SUTU
HIBRIDA
RECIC

13 JUNIO/ 2

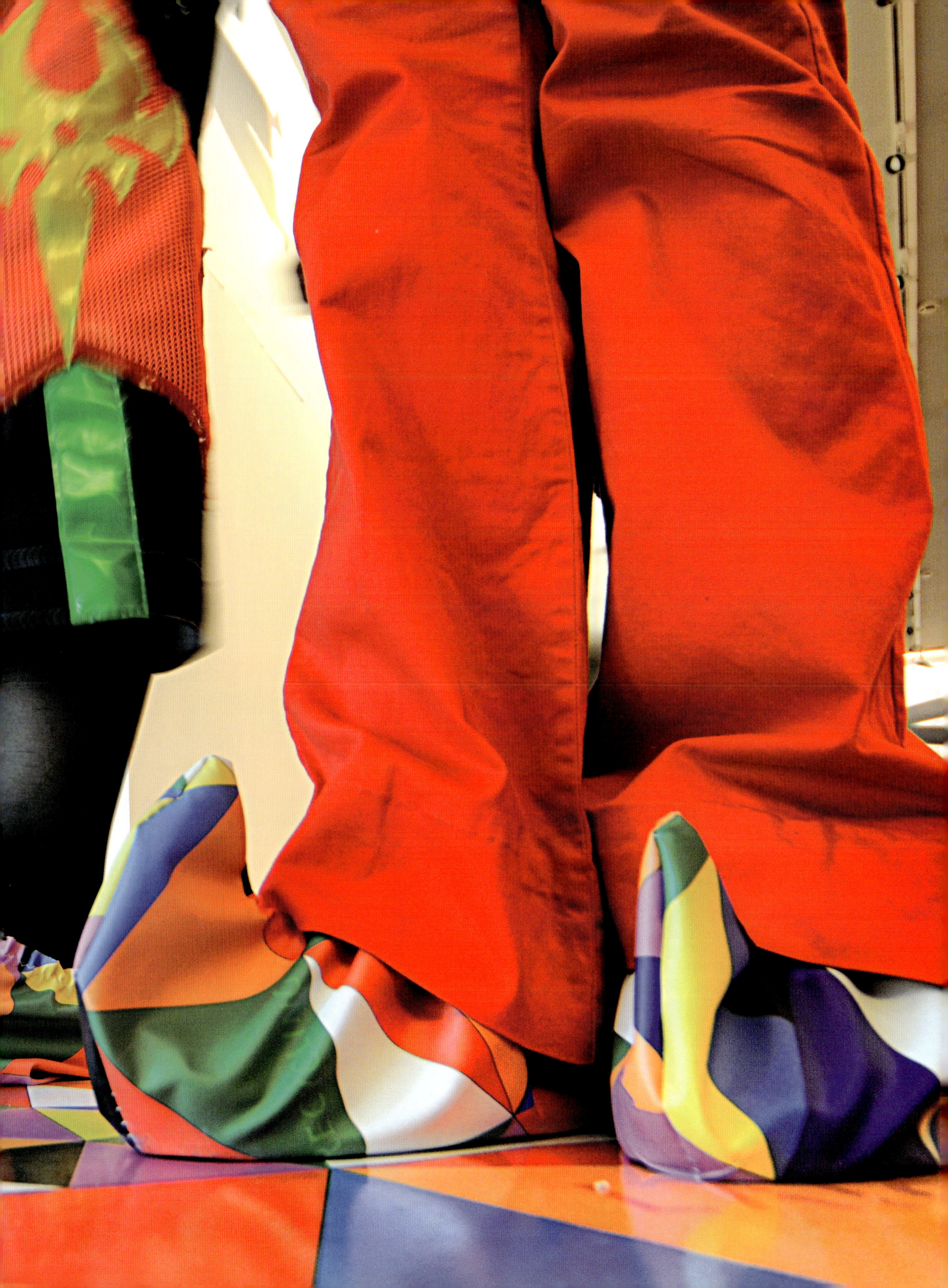

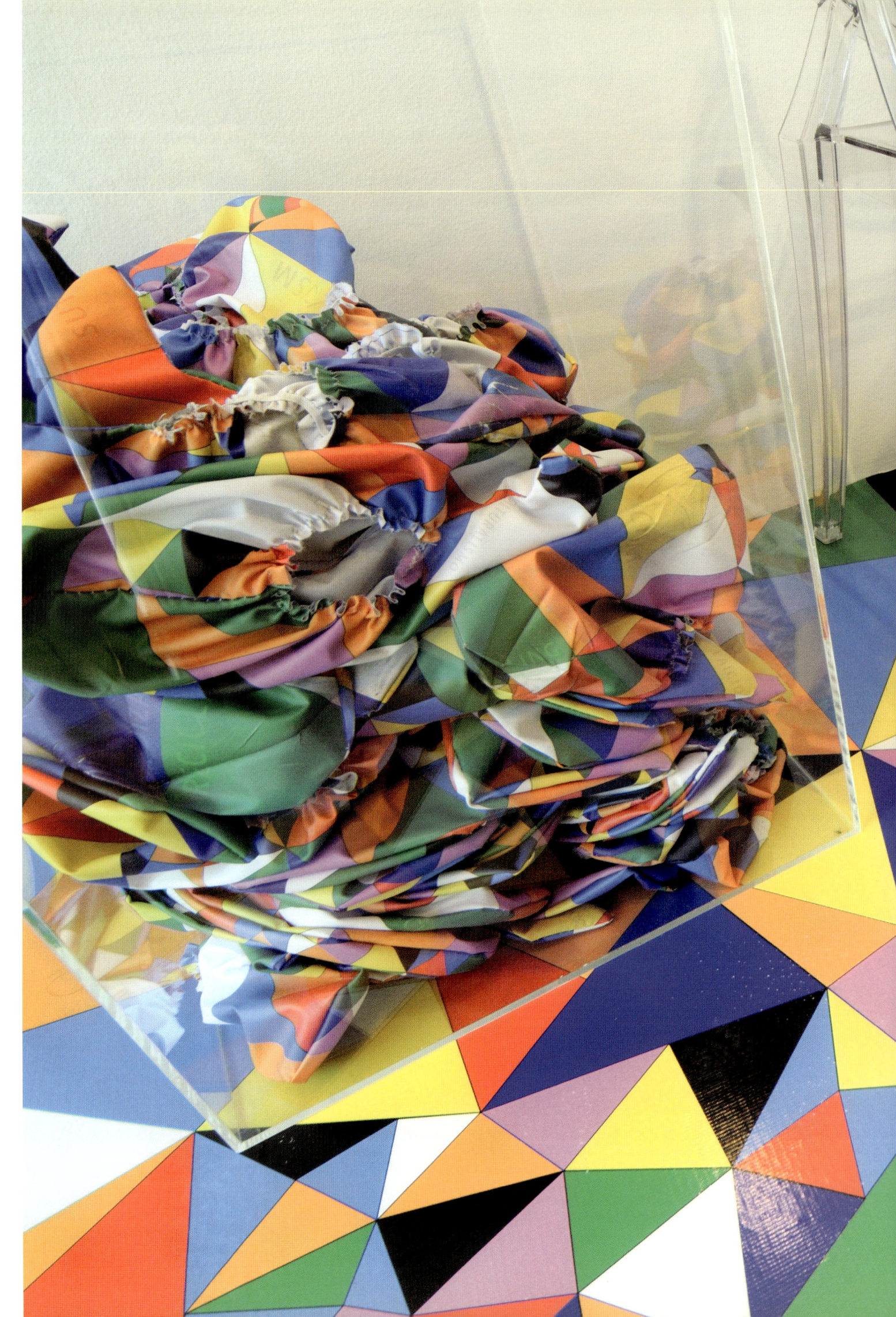

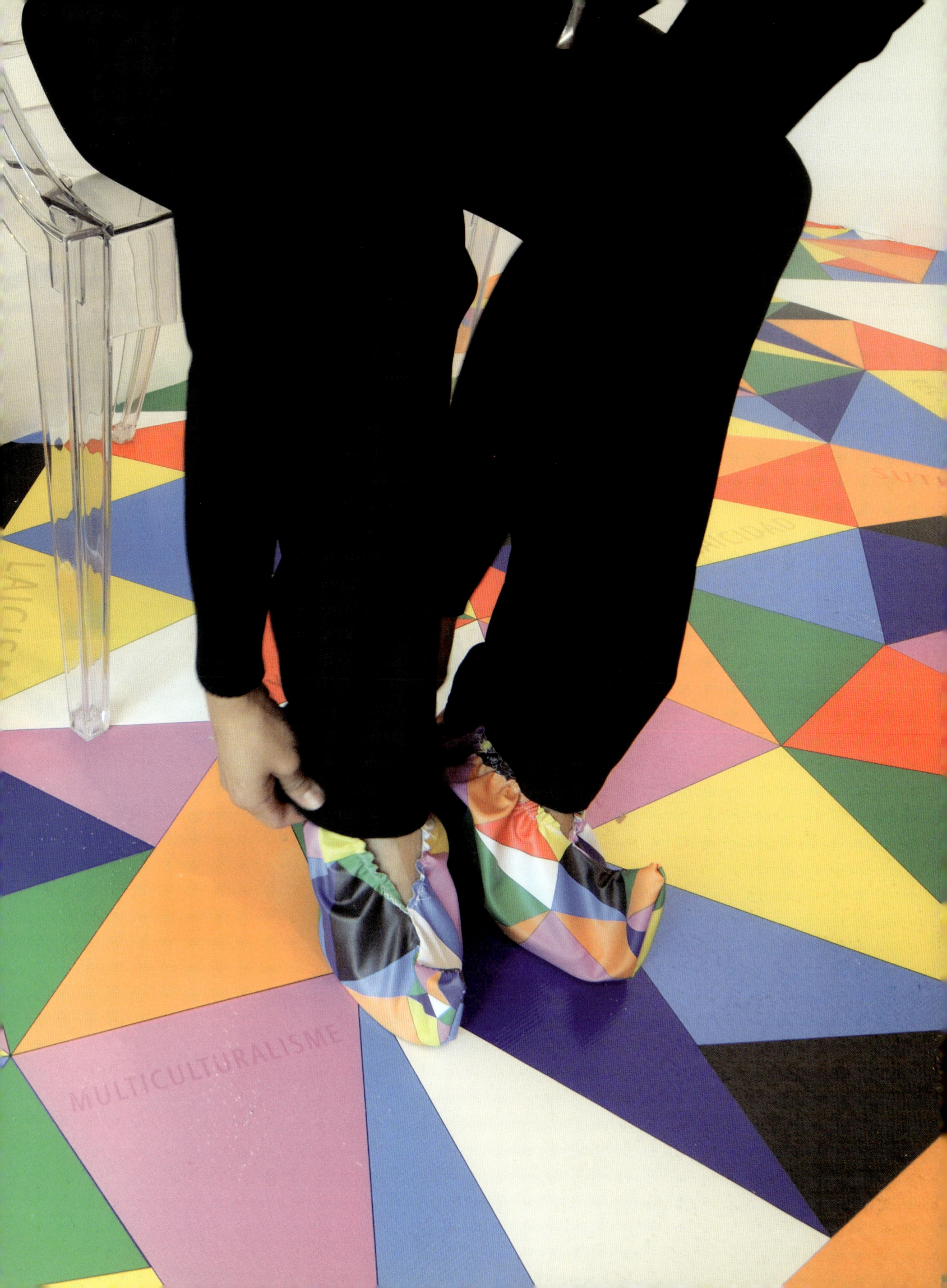

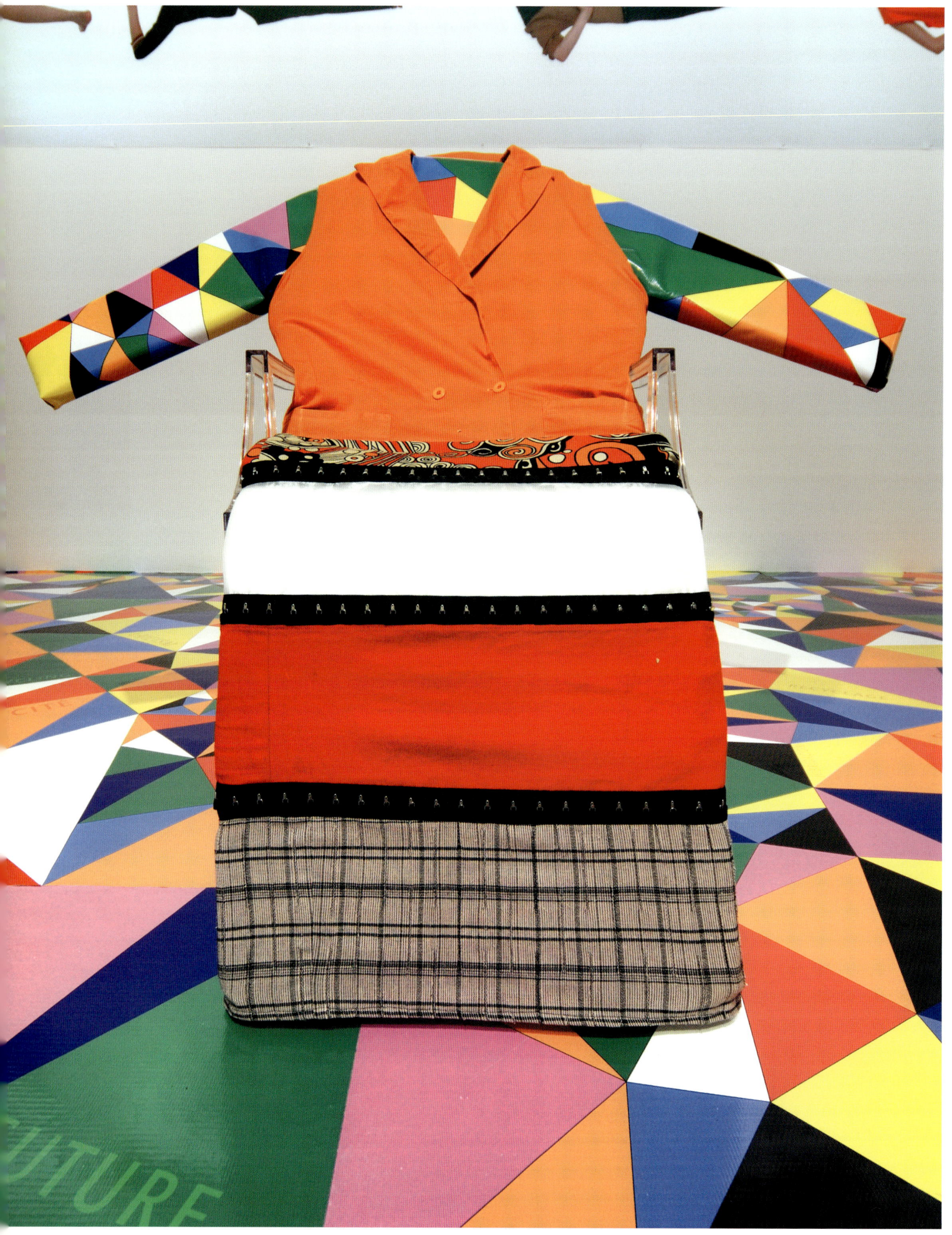

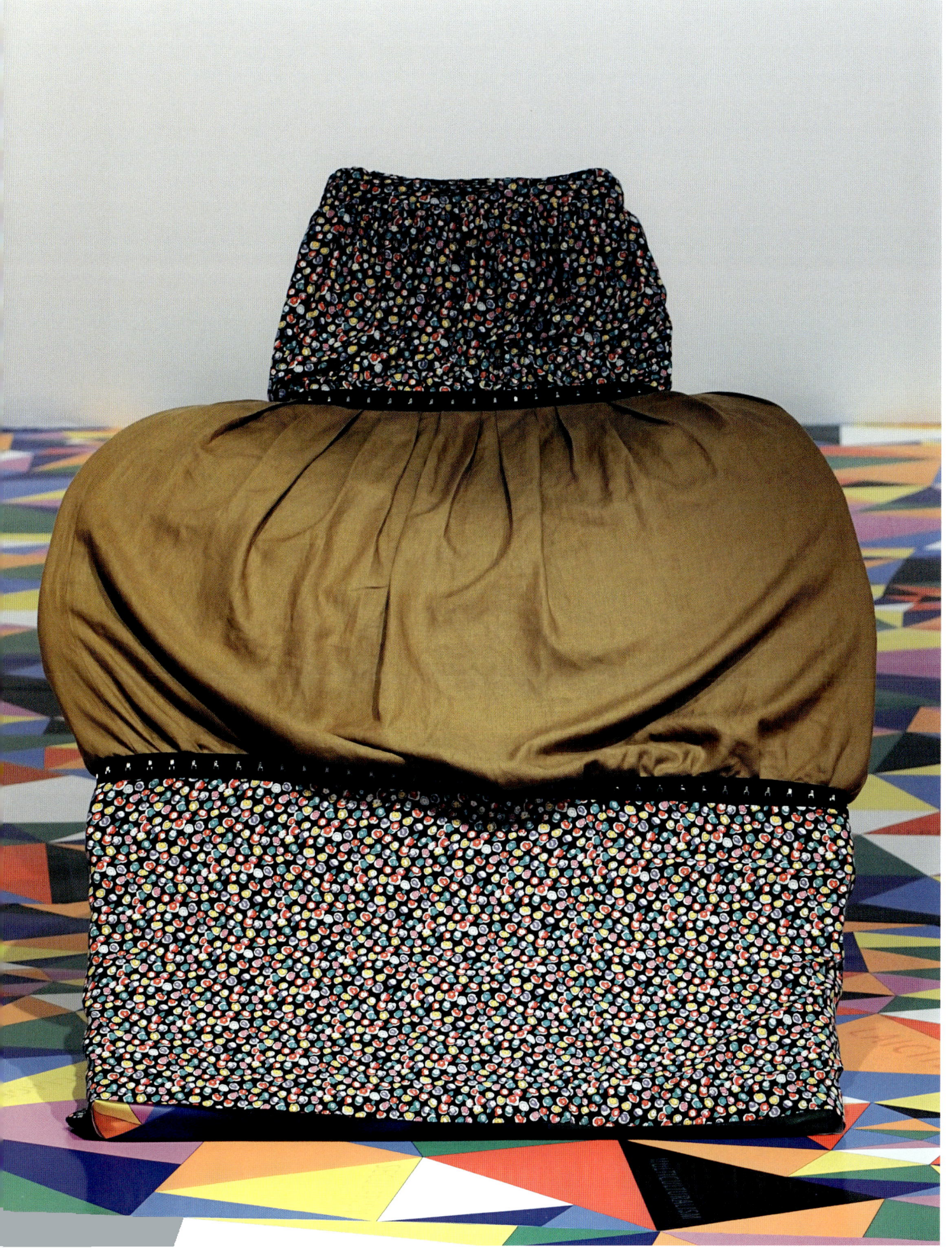

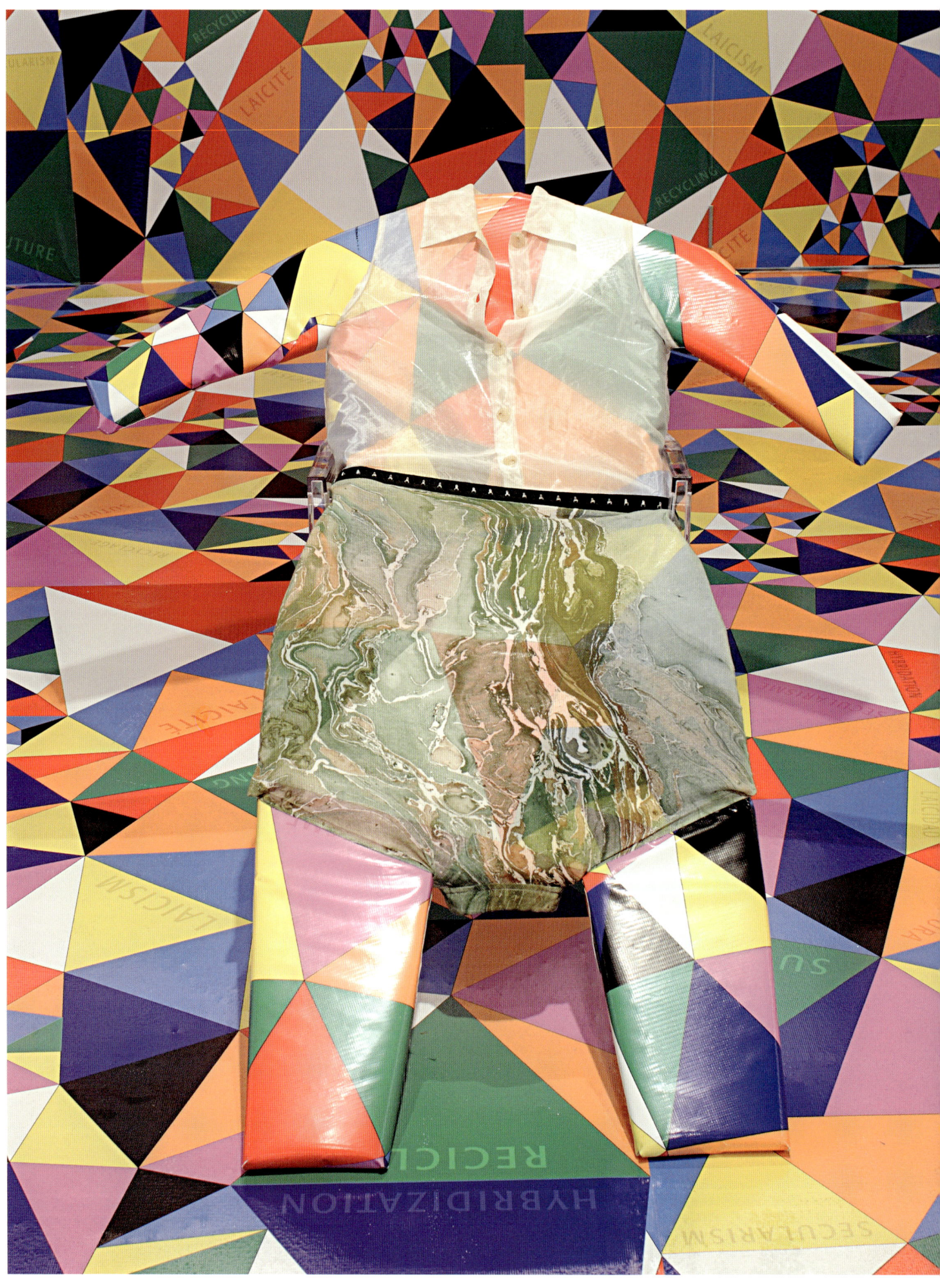

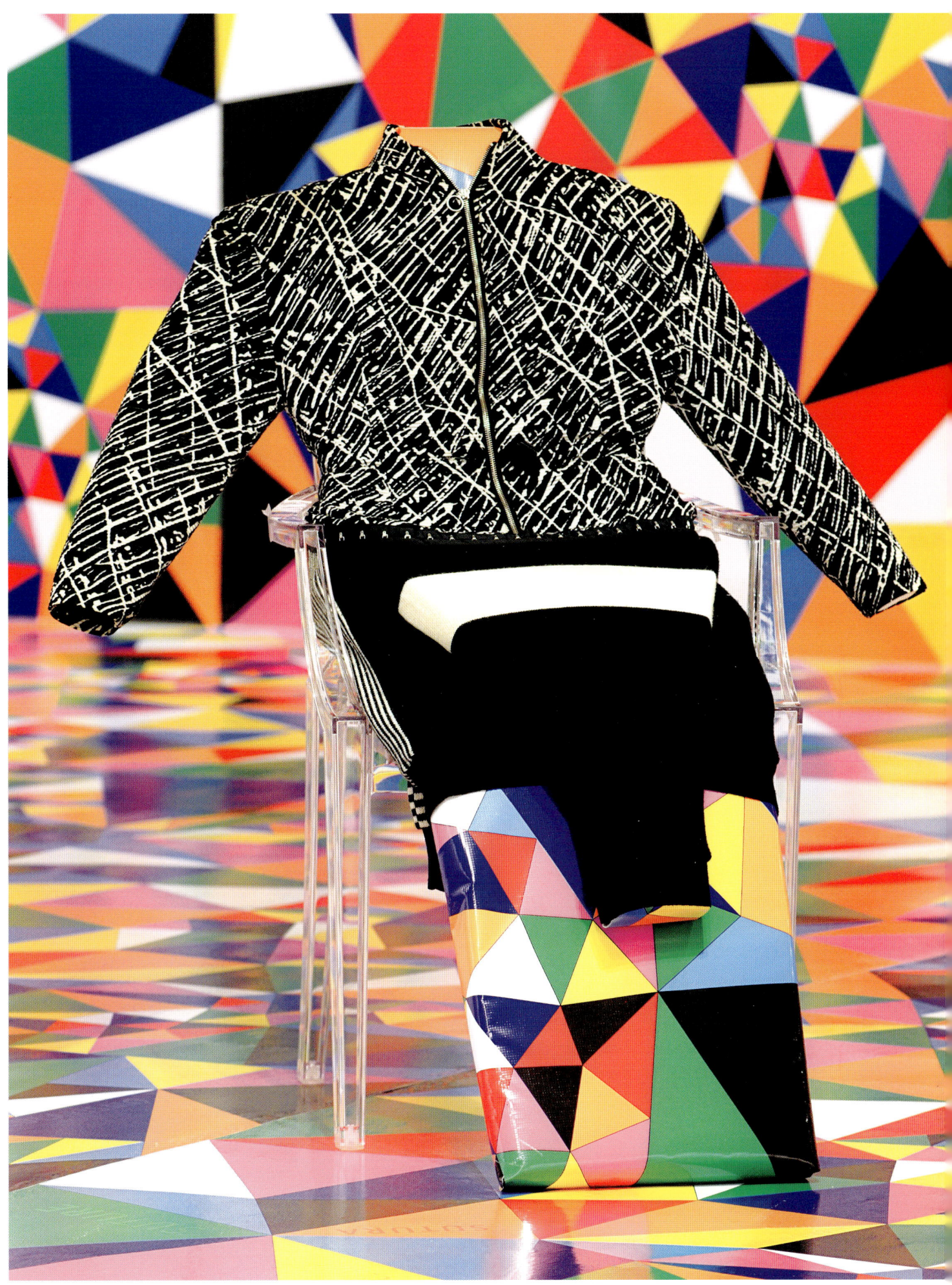

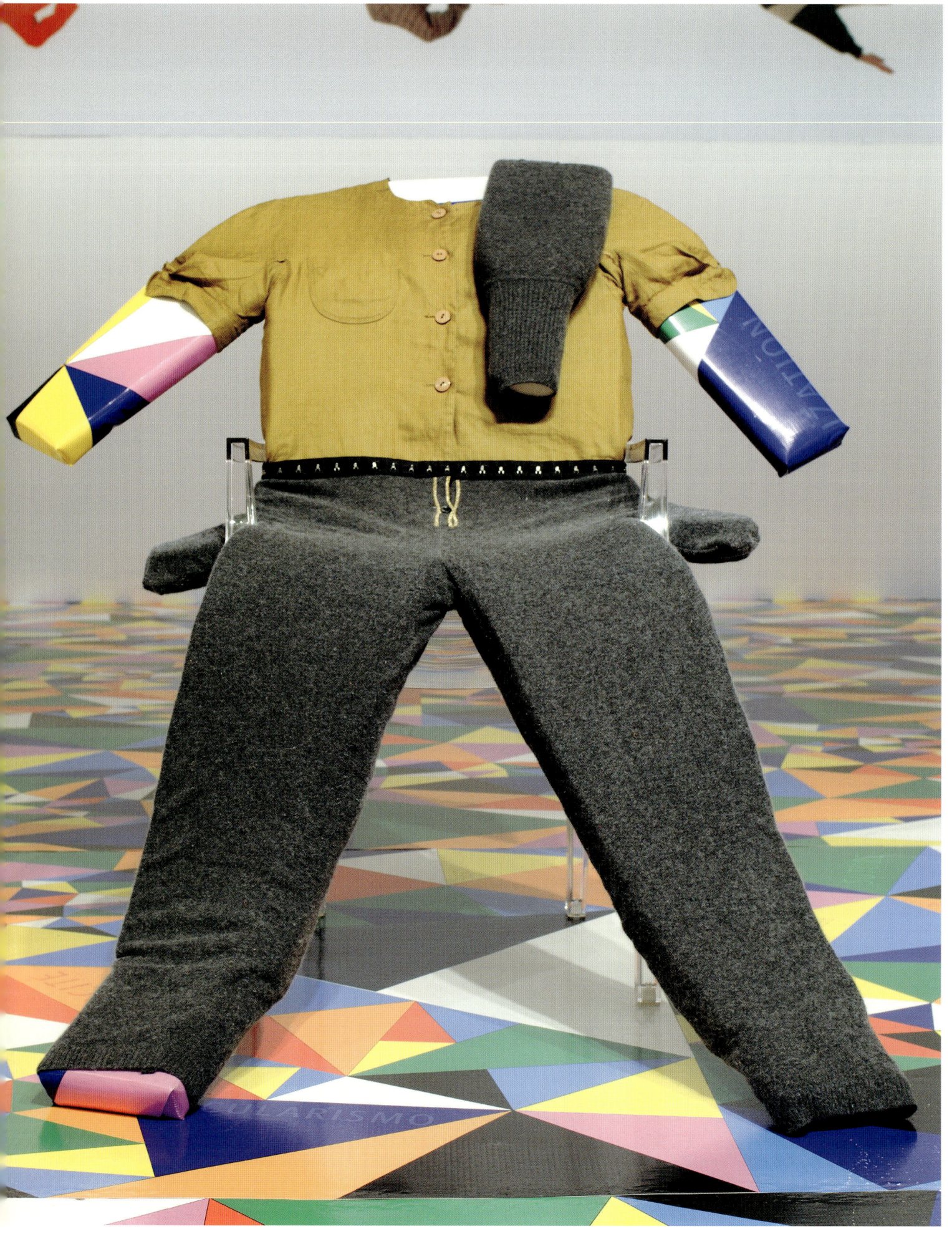

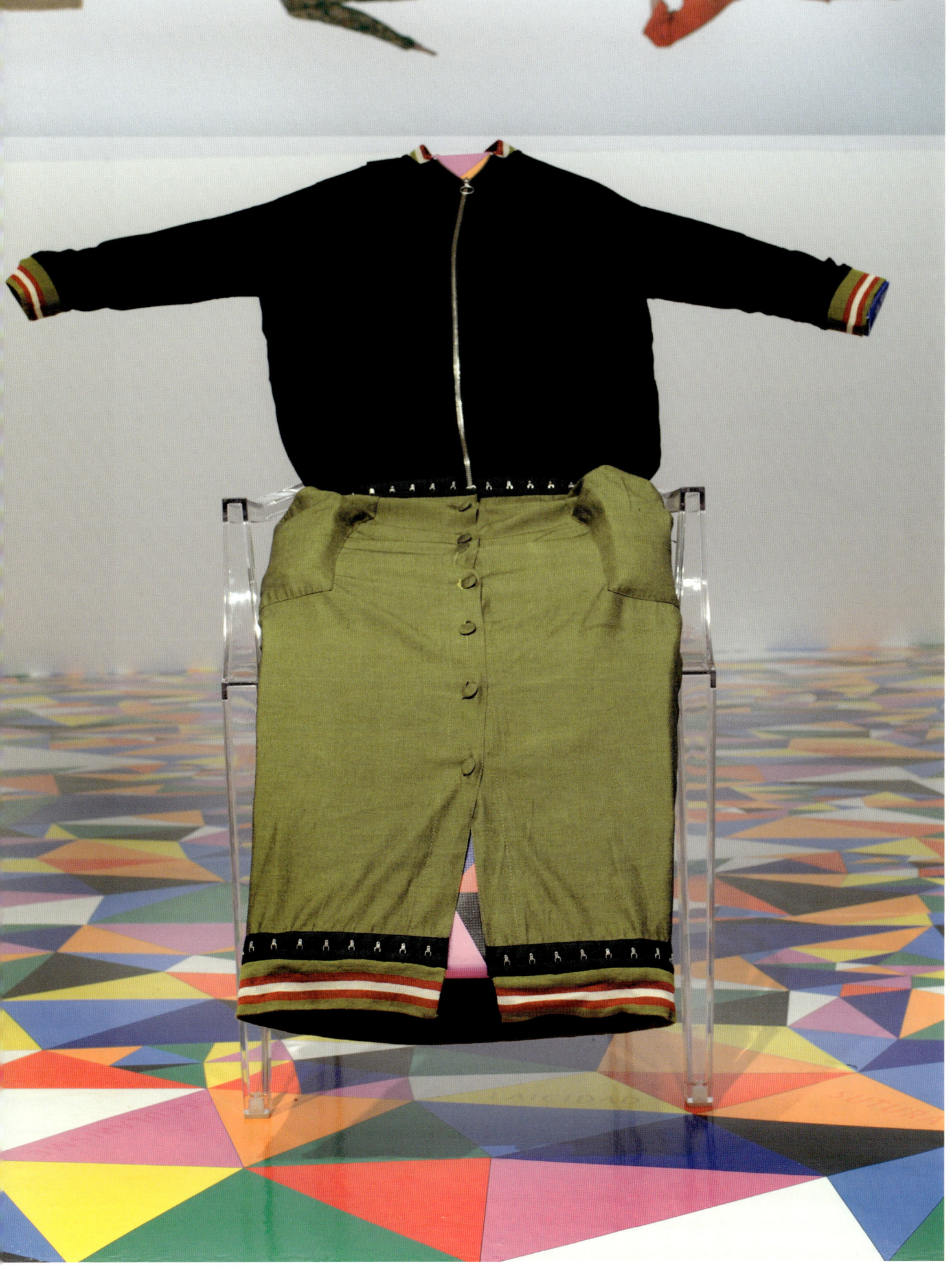

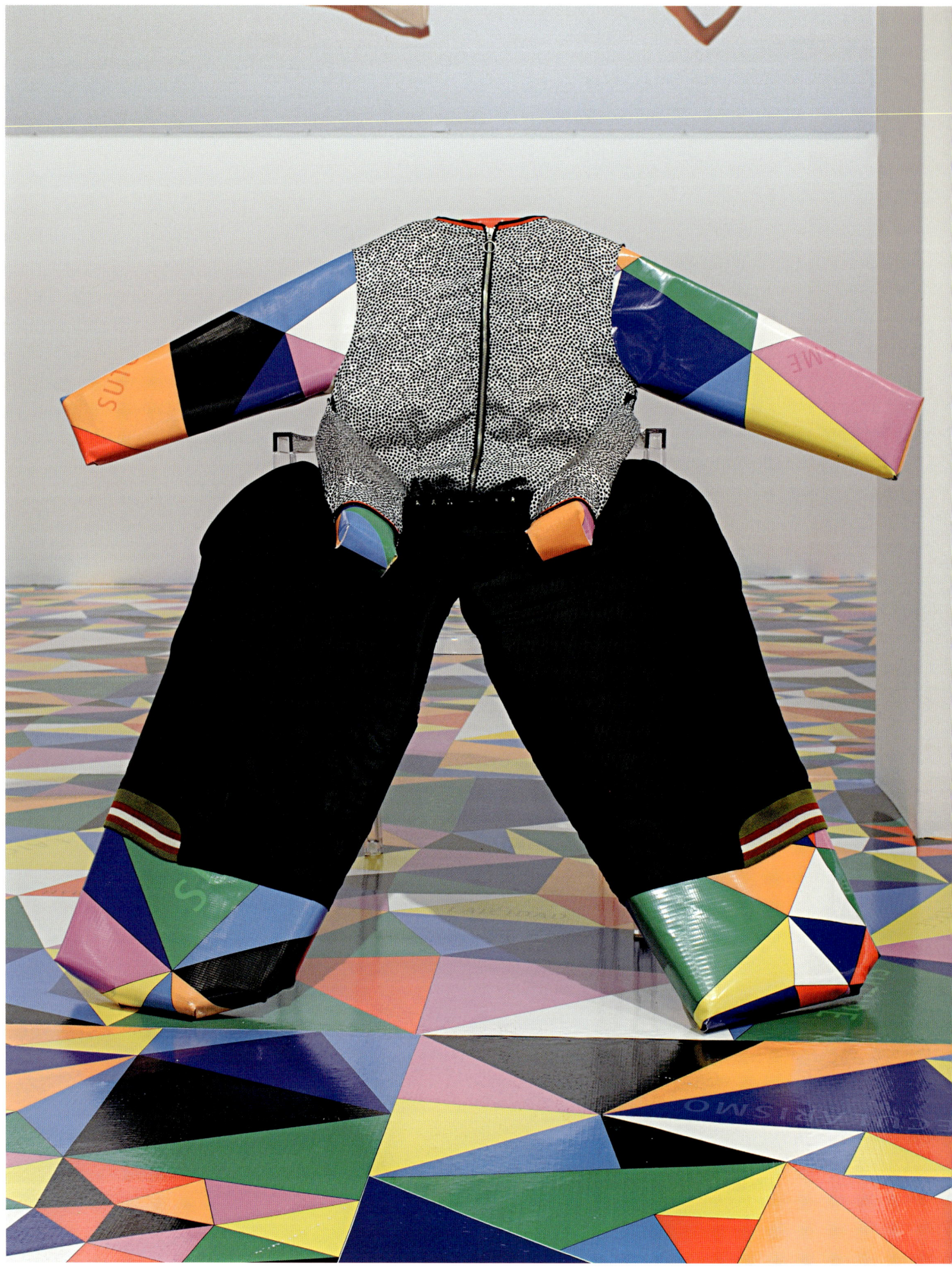

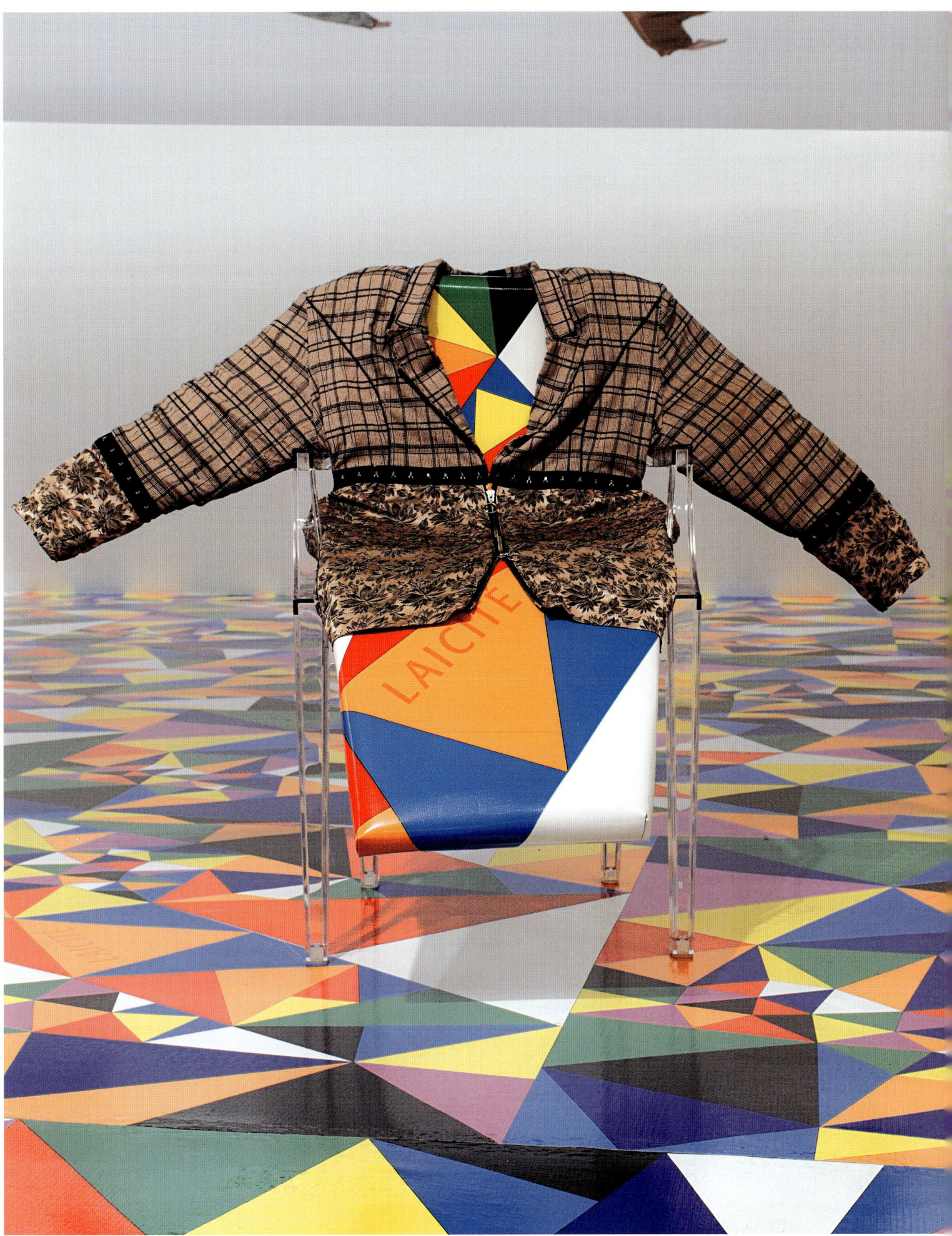

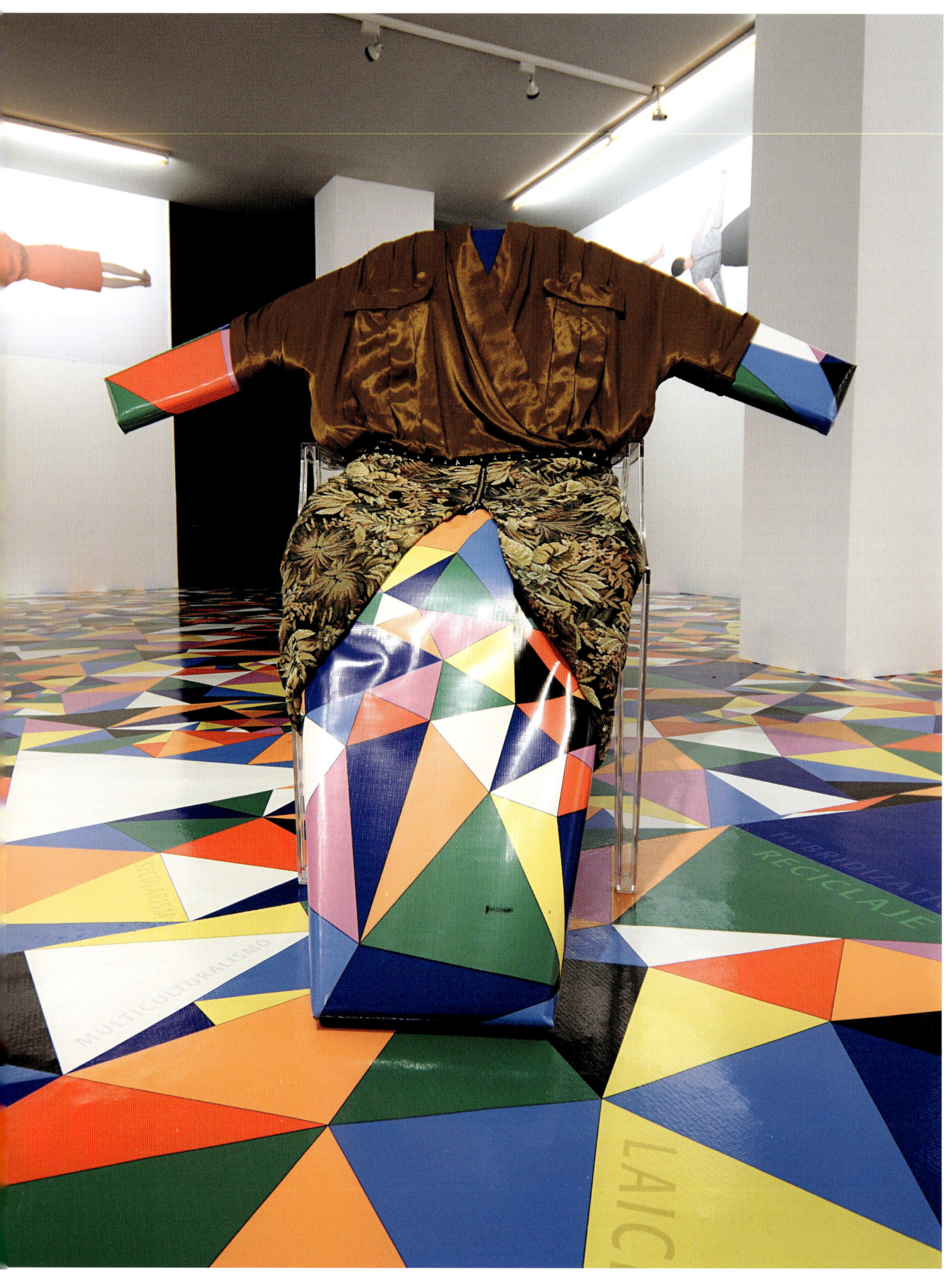

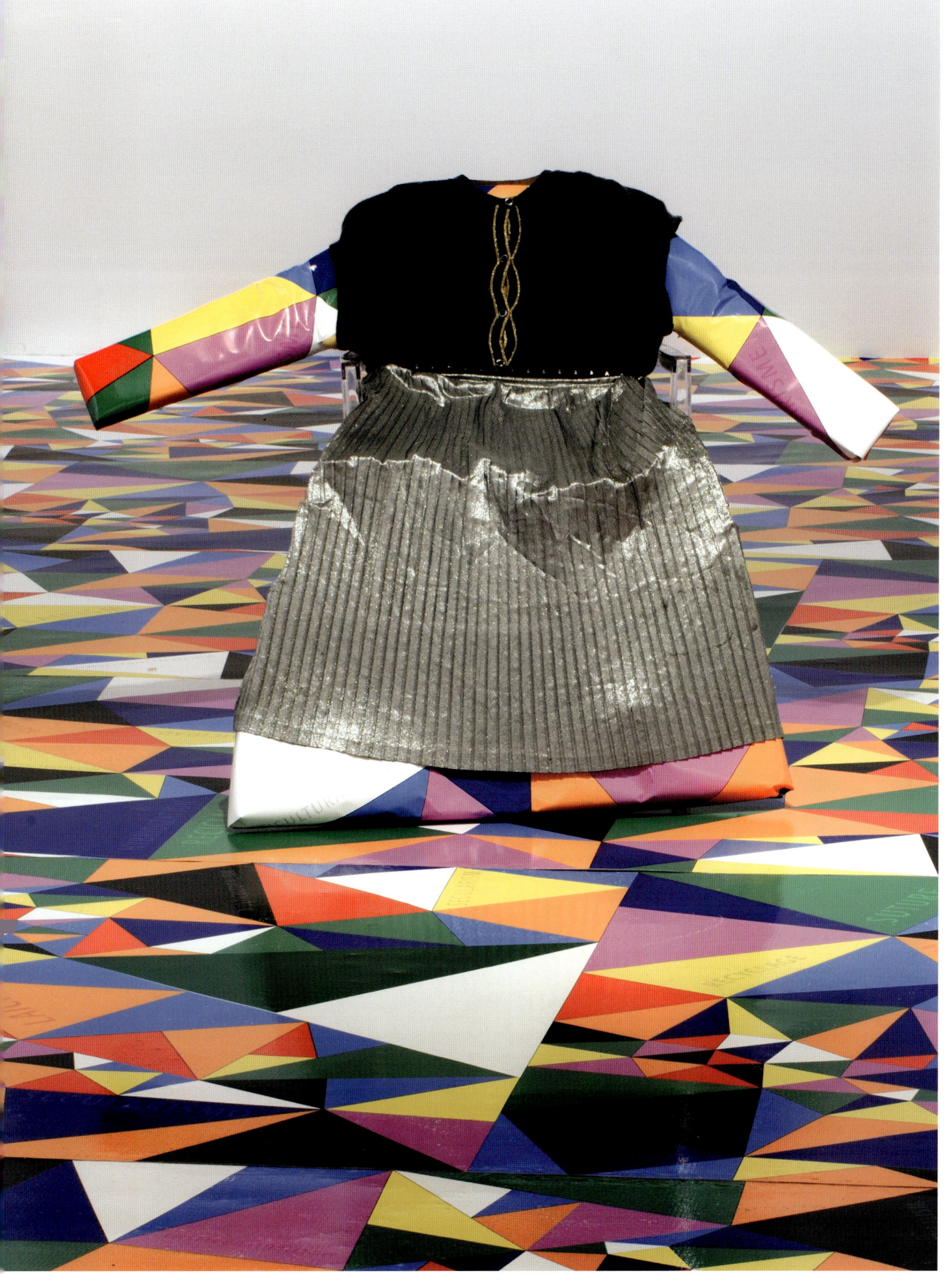

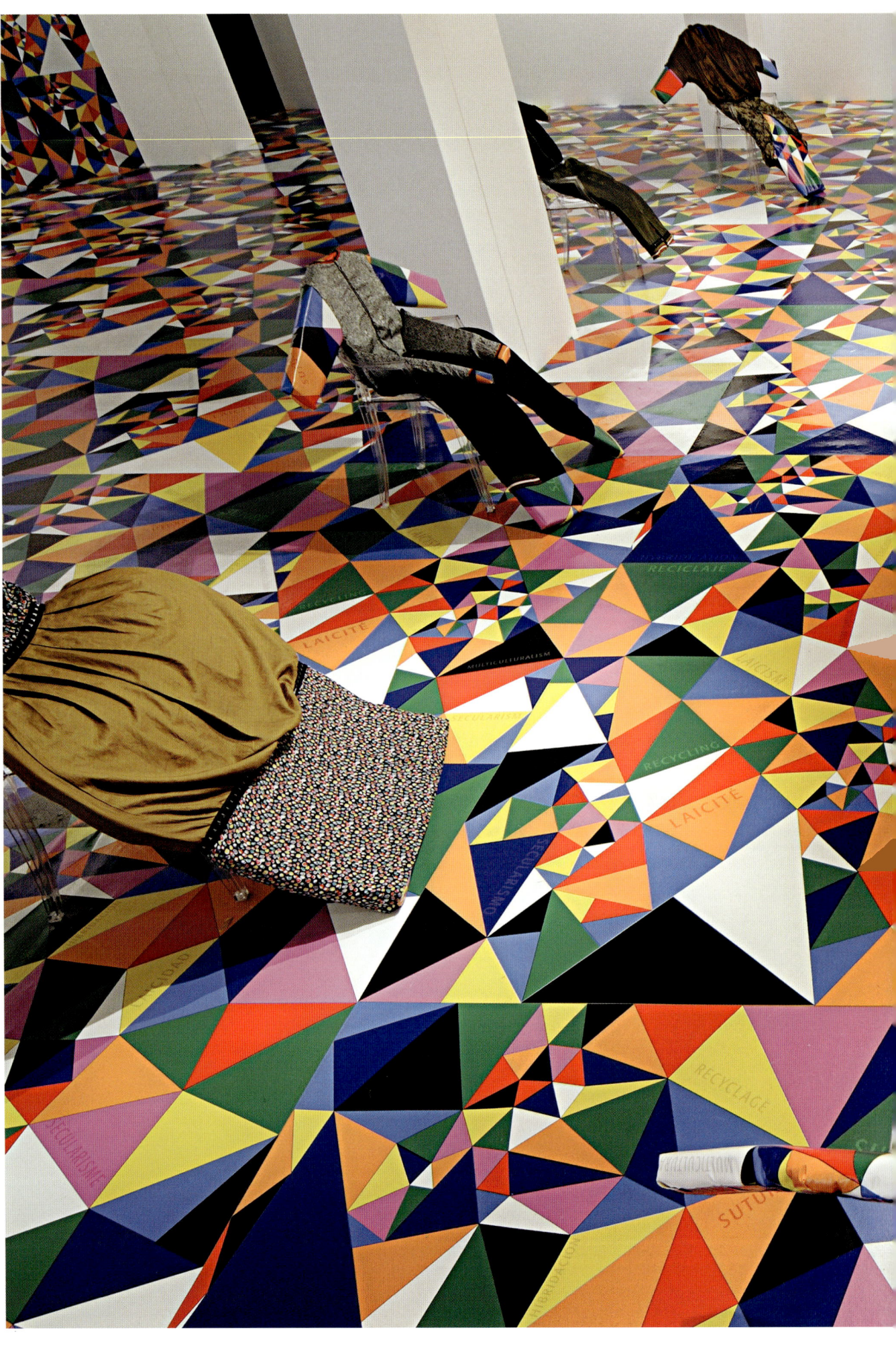

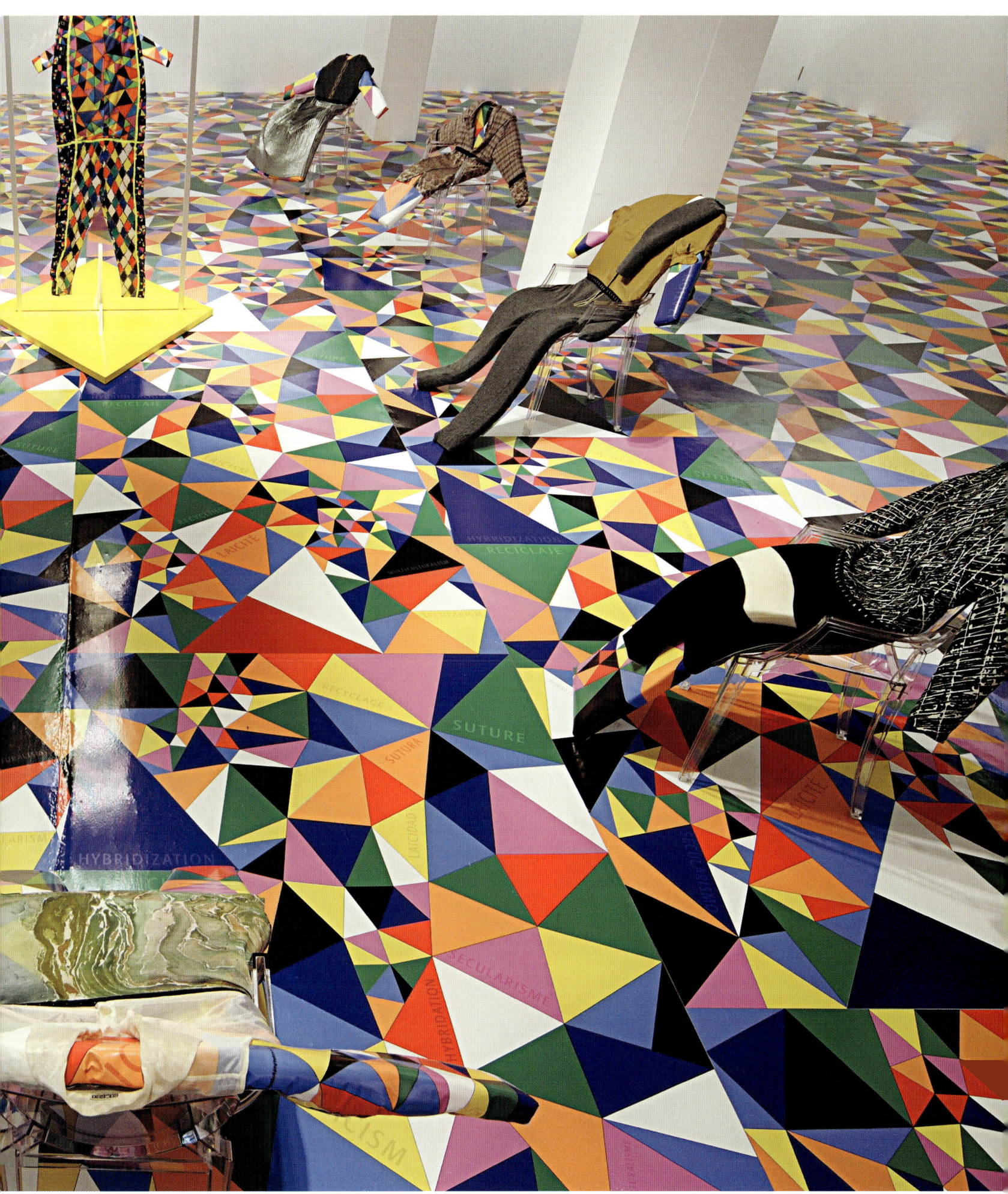

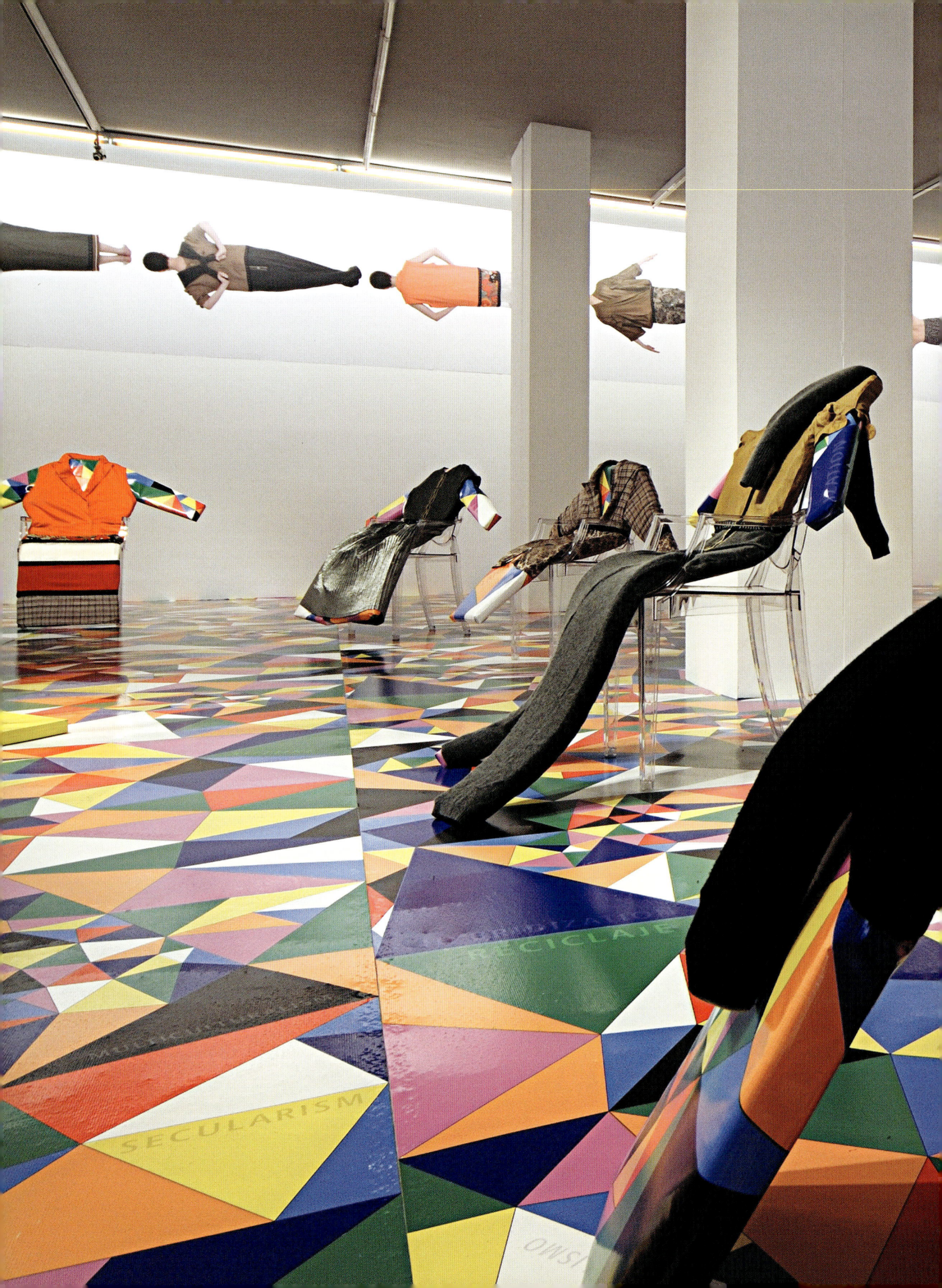

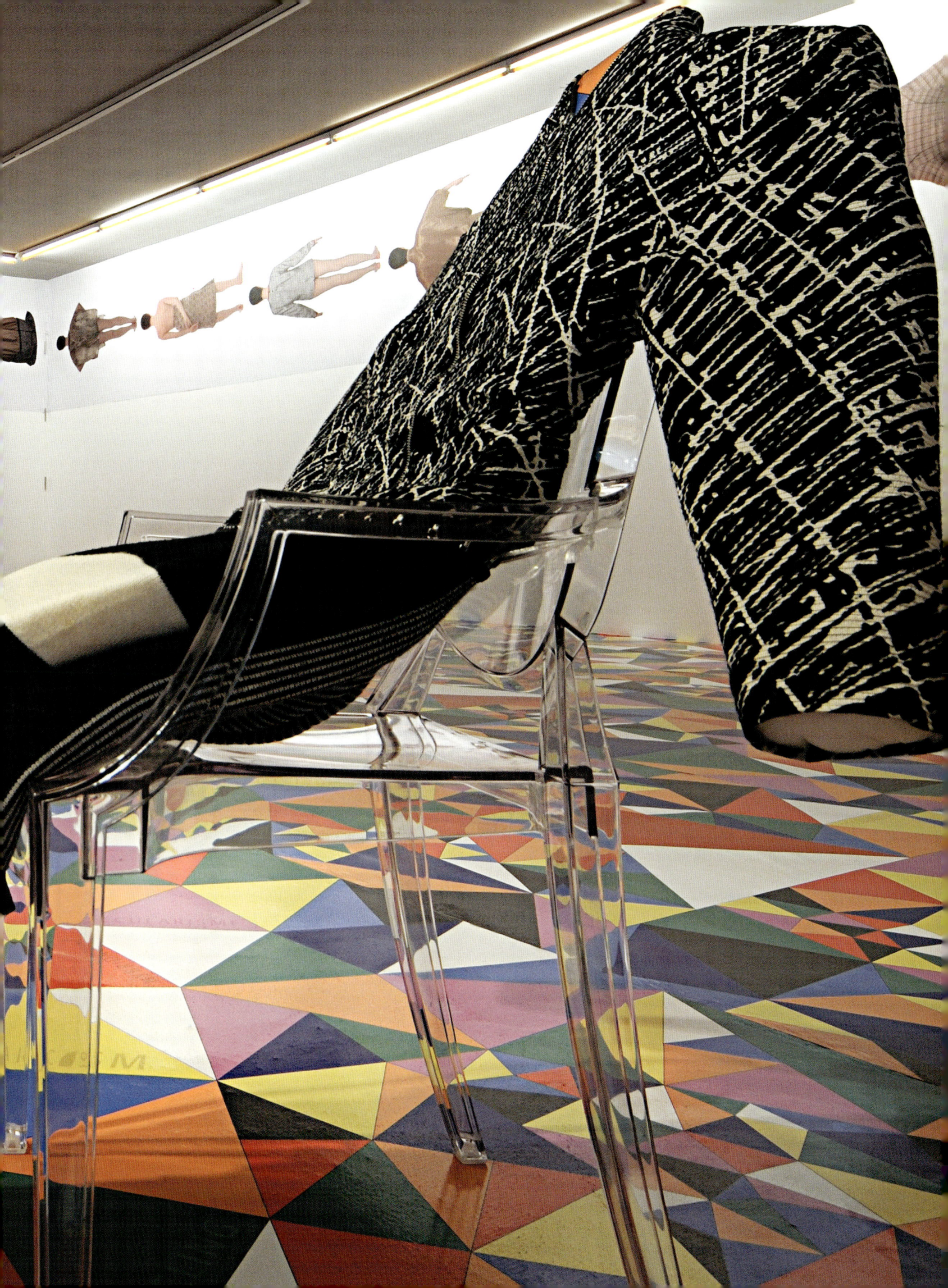

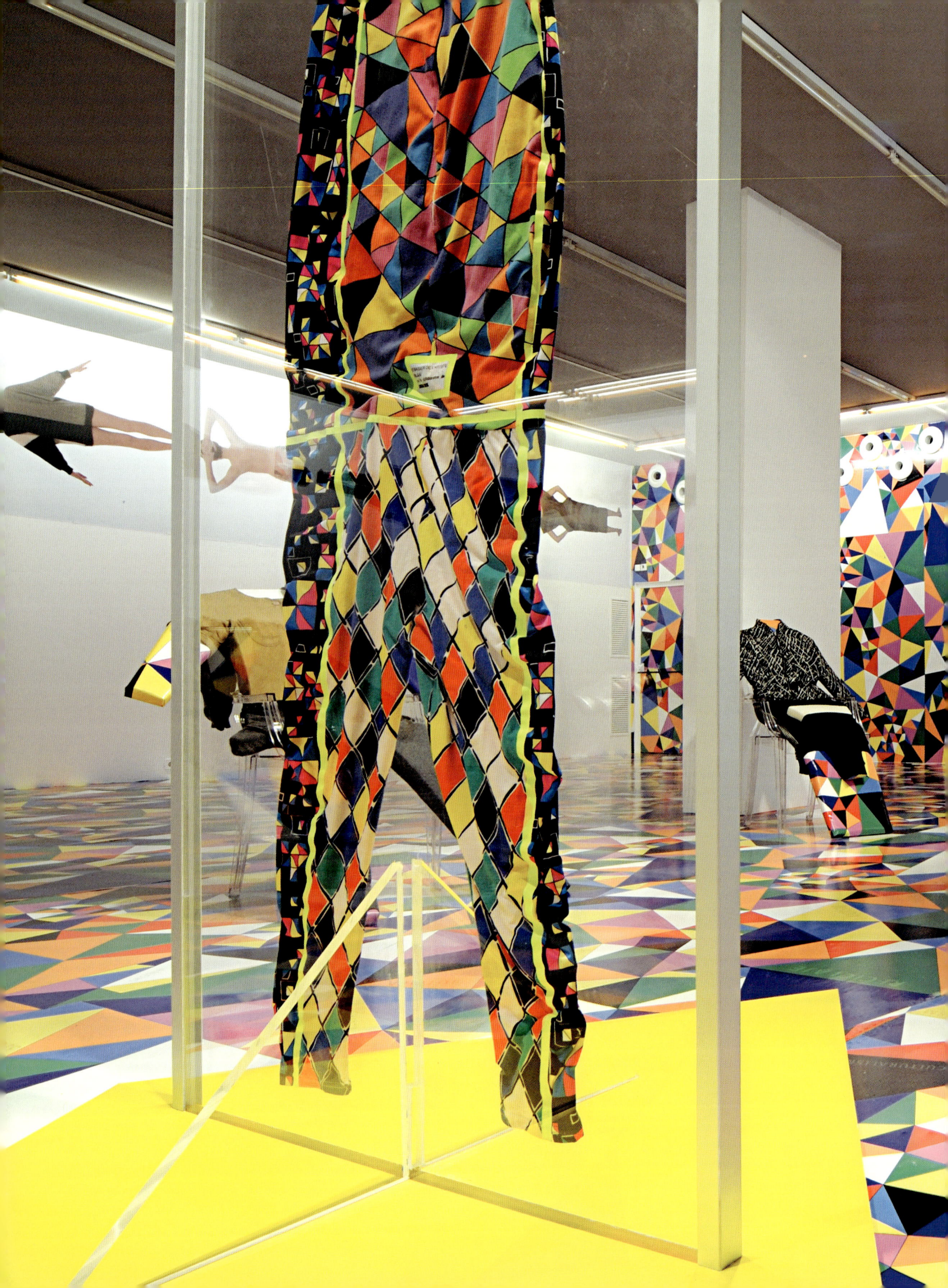

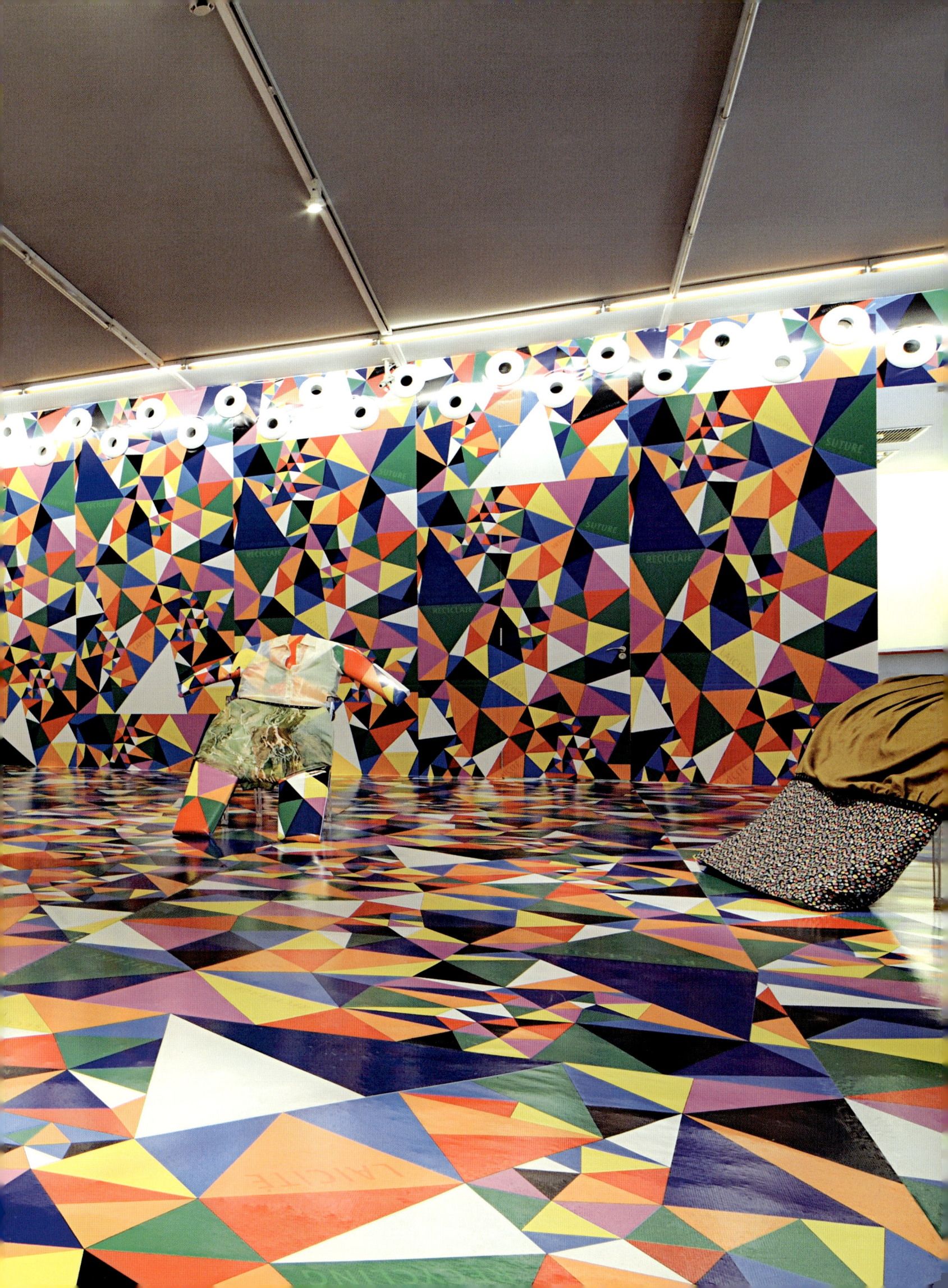

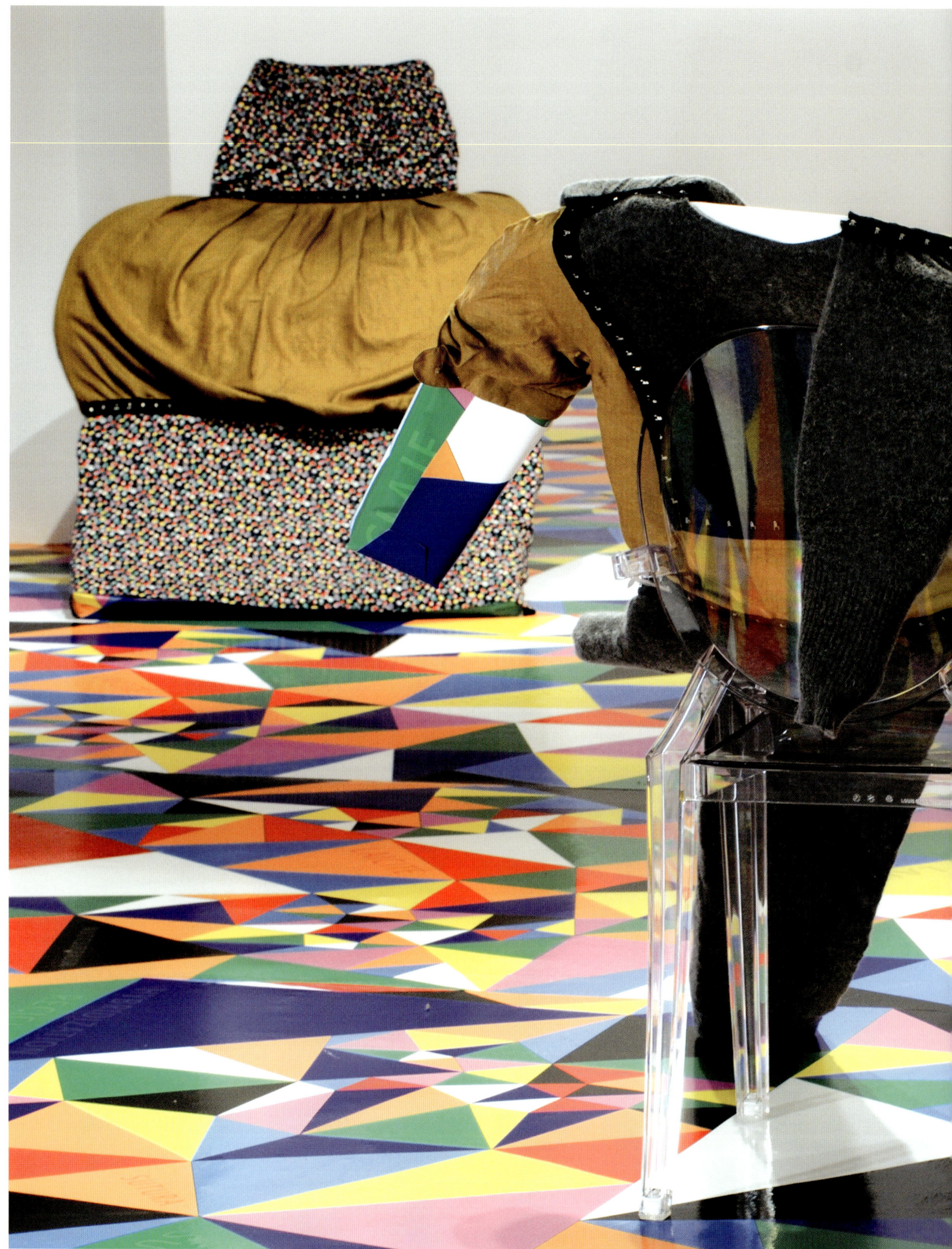

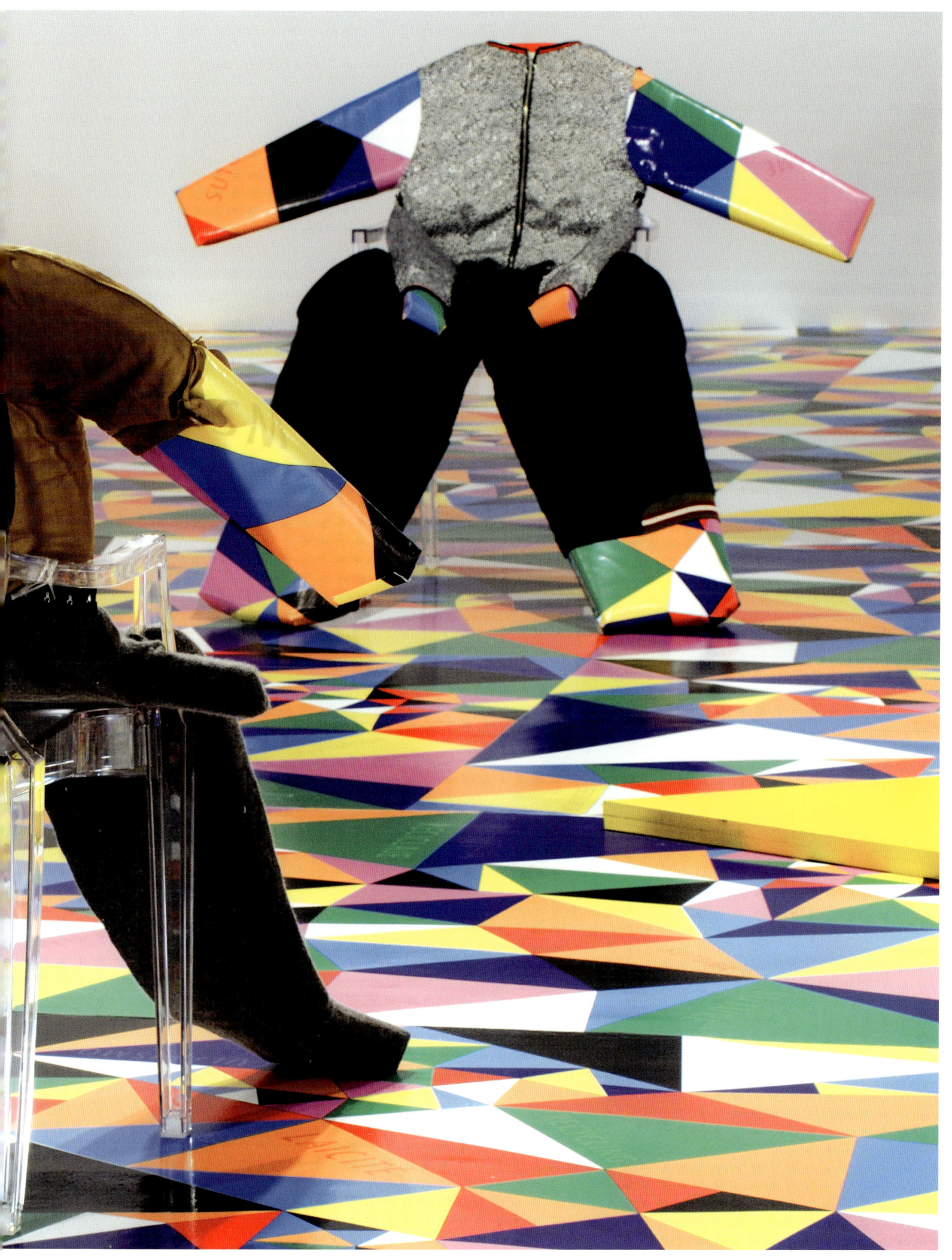

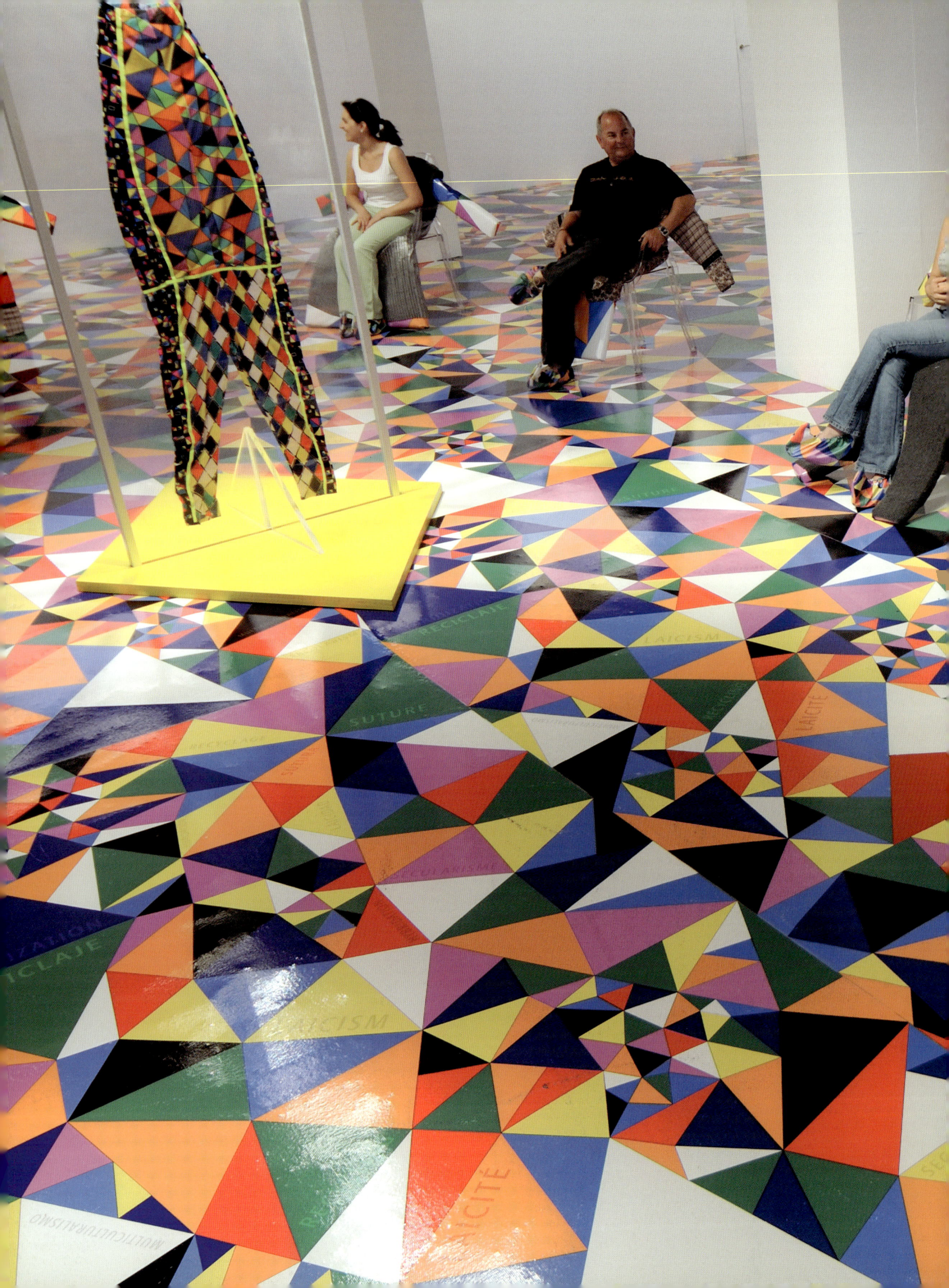

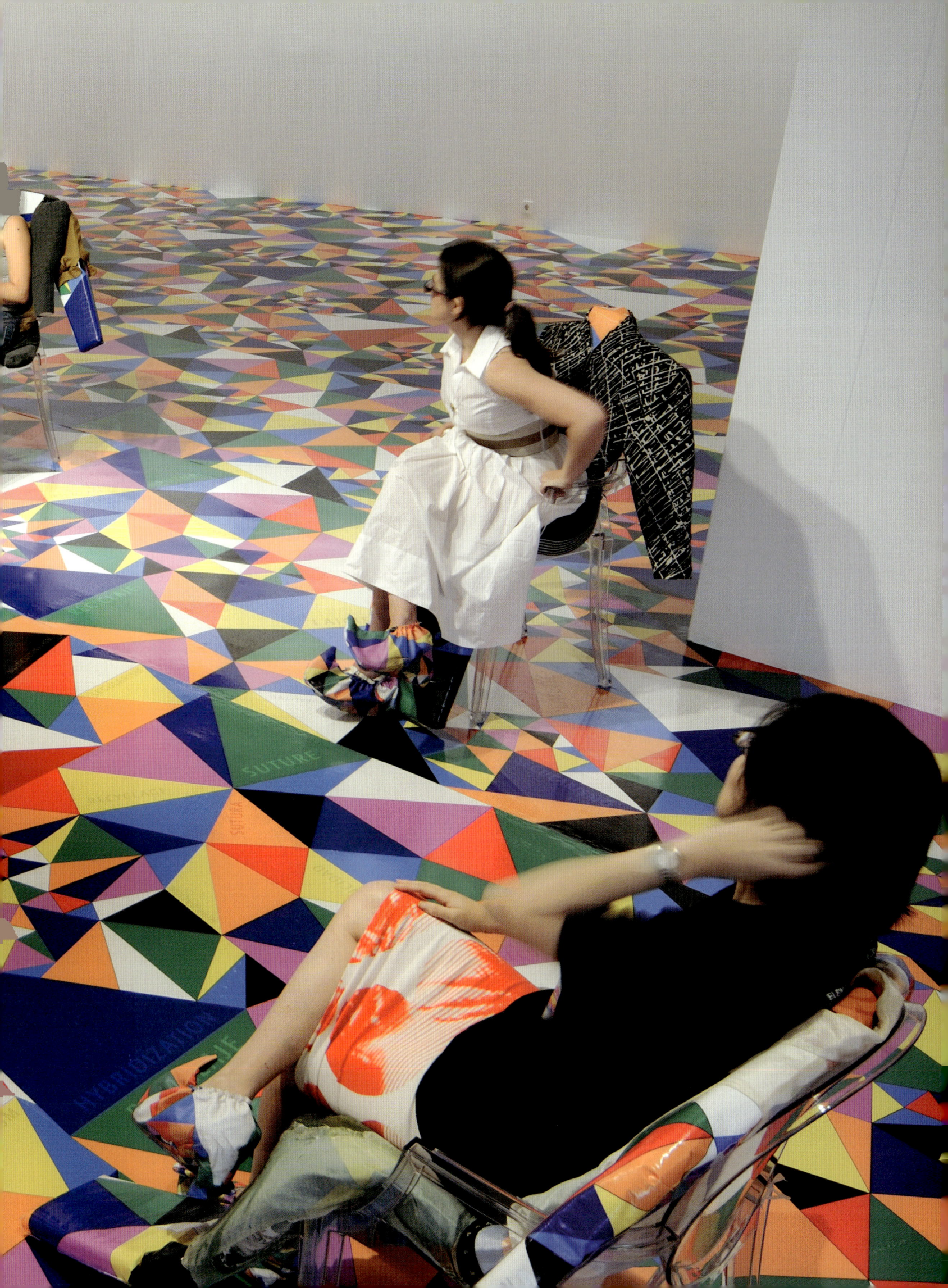

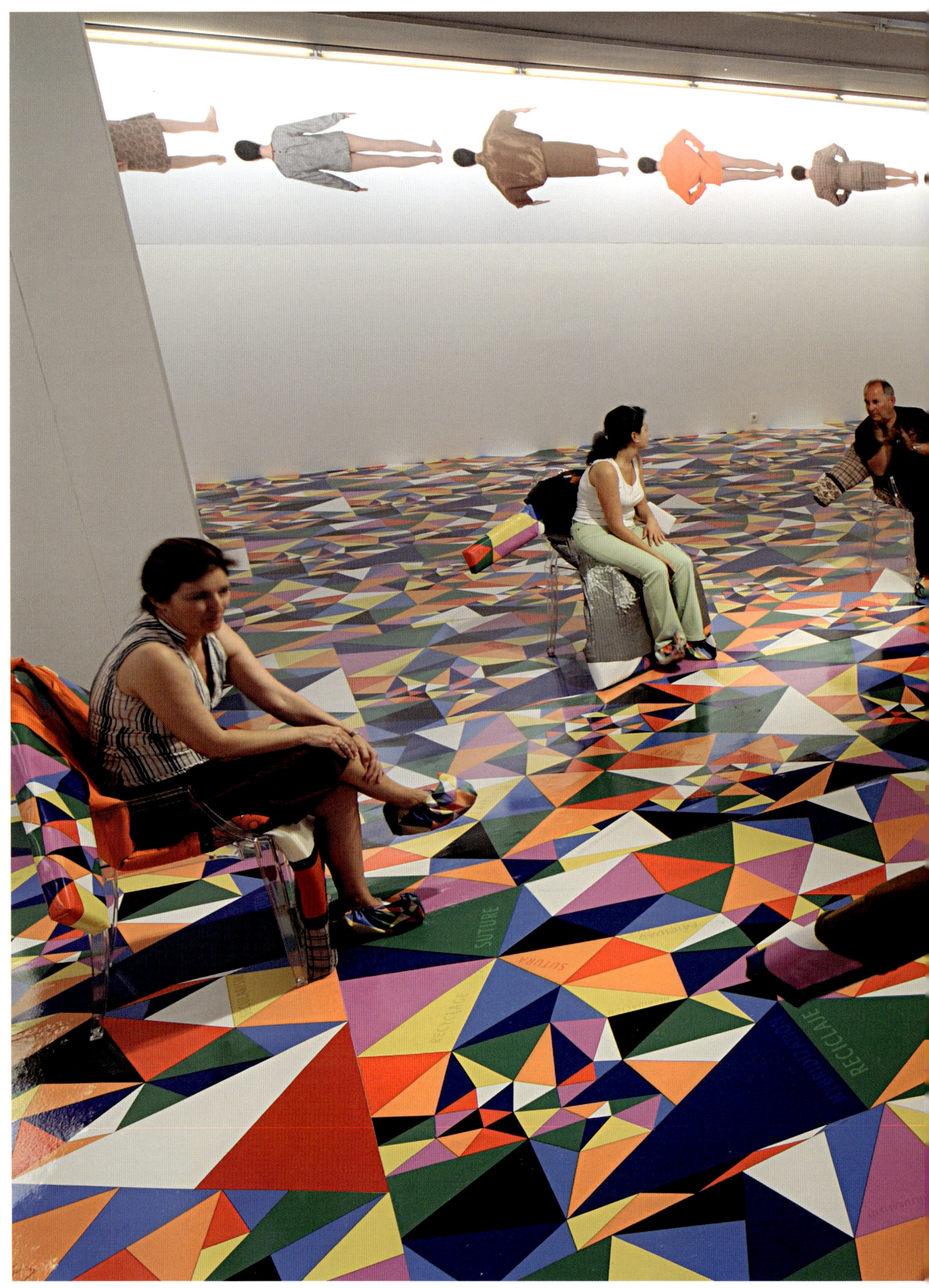

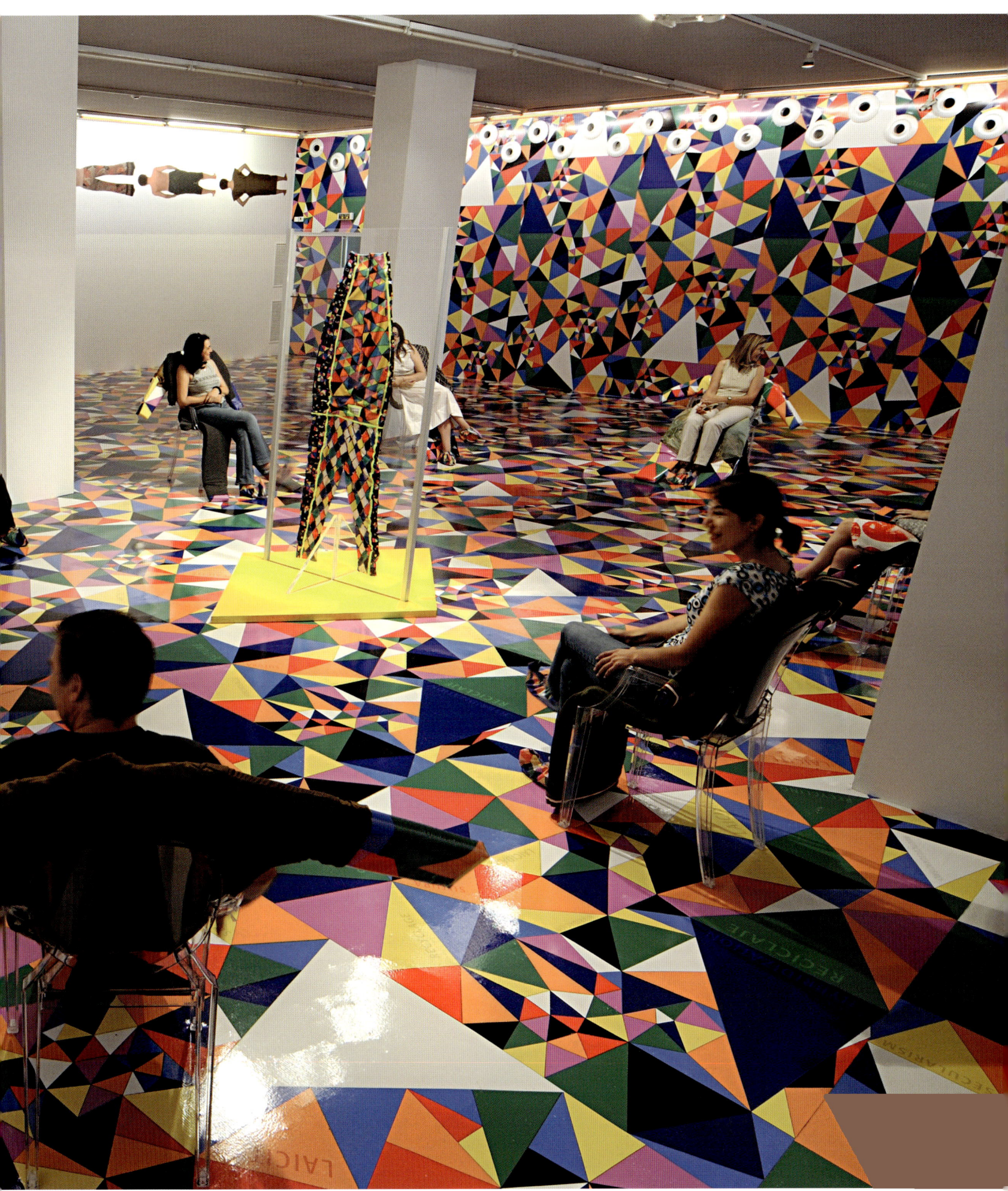

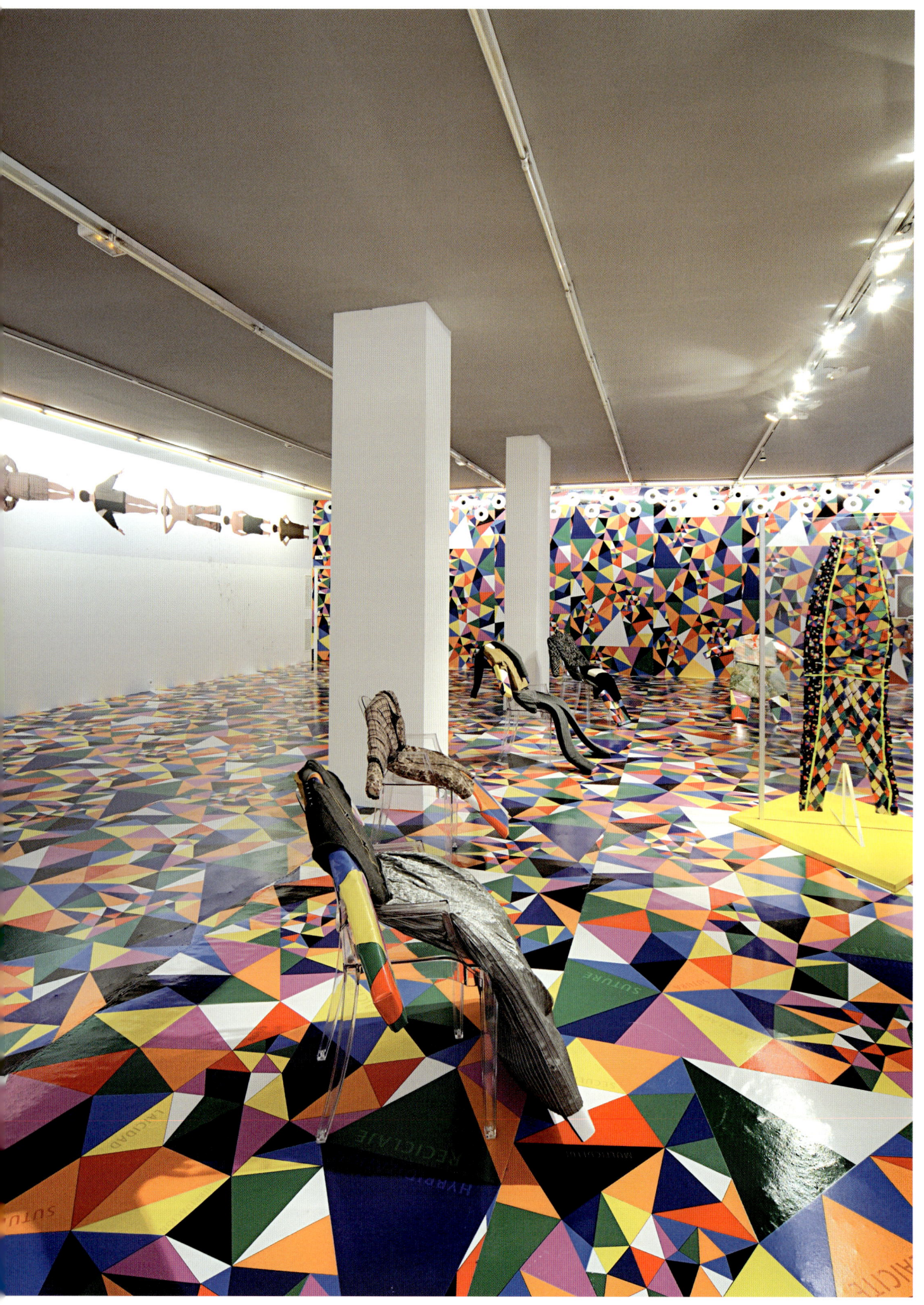

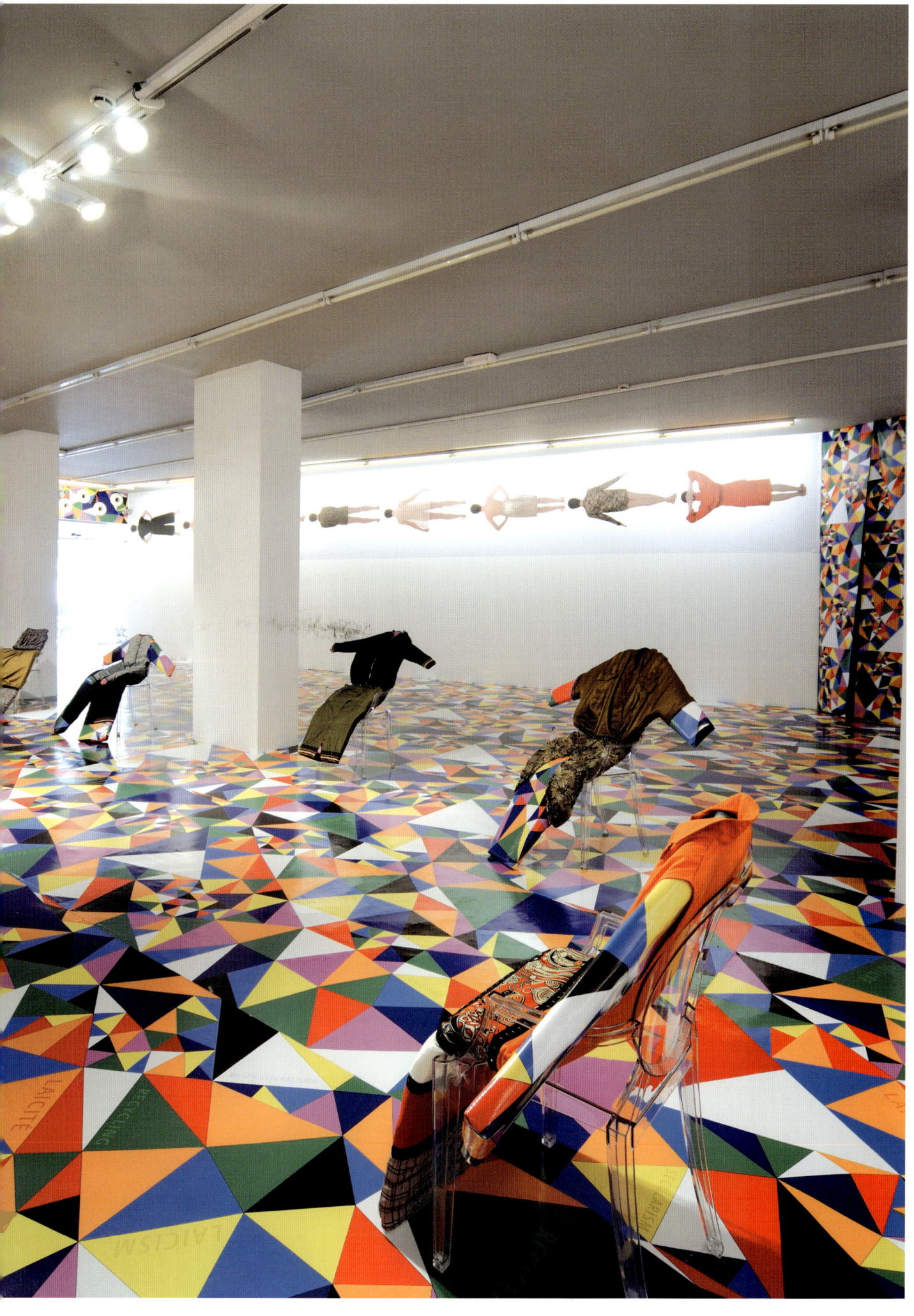

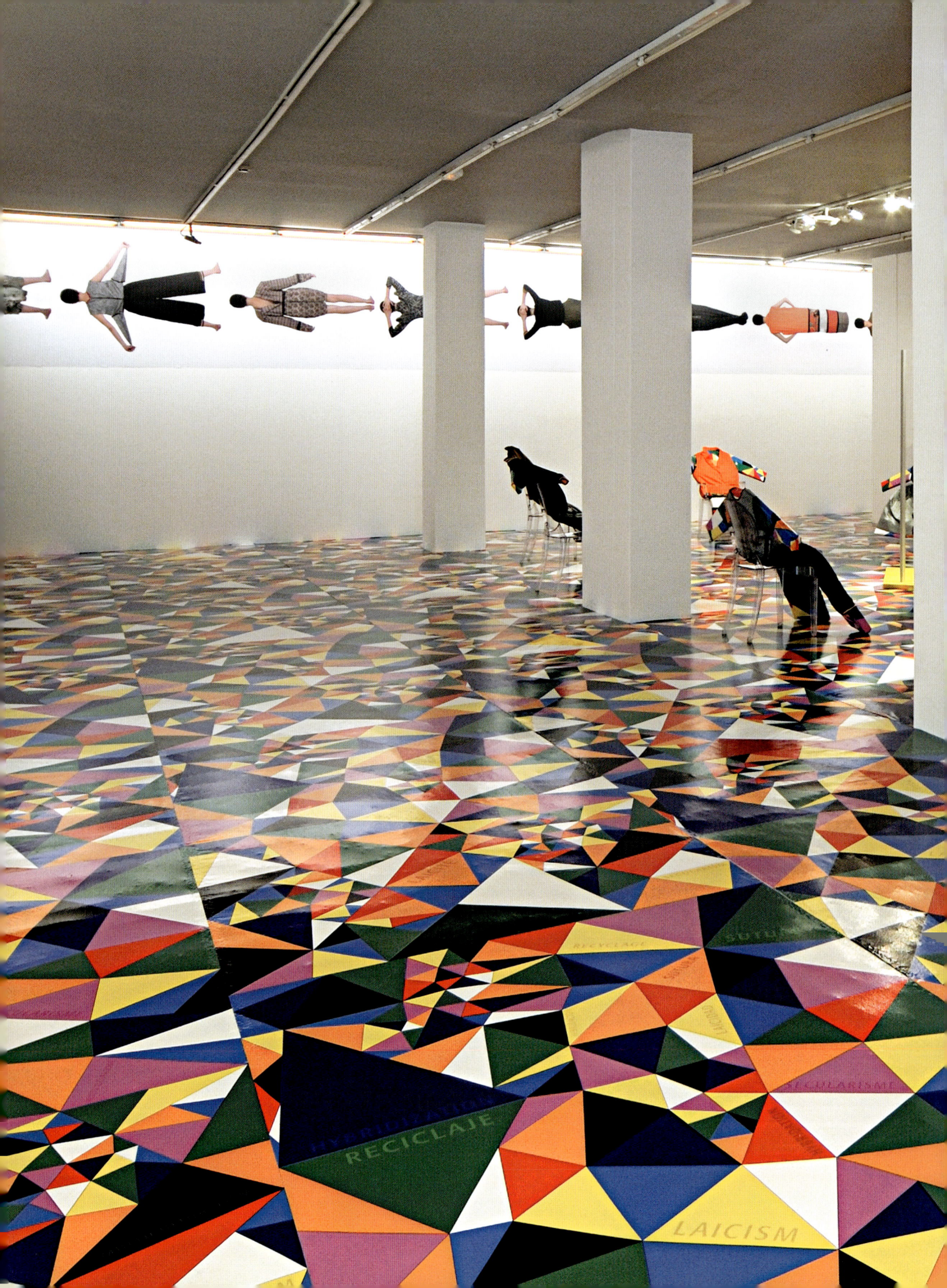

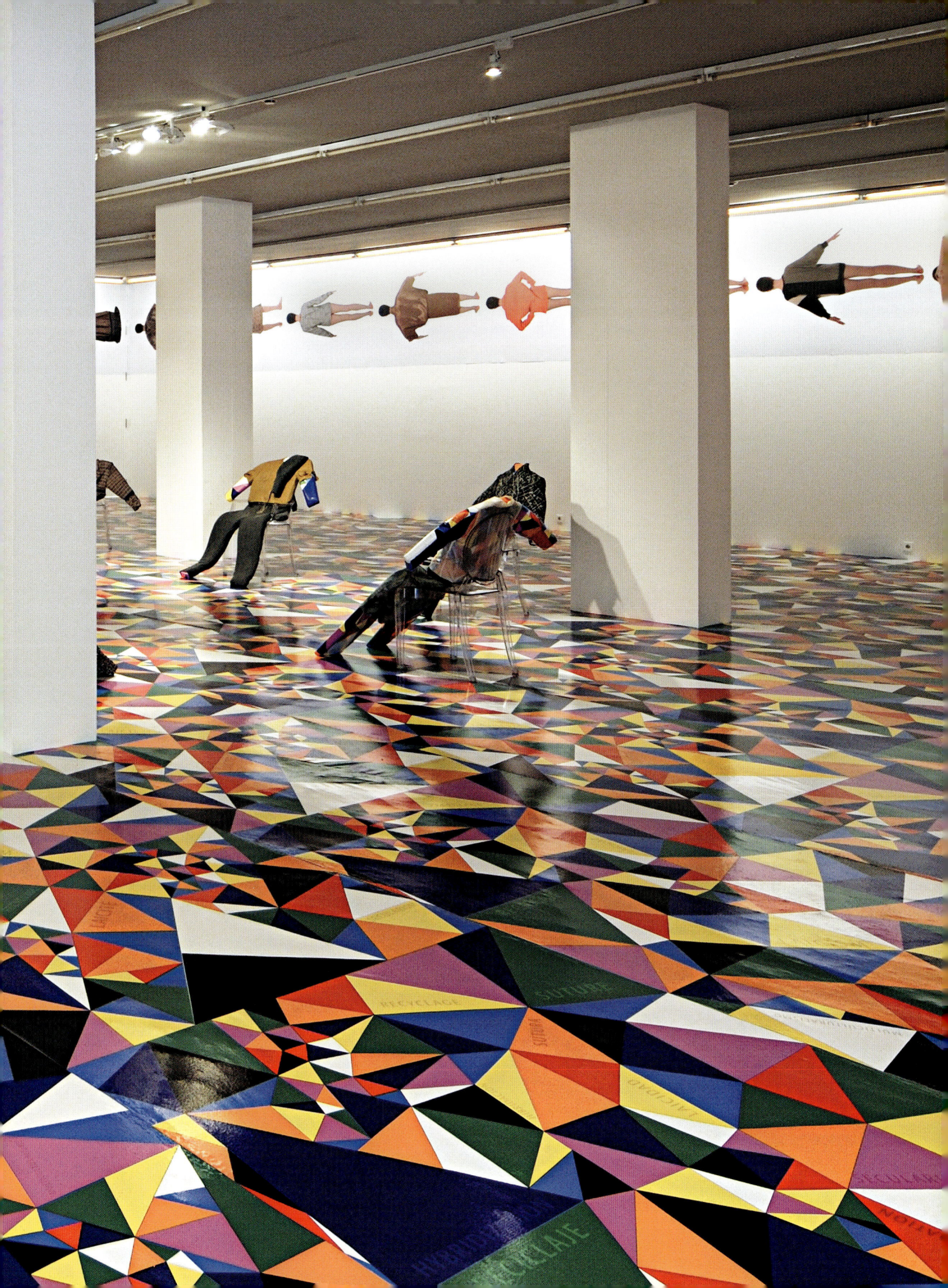

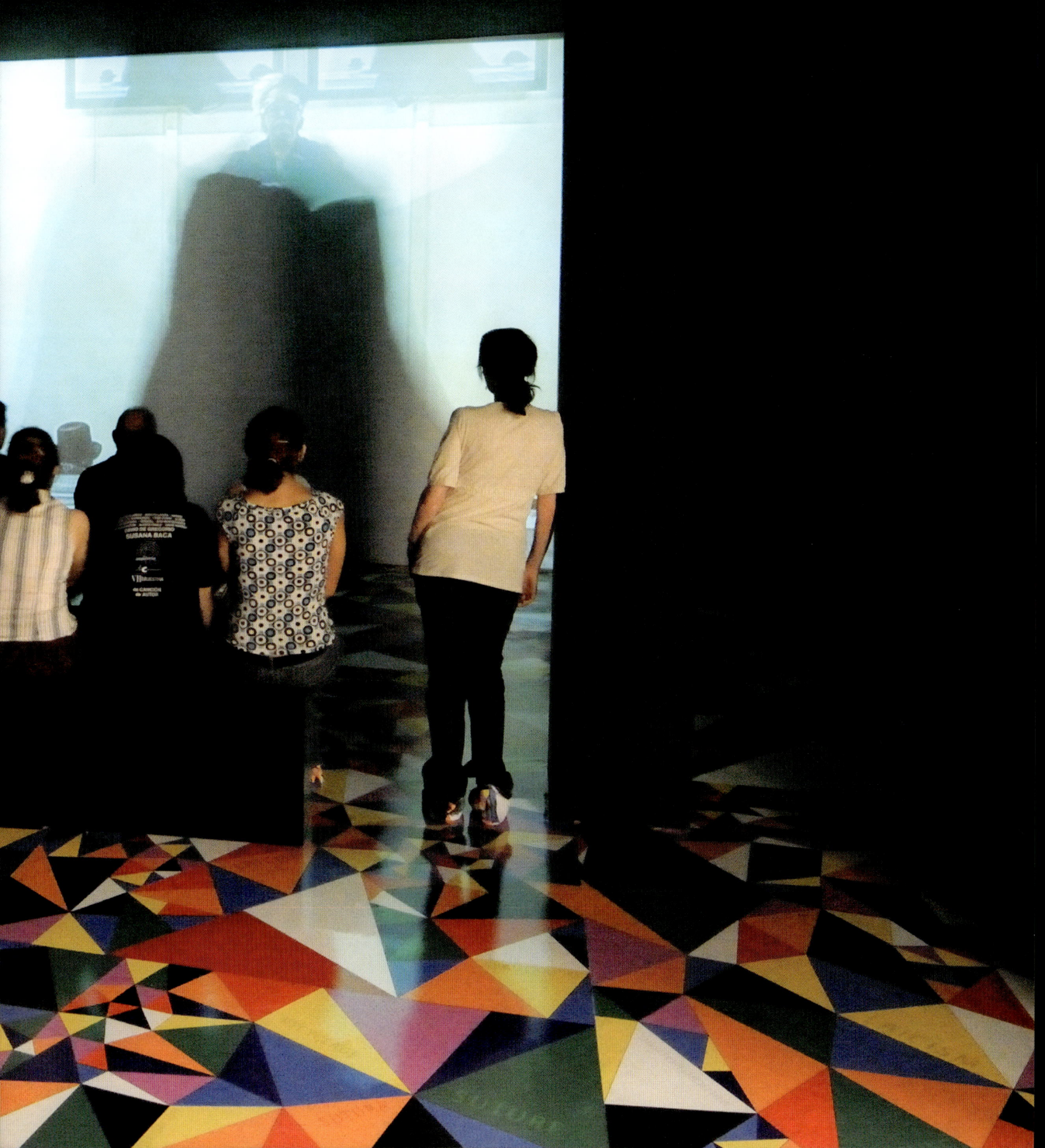

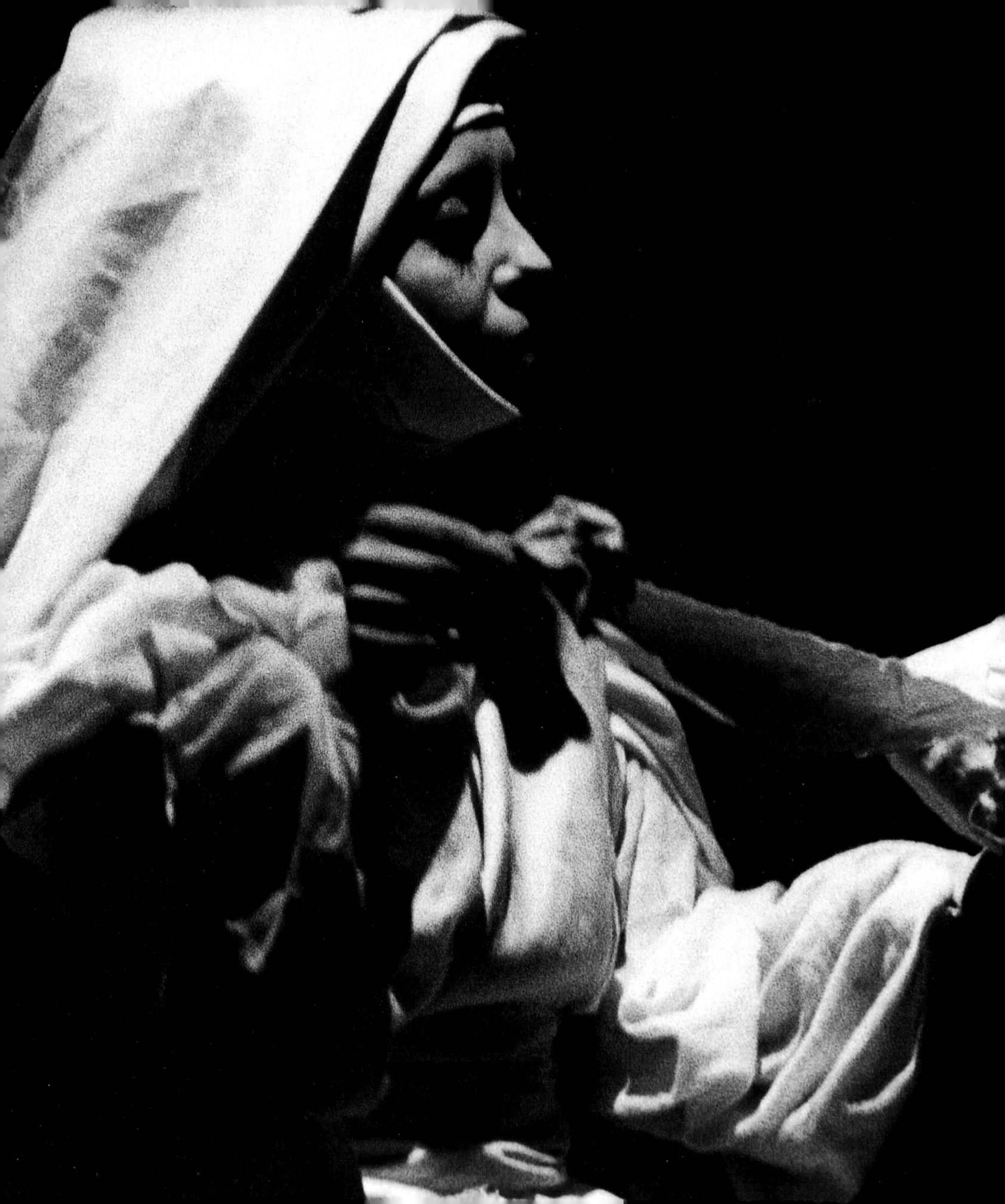

ORLAN WAS BORN MAY 30, 1947, in Saint-Étienne, France. She lives and works between Los Angeles, New York, and Paris. In 2006–2007 she was invited to be a scholar in residence at the Getty Research Institute in Los Angeles.

Since 1965 ORLAN has been active in photography, video, sculpture, installation, and performance, among other things. In 1977 her performance *The Kiss of the Artist*, during the FIAC in Paris, was viewed as somewhat scandalous. In 1978 she created the International Symposium of Performance in Lyon. In 1982 she founded the first online magazine of contemporary art, *Art-Accès-Revue*, on France's precursor to the Internet, the Minitel. She wrote the *Carnal Art* manifesto, and from 1990 to 1993 she conducted her series of nine surgery performances, filmed and broadcast in institutions throughout the world, including the Centre Georges Pompidou in Paris and the Sandra Gering Gallery in New York.

ORLAN has had several retrospectives: in 2002 at FRAC des Pays de la Loire, France (curator Jean-François Taddéi); in 2002 at Centro de Fotografia in Salamanca and in the Museum Artrium in Vitoria, Spain (curators Olga Guinot and Juan Guardiola); in 2004 at CCC, Tours, France (curator Alain Julien-Laferrière); and in 2004 at Centre National de la Photographie, Paris (curator Régis Durand). In 2007 Lorand Hegyi organized a retrospective at the Museum of Modern Art of Saint-Étienne, France, her native city, on the occasion of her sixtieth birthday, and in 2008 the Thallin Art Hall in Estonia presented an exhibition.

In 1998 ORLAN launched *The Self-Hybridizations*, a worldwide tour comparing differing standards of beauty in various civilizations and through history (in Pre-Columbian, African, American Indian, and Chinese cultures). She hybridized her new image (her face modified by surgery) to aesthetic values from other cultures to produce digital photographs. *The Harlequin Coat* was created with skin cells cultivated in vitro, taken from ORLAN and from other people with various skin colors and origins. "Le Plan du Film" (The movie plan), initiated in 1988, was inspired by Godard's comment, "The only great thing about *Montparnasse 19* is that is was not just made back to front, but represents the flip side of cinema to produce a movie the other way around." ORLAN exploited her own image bank to produce a series of movie posters, trailers, and soundtracks for fictitious films. She is also developing a clothing line and a perfume called "Le Baiser de l'Artiste" (The kiss of the artist).

ORLAN has collaborated with many people over the years, including: architect Philippe Chiambaretta (exhibition Luminous Room at the Palais de Tokyo, Paris, 2005); musicians the Tanger Band (for the soundtrack of "Le Plan du film," Al Dante edition, 2001) and Fréderic Sanchez (who created the sound-track of her video installation "Bien que . . . Oui mais!" 2003); film director Stephan Oriach (ORLAN, *Carnal Art*, 2001); fashion designers Walter Van Beirendonck, Jeremie Scott, and Maroussia Rebecqu of Andrea Crews and davidelfin (French and Spanish fashion shows); photographer Jurgen Teller (catalog *Believe*, 1998); choreographer Karine Saporta (Musée des Arts d'Afrique et d'Océanie, Paris, 2002); SymbioticA, a laboratory and a group of artists who use bio-technology (for her project entitled *The Harlequin's Coat* in Perth, Australia); senior perfumer Christophe Laudamiel, with International Flavors & Fragrances, Inc. (IFF), for her perfume, Le Baiser de l'Artiste; and Jan Fabre, performer, for her performance, "MesuRage d'Institution" (Troubleyn/Laboratorium, Anvers, Belgium, 2007).

In 1999 ORLAN was appointed professor at the Ecole Nationale Supérieure d'Arts Paris-Cergy. In 2003 Minister of Culture Jean-Jacques Aillagon conferred on her the honorary title of Chevalier de l'ordre des Arts et des Lettres. In 2005 she was given a one-year residency at the International Studio and Curatorial Program in New York from the AFAA. ORLAN was awarded the Arcimboldo Prize for digital photography by Hewlett Packard France, first prize at the Griffel-Kunst in Hamburg, and first prize of the Moscow Festival of Photography; she also earned the title of Golden Woman by the French art magazine *Connaissance des Arts*.

ORLAN has been featured in the United States at LACMA and MOCA in Los Angeles, at PS1 in New York, and at the Milred Kemper Art Museum in St.

Louis; in Italy at Palazzo Strozzi in Florence and Palazzo delle Esposizioni in Rome; in France at Centre George Pompidou, Centre National de la Photographie, Palais de Tokyo, and Maison Européenne de la Photographie, all in Paris; in Germany at Kunst Museum in Ahlen; in Austria at Kunsthalle and MAK in Vienna; in Luxemburg at Casino of Luxemburg; in Spain at Miro Foundation in Barcelona, Contemporary Art Museum in Vittoria, and Museum of Photography in Salamanca; in Switzerland at Musée de l'Elysée in Lausanne; in Russia at Moscow House of Photography; in South Korea at Center Hall of the National Museum of Contemporary Art in Seoul; and in Japan at Red Brick Warehouse in Yokohama and the National Museum of Art in Osaka.

ORLAN has participated in several biennials of contemporary art in Paris, Venice, Istanbul, Lyon, and Sydney.

ORLAN is represented by Michel Rein Gallery in Paris, Stephan Stux Gallery in New York, Séjul Gallery in Seoul, Ace Gallery in Los Angeles, and Holmes a Court Gallery in Perth, Australia.

In 2004 Flammarion Editions published *ORLAN, Carnal Art* with contributions from Bernard Blistène, Christine Buci-Glucksmann, Caroline Cros, Régis Durand, Eleanor Heartney, Laurent Le Bon, Hans Ulrich Obrist, Vivian Rehberg, and Julian Zugazagoitia.

In 2007, upon ORLAN's large retrospective at the Musée d'Art Moderne de Saint-Étienne, Charta Editions published *ORLAN, The Narrative* by ORLAN with contributions from Lorand Heygi, Donald Kuspit, Marcela Iacub, Peggy Phelan, Joerg Bader, and Eugenio Viola.

The University of Minnesota Press published a book by C. Jill O'Bryan called *Carnal Art: Orlan's Refacing*.

ORLAN's work has inspired many other publications, university works, young artists, films, stylists, theaters, and novels. ORLAN teaches at the Art Center College of Design in Pasadena and at the Ecole Nationale Supérieure d'Art de Paris-Cergy. She is regularly invited to lecture at universities and institutions. Many television and radio programs, as well as various doctoral dissertations, have been dedicated to or written about her. ORLAN's works are part of several public and private collections.

2009

Abbaye de Maubuisson, Maubuisson, France.

2008

Espacio AV., *Sutura/ hybridación/ reciclaje: Orlan + Davidelfin*, curator Isabel Tejeda, Murcia, Spain.

Galeria Michel Rein, *Self-Hybridation, american-indians*, Paris, France.

Tallinn Art Hall, *ORLAN: Post identity strategies*, curators Eugenio Viola and Reet Varblane, Tallinn, Estonia.

ACE Gallery, *Self-Hybridation pre-colombienne*, Los Angeles MOCAca, U.S.

2007

Musée d'Art Moderne de Saint-Étienne, *Le Récit*, curators Lorand Hegyi and Eugenio Viola, Saint-Étienne, France.

Mabel Smith Douglass Galleries Institute for Women and Art, Rutgers University, *Favorite Elements: Works by ORLAN*, curator Ferris Ollis, New Brunswick MOCAnj, U.S.

Getty Research Institute, *Skaï and Sky and Video*, curator Sabine Schlosser, Los Angeles MOCAca, U.S.

Annecy Arthoteque, *Les lendemains du Baroque*, curator Christine Buci-Glucksmann, Annecy, France.

Holmes a Court Gallery, *Skin and Stone*, curator Sharon, Perth, Australia.

2006

Espacio Liquido (in collaboration with B & D Gallery, Milan), *ORLAN*, Gijón, Spain.

Galería Adora Calvo (in collaboration with B & D Gallery, Milan), *Mascaradas*, Salamanca, Spain.

2005

Palais de Tokyo, *Luminous Room*, with architect Philippe Chiambaretta, curators Marc Sanchez and Jerome Sans, Paris, France.

Stephan Stux Gallery, *ORLAN: Digital Photographs and Sculptures, Refiguration / Self-Hybridization, The Pre-Columbian and African Series*, New York MOCAny, U.S.

Cultural Services of the French Embassy, *ORLAN—Recent Works*, curator Blanche Tannery, New York MOCAny, U.S.

Artothèque de la Réunion, *ORLAN*, curator Caroline de Fondaumière, Saint-Denis la Réunion, France.

B & D Gallery, *Self-Hybridations*, curator Francesca Alfano Miglietti, Milan, Italy.

Sejul Gallery, Seoul, South Korea.

Musée des Beaux Arts de Chartres, *Corps primitives Corps numériques*, Chartres, France.

2004

Centre National de la Photographie (CNP), *ORLAN 1964–2004 . . . Méthodes de l'artiste*, retrospective exposition, curators Régis Durand and Claire Guézengar, accompanied by a monograph edited by Flammarion, Paris, France.

Centre de Création Contemporaine (CCC), *ORLAN, 1993*, curator Alain Julien-Laferrière, Tours, France.

Moscow House of Photography, *ORLAN, 2003–2004*, retrospective completed in collaboration with Photobiennale 2004, curator Olga Svlibova, Moscow, Russia.

FRAC Basse Normandie, *Le Plan du Film*, curator Sylvie Froux, Caen, France.

100 Tenson Gallery, *ORLAN*, curators Ark Fongsmut and Philippe Laleu, Bangkok, Thailand.

2003

FRAC des Pays de la Loire, *Éléments favoris*, retrospective, curator Jean-François Taddei, Carquefou, Nantes, France.

Galerie Michel Rein, *Tricéphale, photographs and video installation*, Paris, France.

AFAA, *Le Plan du film*, Paris, France.

2002

FRAC des Pays de la Loire, *Éléments favoris, retrospective*, curator Jean-François Taddei, Carquefou, Nantes, France.

Centro de Fotografía de la Universidad de Salamanca, *Retrospectiva 1964–2001*, curator Olga Guinot, Palacio de Abrantes, Salamanca, Spain.

ARTIUM, Museo de Arte Contemporáneo, curator Juan Guardiola, Vitoria, Spain.

Cannes Film Festival, *Le Plan du film, sequences 3 and 4*, Hôtel Le Martinez, Cannes, France.

Artcore Gallery, *Self-hybridations précolombiennes*, Toronto, Canada.

2001

Sejul Gallery, *ORLAN: Self-hybridations précolombiennes*, Seoul, South Korea.

Forum des Halles, Espace Créateurs, *Le Plan du film, séquence 1*, Paris, France.

Fondation Cartier, *Le Plan du film, séquence 2*, Soirées Nomades, Paris, France.

Le Parvis Centre d'Art Contemporain, *ORLAN, triomphe du baroque*, Ibos, France.

Galerie Bellecour, *Self-hybridations*, Lyon, France.

2000

Bregenzer Kunstverein Magazin 4, Bregenz, Austria.

Galerie de l'École Régionale d'Art de Marseille, *ORLAN: triomphe du baroque*, curator Michel Enrici, Marseille, France.

FIAC, Galerie Yvonamor Palix stand, *One Woman Show*, Paris, France.

1999

Galerie Chelouche, *Omniprésence 2*, Tel-Aviv, Israel.

Art Kiosk Galerie, *ORLAN and Oleg Kulik*, Brussels, Belgium.

Institut Français, *Omniprésences*, curator Sonia Becce, Buenos Aires, Argentina.

1998

Galerie J. and J. Donguy, *Le Mois de la photo à Paris*, Paris, France.

Galerie Yvonamor Palix, *Refiguration-Self-hybridation*, Paris, France.

École Régionale des Beaux-Arts de Nantes, *L'Atelier*, curator Patrick Raynaud, Nantes, France.

1997

Chapter Gallery, *Radical Body*, Cardiff, England.

Camerawork, *This Is My Body . . . This Is My Software*, London, England.

Art Kiosk Gallery, Brussels, Belgium.

CAPC, *ORLAN comme figure de la chimère*, Bordeaux, France.

Galerija s.o.u. Kapelica, *ORLAN*, Ljubljana, Slovenia.

1996

Zone Gallery, *Ceci est mon corps . . . Ceci est mon logiciel*, Newcastle, England.

Portfolio, *This Is My Body . . . This Is My Software*, Edinburgh, England.

Institut Français, Photokina Festival, Cologne, Germany.

Espacio ex Thérésa, Mexico City, Mexico.

SALA 1, *retrospective*, Rome, Italy.

University Museum-Laboratory, Rome, Italy.

Studio Stefania Miscetti, Rome, Italy.

Carte Secrète, *Diagonale*, Rome, Italy.

1995

Centre Georges Pompidou, *Rétrospective video performance*, curator Jean-Michel Bouhours, Paris, France.

1994

Haines Gallery, photograph and video exhibition, San Francisco MOCAca, U.S.

Lab Gallery, video installation, San Francisco MOCAca, U.S.

Camerawork Performance, video conference, San Francisco MOCAca, U.S.

Chassis Post Gallery, *Omniprésence*, Atlanta MOCAga, U.S.

1993

Sandra Gering Gallery, *Omniprésence*, eighth surgical operation-performance (December 8, 1993) and ninth surgical operation-performance (December 14, 1993), New York MOCAny, U.S. Retransmission by satellite to: Centre Georges Pompidou, Paris, Centre MacLuhan, Toronto, and The Multimedia Institute, Banff, Canada.

Sandra Gering Gallery, *Omniprésence*, seventh surgical-intervention-performance (November 21, 1993), New York MOCAny, U.S. Satellite video conference to Quebec, Canada, Belgium, Germany, Latvia, Japan, Switzerland, France (Paris, Nice, Lyon), and United States (New York and Santa Monica MOCAca).

1992

Le Lieu, *Interzone*, curator Richard Martel, Quebec, Canada.

Alliance Française, curator Joël Raffier, Madras, India.

Alliance Française, Bombay, India.

1991

Institut Français, curator Jean-Michel Phéline, Cologne, Germany.

Fifth surgical operation-performance, *Opérationopéra* (July 6, 1991, text by Michel Serres), Paris, France.

1990

First surgical operation-performance, *Art charnel* (July 21, 1990), Paris, France.

Centre d'Art Contemporain de Basse-Normandie, *Les Vingt ans de pub et de cinéma de sainte ORLAN*, curator Joël Savary, Hérouville Saint-Clair, France.

Galea Gallery, *Le Bonheur du jour, vendre du vent . . . vendre du bonheur*, Caen, France.

Second surgical operation-performance, *Opération dite de la licorne* (July 25, 1990, texts by Julia Kristeva), Paris, France.

Third surgical operation-performance (September 11, 1990), Paris, France.

Fourth surgical operation-performance, *Opération réussie* (December 8, 1990, text by Eugénie Lemoine-Luccioni), Paris, France.

1989

Galerie Koppelman, *Die Himmelfahrt oder die Abenteuer de Sainte ORLAN*, Cologne, Germany.

1985

Theâtre et École des Beaux-Arts, *Histoires saintes de l'Art, ORLAN and Léa Lublin*, curators Pierre Restany and Bernard Marcadé, Cergy-Pontoise, France.
FACLIM, *Les Métaphores du sacré*, Limoges, France.

1984

Galerie J. and J. Donguy, *Mise en scène pour une assomption*, photographs and multimedia installation during the month of the photo, Paris, France.
Arleri Gallery, Nice, France.

1982

Espace Sixto/Notes, *ORLAN*, Milan, Italy.

1981

Espace Lyonnais d'Art Contemporain, *Événement ORLAN*, Lyon, France.
Peccolo Gallery, *Installation avec sculpture en marbre et sculpture de pli en drap du trousseau*, Livorno, Italy.
Studio Carrieri Gallery, Martina Franca, Italy.
Gn Gallery, exhibition and *MesuRage*, Gdansk, Poland.

1980

TNP, *Flagrant délit de traces*, Lyon, France.
ICC, *Rétrospective-MesuRage de rue et d'institution*, curator Flor Bex, Antwerp, Belgium.
Nouveau Musée Atrium Tour Caisse d'Épargne, *ORLAN*, Second International Symposium of Performance Art, Lyon, France.
Musée d'Art Moderne, *MesuRage*, Strasbourg, France.

1978

Galerie La Différence, curator Ben, Nice, France.
Galerie Lara Vincy, *Bigeard-bise-art* with Gérard Deschamps, Paris, France.

1976

Casa de Cultura, *MesuRage d'institution*, Caldas da Rainha, Portugal.
Centro de Arte Contemporáneo, First version of *Baiser de l'artiste*, Caldas da Rainha, Portugal.
Performance Festival, *Vendre son corps en morceaux sur les marchés*, Caldas da Rainha, Portugal.
Apartment of Christian Bernard, *MesuRage à façon privé*, Strasbourg, France.
Galerie Rousset Altounian, rue

Lamartine, *MesuRage de rue*, Mâcon, France.

1975

Théâtre du Huitième, paintings, Lyon, France.

1974

Galerie Odile Guerin, presentation of *Sculpture accouchant du bon ventre et du mauvais coeur*, Festival d'Avignon, France.
Festival d'Avignon, *MesuRage de rue*, Plaza central, Avignon, France.

1973

L'Art et la Vie, Fabric works, Lyon, France.
La Mulatière, *Les Tableaux vivants Situation-citations*, Lyon, France.

1972

Vendre son corps en morceaux sur les marchés, performance, Saint-Étienne, Firminy, La Ricamarie, France.

1970

Atelier Claude Delaroa, *Les Tableaux vivants situation-citation*, Saint-Étienne, France.

1969

Atelier Claude Delaroa, *Corps-sculpture*, Saint-Étienne, France.

1967

Action—ORLAN—Corps: "Les Draps du trousseau, souillures," Niza, Saint-Étienne, Rochetaillée, France.
Action Le Père Noël, Saint-Paul-de-Vence, Saint-Tropez, Saint-Étienne, France.
Action Le Déjeuner sur l'herbe, men naked, ORLAN dressed, Rochetaillée, France.

1966

Action—ORLAN—corps, Parcours masqués, Saint-Étienne, France.
Les draps du trousseau souillures, Saint-Étienne, France.

1965

École Municipale des Beaux-Arts, Parcours, Saint-Étienne, France.
Unité Le Corbusier, *Action—ORLAN—corps and Module—or*, *MesuRage*, Firminy, France.
Les Marches au ralenti, Les Marches à rebours and Les Sens interdits, Saint-Étienne, France.

1964

Hotel de ville, *Les Marches au ralenti, Le Gueuloir*, Saint-Étienne, France.
Peintures Trottoirs, Saint-Étienne, Toulon, Marseille, Niza, Saint-Paul de Vence, France.

EXPOSITION COLLECTIONS

2009

Grand Palais, *La force de l´art*, curator Jean Loius Froment, Paris, France.
Casino Luxembourg, *SK-Interfaces*, Luxemburg.

2008

P.S.1 Contemporary Art Center, *"Wack!" Art and the Feminist Revolution*, curator Connie Butler, New York MOCANY, U.S.
Bienal de Busan, Curator Seungbo Jun, Busan, South Korea.
The National Museum of Women in Arts, *"Wack!" Art and the Feminist Revolution*, curator Connie Butler, Washington MOCADC, U.S.
Universidad de Córdoba, Fundacion Rafael Boti, *Exposición sobre Mayo del 68*, curator Michel Hubert, Córdoba, Spain.
Le Plateau, *"l'argent,"* curators Caroline Bourgeois and Elisabeth Lebovici, Paris, France.
Musée des Arts Modestes, *Coquillages et Crustacés*, curator Norbert Duffort, Sète, France.
Tri Postal, *10 ans du prix Arcimboldo*, curator Monique Plon, Lille, France.
Galerie du Petit Chateau de Sceaux, *Compisites*, Sceaux, France.
Exprmntl Gallery, *F for Fakes*, Toulouse, France.
The Vancouver Art Gallery, *"Wack!" Art and the Feminist Revolution*, curator Connie Butler, Vancouver, Canada.
FACT, *Sk-Interfaces*, curator Jens Hauser, Liverpool, England.
Musée d'art moderne de Saint-Étienne, *20 ans de musée*, curator Lorand Hegyi, Saint-Étienne, France.
Espace Peiresc, *Eve-Rêves*, Toulon, France.
Fandazione Solares, *Foodscapes, Art & Gastronomy*, Parma, Italy.
Barbican Museum, *Do Something Different*, international exhibition, London, England.

2007

Osaka National Art Museum, *Skin of / in Contemporary Art*, curator Yukihiro Hirayoshi, Osaka, Japan.
BEAP 07, Biennale of Electronic Arts Perth Stillness, Perth, Australia.
Kunsthius Yellow Art, *Identitites I*, curator Carine Fol, Brussels, Belgium.
Galerie Marion Meyer, *Autofictions*, curator Guy Scarpetta, Paris, France.
Paul Roberson Gallery Cultural Center, Rutgers University, *Imago: The Drama of Selfportraitude in Recent Photography*, curator Daniel Veneciano, Newark MOCANJ, U.S.
Collection Lambert, *J'embrasse Pas*, curator Eric de Mézil, Avignon, France.
Stux Gallery, *Bad Big Love*, curator Joshua Altam, New York MOCANY, U.S.
MOCA Geffen Los Angeles, *Wack! Art and the Feminist Revolution*, curator Connie Butler, Los Angeles MOCACA, U.S.

Palazzo Arti Napoli, *Dangerous Beauty*, curator Manon Slome, Naples, Italy.
Exit Art, *RENEGADES: 25 years of Performance at Exit Art*, curator Papo Colo, New York MOCANY, U.S.
Museo de Bellas Artes de Bilbao, *Kiss Kiss Bang Bang, 45 Años de Arte y Feminismo*, Bilbao, Spain.
Nature (interrupted), curator Pam Posey, 18th Street, Santa Monica MOCACA, U.S.
TROUBLEYN/LABORATORIUM, curator Jan Fabre, Anvers, Belgium.
Bologna Art Fair, *Art Fair*, B & D Stand, Bologna, Italy.
Galerie Michel Rein, *Portraits*, Paris, France.
Chelsea Art Museum, *Dangerous Beauty*, curator Manon Slome, New York MOCANY, U.S.
Museum of Contemporary Art Rome (MACRO), *Into Me / Out of Me*, curator Klaus Biesenbach, Rome, Italy.
Photo L.A., Art Fair, Ace Gallery Stand, Los Angeles MOCACA, U.S.
Kunst Gallery, *Traversée*, curator Judith Bonish, Munich, Germany.
Akureyri Art Museum, *Face to Faces*, curator Isabelle de Montfumat, Reykyavik, Iceland.
ARCO Galería Espacio Liquido, *Feria de arte contemporáneo*, Madrid, Spain.
Palazzo Fortuny, *Artempo*, curators Jean-Hubert Martin and Tijs Visser, Venice Biennale, Venice, Italy.
Museum im Kulturshpeicher, *Diagnose [Kunst], Die Medizin im Spiegel der zeitgenössischen Kunst (Contemporary art reflecting medicine)*, curator Ralf Scherer, Würzburg, Germany.
KW Institute for Contemporary Art, *Into Me / Out of Me*, curator Klaus Biesenbach, Berlin, Germany.
Museum im Kulturspeicher, *Diagnosis*, Würzburg, Germany.
Rutgers University, Foster-Center-Douglass Library, New Brunswick MOCANJ, U.S.
The Bakery ARTRAGE Complex, BEAP Festival, *Still, Living*, Perth, Australia.
AC Institute, Melbourne International Festival, curator Holly Crawford, Melbourne, Australia.
Grand Palais, *Portraits-Souvenirs*, curator Aline Pujo, Paris, France.
Studio Esseci, *Gastronomia nell'Arte Moderna*, curator Lorand Hegyi, Parma, ex-Cinema, Trento, Italy.
Oeuvres de la collèction du Fonds Régional d'Art Contemporain des Pays de la Loire, *Rouge Baiser*, curator Laurence Gateau, Hangar à Bananes, Nantes, France.

2006

P.S.1, *Into Me / Out of Me*, curator

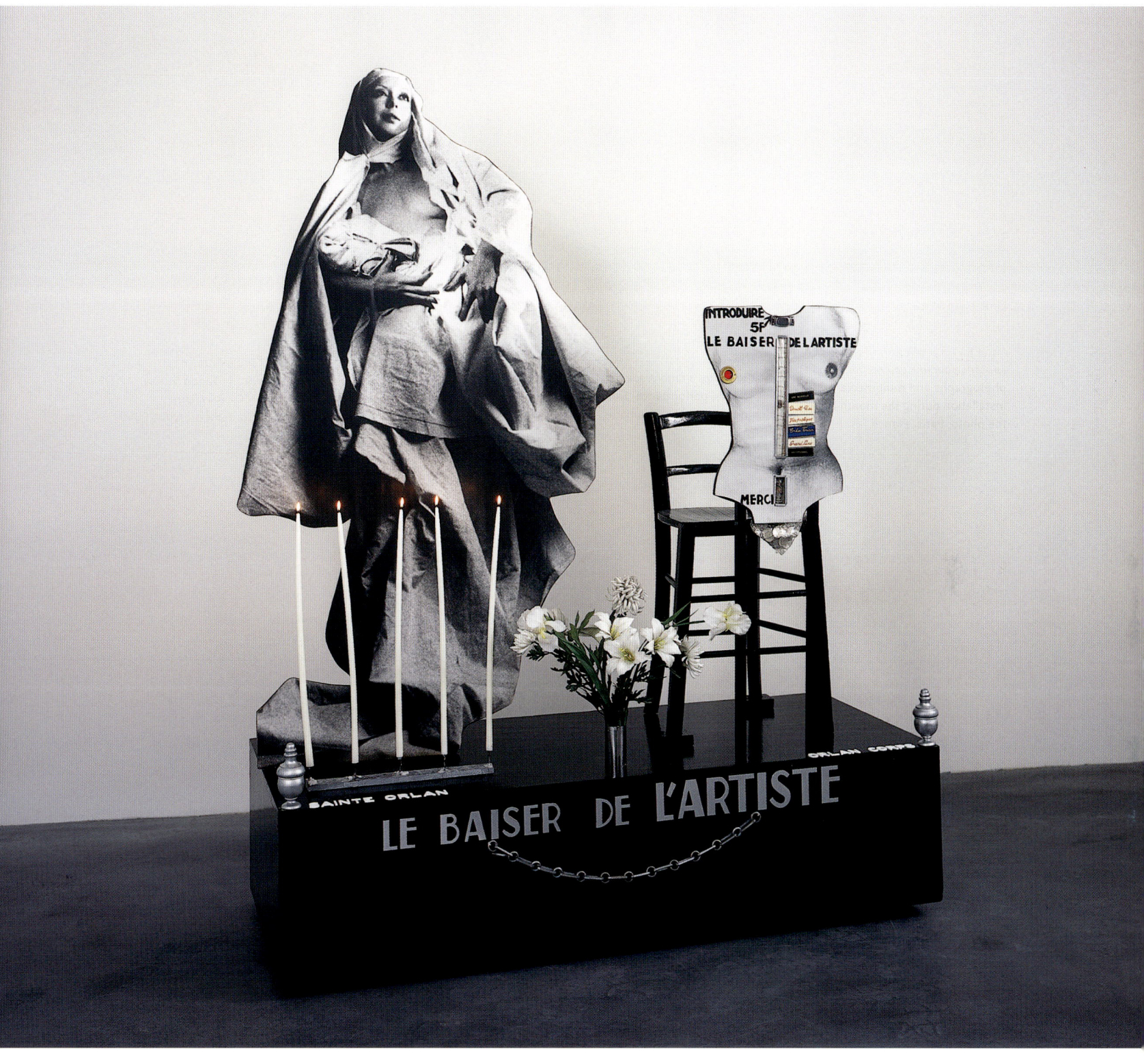

Sculpture and pedestal of the kiss of the artist, 1977. Sculpture and pedestal, photograph in black and white. Wood pedestal, flowers, candles, plastic letters, chair, and sound track. 225.5 cm. x 170 cm. x 70 cm. Photograph by Georges Poncet. Archives of Contemporary Regional Art, Pays de la Loire, France.

Klaus Biesenbach, New York MOCANY, U.S.

Grand Palais, *La Force de l'Art*, curator Eric Troncy, Paris, France.

The New Center for Contemporary Art, *Oh Boy!* Louisville MOCAKY, U.S.

Yokohama Red Brick Warehouse Number 1, *Transimages 4*, curator Anne-Marie Morice, Yokohama, Japan.

KNAP, *Face to Faces*, curator Isabelle de Montfumat, Erevan, Armenia.

Center Art Museum, *Face to Faces*, curator Isabelle de Montfumat, Edinburgh, Scotland.

ARCO, Feria de arte Contemporáneo, B & D Gallery Stand, Madrid, Spain.

Grand Palais, FIAC, Michel Rein Gallery Stand, Paris, France.

Musée d'art et d'industrie de Saint-Étienne, *Bang Bang*, curator Hervé di Rosa, Saint-Étienne, France.

City Art Center, *Face to Faces*, curator Isabelle de Montfumat, Edinburgh, Scotland.

Brussels Art Fair, B & D Gallery Stand, Brussels, Belgium.

Fotografins Haus, *Face to Faces*, curator Isabelle de Montfumat, Stockholm, Sweden.

Slovak National Gallery, *Autopoesis*, Bratislava, Slovakia.

Photo Espana 2006 (in collaboration with B & D, Milano), Madrid, Spain.

Musée des Arts Modestes de Sète, *Bang Bang*, curator Hervé di Rosa, Sète, France.

ART COLOGNE, Sejul Gallery Stand, Cologne, Germany.

2005

Mildred Kemper Art Museum, *Inside Out Loud: Visualizing Women's Health*, curator Janine Mileaf, St Louis MOCAMO, U.S.

Kunsthalle & Kunstforum Wien, *Superstars*, curator Thomas Miessgang, Vienna, Austria.

Artcurial, *Face à Faces*, curator Isabelle de Montfumat, Paris, France.

Bass Museum, *L'art en France*, curators Catherine Francblin y Jean-Marc Prevost, Miami MOCAFL, U.S.

Galerie Nikki Diana Marquardt, *Portaits de femmes, inspirés des femmes de la Bible*, curator Patrick Amsellem, Paris, France.

National Museum of Australia, *Mirror Mirror: Reflections on Beauty*, Canberra, Australia.

Bruce Silverstein Gallery, *Jesus Christ Superstar*, New York MOCANY, U.S.

Museo de Arte Moderno de Buenos Aires, *Projet Cone Sud*, curators Bernard Goy and Gusto Pastor Mellado, Buenos Aires, Argentina.

Fundación Miró, *La dona, metamorfosis de la modernitat*,

curator Gladys Fabre, Barcelona, Spain.

ArtLA FAIR, Brown Bag Contemporary, Los Angeles MOCACA, U.S.

BAC Festival, La Santa, Barcelona, Spain.

FIAC, Michel Rein Gallery Stand, Paris, France.

Breda's Photo Festival, *Irréelle Beauté*, curator Harry Pennings, Breda, The Netherlands.

The Curzon Soho Cinema, *International Exhibitionist (18)*, curators Cyril Lepetit and Lindsay O'Nions Soho, London, England.

Museo Nacional de arte Montevideo, *Projet Cone Sud*, curators Bernard Goy and Gusto Pastor Mellado, Montevideo, Uruguay.

Galerie Artcore, *L'association les 7 péchés capitaux*, curator Christian Alandete, Paris, France.

Musée d'Art Contemporain de Lille, *Marie-Madeleine Contemporaine*, curator Annie Delay, Lille, France.

ARCO, B & D Gallery Stand, Madrid, Spain.

Musée des Arts Décoratifs de Lausanne, *Body Extensions*, Lausanne, Switzerland.

National Gallery of Victoria, *Mirror Mirror: Reflections on Beauty*, Melbourne, Australia.

Brussels Art Fair, B & D Gallery Stand, Brussels, Belgium.

Galerie Traversée, *Statement*, Munich, Germany.

FRAC Basse Normandie, *Strangers in the Night*, curator Sylvie Froux, Caen, France.

FIAC, B & D Gallery Stand, Paris, France.

La Galerie de la Filature, *Images du monde et inscription de la guerre*, Mulhouse, France.

Centre d'art de l'Yonne, *Les métamorphoses de l'ange*, curator Christine Buci-Glucksmann, France.

2004

Musée de l'Élysée (Musée de la Photographie), *Je t'envisage, La disparition du portrait*, Lausanne, Switzerland.

UNESCO, *In Movement: UNESCO Salutes Women Video Artists of the World*, curator Kim Airyung, Paris, France.

Galleria d'Arte Moderna, *La Creazione ansiosa, da Picasso a Bacon*, curator Giorgio Cortenova, Verona, Italy.

Luxembourg Museum, *Moi! Autoportraits du XXe siècle*, curator Pascal Bonafoux, Paris, France.

Kunstverein Bad Salzdetfurth, *Bocca della verità*, curator Hans-Werner Kalkmann, Bad Salzdetfurth, Germany.

ZKM, *Media Art Net*, curator Peter Weibel, Karlsruhe, Germany.

Deutsches Hygiene Museum, *The*

Ten Commandments, curator Klaus Biesenbach, Dresden, Germany.

Sejul Gallery, *Pop culture*, curator Agnes Gouvion de St. Cyr, Seoul, South Korea.

Old Parliament House, *Pop Culture*, curator Agnes Gouvion de St. Cyr, Singapore.

Tadu Contemporary Art Gallery (for the Month of the Photography), *Pop Culture*, curator Agnès Gouvion de St. Cyr, Bangkok, Thailand.

Cristinerose-Josee Bienvenu Gallery, *Revisiting History: Self-Portrait Photography*, New York MOCANY, U.S.

Fonds Régional d'art contemporain d'Ile-de-France / Fondation Guerlain, *Du corps à l'image*, curator Bernard Goy, Paris, France.

FRAC Pays de la Loire, *Pour les oiseaux*, curator Christian Bernard, Carquefou, France.

Hayward Gallery, *About Face*, London, England.

Musée d'art de Toulon, *Marie Madeleine Contemporaine*, Toulon, France.

Musée des Moulages, *Immobilis*, curator Céline Moine, Lyon, France.

Deichtorhallen, *Révélation*, curator Nissam Perez, Hamburg, Germany.

Palazzo Strozzi, *Moi! Autoportraits du xxe siècle*, curator Pascal Bonafoux, Florence, Italy.

Photobiennale 2004, *Identification*, curator Agnès Gouvion de St. Cyr, Moscow, Russia.

Museum of Art & Design, *Identity*, New York MOCANY, U.S.

Château de Linardié, *Mutations*, curator Claude Lelouche, Toulouse, France.

Galerie des Filles du Calvaire, *Femina*, curator Christine Ollier, Paris, France.

Museo de Arte de Lima, *Projet Cone Sud*, curators Bernard Goy and Gusto Pastor Mellado, Lima, Peru.

Mattucana 100 Centro Cultural en Santiago, *Projet Cone Sud*, curators Bernard Goy and Gusto Pastor Mellado, Santiago, Chile.

Fundación Miró, *Mujer y modernidad*, curator Gladys Fabre, Barcelona, Spain.

Musée des Arts Derniers, *Les Afriques*, curator Olivier Sultan, Paris, France.

Museum of Decorative Art of Lausanne, *Body Extensions*, Lausanne, Switzerland.

Musée des Beaux-Arts de Tourcoing, *De leur Temps, Collections Privées Françaises*, Tourcoing, France.

2003

Musée de l'Élysée (Musée de la Photographie), *Face*, Lausanne, Switzerland.

Zabriskie Gallery, *Role Play in Photography Self-Portrait*, New York MOCANY, U.S.

Galeria Espacio Liquido, *Fragiles*, Gijón, Spain.

University of Paris—VIII—Saint-Denis, *Campus Euro(pe) Art*, curator Claude Mollard, Saint-Denis, France.

ART COLOGNE, Galerie Michel Rein Stand, Cologne, Germany.

University of Champagne Ardennes, *Campus Euro(pe) Art*, curator Claude Mollard, Reims, France.

FIAC, Galerie Michel Rein Stand, Paris, France.

University of Aix-Marseille III, *Campus Euro(pe) Art*, curator Claude Mollard, Aix-en-Provence, France.

Culturgest, *Cara a Cara*, Lisbon, Portugal.

University of Marne-la-Vallée, *Campus Euro(pe) Art*, curator Claude Mollard, Marne-la-Vallée, France.

Musée des Beaux-Arts du Québec, *Doublures*, Quebec, Canada.

Free University of Belgium, *Campus Euro(pe)art*, curator Claude Mollard, Brussels, Belgium.

Valencia Bienal de Arte Contemporáneo, *La Ciudad Ideal*, curator Lorand Hegyi, Valencia, Spain.

Galleria d'Arte Moderna, *La Creazione ansiosa, da Picasso a Bacon*, Verona, Italy.

Briggs Robinson Gallery, *9 Women in the Same Coat*, curator Nicola L., New York MOCANY, U.S.

Rencontres de la Photographie d'Arles, 2003, Saint-Anne Chapel, *Les 20 ans des FRAC*, curator Bernard Blistène, Arles, France.

University of Grenoble library, *Campus Euro(pe) Art*, curator Claude Mollard, Grenoble, France.

David Gill Gallery, *Made in Paris Photo/Vidéo*, London, England.

Le Divan, LHOOQ, Paris, France.

University of Littoral Côte-d'Opale, *Campus Euro(pe) Art*, curator Claude Mollard, Dunkerque, France.

Sorbonne chapel, University of Paris IV, *Campus Euro(pe) Art*, curator Claude Mollard, Paris, France.

CRDP de Poitou-Charentes, *Campus Euro(pe) art*, curator Claude Mollard, Poitiers, France.

University of Angers, Library gallery, *Campus Euro(pe) Art*, curator Claude Mollard, Angers, France.

Galerie der HGB, Academy of Visual Arts, *Bellissima*, Leipzig, Germany.

Musée Départemental d'Art Ancien et Contemporain, *Art contemporain*, Épinal, France.

Prisme Escape, Les Voûtes, *ORLAN, Charnel Art*, Paris, France.

La Galerie des Galeries, Galeries Lafayette, *Avatars*, Paris, France.

Elga Wimmer Gallery PCC, *Body Politics*, New York MOCANY, U.S.

Art in General, *Time Capsule*, New York MOCANY, U.S.

Institut d'Art Contemporain, *Collection 001*, Villeurbanne, France.

Hungarian Photography House, *La Fabrication du réel*, Budapest, Hungary.

Place Saint-Sulpice, *Rencontres A3*, Paris, France.

2002

Center Hall of the National Museum of Contemporary Art, Seoul, South Korea.

Chicago Fair, Artcore Gallery Stand, Chicago MOCAɪʟ, U.S.

Jewish Community Center in Manhattan, *Dangerous Beauty*, New York MOCAɴʏ, U.S.

Kunsthalle Wien, *Tableaux vivants*, Vienna, Austria.

Modern Art Museum, *International Contemporary Art*, México MOCAᴅꜰ, Mexico.

Magazin 4, *Vorarlberger Kunstverein*, Bregenz, Austria.

78 International Contemporary Art, *Shock & Show, Reality & Alternatives*, Trieste, Italy.

Cologne Fair, Artcore Stand, Cologne, Germany.

Art Basel Miami Fair, Artcore Stand, Miami MOCAꜰʟ, U.S.

2001

Museum of Modern Art, *Between Earth and Heaven: New Classical Movements in Art Today*, curator W. Van den Bussche, Ostende, Belgium.

Galería Luis Adelantado, Valencia, Spain.

Marella Gallery, *Metamorfosi del corpo*, Milan, Italy.

Borusan Foundation, *Les Voluptés*, curator Elga Wimmer, Istanbul, Turkey.

Chicago Fair, Galerie Yvonamor Palix Stand, Chicago MOCAɪʟ, U.S.

Festival E-Phos 2001, *The Hybrid Body and the Monster*, Athens, Greece.

Musée de Cholet, *Jocondissima*, Cholet, France.

Casa del Mantegna Museum, *Totemica*, Mantua, Italy.

Musée d'Art Contemporain d'Anvers, *Mutilate Mode and Body Art 2001: Landed/Geland*, Antwerp, Belgium.

Centro Bice Piacentini per le Arti Visive, *Le Arti della Critica*, San Benedetto del Tronto, Italy.

Rencontres de la Photographie d'Arles, Abbaye de Montmajour, curator Alain Say, Arles, France.

Le Parvis Centre d'Art Contemporain, *Réjouissez-vous*, Ibos, France.

FIAC, Galerie Yvonamor Palix Stand, Paris, France.

Festival des Arts Électroniques, Rennes, France.

ISELP, *Le Clonage d'Adam*, Brussels, Belgium.

Musée de la Villette-Cité des Sciences et de l'Industrie, *L'Homme transformé*, Paris, France.

Musée d'Art Contemporain de

Roubaix-tourcoing, *Sous le drap, les temps des plis*, Roubaix-tourcoing, France.

2000

Centre Georges Pompidou, *La Grâce* (with Michel Maffesoli), Revue Parlée, Paris, France.

Musée de l'Élysée, *Le Triomphe de la chair*, Lausanne, Switzerland.

Deste Foundation, curator Daniel Abadie, Athens, Greece.

Palazzo Reale, *Arte in vivo*, curator Francesca Alfano Miglietti, Turín, Italy.

Metropolitan Museum of Tokyo, *The One Hundred Smiles of Mona Lisa*, curator Jean-Michel Ribettes, Tokyo, Japan.

Le Printemps, *Excentrique, un manifeste de l'apparence*, curator Florence Müller, Paris, France.

Artists in the City Festival, Bregenz, Austria.

Galerie Verney Carron and Maison du Livre, de l'Image et du Son, Villeurbanne, France.

Studio Stefania Miscetti, *Anableps*, curator Mario de Candia, Rome, Italy.

Artothèque Amiens, *Résonance*, Amiens, France.

Passage de Retz, *Narcisse blessé*, curator Jean-Michel Ribettes, Paris, France.

Galerie Enrico Navarra, *Le Corps mutant*, curator Jacques Ranc, Paris, France.

Arken Museum of Modern Art, *Man*, Arken, Denmark.

Kulturamt Stadt Oldenburg, *Reality Checkpoint*, Körperszenarien, Oldenburg, Germany.

Lyon Cotemporary Art Biennale, *Partage d'exotisme*, curator Jean-Hubert Martin, Lyon, France.

Staatliche Kunsthalle, curator Silvia Eiblmayer, Baden-Baden, Germany.

Culturgest, Lisbon, Portugal.

Zentrum für Kunst und Medientechnologien, *Anagrammatische der Körper und seine mediale Konstruktion*, curator Peter Weibel, Karlsruhe, Germany.

Anne Faggianato Gallery, *Art and Anatomy*, Londres, England.

Art Kiosk Gallery, *Zizi 2000*, Brussels, Belgium.

Sapporo Prefectural Museum, *Focus on Genes*, curator Jean-Michel Ribettes, Sapporo, Japan.

Kunsthaus-Galerie im Lenbachhaus and Kunstverein, *The Wounded Diva Hysteria, the Body and Technology in Art*, curator Silvia Eiblmayer, Munich, Germany.

Centre d'Art Contemporain d'Auvers-sur-Oise, *L'Invention des femmes*, curator Marie-Hélène Dumas, Auvers-sur-Oise, France.

Château Pommery les Crayères, *Stratégies charnelles*, curator Adrien Sina, Reims, France.

Kunstsammlung NRW 235 Media Vidéo, *The Self Is Something Else*, Düsseldorf, Germany.

Galerie im Taxispalais, curator Silvia Eiblmayer, Innsbruck, Austria.

Shizuoka Prefectoral Museum, *Focus on Genes*, curator Jean-Michel Ribettes, Shizuoka, Japan.

Winnipeg Art Gallery, Manitoba, Canada.

1999

LACMA, *Ghost in the Shell*, curator Robert Sobieszeck, Los Angeles MOCAᴄᴀ, U.S.

Musée de l'Élysée, *Le Siècle du corps: Photographie 1900–2000*, Paris, France.

Maison Européenne de la Photo, first prize in the Prix Arcimboldo, Paris, France.

MOCA, *The One Hundred Smiles of Mona Lisa*, curator Jean-Michel Ribettes, Tokyo, Japan.

Tate Gallery of Liverpool, curator Doreet Levitte-Harten, Liverpool, England.

Contemporary Art Pavilion, Rosso, *Transfiguration and Blood in Contemporary Art*, curator Francesca Alfano Miglietti, Milan, Italy.

Maison du Citoyen, *L'Invention des femmes*, curator Marie-Hélène Dumas, Fontenay-sous-Bois, France.

The Israel Museum, *Skin-Deep*, curator Suzanne Landau, Jerusalem, Israel.

National Museum, *The One Hundred Smiles of Mona Lisa*, curator Jean-Michel Ribettes, Osaka, Japan.

Art Brussels, Galerie Palix Stand, Brussels, Belgium.

Städtische Kunsthalle, *Heavenly Figures*, Düsseldorf, Germany.

Galerie Enrico Navarra, *Corps mutant*, curator Jacques Ranc, Paris, France.

Encontros da imagem Festival de fotografía, Braga, Portugal.

Galerie Khan Strasbourg, *Photographies portraits de corps*, Strasbourg, France.

Neue Galerie am Landesmuseum, *Anagrammatical Body*, curator Peter Weibel, Graz, Austria.

Carrillo Gil Museum, *Tour exhibition "Le sang, le Coeur et le nid de l'aigle,"* Mexico City, Mexico.

MCNARS Centro Reina Sofia, *Année de la France en Espagne*, Madrid, Spain.

Art Space, *AU-International*, Japan.

1998

MOCA, *Out of Actions: Between Performance and the Object 1949–1979*, curator Paul Schimmel, Los Angeles MOCAᴄᴀ, U.S.

International Short Film Festival, Cologne, Germany.

MAK, *Out of Actions, Between Performance and the Object 1949–1979*, curator Paul Schimmel, Vienna, Austria.

Maison de la Culture, *Violence*, Dieppe, France.

Palazzo Branciforte, *Disidentico*, curator Achille Bonito Oliva, Palermo, Italy.

ARCO, Galerie Yvonamor Palix Stand, Madrid, Spain.

La Coscienza Luccicante, curator Carmelo Strano, Cefalù, Sicily, Italy.

Chicago Fair, Galerie Palix stand, Chicago MOCAɪʟ, U.S.

Observatoire de l'Image, *Made in Corpus*, Toulouse, France.

Galeries Contemporaines Sextius, *L'Art dégénéré II, Des artistes contre l'extrême-droite*, exhibition conceived and completed by the CAAC (Aix Contemporary Art Collective), Aix-en-Provence, France.

Living Art Museum, Reykjavik Festival, *The Human Body*, curator Hannes Sigurdsson, Reykjavik, Iceland.

Galerie Yvonamor Palix, *Hygiène*, Paris, France.

By the Way, *Mutation*, Paris, France.

Galerie Passage de Retz, *Fétiche-fétichisme*, curator Jean-Michel Ribettes, Paris, France.

Galerie Cargo, Marseille, France.

Palazzo delle Esposizioni, *La Coscienza Luccicante: electronic art*, curator Carmelo Strano, Rome, Italy.

Art Kiosk Gallery, *Flesh and Field*, Brussels, Belgium.

Histories of the Present Fourth South African Qualitative Methods, Johannesburg, South Africa.

Expo Arte, Galerie Yvonamor Palix Stand, Guadalajara, Mexico.

FIAC, Galerie Yvonamor Palix Stand, Paris, France.

MACBA, *Out of Actions: Between Performance and the Object, 1949–1979*, curator Paul Schimmel, Barcelona, Spain.

Phoenix Arts, Leicester and The Centre for Contemporary Arts of Montfort University, *Rethinking the Avant-garde*, international conference and multimedia festival, Leicester, England.

1997

Venice Biennale of Contemporary Art, *Unimplosive Art Exhibition*, Zitelle, Venice, Italy.

Serpentine Gallery, *Art Vidéo*, curator Anthony Howell, London, England.

P.S.1, *Heaven*, curator Jean-Michel Ribettes, New York MOCAɴʏ, U.S.

The Community Museum of Art, Palm Beach, *Is It Art*, curator Linda Weintraub, Palm Beach, Florida, U.S.

Miami State University, *Endurance*, Miami MOCAꜰʟ, U.S.

ARCO, Galerie Palix Stand, Madrid, Spain.

Vancouver Art Gallery, *Endurance*, Vancouver, Canada.

MACBA, *La máscara y el espejo*, curator Anatxu Zabalbeascoa,

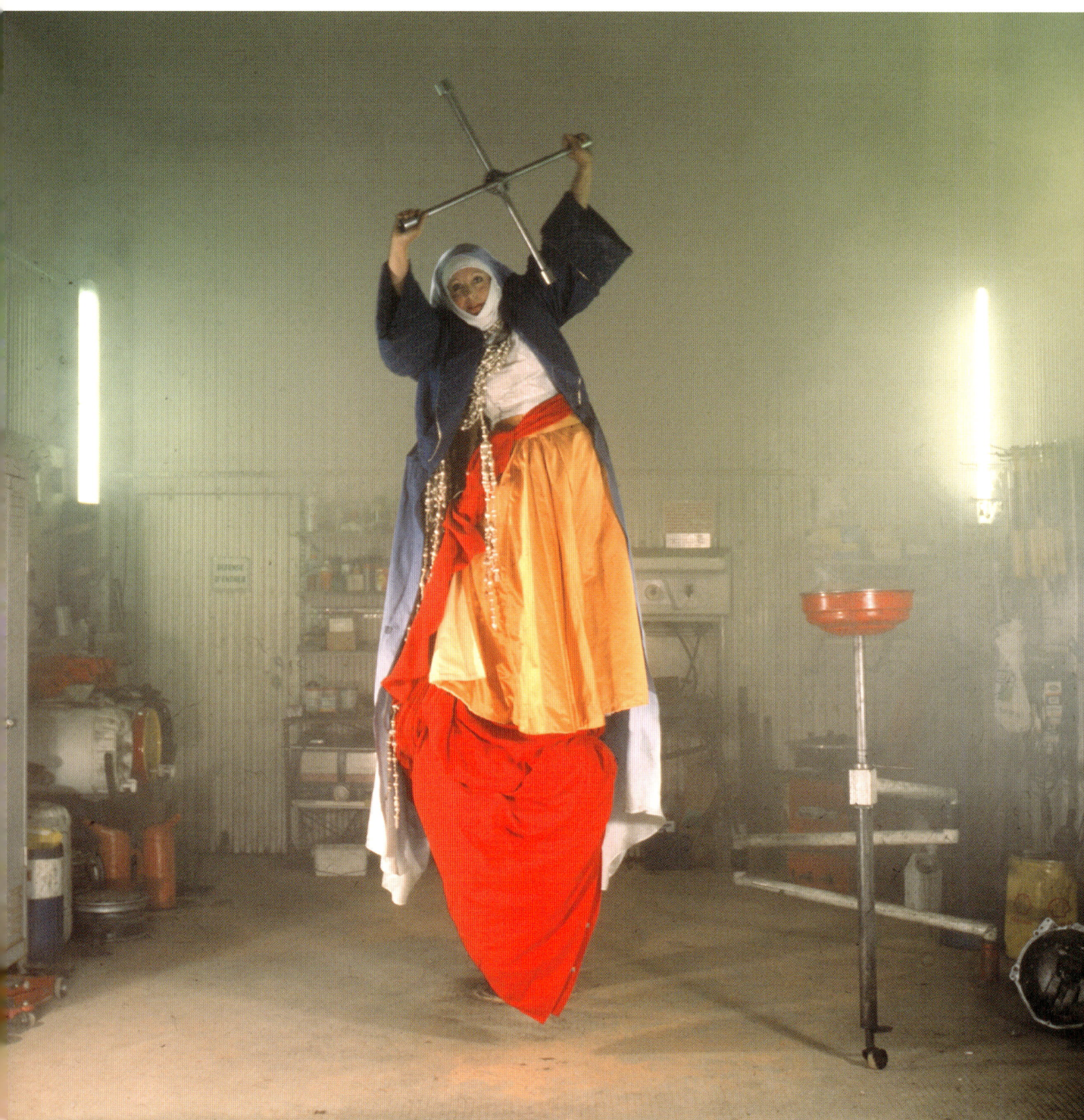

*Assumption of the Madonna of the tire iron,
on pneumatic jack*, 1990. Cibacrome.
120cm. x 120 cm. Photograph by Joel Savary.
Courtesy of the Michel Rein Gallery, Paris.

Barcelona, Spain.

Laguna Museum of Art, *Is It Art*, Laguna MOCAFL, U.S.

Fundacion Miró, *Corps et technologie*, Barcelona, Spain.

Community Museum of Art, Lakeworth, *Is It Art*, curator Linda Weintraub, Lakeworth MOCAFL, U.S.

Centro da arte contemporánea de Belem, *Atlantico Festival*, Lisbon, Portugal.

Lattuada Gallery, curator Francesca Alfano Miglietti, Milan, Italy.

Contemporary Art Fair, Milan, Italy.

Magazin Général, Curator Francesca Alfano Miglietti, Milan, Italy.

Le Magasin, *Vraiment féminisme et art*, curator Laura Cottingham, Grenoble, France.

Musée Saint-Pierre, *Hommage à R. Déroudille*, Lyon, France.

University of Washington, video and conference, Seattle MOCAWA, U.S.

Exogène, *Principe d'extériorité*, exhibition with the help of police forensic services and the Internet, curators Bruno Guigonti and Morten Selling, Copenhagen, Denmark.

Galerie Gilles Peyroulet, *Le Rose de la vie*, Paris, France.

Museum voor Hedendaagse Kunst, video and conference, Ghent, Belgium.

Troisième Manifestation Internationale Vidéo et Art Électronique, Champ Libre, Montreal, Canada.

FIAC, Galerie Palix Stand, Paris, France.

Kunstforening af 1847, SUM, Arhus, Denmark.

Contemporary Art Museum of Trento, *Trash*, curator Lea Vergine, Trento, Italy.

Café-crème, *The Mimeties a Family of Man*, Luxembourg City, Luxembourg.

New Media Department, Faculty of Fine Arts, *Symptoms and Home Remedies*, Hi-Tech/Art Brno, Ostrava, Czech Republic.

Albany Institute of History and Art, *Is It Art*, curator Linda Weintraub, Albany MOCANY, U.S.

Horsens Kunstmuseum, *Woman à*, curator Christin Juerstesens, Horsens, Denmark.

Lichthaus Center, curator Claudia Ruche, Bremen, Germany.

1996

Spaces, *Is It Art*, curator Linda Weintraub, Cleveland MOCAOH, U.S.

Beaver College, *Endurance*, Beaver MOCAPA, U.S.

Kunsthallen Brandts Klaedefabrik, *Body as Membrane*, Odense, Denmark.

ICA, *Totally Wired—Live Arts—Femme avec tête*, curator Lois Keidan, London, England.

Zacheta, *J'ai donné mon corps à l'art*, Warsaw, Poland.

Multi Link, Bari Festival, Bari, Italy.

Ivan Dougherty Gallery, Sydney, Australia.

Contemporary Arts Center, *Is It Art*, curator Linda Weintraub, Cincinnati MOCAOH, U.S.

Rencontres de la Photographie d'Arles, *Le Masque et le Miroir*, curator Anatxu Zabalbeascoa, Arles, France.

Basel Fair, Palix Gallery Stand, Basel, Switzerland.

De Appel, *Hybrids*, Amsterdam, The Netherlands.

Dr Richard Kimble Syndrom, Wolfgang Mentzel, Berlin, Germany.

NGKB Gallery, *Der Körper und der Computer*, curator Richard Wagner, Berlin, Germany.

Musée d'Art Contemporain, *L'Art au corps*, curators Philippe Vergne and Bernard Blistène, Marseille, France.

Salle Gaveau, *Brut de Culture, Schizophrénies*, Paris, France.

École Supérieure des Beaux-Arts de Paris, *Plastic*, curator Robert Fleck, Paris, France.

Art Space, *ORLAN Carnal Art*, Auckland, New Zealand.

Feria Internacional de Guadalajara, Galerie Palix and MOCAfiat Stand, Guadalajara, Mexico.

Museum of Contemporary Art, Endurance, Helsinki, Finland.

Proton I.C.A. *Endurance*, Amsterdam, The Netherlands.

The Katonah Museum of Art, *Is It Art*, curator Linda Weintraub, Katonah, New York, U.S.

GAK, *Endurance*, Bremen, Germany.

La Ferme du Buisson, *Fluctuations fugitives*, curators Chantal Cuzin-Berche and Andrieu Sina, Marne-la-Vallée, France.

Kulturhusset, *Endurance*, Stockholm, Sweden.

FIAC, Galerie Palix stand, Paris, France.

Espace Belleville, *Le Corps dans tous ses états*, Paris, France.

Maine College of Art, *Endurance*, Portland MOCAOR, U.S.

La Laverie Automatique y Galerie Lara Vinci, *Laver l'art*, Ben and Youri, Paris, France.

Nikolaj Church—Contemporary Art Center, *Nemo*, curator Elisabeth Delin-Hansen, Copenhagen, Denmark.

Gallery 400, *Endurance*, Chicago MOCAIL, U.S.

Galerie Lara Vincy, *Les rencontres de Dépanne Machine*, Paris, France.

1995

Galerie Satellite, *Paquets*, Paris, France.

Galerie Janos, *Extrême limite*, curators Joël Hubaut and Arnaud Labelle-Rojoux, Paris, France.

Illinois State University, *Endurance*, Normal MOCAIL, U.S.

Galerie Satellite, *Riquiqui*, Paris, France.

Kunsthalle of Kiel, *Positionem zum Ich*, curator Beate Ermacora, Kiel, Germany.

Kamerabilder, Berlin, Germany.

MNCARS Centro Reina Sofia, *Art futura*, curator Agnès de Gouvion Saint-Cyr, Madrid, Spain.

Clark & Co. Gallery, *Fat Form and Taste*, Washington MOCADC, U.S.

Atelier Brouillard Précis, *Art transit*, Marseille, France.

California College of the Arts, *Mirror Gender Roles and the Historical Significance of Beauty*, San Francisco MOCACA, U.S.

Festival of New Technologies, Warwick, England.

Triple X Festival, Amsterdam, The Netherlands.

Locarno Video Festival, curator Pierre Restany, Locarno, Switzerland.

Studio Stefania Miscetti, *L'Arte "Riparte,"* curator Achille Boniti Oliva, Rome, Italy.

Galerie Agnès b, *Les Tétines noires*, Paris, France.

Sculpture Biennale, *Oltre di scultura*, curator Ernesto L, Francalanci, Padua, Italy.

Virginia Beach Center, *Endurance*, Virginia Beach MOCAVA, U.S.

Biennale d'Art Contemporain et de Nouvelles Technologies, curators Georges Rey, Thierry Raspail, and Thierry Prat, Lyon, France.

Artpool, *Video-Expedition in the Performance-World*, Budapest, Hungary.

1994

Centre Georges Pompidou, *Hors limites*, curator Jean de Loisy, Paris, France.

ICA, *The Body as Site*, video performance, London, England.

Galleria d'Arte Moderna, *French Art from 70 to 90*, curators R. Barilli and Pierre Restany, Bologna, Italy.

Kariya City Museum, *French Portrait Art in the Nineteenth and Twentieth Centuries*, curator Jean-Michel Ribettes, Aichi, Japan.

La Giarrina Gallery, *Shape your Body*, curator Francisco Conz, Verona, Italy.

Shoto Museum of Art, *French Portrait Art in the Nineteenth and Twentieth Centuries*, curator Jean-Michel Ribettes, Tokyo, Japan.

Nexus Center, Atlanta MOCAGA, U.S.

Onomichi Municipal Museum of Art, *French Portrait Art in the Nineteenth and Twentieth Centuries*, curator Jean-Michel Ribettes, Onomichi, Japan.

Kunstverein, *Suture*, curator Sylvia Eiblmayr, Salzburg, Austria.

Tour du Roi René, Brouillard précis, *Art and New Technologies*, Marseille, France.

Kunsthalle of Kiel, curator Beate Ermacora, Kiel, Germany.

NGBK, *Fabricated realities (Bec,* *Stelarc, ORLAN)*, Berlin, Germany.

San Francisco Museum, *Mirror Mirror*, curator Terri Cohn, San Francisco MOCACA, U.S.

Akita Museum of Modern Art, *French Portrait Art in the Nineteenth and Twentieth Centuries*, curator Jean-Michel Ribettes, Hiroshima, Japan.

Parc Floral, *Actuel*, all-night performance, Paris, France.

1993

Musée de la Villette, *Van Gogh TV Piazza Virtuale*, curator Christian Van der Borgh, Paris, France.

Penine Hart Gallery, *Bodily*, New York MOCANY, U.S.

Ars Electronica, Landesmuseum, Linz, Austria.

Bali, Amsterdam, The Netherlands.

Rijksakademie van beeldende kunsten, *ORLAN*, Amsterdam, The Netherlands.

Postmuseum Frankfurt, *Borderlines*, curator Hildegard M. Wilms, Photography Biennial, Fototage, Frankfurt, Germany.

Nederlands Filmmuseum, *Festival Video and Film Skrien*, Amsterdam, The Netherlands.

V2, video installation *The Body in Ruins*, Hertogenbosch, The Netherlands.

Galerie Satellite, *De l'amour*, Paris, France.

Sandra Gering Gallery, *Omniprésence 1*, New York MOCANY, U.S.

Cirque Divers, *Sacrifice*, Sixth operation surgery-performance (text by Antonin Artaud) and multimedia exhibition, Liège, Belgium.

Galerie du Cirque Divers, *Deux soirs à l'autel*, Liège, Belgium.

Penine Hart Gallery, *My Flesh, the Text and the Languages*, New York MOCANY, U.S.

Webster Hall, *Vidéo Party*, curator Jacques Ranc, New York MOCANY, U.S.

Biennale of Contemporary Art, Private Exhibition, Jean-Claude Binoche, curator Jacques Ranc, Venice, Italy.

Galerie Sylvana Lorenz, *Le printemps de Beaubourg*, Paris, France.

1992

Sydney Biennial of Contemporary Art, *Vidéo installation pour le plafond*, curator Anthony Bond, Sydney, Australia.

Lallit Kala Academy, *Scholarship from the FIACRE for a Trip to India*, Madras, India.

Buro Performance and Video, Koning, Poland.

Emily Harvey and Pat Hearn Gallery, New York MOCANY, U.S.

1991

Musée de la Poste, *Les Couleurs de l'argent*, curator Jean-Michel Ribettes, Paris, France.

L'Espace d'un instant, curators Emmanuel Javogue and Édouard Fabre, Paris, France.

Molkerei-Werkstatt Performance Multimedia, Cologne, Germany.

L'Artiste en représentation, curators Arnauld Labelle-Rojoux and Guy Scarpetta, Avignon, France.

Espace Art-Brenne, *Écran icône*, curator Christian Gattinoni, Concremiers, France.

Galerie de l'École Régionale des Beaux-Arts, Clermont-Ferrand, France.

Fondation Cartier, *Vraiment faux*, Munich, Germany.

1990

Centre Georges Pompidou, *Performance of Art and Pub*, Arzapub, Paris, France.

FIAC Grand Palais, curator Éric Fabre, Paris, France.

Grand Palais, *Europe des créateurs*, *Actuel magazine*, Art Planète Stand, Intermaco advertising agency, Video-fax-telematics installation with Jean-Christophe Bouvet and François Berheim, Paris, France.

Edge Festival, *L'Art et la Vie dans les années 90*, Beginning of surgical operation performances: *La Réincarnation de sainte ORLAN ou Image(s) nouvelle(s) images* (May 30, 1990), Newcastle, England.

Biennal of Innovative Visual Art, Glasgow-London, England.

Edge, Rotterdam, The Netherlands.

The Gallery, *Désir et désordre*, curator Jean-Jacques Lebel, Milan, Italy.

Centre Wallonie-Bruxelles, *La vidéo casse le baroque*, videos and installations, Paris, France.

Espace Paul Ricard-Fondation Camille, Paris, France.

La Manufacture, Ivry-sur-Seine, France.

CREDAC, *Un peu de temps et vous ne me verrez plus . . . Encore un peu de temps et vous me verrez*, curator Thierry Sigg, Ivry-sur-Seine, France.

Performance de La Réincarnation de sainte ORLAN ou Image(s) nouvelle(s) images, Paris, France.

L'Enlèvement d'Europe, Project Caravan and Container Seven and a Half, Sète, France.

G. Descossy Gallery, *Salon*, Paris, France.

L'Enlèvement d'Europe, Project Caravan and Container Seven and a Half, Tanger-Casablanca, Morocco.

Espace Lamartine-Fondation France Télécom, Paris, France.

ARCADE, Center for research and contemporary creation, *Le corps le sacré*, Carcassonne, France.

Galerie de l'Ecole des Beaux-Arts, Clermont-Ferrand, France.

1989

Grand Palais, *Europe des créateurs*, Paris, France.

Palais de Tokyo, *La Madonne au minitel*, Paris, France.

International Video Festival Simone de Beauvoir, *Femmes cathodiques*, Paris, France.

Espace d'Art Brenne, *Écrans-icônes*, Concremiers, France.

Bilder Streit, Cologne, Germany.

ISELP, *Utopies 89*, Brussels, Belgium.

Galerie J. and J. Donguy, *yet more performances*, Paris, France.

Centre Georges Pompidou, *Polyphonix (Fluxus et Happenings)*, curators Jean-Jacques Lebel y Jacqueline Cahen, Paris, France.

Fondation Camille Claudel, Fort-de-France, Martinique.

Fondation Danaé, *Espaces affranchis*, Pouilly-en-Auxois, France.

Sixièmes Rencontres Internationales de Poésie Contemporaine, curator Julien Blaine, Tarascon, France.

Video Festival, San Francisco MOCAca, U.S.

ISELP, *Pages d'artistes hors mesure*, Brussels, Belgium.

MacLuhan Science Center, *Les Transintéractifs*, curator Fred Forest, Toronto, Canada, performance retransmitted via satellite to Paris, France.

Atelier 03, *Fin de siècle et début de mois*, Ivry-sur-Seine, France.

Le Palace, *Le Palace, l'acte pour l'art*, curator Arnauld Labelle-Rojoux, Paris, France.

Rencontre Vidéo-Art-Plastique, Hérouville Saint-Clair, France.

Locarno Video Festival, curator Pierre Restany, Locarno, Switzerland.

University of Louvain-la-Neuve, *Atelier Télématique*, Louvain-la-Neuve, Belgium.

1988

Centre Français du Commerce Extérieur, for the city of Science and Industry, *Tran Interactifs*, videoconference, Paris-Toronto, Paris, France.

Galea Gallery, *Bande à part*, Caen, France.

Le Lieu, installation, curator Richard Martel, Quebec, Canada.

Fondation Danaé, *Hommage à Robert Filliou*, Pouilly-en-Auxois, France.

1987

Centre Georges Pompidou, *Polyphonix 11*, International festival of poetry, music, and performance, Paris, France.

Galerie Chambre Claire, *Baroques photographiques*, Paris, France.

ELAC, *videos and movies*, curator Georges Rey, Lyon, France.

FNAC, Palais de Tokyo, *Nuit de la vidéo*, curator Brigitte Castel, Lyon, France.

Les Troisièmes Rencontres photographiques de Saintes, *Le Baroque en photo*, curator Christian Gattinoni, Abbaye-aux-Dames, Saintes, France.

CCI Centre Georges Pompidou, Telematics and creation, Paris, France.

Fondation Danaé, *Espaces affranchis*, Pouilly-en-Auxois, France.

International Biennale MOCAcd 87, Ljubljana, Slovenia.

International Multimedia Center, *Aesthetic diffuse*, Salerno, Italy.

Museu Municipal Dr. Santos Rocha, Figueira da Foz, Portugal.

Le lieu, Contemporary Art Center, Quebec, Canada.

1986

Festival des Arts Électroniques, *Light Show*, laser graphic, Rennes, France.

Venice Biennale of Contemporary Art, section "Art and Science," curator Dan Foresta, Venice, Italy.

2nd Videonale, Bonn, Germany.

3rd International Festival of Poetry of Cogolin, curator Julien Blaine, Cogolin, France.

École Nationale Supérieure des Beaux-Arts, *Art Com 86*, curator Robert Fleck, Paris, France.

Gare de l'Est, *Culture-future*, Paris, France.

Stedelijk Museum, *Rétrospective vidéo*, Amsterdam, The Netherlands.

Art Jonction, Nice, France.

FAUST, Toulouse, France.

L'Élan avec le MIT *Buses and bus shelters*, Paris, France.

Mouvements-recouvrements, with the collaboration of Daniel Buren and with the help of Art-Accès, Reims, France.

1985

Centre Georges Pompidou, Les Immatériaux, curator François Lyotard, Paris, France.

FIAC Grand Palais, Paris, France.

Modern Art Museum, *Kunst mit eigensinn*, Vienna, Austria.

Electronic Image Congress, Bologna, Italy.

Vidéo Belvédère, Geneva, Switzerland.

Ars Machina Festival, Turin, Italy.

Cultural Center of Belgrade, Serbia.

2nd International Festival of Poetry of Cogolin, Cogolin, France.

Locarno International Video Festival, curator Pierre Restany, Locarno, Switzerland.

Créatique, Saint-Quentin-en-Yvelines, France.

1984

Musée d'Art Moderne de la Ville de Paris, *Electra Documentary Study*, no. 101: *La Lumière mise en scène pour un grand Fiat*, curator Dany Block, Paris, France.

Tate Gallery, *Sélection French Video*, London, England.

Sociedade Nacional de Belas Artes, *Corperformance 84*, curator Manoel Barbosa, Lisbon, Portugal.

Lantaren Perfo 2 Festival, Rotterdam, The Netherlands.

Ubu à Saint-Vorles, contemporary art show, *Sainte-orLAN multi faces*, Châtillon-sur-Seine, France.

Locarno Festival, curator Pierre Restany, Locarno, Switzerland.

1983

Guggenheim Museum, *MesuRage d'institution*, New York MOCAny, U.S.

Moderna Museet, *L'Art expérimental*, Stockholm, Sweden.

Rheinisches Landesmuseum, photo-installation, Bonn, Germany.

Palazzo dei Diamanti, Argillière presse, curator Lea Bonora, Ferrrara, Italy.

Ars Viva Gallery, curator Pierre Restany, Milan, Italy.

Festival International de Performance de Lyon, *Sainte: orLAN bénit la performance, instalación multimedia*, Lyon, France.

Geneva Festival, *Andata Ritorno*, laser show and giant projection accompanying the orchestra of the Geneva Opera, Switzerland.

Kunst Museum, Norköping, Sweden.

2e Rencontres Vidéo, Roubaix, France.

1982

Centre Georges Pompidou, *Revue parlée*, Paris, France.

Alain Oudin Gallery, *Autoportraits de femmes*, Paris, France.

Art-Prospect, actions in the urban landscape, "Avenir Publicité" advertising posters, Lyon, France.

Contemporary Art Fair, Bilbao, Spain.

Albi Festival of Technology of the Future and the Future of the Culture, video and laser projections, Albi, France.

Modern Art Museum, selection from the Paris Biennale, Helsinki, Finland.

Bari Art Fair, Galerie Lattuada Stand, Bari, Italy.

La Chambre Blanche, Quebec, Canada.

Living Art Festival, Almada, Portugal.

Gallerie J. & J. Donguy, *Pastiches 54*, curator Jean Donguy, Paris, France.

1981

Centre Georges Pompidou, *L'Autoportrait*, curator Alain Sayag, Paris, France.

Fundación Gulbenkian, selection from the Paris Biennale, Lisbon, Portugal.

Espace Lyonnais d'Art Contemporain, *Made in France*, curator Marie-Claude Jeune, Lyon, France.

Seventh Paris Biennale in Nice, Nice, France.

Pinacoteca, curator Renato Barilli, Ravena, Italy.

Sofitta Theater, *Fifth International Week of Performance*, curator Renato Barilli, Bologna, Italy.

Teatro Municipale Ariosto Reggio, curator Renato Barilli, Reggio Emilia, Italy.

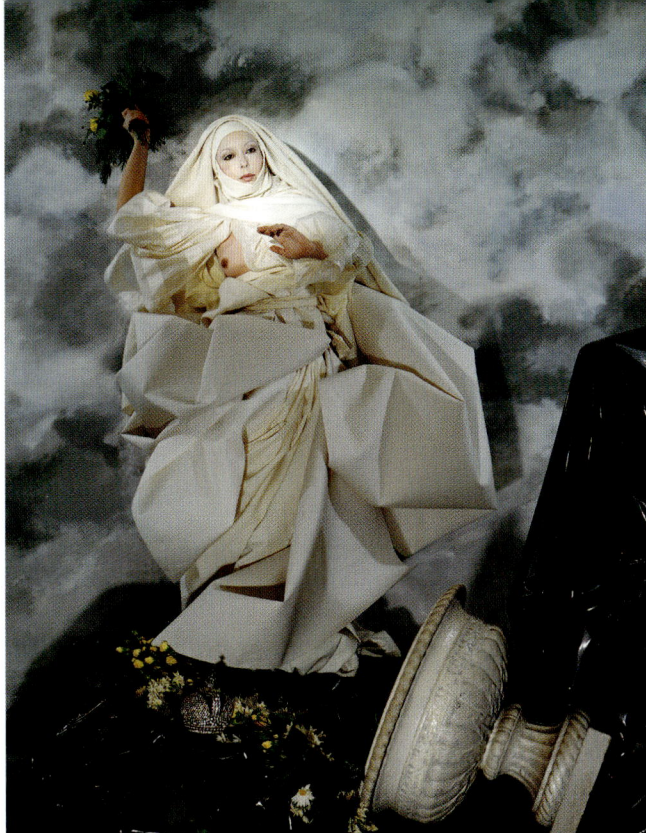

Museo de Bellas Artes, curator
Renato Barilli, Piacenza, Italy.
Performance Festival, Wuppertal and
Cologne, Germany.
Drawing Triennale, Wroclaw, Poland.
Art Forum Gallery, Lodz, Poland.

1980

Centre Georges Pompidou, *Exposition
photocopie*, curator Alain Sayag,
Paris, France.
Musée d'Art Moderne de la Ville de
Paris, *Vidéo à l'ARC*, curator Dany
Block, Paris, France.
Goethe Institut, Manifestation video
performance, Paris, France.
*Symposium International de
Performance*, Lyon, curators ORLAN
and Hubert Besacier, Lyon, France.
Espace Lyonnais d'Art Contemporain,
Made in France, ORLAN presents
the multimedia installation, *Mise en
scène pour une sainte*, curator Marie-
Claude Jeune, Lyon, France.
Art Biennale de Paris, Paris, France.
Musée Chéret, selection from the
Paris Bienalle, Nice, France.

1979

Centre Georges Pompidou,
Rencontre Internationale d'Art
Corporel, *ORLAN is delivered to the
Centre in a container, like a work of
art*, curator Jorge Glusberg, Paris,
France.
Symposium International de
Performance, *urgent surgical
operation GEU*, Lyon, France.
Palazzo Grassi, *Incontri Internazionali
di Performance*, curator Jorge
Glusberg, Venice, Italy.
Bologna Fair, Galerie Pellegrino
Stand, Bologna, Italy.
Théâtre d'en face, *Performances-
bouffe*, Paris, France.

1978

Musée du Louvre, Action minute,
Performance of *À poil sans poils*,
curators Jean Dupuy y A. Lemoine,
Paris, France.
Musée d'Angoulême, *Les Artistes sur
les pavés*, curators Monique Bussac
y Joël Capella-Lardeux, Angoulême,
France.
Espace Lyonnais d'Art Contemporain,
Langages au féminin, ORLAN
presents *Le Baiser de l'artiste*,
curator Jean-Louis Maubant, Lyon,
France.
Galerie N.R.A., *Livre d'art et d'artiste*,
curator hristian Parisot, Paris,
France.
MesuRage de rue, curator Ben, Nice,
France.
Neue Galerie Sammlung Ludwig,
*Symposium International de
Performance*, Aix-la-Chapelle,
Germany.

1977

Grand Palais—Foire Internationale
d'Art Contemporain, *Le Baiser de
l'artiste*, Paris, France.
Espace Lyonnais d'Art Contemporain,
Contemporary trends of Rhone-
Alpes, ORLAN presents the
installation *1000 et une façons de
ne pas dormir*, curator Jean-Louis
Maubant, Lyon, France.
Galerie NRA, *Piège, casserole et chaîne
and Panoplie de la mariée mise à
nue*, Paris, France.
Studio d'Ars, curator Pierre Restany,
Milan, Italy.

1976

Galerie des Ursulines, con el grupo
Untel, Mâcon, France.
Municipal Theater, *Concert Fluxus*,
curator Ben, Nice, France.

1975

La Mulatière, *Les Tableaux vivants
Situation-citation*, Lyon, France.
Basel Art Fair, *Pellegrino Gallery stand*,
Basel, Switzerland.
Maison de la Culture et des Loisirs
de Saint-Étienne, *Triennale de la
Peinture*, curator Lydia Artias, and
MesuRage, Saint-Étienne, France.
Atelier Claude Delaroa, *Strip-tease
occasionnel à travers les draps du
trousseau*, Lyon, France.
Manifestation Internationale
des Jeunes Artistes, Neuvième
Biennale, Paris, France.

1974

Salon du Sud-Est, *pinturas y
abstracciones líricas*, Lyon, France.

1973

Wuppertal Museum, *Expo 63/42*,
curator Lydia Artias, Wuppertal,
Germany.

1972

Maison de la Culture, *MesuRage dans
Expo 63/42*, curator Lydia Artias,
Saint-Étienne, France.
Atelier Claude Delaroa, *Les Tableaux
vivants Situation-citation*, Saint-
Étienne, France.

1971

L'Art et la vie, Lyon, France.
Universidad de Toulouse, Mirail
Action, *Je suis une homme et un
femme*, feminist colloquium,
Toulouse, France.
Atelier Claude Delaroa, *Situation-
citation*, Saint-Étienne, France.
L'Art dans la rue, Saint-Étienne, France.

1970

Salon du Sud-Est, *Peinture,
abstractions géométriques*, Saint-
Étienne, France.

1969

Sous chapiteau, Festival de Peinture,
La Ricamarie, France.
Action contravention, Saint-Étienne,
Lyon, Bourges, Marseille, Avignon,
France.

1968

MesuRage Performance, Saint-
Chamond, France.
Atelier Claude Delaroa, *Couture en
clair obscur, broderies des tâches de
sperme sur les draps du trousseau*,
blindfolded performance, Saint-
Étienne, France.
Place des Ursules, *Les Peintres dans la
rue*, Saint-Étienne, France.
*Street actions: Contraventions of the
brigade anti-norm*, itinerant, France.

1967

Atelier Peagno, exhibition and
signing of *Prosésies écrites*, Saint-
Étienne, France.

1966

Auberge de Dargoire, *Peintures-
Matières*, Dargoire, France.

PUBLIC COLLECTIONS

Centre Georges Pompidou, National
Museum of Contemporary Art,
Paris, France.
Maison Européenne de la
Photographie, Paris, France.
FNAC, National Fund of
Contemporary Art, Paris, France.
National Fund of Photography, Paris,
France.
MAC/VAL, Contemporary Art
Museum of the Val-de-Marne, Vitry-
sur-Seine, France.
FRAC, Regional Fund for
Contemporary Art, Rhônes-Alpes,
France.
FRAC, Regional Fund for
Contemporary Art, Pays de Loire,
France.
FRAC, Regional Fund for
Contemporary Art, Ile de France,
France.
FRAC, Regional Fund for
Contemporary Art, Limoges,
France.
Neuflize Vie Collection, France.
Marseille Municipal Collection,
Marseille, France.
Fine Arts Museum of Tourcoing,
Tourcoing, France.
Bièvre Museum of Photographie,
Bièvre, France.
Camille Foundation, Epinal, France.
Departemental Museum of Ancient
and Contemporary Art of Epinal,
France.
Le Magasin, Contemporary Art
Center, Grenoble, France.
Artothèque du Département de la
Réunion, France.
MOCAlacma, Los Angeles MOCAca,
U.S.
Getty Research Institut, Los Angeles
MOCAca, U.S.
Getty Museum, Los Angeles
MOCAca, U.S.
Banca di Santo Spirito, Lisbon,
Portugal.
Daelim Contemporary Art Museum,
Seoul, South Korea.
Hanlim Art Museum, Seoul, South
Korea.
Universidad de Salamanca,
Salamanca, Spain.
MOCAartium, Vitoria, Spain.
Museum Kunst Palast, Düsseldorf,
Germany.

*Documentary Study, no. 1. The Draped—
The Baroque or, Saint ORLAN with
flowers against a backdrop of clouds*, 1983.
Cibachrome, 160 cm. x 120 cm., edition
of seven. Photograph by Anna Garde.
Courtesy of the Michel Rein Gallery, Paris.

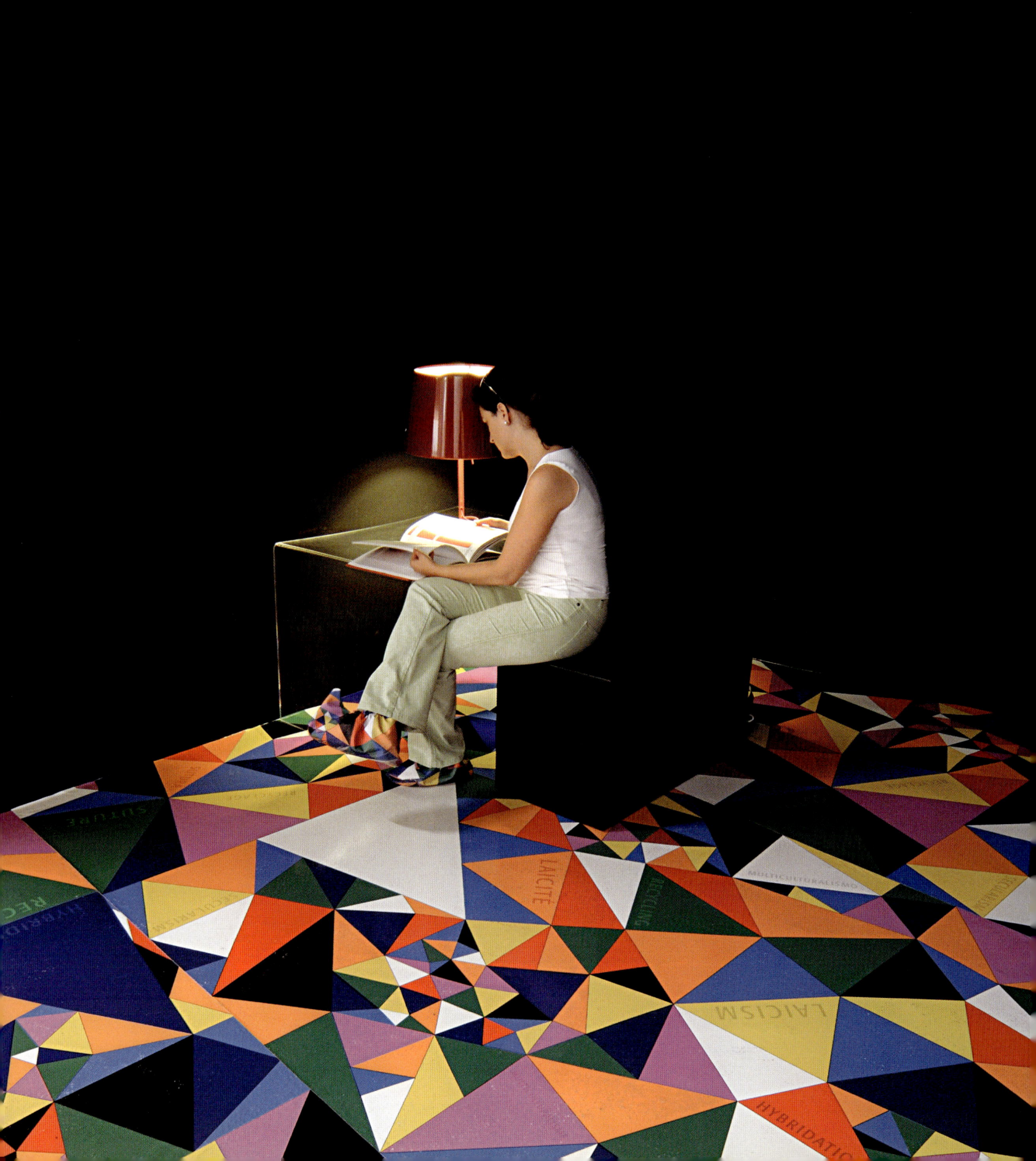

MONOGRAPHS

2008

Cruz, Pedro Alberto, Rhonda Garelick, ORLAN, Michel Serres, Isabel Tejeda, Rocío y de la Villa, and Lan Vu. *ORLAN+davidelfin: sutura, hibridación, reciclaje: la ropa y los vestidos encarnados en la obra de ORLAN*. Catálogo de la exposición en el Espacio AV, Murcia, Spain: Comunidad Autónoma Región de Murcia, Consejería de Cultura y Turismo, Dirección General de Promoción Cultural, Murcia Capital Creativo, 2008.

2007

Barjou, Nathalie, Laurent Deflandre, Antonia Dubrulle, Clémence Laot, Charlène Marquis, Cécile Noesser, and Olivier Normand. *ORLAN, Morceaux choisis*. Lyon, France: Ecole Nationale Supérieur editions / Musée d'art moderne de Saint-Étienne Métropole, 2007.

Hegyi, Lorand, Donald Kuspit, Marcela Iacub, Peggy Phelan, Joerg Bader, and Eugenio Viola. *ORLAN: The Narrative*. Milan, Italy: Éditions Charta, 2007.

ORLAN. *Pomme Cul et petites fleurs*. Paris: Editions Baudoin Janninck, 2007.

2005

Francesca, Alfano Miglietti. Milan, Italy: Catálogo de las *Self-Hybridations* expuestas por B & D, 2005.

O'Bryan, Jill. *Carnal Art: ORLAN's Refacing*. Minneapolis MN: University of Minnesota Press, 2005.

2004

Blistène, Bernard, Christine Buci-Glucksmann, Caroline Cros, Régis Durand, Eleanor Heartney, Laurent Le Bon, Hans Ulrich Obrist, Vivian Rehberg, Julian y Zugazagoitia, and ORLAN. *ORLAN: Carnal Art*. Paris: Editions Flammarion, 2004.

2002

ARTIUM. Vitoria, Spain: Centro de Fotografía de la Universidad de Salamanca, 2002.

Blistène, Bernard, Christine Buci-Glucksmann, Juan Guardiola, Olga Guinot, Juan Antonio Ramirez, and Julian Zugazagoita. *ORLAN 1964–2001*. Catálogo de la retrospectiva en el Centro de Fotografía de la Universidad de Salamanca, Salamanca, España, 2002.

2001

Baqué, Dominique, Marek Bartelik, and ORLAN. *ORLAN: Refiguration Self-hybridations*. Pre-Columbian Series. Paris: Éditions Al Dante, 2001.

Rehm, Jean-Pierre, and Serge Quadruppani. *Le Plan du Film*. Séquence 1, libro y del CD del grupo Tanger. Romainville, France: Éditions Laurent Cauwet/ Al Dante, 2001.

Yun, Jin-Sup, and Dominique Baqué. *ORLAN: Re-figuration Self-hybridations*. Seoul, South Korea: Catálogo de la galleria, 2001.

2000

Buci-Glucksmann, Christine, and Michel Enrici. *ORLAN: triomphe du baroque*. Marseille, France: Éditions Images en Manoeuvres, 2000.

Ince, Kate, and ORLAN. *Millennial Female*. Oxford, England: Berg, 2000.

Partouche, Marc, Carole Boulbès, Jean-Michel Ribettes, Norbert Hillaire, Hugues Marchal, Jean-Pierre Nouhaud, and ORLAN. *Multimedia Monograph*. Paris: Éditions Jeriko, 2000.

1999

Becce, Sonia, Roberto Jacoby, and Serge François. *ORLAN: Omniprésence*. Buenos Aires, Argentina: Galérie L'Alliance, 1999.

Bourgeade, Pierre. *ORLAN: Self-hybridations*. Romainville, France: Éditions Al Dante, 1999.

1998

Bastille, Marie-José, Christian Gattinoni, Bernard Lafargue, ORLAN, Lydie Pearl, Isabelle Rieusset Lemarié, and Joël Savary. *Une OEuvre d'ORLAN*. Marseille, France: Éditions Muntaner, collection Iconotexte, 1998.

1997

Alfano, Miglietti Francesca, Ernesto Francalanci, and Jean-Michel Ribettes. *ORLAN*. Catálogo de la exposición. Milan, Italy: Lattuada Studio, 1997.

Fabre, Gladys, Flor Bex, Sarah Wilson, Bernard Ceysson, Julien Blaine, David Moos, Ulla Karttunen, Malgorzata Listewicz, Philippe Vergne, August Ruhs, Patrick Desmons, Parveen Adams, Louis Bec, Jean-Michel Ribettes, Michel Onfray, Hubert Besacier, Alain Charre, Jacques Donguy, Christian Gattinoni, Linda Weintraub, Catherine Millet, Françoise Eliet, and Abraham Moles. *ORLAN, de L'Art charnel au Baiser de l'artiste*. Collection Sujet-Objet. Paris: Éditions Jean-Michel Place & Fils, 1997.

1996

Alfano Miglietti, Francesca. *ORLAN*. Milan, Italy: Virus Productions, 1996.

Bonito, Oliva Achille, Bernard Ceysson, Bruno Di Marino, Vittorio Fagone, Ulla Karttunen, and Mario Perniola. *ORLAN 1964–1996*. Rome: Diagonale, 1996.

Wilson, Sarah, Michel Onfray, Rosanne Stone Allucquére, Serge François, and Parveen Adams. *ORLAN. Ceci est mon corps, ceci est mon logiciel*. London: Black Dog, 1996.

1994

Fabre, Gladys, Dominique Gilbert-Laporte, and Jacques Donguy. *Skaï and Sky et Vidéo*. Paris: Éditions Tierces, 1994.

Raffier, Joël. *L'Art Ushuaïa, l'extrême ORLAN. Gervais Lescure ou l'art somatique*. Auroville, India: Editions ACI, 1994.

1990

Ceysson, Bernard, and Joël Savary. *ORLAN: l'ultime chef-d'oeuvre. Les 20 ans de pub et de cinéma de sainte ORLAN*. Catálogo de la exposición. Saint-Clair, France: Editions du Centre d'Art contemporain de Basse-Normandie, Hérouville, 1990.

1986

Fabre, Gladys, and Dorine Mignot. *ORLAN. Art Access online revue*. Amsterdam, Holland: Stedelijk Museum, 1986.

1984

Fabre, Gladys, Dominique Gilbert-Laporte, and Jacques Donguy. *Skaï and Sky and Vidéo*. Catálogo de la exposición en la galería J.& J. Donguy. Paris: Tierces, 1984.

CATALOGS OF COLLECTIVE EXHIBITIONS

2008

Alizart, Mark, and Jean de Loisy. *Traces du Sacré*. Paris: Éditions du Centre Pompidou, 2008.

Baptiste, Essevaz-Roulet. *Les Arts font évènement*. Paris: Art saint-germain des prés, 2008.

Fuchs, Daniel and Geo. *Famous Eyes*. Munich, Germany: Edition Reuss, 2008.

Heartney, Eleanor. *Art and Today*. London: Phaidon, 2008.

Janus23. *A White Box for a Black Cube*. Gabriel Kuri, Anish Kappor, Edith Dekyndt, Olaf Nicolai, Eric Van Hove. Ghent, Belgium: Janus VZW in association with MER, 2008.

Museo Tridentino di Scienze Naturali, Avatar, Italy, 2008.

2007

BEAP 07. Biennale of Electronic Arts Perth Still-ness. Australia: Edition BEAP, 2007.

Belleza, Pericolosa. *Dangerous Beauty*. Naples: Edition Palazzo delle, 2007.

Butler, Cornelia. *WACK! Art and the Feminist Revolution*. Cambridge MA: MIT Press, 2007.

Collection du Centre Pompidou. Collection Photographies. Musée national d'art moderne, Edition du Centre Pompidou, Quentin Bajac, Clément Chéroux. Paris: Centre Pompidou, Éditions du Panama, 2007.

GNAM gastronomia nell'arte moderna. Rome, Italy: Frederico Mosta Editore, 2007.

Kozloff, Max. *The Theatre of the Face: Potrait Photography since 1900*. London: Phaidon, 2007.

Leismann, Scherer. *Diagnose Kunst Diagnosis Art*. Cologne, Germany: Wienand Verlag-Gmbh, 2007.

Nehamasm, Alexander. *Only a Promise of Happiness: The Place of Beauty in a World of Art*. Princeton NJ: Princeton University Press, 2007.

Slovak National Gallery, Autopoesis. *Irena Kucharova (Ed)*. Bratislava, Slovakia: Slovak National Gallery Bratislava, 2006.

Vervoordt, Axel. *Artempo: Where Time becomes Art*. Brussels, Belgium: MER Editions, 2007.

Zidianakis, Vassilis. *RRRIPP!! Paper Fashion*. Athens, Greece: Atopos, 2007.

2006

Carey, John. *What Good Are the Arts?* Cambridge, England: Oxford University Press, 2006.

Carpio, Francisco, Fernando Castro, and Javier Panera. *Mascarada, Explorafoto*. Salamanca, Spain: Universidad de Salamanca, 2006.

Marquard Smith, Joanne Mora. *The Prosthetic Impulse: From a Posthuman Present to a Bocultural Future*. Cambridge MA: MIT Press, 2006.

Mayeur, Christian. *Le manager à l'écoute de l'artiste*. Paris, France:

Éditions d'Organisation, 2006.
Montfumat, Isabelle de (dir.). *Face à Face*. Tours, France: Collection privée ADP, Corpus initial/AFAA2006.
Salmon Dimitri, Ingres. *La Grande Odalisque*. Paris: Musée du Louvre Editions, 2006.

2005

Blasco, Lorena Amorós. *Abismos de la mirada: La experiencia límite en el autorretrato último*. Cendeac, Spain: Cendeac, 2005.
Buci-Glucksmann, Christine. *Les vanités dans l'art contemporain*, Charbonneaux Anne-Marie (dir.). Paris: Flammarion, 2005.
David, Julie (dir.). *Parcours #1 2005/2006, collection du MAC/ VAL, éditions du MAC/VAL*. Paris: Musée d'art contemporain du Val-de-Marne, 2005.
Jeffet, William, Diane Camber, Olivier Kaeppelin, and Olivier Poivre d'Arvor. *Shortcuts between Reality and Fiction: Video, Installations, and Paintings from le Fond National d'Art Contemporain*. Exhibition catalogue. Miami FL: Bass Museum of Art, 2005.
Rouille, André. *La Photographie*. Paris: Gallimard, 2005.
Sánchez, Pedro A. Cruz, and Miguel Á Hernández-Navarro Miguel, eds. *Cartografías del Cuerpo: La dimensión corporal en el arte contemporáneo*. Barcelona, Spain: Cendeac, 2004.
Viola, Eugenio. "Itinerari del Post-Human." In *Figure dell'Arte 1950–2000*, Stefania Zuliani (dir.) Parma, Italy: Modo, 2005.
Warr, Tracey, and Amelia Jones. *Le corps de l'artiste*. London: Phaidon, 2005.

2004

Airyung, Kim. *In Mouvement: UNESCO Salutes Women Video Artists of the World*. Paris: Section for Women and Gender Equality, Bureau of Strategic Planning, UNESCO, 2004.
Bonafoux, Pascal. *Moi! Autoportraits du XXè siècle*. Paris: Éditions Skira, Musée du Luxembourg, 2004.
Delay, Annie. *Marie Madeleine Contemporaine*. Paris: Espace-Temps et Création, 2004.
Ewing, William A. *About Face: Photography and the Death of the Portait*. London: Hayward Gallery, 2004.
Heathfield, Adrian (dir.). *Live, Art and Performance*. London: Tate, 2004.
Kalkmann, Hans Werner. *Bocca Della Verità*. Bad Salzdetfurth, Germany: KunstvereiN Bad Salzdetfurth, 2004.
Lamy, Franck. *Du corps à l'image*. Collection du Fonds Régional d'art contemporain d'Ile-de-France, Conseil Général des Yvelines. Le

Frac Ile-de-France: La Fondation d'Art Contemporain Daniel & Florence Guerlain, 2004.
Mileaf, Janine. *Inside Out Loud: Vizualizing Women's Health in Contemporary Art*. Edited by Jane E. Neidhardt. St. Louis MO: Mildred Lane Kemper Art Museum, Washington University, 2004.
Mollard, Claude, Marie-Christine Burguillo, and Jean-Luc Chalumeau. *Campus Euro(pe) Art*. Paris, France: Éditions Scérén, 2004.
Prix Arcimboldo 2004. Paris: Maison Européenne de la Photographie, 2004.
Sultan, Oliver. *Les Afriques-36 Artistes contemporains*. Paris: Autrement, 2004.
Sviblova, Olga. *Cinquième Mois International de la Photographie à Moscou "Photobiennale 2004."* Moscow: Maison de la Photographie de Moscou, 2004.
Walter, Herbert. *Die Zhen Gebote*. Dresden, Germany: Deutschen Hygiene Museum, 2004.

2003

Barak, Ami, Katie Baudin, Bernard Blistène, and Olivier Zahm . *Trésors publics, 20 ans de creation dans les Fonds régionaux d'Art contemporain*. Catálogo de la exposición. Paris: Flammarion, 2003.
Bethenod, Martin, and Jacques Kerchache. *Portraits croisés*. Paris: Gallimard, Musée du Quai Branly, 2003.
Cortenova, Giorgio. *La Creazione ansiosa da Picasso a Bacon*. Verona, Italy: Marsilio, Palazzo Forti, 2003.
Deschamps, Gérard. *Retrospective 1956–2003*. Musée de l'hospice Saint-Roch, Issoudun, Musée des Beaux-Arts, Dole, 2003.
Durand, Régis, Jean-Louis Milin, and André Pessel. *Fables de l'identité, oeuvres photographiques et vidéo de la collection NSM Vie/ABN AMRO*. Paris: Centre National de la Photographie, 2003.
Galán, Fernando Martin, Nuria Fernández, and Fernando Castro, . *Frágiles*. Gijón, Spain: Catálogo de la exposición Galería Espacio Liquido, 2003.
Haenning, Marie, Shirley Veer, and Matthieu Gilles. *Art contemporain, 20 ans d'acquisitions avec l'aide du FRAM*. Épinal, France: Catálogo de la exposición, 2003.
Katz-Freiman, Tami, and Holly Block. *Time Capsule*. New York: Art in General, 2003.
Késenne, Joannes. *Eva Venus Madonna*. Louvain, Belgium: Alle deelnemende kunstenaars en bruikleengevers, 2003.
Lamoureux, Johanne. *Doublures, vêtements de l'art contemporain*. Quebec, Canada: Catálogo de la exposición, Musée National des

Beaux-Arts du Québec, 2003.
Perez, Nissan. *Révélation, représentation du Christ dans la photographie*. Jerusalem: Merrell, en asociación con the Israel Museum, 2003.
Pierret, Stanislas, Daniel Dumont, Daniel, Jean-Luc Monterosso, Isabelle Chesneau, and Pascal Hoël. *La Fabrication du réel, 1980–2000*. Paris: Collection of the Maison Européenne de la Photographie, Hungarian Institute of Photography, Budapest, Hungary, 2003.
Pitts, Victoria L. *In the Flesh: The Cultural Politics of Body Modification*. New York: Palgrave MacMillan, 2003.
Rencontres de la photographie d'Arles. Arles, France: Actes Sud, 2003.
Settembrini, Luigi. *Segunda Bienal de Valencia, La Ciudad Ideal*. Valencia, Spain: Charta, 2003.
Seung-Wan, Kang, and Ryu Han-Seung. *New Acquisitions 2002*. Seoul, South Korea: National Museum of Contemporary Art, 2003.

2002

Babel 2002. Seoul, South Korea: National Museum of Contemporary Art, 2002.
Buci-Glucksmann, Christine. *Le Temps des plis*. Tourcoing, France: Musée des Beaux-Arts de Tourcoing, 2002.
Campitell, Marina, Lorenzo Michelli, and Nicoletta Vallorani. *Shock & Show*. Trieste, Italy: Catálogo de la exposición, 2002.
Dangerous Beauty. New York: Catálogo de la exposición, The Jewish Community Center in Manhattan, 2002.
Degott, Ekatérina. *Corps et mouvements, Fourth International Month of Photography.Photobiennale 2002*. Moscow, Russia: Catálogo de la exposición, Moscow Institute of Photography, 2002.
Electric Body. Le corps en scène. Paris: Catálogo de la exposición, Beaux-Arts Magazine y Cité de la Musique, 2002.
FIAC 02. Paris: Galerie Rabouan Moussion, 2002.
Folie Sabine, Michael Glasmeier, Christine Buci-Glucksmann and Mara Reissberger. *Tableaux vivants*. Kunsthalle Wien, Austria: Lebende Bilder und Attitüden in Fotografie, Film und Video, 2002.
Le Breton, David. *Signes d'identité, tatouages, piercing et autres marques corporelles*. Paris: Métailié, 2002.
Luc, Virginie. *Art à mort*. Paris: Léo Scheer, 2002.
Mießgang, Thomas. *Dem Absurden Sinn geben, Magazin im Magazin-Revisited 2, no. 4*. Bregenz, Austria: Vorarlberger Kunstverein, 2002.
Mondadori, Bruno. *Fotografia, First

International Festival of Rome, SIAE*. Rome: SIAE, 2002.
Morsillo, Sandrine, Richard Conte, and Alain Douté. *L'Art contemporain au risque du clonage*. Paris: Publications de la Sorbonne, 2002.
Perez, Nissan N. *Corpus Christi: Les representations du Christ en photographie, 1855–2002*. Paris: Marval, 2002.
Polyphonix. Paris: Léo Scheer, Centre Georges Pompidou, 2002.
Taddeï, Jean-François. *La collection du FRAC des Pays de la Loire 2002*. France: FRAC des Pays de la Loire, 2002.

2001

Abadie, Daniel. *Tongue in Cheek*. Athens, Greece: Deste Foundation, 2001.
Freeland, Cynthia. *But Is It Art?* London: Oxford University Press, 2001.
Marella, Maria Rosa. *La metamorfosi del corpo*. February 21–March 24. Milan, Italy: Marella Arte Contemporanea, 2001.
Margat, Jean. *Jocondissima*. Cholet, France: Catálogo de la exposición, éditions des Musées de Cholet, 2001.
McDonald, Helen. *Erotic Ambiguities: The Female Nude in Art*. London: Routledge, 2001.
Mennesket, Et halvt arhunderde set gennem kroppen. Arken, Denmark: Catálogo de la exposición, Arken Museum of Modern Art, 2001.
Mutilate. Antwerp: Catálogo de la exposición, Antwerpen Open VZW, Flanders Fashion Institute, 2001.
Riva, Alessandro. *Totemica, Feticci e rituali del contemporaneo*. Mantua, Italy: Casa del Mantegna, 2001.
Smith, Lucie. *Between Earth and Heaven*. Ostende, Belgium: Museum voor Moderne Kunst, 2001.
Sojcher, Jacques, Gita Brys-Schatan, and Ben Durant. *Le Clonage d'Adam*, Brussels: ISELP, 2001.
Vezzosi, Alessandro. *Raffaello e l'idea della bellezza, Raffaello vive*. Relitalia studi editoriali. Rome: Exposición en San Benedetto del Tronto, 2001.
Wimmer, Elga. *Arzulananlar/Les Voluptés*. Istanbul, Turkey: Borusan Sanat Galerisi Estambul, 2001.

2000

Beauty Now, Die Schönheit in der Kunst am Ende des 20. Mönchen Hatje Cantz, Germany: Jahrhunderts, Hirshhorn Museumhaus für Kunst, 2000.
De Candia, Mario. *Anableps*. Rome: Studio Stefania Miscetti, 2000.
Delarge, Alexandre, and Évelyne Coutas. *Résonances ou Le Musée au risque de l'art*. Fresnes, France: Écomusée de Fresnes, 2000.
Dumas, Marie-Hélène. *Femmes & art au xxe siècle: le temps des défis*. Paris: Lunes, 2000.

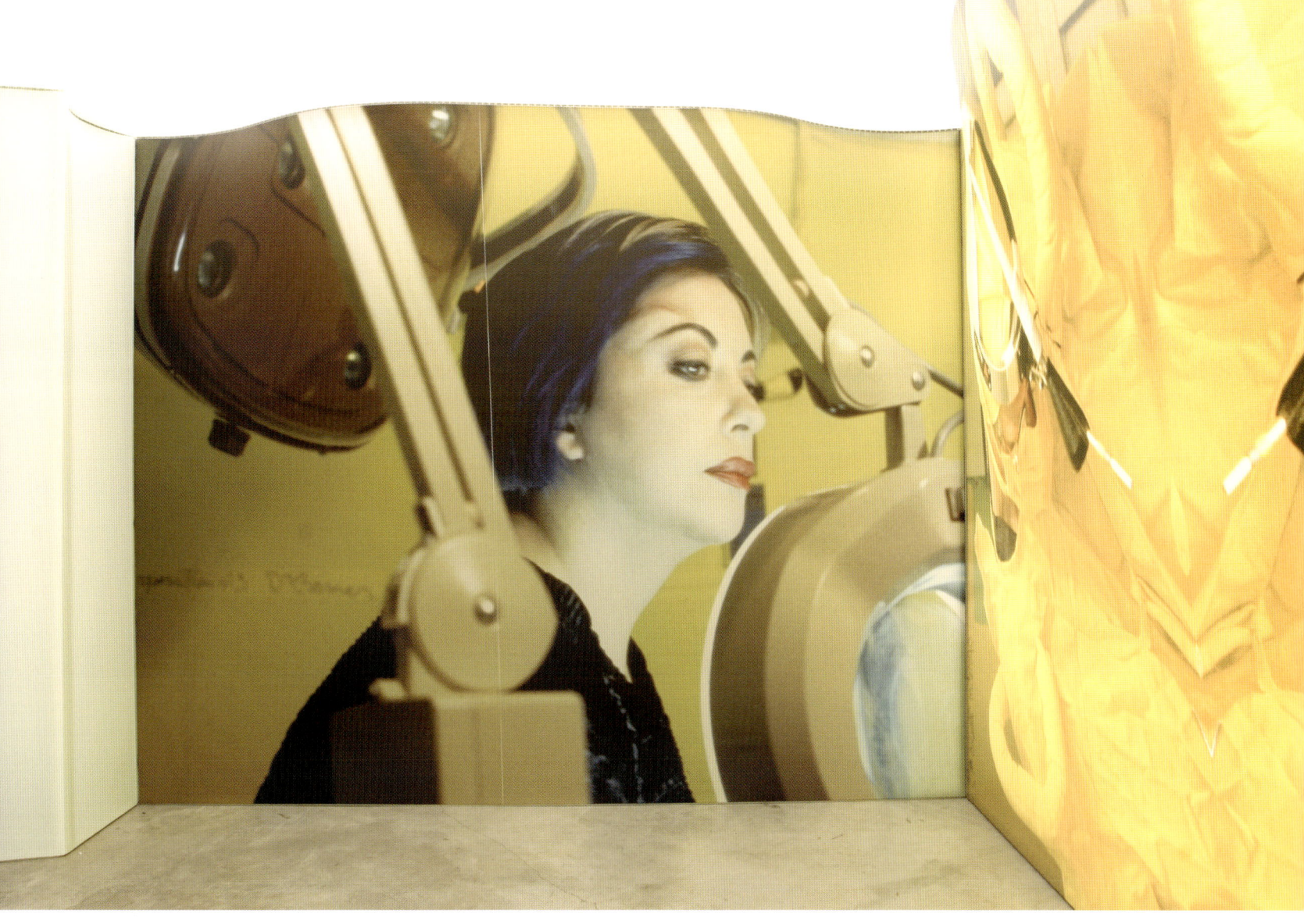

———— L'Invention des femmes. Augers-sur-Oise, France: Catálogo publicado por el Departamento de Cultura de Auvers-sur-Oise, 2000.

Eiblmayr, S., D. Snauwaert, U. Wilmes, and M. Winzen. *Die Verletzte Diva, Hysterie, Körper, Teknik in der Kunst des 20.*

Grünberg, Serge, and Axel Kahn. *Le Corps mutant.* Paris: Catálogo de la exposición, Galerie Enrico Navarra 2000.

Jahrhunderts. Innsbruck, Austria: Kunstverein München, Alemania, Galerie Im Taxispalais, Oktagon, 2000.

ISEA 2000, Tenth International Symposium of Electronic Arts. Catálogo de la exposición. Paris: coeditado por Musica Falsa y Art3000, 2000.

Hugues, Ribettes Jean-Michel. *Les 100 Sourires de Mona Lisa.* Shimbun, Japan: Nihon Keizai, 2000.

Labelle-Rojoux, Arnaud. *Leçons de scandale.* Paris: Yellow Now—Côté Arts, 2000.

Levitté, Harten Doreet. *Heaven: An Exhibition that Will Break Your Heart.* Catálogo de la exposición. Liverpool, England: Kunsthalle Düsseldorf, Hatje Cantz Publishers, Alemania y Tate Gallery, 2000.

LKW Kunst in der Stadt 4. Catálogo de la exposición. Kunsthaus Bregenz: KUB, 2000.

Martin, Jean-Hubert. *Partage d'exotisme, Fifth Lyon Biennial of Contemporary Art.* Lyon, France: RMN, 2000.

Navarra Enrico, Jacques Ranc, David Le Breton, Nicolas Bourriaud, Pierre Restany, Florence Müller, Jin-sup Marchal Yun, and Hong Sun-hoan. *Seoul International Performance Art Festival.* Seoul: Catálogo SIPAF, 2000.

1999

Combalia, Victoria, and Jean-Jacques Lebel. *Jardin d'Eros, Institut de Cultura.* Barcelona: Electa, 1999.

Hegyi, Lorand. "The competence of Utopia-Reflection on ORLAN's oeuvre." Tel Aviv: En el catálogo de la exposición en Chelouche Gallery, 1999.

Jeux et simulacres. Madrid: MNCARS Librería, 1999.

Miglietti, Alfano Francesca. *Rosso vivo, mutazione, trasfiguratione e sangue nell'arte contemporanea.* Milan, Italy: Electa, 1999.

Ribettes, Jean-Michel. *Fétiches et fétichisme, Le Défaut de l'objet religieux, économique & sexuel.* Paris: Blanche, Passage de Retz, 1999.

Skin-Deep: Surface and Appearance in Contemporary Art. Jerusalem: Israel Museum, 1999.

Sobieszek. Robert. *Ghost in the Shell: Photography and the Human Soul, 1850–2000.* Los Angeles: lacma—mit Press, 1999.

1998

L'Art dégénéré. Aix-en-Provence, France: Al Dante/CAAC, 1998.

Baqué, Dominique. *La Photographie plasticienne: Un art paradoxal.* Paris: Regard, 1998.

Bonito, Oliva Achille. *Distentico: Maschile Femminile e Oltre.* Rome: Panepinto Arte, 1998.

ERBAN / Patrick Raynaud. *La Nouvelle Interlope.* Nantes, France:

Illuminated room (detail), 2004. In collaboration with architect Philippe Chiambaretta. Barisol TM, aluminum structure, internal lighting, and Video/Barisol TM. Variable dimensions (8 cm. x 16 cm. x 3.5 cm). CCC from Tours and the Palais de Tokyo, Paris.

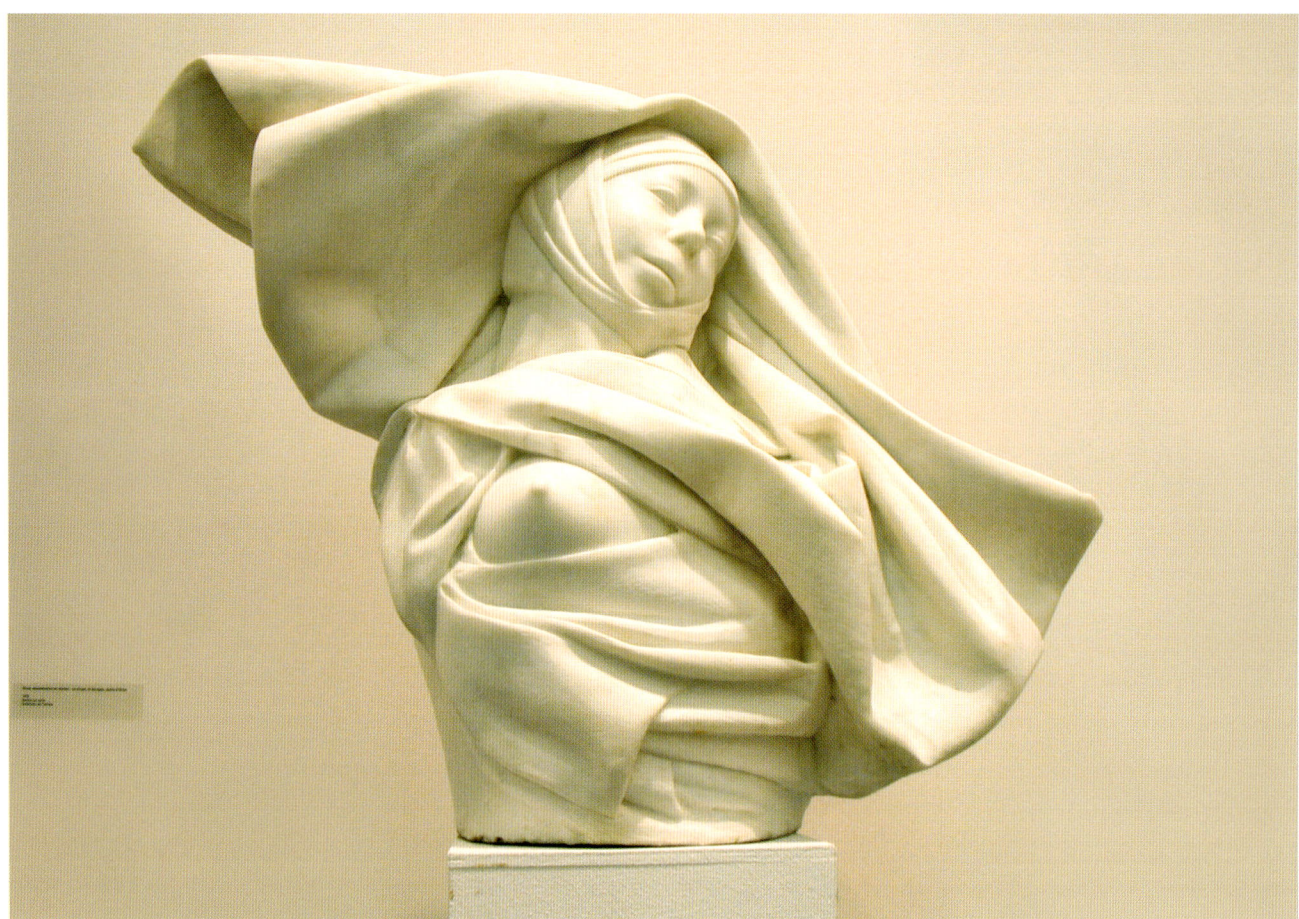

*Documentary study: The Draped—
The Baroque. Marble bust of ORLAN
as Saint ORLAN*, 1978. Marble,
70 cm. x 80 cm. x 45 cm. Courtesy
of the Michel Rein Gallery, Paris.

École Régionale des Beaux-Arts,
1998.
*Griffelkunst-Vierter Graphikpreis der
Mitglieder, Kunst und Computer.*
Hamburg, Germany: Griffelkunst,
1998.
Hagedorn-Olsen, Claus, Birgit
Hessellund, Tove Nyholm, and
Anette Lerche. *Trolle, Kvinden.*
Horsens, Denmark: Horsens
Kunstmuseum, 1998.
Harrison, Espace D. René. *De la
monstruosité, expression des passions.*
Montreal: Jaune-Fusain, 1998.
Lamarche-Vadel, Bernard, and Marie-
José Mondzain. *Mois de la Photo
à Paris.* Paris: Paris Audiovisuel,
1998.
Prosser, Jay. *Second Skins: The Body
Narratives of Transsexuality.* New
York: Columbia University Press,
1998.
Schimmel, Paul, and Kristine Stiles.
*Out of Action (1949–1976): Between
Performance and the Object.* New
York: Moca-Thames & Hudson,
1998.

Sega, Paola, Serra Zanetti, and Maria
Grazia Tolomeo. *La Coscienza
luccicante, dalla Videoarte all'arte
Interattiva.* Rome: Palazzo delle
Esposizioni, Gangemi, 1998.
Sigurósson, Hannes, and Jón Proppé.
Flögó og fögur skinn. Rekjavik,
Iceland: Ritstjó, Flögd, 1998.
Strano, Carmelo. *Europe–U.S.A.
and the Epoch of Unimplosive Art.*
Palermo, Italy: Bienal de Venecia
1997, 1998.
Troncy, Eric. *Le Colonel Moutarde dans
la bibliothèque avec le chandelier*
(textes 1988–1998). Dijon, France:
Les Presses du réel, 1998.
Van Beirendonck, Walter. *Wild and
Lethal Trash: Believe, Kiss the Future.*
Rotterdam, Holland: Boijmans Van
Beuningen Museum, 1998.

1997
Blessin, Jennyfer. *Rose Is a Rose Is
a Rose: Gender Performance in
Photography.* New York: Solomon R.
Guggenheim Foundation, 1997.
Cottingham, Laura. *Vraiment
féminisme et art.* Grenoble,
France: Centre National d'Art
Contemporain, 1997.
Eurokaz. *Festival novog kazalista.*
Frakcua, Macedonia: FRAKCIJA,
1997.
*Festival Atlantico, Arte Performance
Tecnologia.* Catálogo de la

exposición. Lisbon: Zé Dos Bois
Galeria, 1997.
*Hommage à René Déroudille, Un
combat pour l'art moderne.* Lyon,
France: Musée des Beaux-Arts, 1997.
Luces, Càmara. *accion (. . .) !Corten
!: Videoaccion: el cuerpo y sus
fronteras.* Madrid, Spain: MNCARS
Librería, 1997.
Lunghi, Enrico, and Paul di Felice.
*The 90's "A Family of Man": Images
de l'homme dans l'art contemporain.*
Casino, Luxemburg: Café-Crème,
1997.
Martinez, Rosa. *On Life, Beauty,
Translations and Other Difficulties.*
Istanbul, Turkey: Fifth Istanbul
Biennial, 1997.
Strano, Carmelo. *Unimplosive Art.*
Venice, Italy: Bienal de Venecia,
1997.
Ravin, Inge-Lise, and Steen
Rasmussen. *Sum, Århus
Kunstbygning.* Kirke Såby, Denmark:
Jubilæumsudstilling II, 1997.
Van Duyn, Edna. *Hybrids.* Catálogo de
la exposición. Amsterdam: Appel
Foundation, 1997.

1996
"Art charnel: ORLAN." *Internationale
Photoszene Köln.* Catálogo de la
exposición. Cologne, Germany,
1996.
Donguy, Jacques. *Le corps obsolète:*

"*ORLAN de l'art performance à l'art
charnel.*" Catalog *L'art au corps.*
Marseille, France: MAC, galleries
contemporaines des Musées de
Marseille, 1996.
Eiblmayer, Silvia, and August Ruhs.
Body as Membrane. Kunsthallen,
Denmark: Brandts Klædefabrik,
1996.
Expoarte-Guadalajara. Guadalajara,
México: Museo des Artes–
University of Guadalajara, 1996.
Fontcuberta, Joan, and Anatxu
Zabalbeascoa. *Màscara i Mirall.*
Barcelona: MACBA, Museo de Arte
Contemporáneo, 1996.
Macri, Teresa. *Corpo Estremo.*
Riminicinema Catalogo generale
1996.
Nemo. *Drommen om det ny
menneske: The Dream of New
Man.* Copenhagen, Denmark:
Copenhague Contemporary Art
Center, 1996.
Parent, Francis. *Le Corps dans tous
ses états.* atálogo de la exposición.
Paris: Espace Belleville, CFDT.
1996.
*Übergangsbogen und
Überhöhungsrampe,
naturwissenschaftliche und
künstlerische Verfahren, Symposion
I und II.* Hochschule für Bildende
Künste, Lerchenfeld 2. Hamburg,
Germany: Material-Verlag, 1996.

Vergne, Philippe, and Jacques Donguy . *L'Art au corps, le corps exposé, de Man Ray à nos jours.* Marseille, France: Galeries Contemporaines des Musées de Marsella, 1996.

Weintraub, Linda, Arthur Danto, and Thomas McEvilley. *Art on the Edge and Over: ORLAN, Self-Sanctification.* New York: Art Insights, 1996.

Zabalbeascoa, Anatxu. *Réels, fiction, virtuel, Rencontres internationales de la photographie.* Arles, France: Éditions Actes-Sud, 1996.

1995

De Loisy, Jean, Arnaud Labelle-Rojoux, and Jacques Donguy Jacques. *Hors limite: L'Art et la vie, 1952–1994.* Paris: Éditions du Centre Georges Pompidou, 1994–1995.

Francalanci, Ernesto L. *Scultura e oltre, sedicesima biennale internazionale del bronzetto piccolo scultura Padova.* Padua, Italy: Il Poligrafo, Scultura e Oltra, 1995.

Klaniczay, Júlia. *Video Expedition in the Performance World.* Budapest, Hungary: Artpool Art Research Center, 1995.

Le Grand Jardin du paradoxe et du mensonge universels, 18 ans de la galerie du Cirque Divers. Liège, Belgium: Musée d'Art Moderne et d'Art Contemporain, Éditions du Cirque Divers, 1995.

Raspail, Thierry, Thierry Prat, Georges Rey, and Gladys Fabre. *Installation, cinéma, vidéo, informatique: Third Contemporary Art Biennial of Lyon.* Paris: RMN, 1995.

Straus, Marc J. *ORLAN: Inside Out, Psychological Self-Portraiture.* Ridgefield CT: Aldrich Museum of Contemporary Art, May–September 1995.

Wilson, Sarah. *Féminin=Masculin: le sexe de l'art.* Catálogo de la exposición. Paris: Centre Georges Pompidou, Gallimard-Electa, 1995.

1994

Bianda, Rinaldo. *Video Art.* 15th Internation Festival of video and electronic arts, forum of new images and emerging culture. Locarno, Italy: AVArt Associazione per la VideoArte, 1994.

Eiblmayr, Silvia. *Suture Fantasies of Totality.* Salzburg, Austria: Salzburger Kunstverei, 1994.

Ermacora, Beate. *Positionen zum Ich, Kamerabilder.* Keil, Germany: Kunsthalle zu Kiel, 1994.

Restany, Pierre, and Renato Barilli. *Art en France de 1970 à 1993.* Bologna, Italy: Mazzota, 1994.

Ribettes, Jean-Michel. *L'Art du portrait aux XIXe et XXe siècles en France.* Tokyo: Musées d'art de Shoto, 1994.

Stiegler, Bernard, Ines Linder, and Nathalie Ergino. *Neuen Gesellschaft für Bildende Kunst.* Catálogo de la exposición. Berlin: NGBK, 1994.

1993

Blaine, Julien. *Dix ans de poésie directe 1984–1993): Attendez-moi, je reviens.* Paris: Musée de Marsella, RMN, 1993.

The Body in Ruin, Manifestatie voor de instabiele Media; ORLAN: My Flesh. The Text and the Languages. Rotterdam, The Netherlands: Institute for Unstable Media, 1993.

Bond, Anthony. *The Boundary Rider: Ninth Sydney Biennial.* Sydney, Australia: National Library of Australia, 1992–1993.

Pusch Huskes Werbeage Natur. Performance by ORLAN. Berlin: Kunstlerhaus Bethanien 1993.

Sex Quake Show: Art after the Apocalypse. [Anonymous]: First Art-Genes Portable Museum, 1993.

Wilms, Hildegard M. *Borderlines.* Frankfurt, Germany: Fotomuseum, 1993.

1992

Spotkania Sztuki aktywnej. Konin, Poland: Galeria Wieza Cisnien, 1992.

Ribettes, Jean-Michel. *Les Couleurs de l'argent.* Poste, France: Musée de la Poste, 1991–1992.

1990

Buci-Glucksmann, Christine, and Christian Gattinoni. *Écrans-icônes.* Brenne, France: Édition Argraphie, 1990, portada de ORLAN. And "Art and Life in the Nineties," *Mediamatic,* vol. 4, no. 4.

Video Ch'ti choc de Roubaix. Roubaix, France: Deuxième Rencontres de vidéo de Roubaix, 1989.

Situation(s). Catálogo de la exposición. Ivry-sur-Seine, France: CREDAC, Centre d'Art Contemporain, 1990.

1989

Nardin, Anne. *Vierge noire aux deux Chevalets.* Paris: Fonds National d'art contemporain (acquisition 1989), Ministre Culture et Communication, 1989.

1985

Faux, Monique, Vottorio Fagone, ORLAN, Dominique-Gilbert Laporte, and Pierre Restany. *Histoire sainte de l'art: ORLAN, Léa Lublin.* Cergy-Pontoise, France: Lacertidé, 1985.

Fagone, Vittorio. *Vidéo d'artistes.* Geneva, Switzerland: Salle Patino, 1985.

Lyotard, Jean-François. "Les Immateriaux. Album et inventaire." Paris: Centre Georges Pompidou, 1985.

1984

Donguy, Jacques. *Mois de la photo à Paris.* Paris: texto Mise en scène pour une assomption, étude documentaire n°100, 1984.

Charre, Alain. "Orlan" in *Cinq ans d'Art Performance à Lyon.* Lyon, France: Éditions Comportement, 1984.

Ubi à Saint-Vorles, contemporary art event. Châtillon-sur-Seine, France: Espace Lyonnais d'Art Contemporain, 1984.

1983

Popper, Frank. *Electra, l'électricité et l'électronique dans l'art du xxe siècle.* Paris: Musée d'Art Moderne de la Ville, 1983.

1982

ORLAN, Hugh Adams, Hubert Besacier, Jean de Breyne, Enrico Crispolti, René Déroudille, Vittorio Fagone, Elisabeth Jappe, and Gray Watson. *Fourth International Symposium of Performance Arts.* Lyon, France: Comportement-Environnement-Performance, 1982.

1981

Alvaro, Egidio. *Performances, rituels, interventions en espace urbain.* Lyon, France: 'Éditions du Cirque Divers/ Centre Georges Pompidou, 1981.

Eleventh Paris Biennale in Nice. Catálogo de la exposición. Paris: Musee d'art Moderne, 1981.

Identité: illusion-allusion no 1, Eleventh Paris Biennial. Lisbon: Galería Nacional de Arte, 1981.

Publication on visual arts by performance artists. Lyon, France: ELAC, 1981.

Roche, Denis. *Brèves rencontres (l'autoportrait en photographie), self-portrait photographs.* Paris: Centre Georges Pompidou, Herscher, 1981.

1980

Ainardi, A propos de Flagrant délit de traces. Catálogo de la exposición. Lyon, France: TNP, 1980.

Bonnaval, Jacques. "ORLAN, mise en scène pour une sainte." In *Analysis of an installation presented in Made in Bex Flor.* Paris: ICC Anvers, 1980.

France. Lyon, France: Espace Lyonnais d'Art Contemporain, December 1980.

Gerome, Élyane. "Tendances contemporaines Rhône-Alpes, état 1." Lyon: En la exposición en el *Espace Lyonnais d'Art Contemporain,* May–June 1980.

Made in France, con Mise en scène pour une sainte. Lyon, France: ELAC, 1980.

Von Mulders, Vim. "Aspects du mythe dans l'oeuvre d'ORLAN." Antwerp: Retrospective de The MesuRage, Septiembre 1980.

1979

Charre, Alain. Notes à partir du mesurage du Musée St Pierre de Lyon. Lyon: *First International Symposium for Performance Arts in Lyon,* 1979.

Kent, Sarah, Helena Kontova, Malitte Matta, Tadeusz Pawlowski, and Poli Francesco. Lyon, France: *First International Symposium for Performance Arts,* 1979.

1978

Besacier, Hubert. *ORLAN a choisi son corps comme matériau en el Centro Georges Pompidou.* Catálogo para The Das of Corporal Art and Performance. Paris: Pompidou Center, Febrero 1978.

Maubant, J. L. *Catalogue for the National Fine Arts School of Macon's Teachers' exhibition,* April 1978.

1977

Besacier, Hubert. Face à une société de mères et de marchands. Catalogue Le baiser de l'artiste. Paris: FIAC, 1977.

Gérome, Élyane. *Tendances Contemporaines Rhône-Alpes.* Lyon, France: ELAC, 1977.

Feminie 77. Catálogo de la tercera exposición. Paris: Dialogue Group, UNESCO, 1977.

1976

Besacier, Hubert. Catálogo *Langage au féminin.* France: ELAC, 1976.

1975

Artias, Lydia. *Triennial, Sculptures, Paintings.* Saint-Étienne, France: Maison de la Culture et des Loisirs, 1975.

1972

Artias, Lydia. *63/42.* Saint-Étienne, France: Maison de la Culture et des Loisirs, 1972.

1971

Séptima Bienal de Paris. Paris: Musee d'art Moderne, 1971.

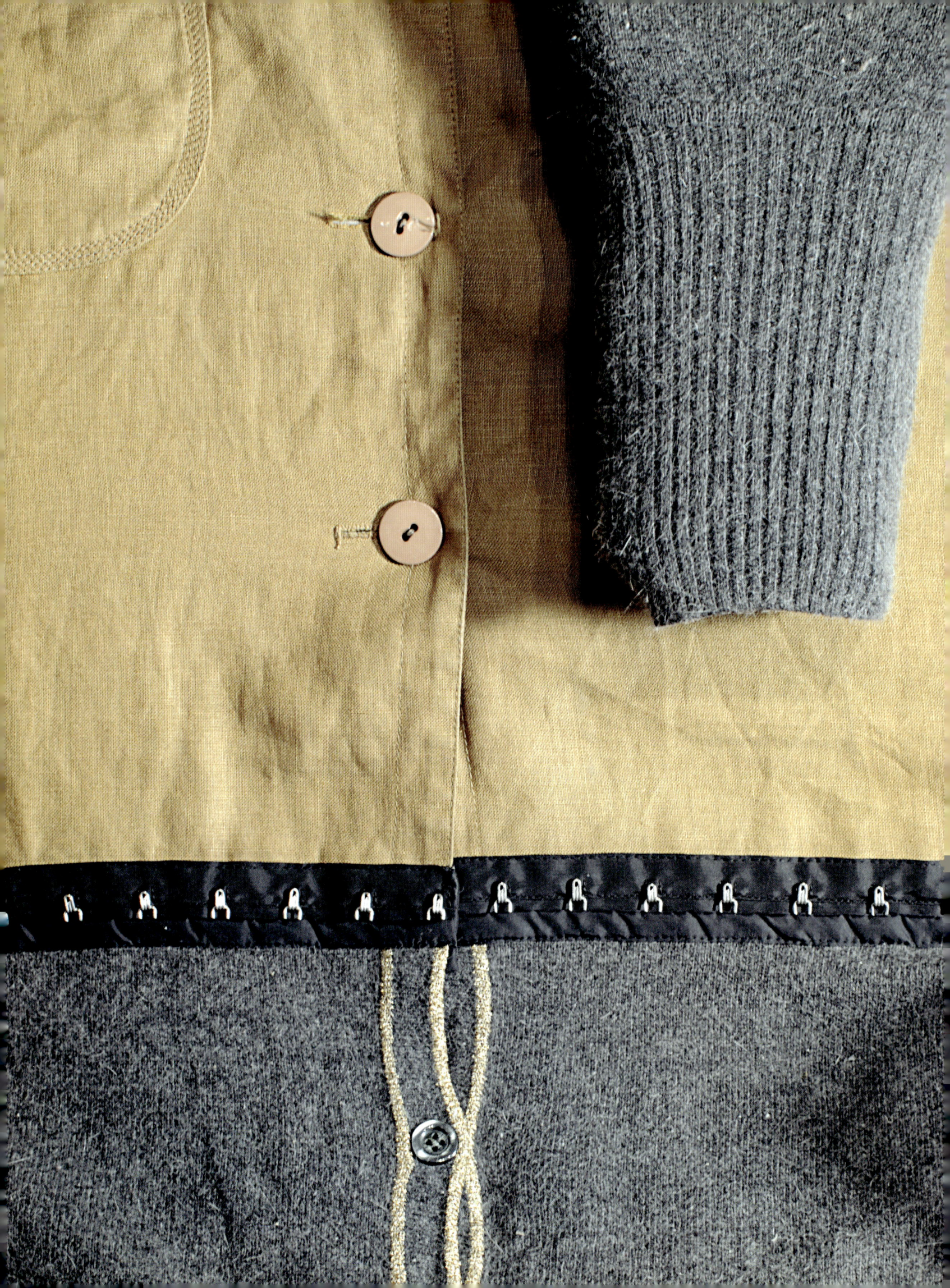

davidelfin CHRONOLOGY

163

2008

DIASTEMA Spring-Summer Collection 2009. Madrid Fashion Week.

Creative Process and Fashion Show-Action at the Guggenheim for "Cosa del Surrealismo" Exhibition.

Collaboration with ORLAN for the exhibition "SUTURE, HYBRIDISATION- RECYCLING: The Sculpture of Pleats, the Clothes, and the Costumes Personified in the Work of ORLAN," at Espacio AV, Murcia, Spain.

The Season's Book International Prize for the Best Autumn-Winter Collection at Madrid, Milan, and London.

INTIMIDAD Autumn-Winter Collection 2008/2009. Madrid Fashion Week.

2007

DA davidelfin Collection, Spring-Summer 2008.

DUAL Spring-Summer Collection 2008. Madrid Fashion Week.

Best Designer of the Year from *SHANGAY* magazine.

Best Designer of the Year from *Men's Health* magazine.

Graphic design for the launch of HPNOTIQ cocktail drink at the Penthouse Hotel ME, Madrid.

Launch of second line DA davidelfin, Autumn-Winter 2007/2008.

DÉMÉNAGEMENT Autumn Winter collection 2007/2008. Madrid Fashion Week.

Design of mini-collection CONVERSE Spring Summer 2007.

Art director for CD "PAPITO" by Miguel Bosé, Warner Music.

2006

Design of image for Málaga Film Festival.

DAFO Spring-Summer Collection 2007. Madrid Fashion Week.

PATER Autumn-Winter Collection 2006/2007. Madrid Fashion Week.

2005

THIS IS THE CHIVAS LIFE," conceptualized party for AROLA Restaurant

Carpet and rug design, davidelfin Proyecto DAC.

Design of oil packaging Proyecto A LA MODA.

Member of ACME (Association of Spanish Fashion designers).

Design of cover for SONY PSP console.

"LOS MORTALES" Spring-Summer Collection 2006. Madrid Fashion Week.

Design of uniform for AROLA Restaurant. Museo de Arte Contemporáneo Reina Sofía.

"LADIES AND GENTLEMEN" Autumn-Winter Collection 2005/2006. Madrid Fashion Week.

2004

Opening of DAVIDELFIN store at Jorge Juan no. 31, Madrid.

Art director for CD "VELVETINA," Miguel Bosé, Warner Music.

Videos "OJALÁ, OJALÁ" and "LA MANO DE DIOS."

"PASSWORD" Spring-Summer Collection 2005. Madrid Fashion Week.

Live audiovisuals for tour, "ARQUITECTURA EFÍMERA," Fangoria.

Exhibition "CUERPO EXTRAÑO" Autumn-Winter Collection 2004/2005. Madrid Fashion Week.

Costume design for ARCO Art Fair, 2004.

"EXTIMIDAD" Project, davidelfin Galería Soledad Lorenzo, Madrid.

2003

Fashion Award from *Marie Claire* for Best New Designer of the Year.

"MI MANCHI" Spring-Summer Collection 2005. Madrid Fashion Week.

"TRAS EL ESPEJO. MODA ESPAÑOLA" MNCARS. Madrid.

Shangay Award to Best Spanish Designer.

Art director for CD, "LO SIENTO, FRANK," by Ariel Roth, DRO EAST WEST.

"IN LOVING MEMORY" Autumn-Winter Collection 2002/2003.

L'oreal Prize for Best Collection by Young Designers. Madrid Fashion Week.

Collaboration in "ANTI_DOG" exhibition with Alicia Framis at Galería Helga de Alvear, Venice Biennale 2003 and ARCO 2003.

Art director and costume designer, "ORDEN DE APARICIÓN," for Dani Pannullo Dance Theater. Teatro Lliure Barcelona and Centro de Nuevos Creadores. Sala Mirador Madrid.

2002

"COUR DES MIRACLES" Spring-Summer Collection 2003. Madrid Fashion Week.

"DAVIDELFIN2" Autumn-Winter Collection 2002/2003. Circuit V Barcelona.

2001

"OPENIN NITE" Collection. Circuit IV, Barcelona.

Art director for short "V.O." by Antonia Sanjuan. Nominated for Goya Awards in 2002.

1999

"SANS TITRE," Project davidelfin vs Joseph Beuys.

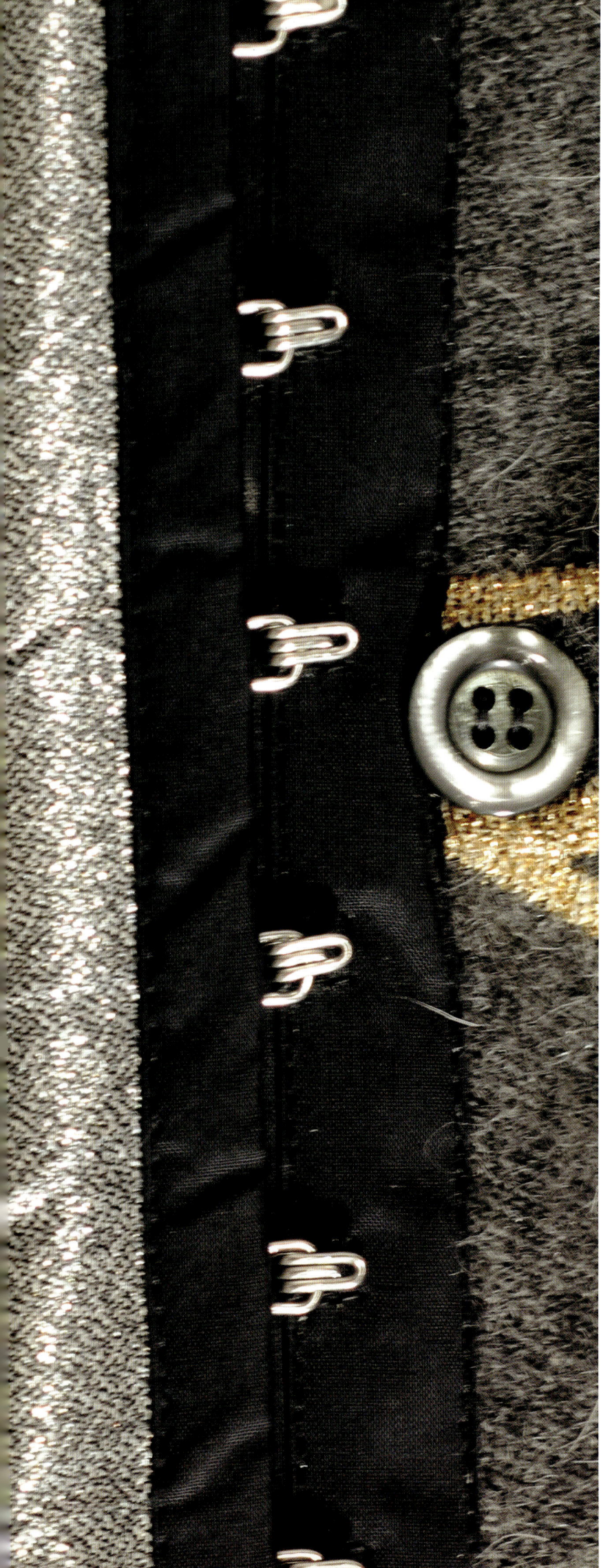

HOMI K. BHABHA is a professor of the humanities in the Department of English at Harvard University. Educated at the University of Bombay and the University of Oxford, Bhabha advises key arts institutions including the Institute of Contemporary Arts London, the Whitney Museum of American Arts, New York, and the Rockefeller Foundation. Bhabha sits on the editorial board of, among others, *October*, *Critical Inquiry*, and *New Formations*, and is a regular contributor to *Artforum*. Bhabha is the Director of the Humanities Center at Harvard and Distinguished Visiting Professor in the Humanities at University College London. His book, *Location of Culture*, has recently been reprinted as a Routledge Classic and has been translated into Korean, Spanish, Italian, Slovenian, German, Arabic, and Portuguese. Bhabha has given the keynote addresses for the Colloquium on Research and Higher Education organized by the United Nations Educational, Scientific, and Cultural Organization (unesco), the Beckman Lectures at the University of California–Berkeley, and the Presidential Lectures at Stanford University. Bhabha has served twice as Faculty Advisor to the davos World Economic Forum. In 1997, *Newsweek* named Homi Bhabha among the "100 Americans for the Next Century."

RHONDA K. GARELICK, a scholar of performance and visual culture, is the author of *Electric Salome: Loie Fuller's Performance of Modernism* (Princeton University Press 2007), *Rising Star: Dandyism, Gender and Performance in the Fin-De-Siècle* (Princeton University Press 1998), and the forthcoming, *Antigone in Vogue: Coco Chanel's Theatrical Collaborations*. Her cultural criticism has appeared in scholarly journals as well as popular venues including the *New York Times*, *New York Newsday*, and the *Sydney Morning Herald*. She is the recipient of a Guggenheim Fellowship as well as awards from The Dedalus Foundation, The Getty Research Institute, The American Council of Learned Societies, The National Endowment for the Humanities, and the American Association of University Women. Garelick is a professor in the Department of English and at the Hixson-Lied School of Fine and Performing Arts at the University of Nebraska–Lincoln. She received her PhD from Yale University and is an Ancienne Pensionnaire Étrangère of the École Normale Supérieure in Paris.

MICHEL SERRES was born in Agen, France. A philosopher and historian of science, he began his studies at the Naval College, later taking a Doctorate in philosophy. He is a member of the Academie Francaise and the European Academy of the Arts and Sciences. He teaches history of science at Stanford University. Author of around thirty books, his work analyzes the development of new technologies, locating current transformations within the continuing evolution of mankind. His books include: *Le Système de Leibniz et ses modèles mathématiques* (1968); *Hermès* (4 vols., 1969–1977); *Jouvences sur Jules Verne* (1974); *Feuz et signaux de brume: Zola* (1975); *Esthétiques sur Carpaccio* (1975); *Auuste Comte: Leçons de philosophie positive* (1975); *La Naissance de la physique dans le texte de Lucrèce: Fleuves et turbulences* (1977); *Le Parasite* (1980); *Genèse* (1982); *Rome, Le livre des foundations* (1983); *Détachment* (1983); *Les cinq sens* (1985); *L'hermaphrodite* (1987); *Statues* (1987); *Éclaircissements, Entretiens avec Bruno Latour* (1991); and *Le Tiers-Instruit* (*The Troubadour of Knowledge*) (1997).

ISABEL TEJEDA is the head of the Visual Arts Department at Murcia Cultural S.A. in Murcia, Spain, and a professor of fine arts at the University of Murcia. Tejeda is curator of various exhibition projects on issues of gender, such as *Territorios Indefinidos, discursos sobre la construcción de la identidad femenina*, *Mary Kelly—La Balada de Kastriot Rexhepi* and *Carne de Marina Núñez*, as well as the exhibitions *Tadeusz Kanto-La clase muerta*, *Espacio, tiempo y espectador*, and *Instalaciones y nuevos medios en las colecciones del ivam*. She is the author of the book *El montaje expositivo como traducción, fidelidades, traiciones y hallazgos en el arte contemporáneo desde los años 70*. Tejeda has been awarded the Premio Espais Art Critic Prize and was a finalist in the Fundación Arte y Derecho Essay Prize.

JORGE DANIEL VENECIANO is director of the Sheldon Museum of Art and former director of the Paul Robeson Galleries at Rutgers University, Newark. Recent publications include *Play's the Thing: Reading the Art of Jun Kaneko* (2009); *Neo-Constructivism: Art, Architecture, and Activism* (2008); *Imago: The Drama of Self-Portraiture in Recent Photography* (2007); and *Night of the Khmer Rouge: Genocide and Justice in Cambodia* (2007). He has published arts criticism in *Art Journal*, *Afterimage*, *New York Newsday*, *New Art Examiner*, *L.A. Weekly*, *Artweek*, and *Visual Arts Quarterly*, among other venues, since 1991. He received his PhD from Columbia University in the Department of English and Comparative Literature. His areas of research include the intersection of aesthetic and democratic theory.

PAUL VIRILIO is a renowned theorist with a special interest in urbanism and the strategic implications of new technologies. The creator of concepts such as the "war model," "dromology," and the "aesthetics of disappearance," Virilio's phenomenologically grounded and controversial cultural theory draws on the writings of Maurice Merleau-Ponty, with whom he studied while at the Sorbonne. He was teacher at the École Speciale de Architecture until 1968, becoming director of studies in 1973, and chairman of the board in 1989. In 1987 Virilio won the Grand National Prize for Architecture Critique. In 1989 he became the director of the program of studies at the College International de Philosophie de Paris, under the direction of Jacques Derrida, then a member of the High Committee for the Housing of the Disadvantaged in 1992. Paul Virilio has published over twenty-five books, including *Speed & Politics: An Essay on Dromology* (1986 [1977]); *Pure War* (his first in English) (1988); *The Information Bomb* (2000 [1998]); and, most recently, *Art as Far as the Eye Can See* (2007). Virilio retired from teaching in 1998. He currently devotes himself to writing and working with private organizations concerned with housing the homeless in Paris.

LAN VU is the creative director of lance and has worked as a creative consultant and trend forecaster for London Fog Industries, *Marie Claire Singapore Magazine*, and *Collezioni Trends Magazine* in Italy. In 1993 Vu managed a team of designers and graphic artists responsible for creating original costumes for the surgical performances included in ORLAN's *Omnipresence* series, which were then transmitted live to galleries and museums worldwide (Paris, Centre Georges Pompidou). Vu has worked in fashion design and merchandising for Gruppo GFT (Valentino & Ungaro Mens Furnishings), Liz Claiborne, Inc., and Philips VanHeusen, Inc. She is a graduate of the Fashion Institute of Technology and Virginia Commonwealth University.

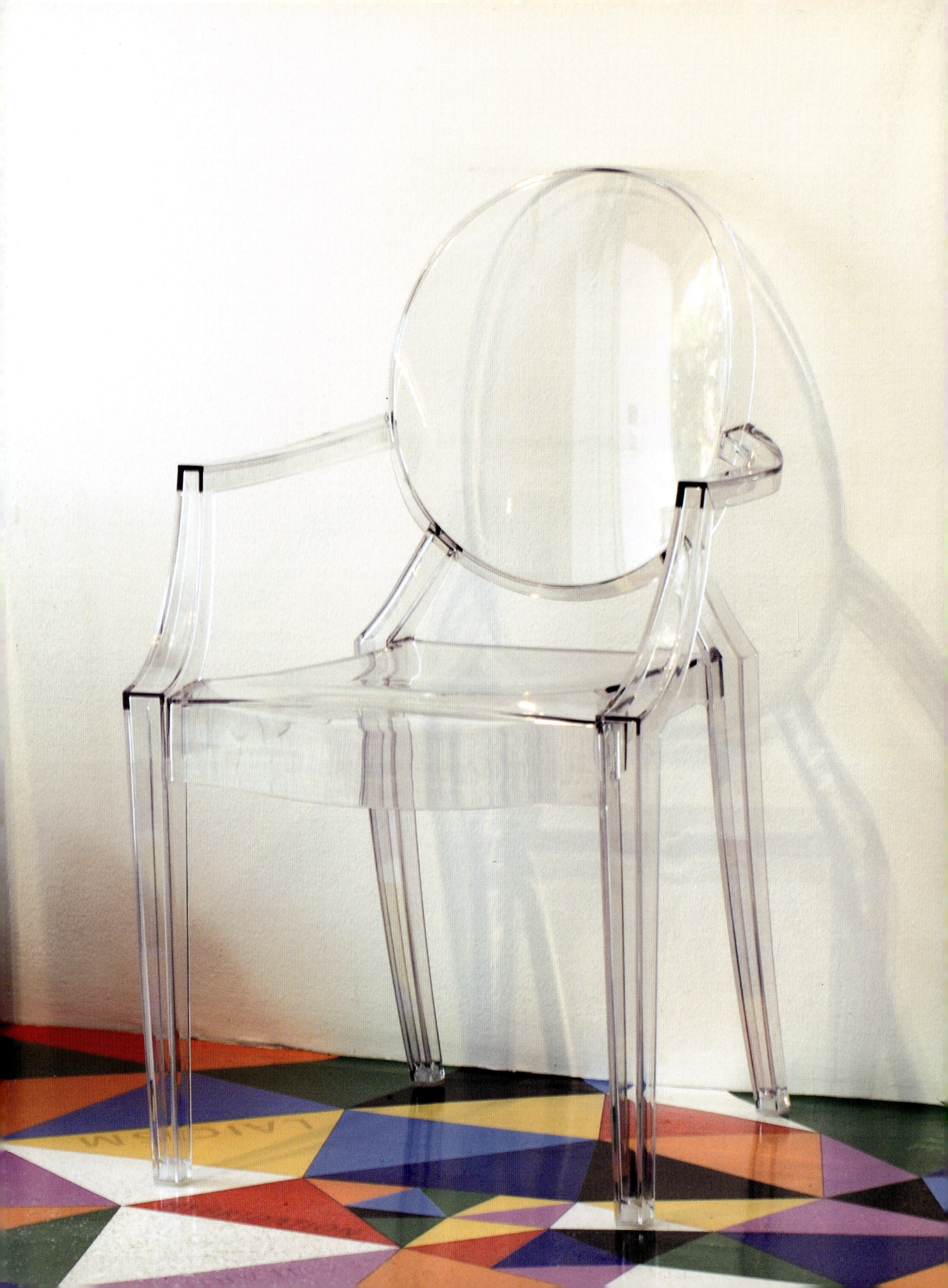